GENTLEMEN
AND TARPAULINS

The Officers and Men of the
Restoration Navy

J. D. DAVIES

CLARENDON PRESS · OXFORD
1991

Oxford University Press, Walton Street, Oxford OX2 6DP
Oxford New York Toronto
Delhi Bombay Calcutta Madras Karachi
Petaling Jaya Singapore Hong Kong Tokyo
Nairobi Dar es Salaam Cape Town
Melbourne Auckland
and associated companies in
Berlin Ibadan

Oxford is a trade mark of Oxford University Press

Published in the United States
by Oxford University Press, New York

British Library Cataloguing in Publication Data

(Data available)
ISBN 0–19–820263–6

Library of Congress Cataloging in Publication Data

Davies, J. D.
Gentlemen and tarpaulins: the officers and men of the restoration
navy/J. D. Davies.
p. cm.—(Oxford historical monographs)
Based on the author's thesis (D. Phil.)—Oxford University, 1986.
Includes bibliographical references and index.
1. Great Britain. Royal Navy—History—17th century. 2. Great
Britain. Royal Navy—Officers—History—17th century. 3. Seamen—
Great Britain—History—17th century. I. Title. II. Series.
VA454.D38 1992
359'.00941'09032—dc20 91–12205
ISBN 0–19–820263–6

Typeset by Best-Set Typesetter Ltd.
Printed and bound in
Great Britain by Bookcraft Ltd
Midsomer Norton, Bath

For
My Parents

PREFACE

THIS book is based on an Oxford University D.Phil. thesis, funded by the British Academy and completed in 1986. In both forms, it has owed an incalculable amount to the influence of Gerald Aylmer, first as supervisor of the thesis and then as sub-editor of the book. Like others of Gerald's pupils, past and present, I have benefited from his incisive criticisms of conceptual and technical shortcomings, his quiet but persuasive encouragement, and above all his genuine and abiding interest—an interest enhanced, in this case, by his own past naval service and his relationship to one of the officers who figure largely in the later chapters of this study, Matthew Aylmer of Balrath. His influence on this work has been immeasurable. I owe another long-standing debt to John Walsh, my undergraduate tutor at Jesus College, Oxford, who, in addition to being the greatest influence on my original development as a historian, played a crucial part in helping to arrange my return to Oxford at a time when, as a teacher in Cornwall, I was geographically too remote and professionally too busy to pursue my application in person.

In consulting manuscript and printed sources, I can vouch for the patience, good humour, and helpfulness of the staffs of each and every repository listed in the Bibliography, all of whom coped admirably with my frequent requests for the obscure, the bizarre, and sometimes the impossible. I am grateful to the Warden and Fellows of All Souls College, Oxford, the Master and Fellows of Magdalene College, Cambridge, the Marquis of Bath, and the Earl of Dartmouth for granting permission to study and cite their respective manuscript collections. Inevitably for a study of this sort, I owe a great deal to conversations and correspondence, formal and informal, with many historians working in related fields. My examiners, Anne Whiteman and Bernard Capp, made many valuable suggestions as to ways in which the thesis could be revised prior to publication. Dr Capp's own work on *Cromwell's Navy* appeared at a late stage in the present work's gestation, though it had already become apparent that our independent researches had produced conclusions which were mutually supportive to a considerable extent. I should like to hope that this book carries on where Dr Capp leaves off: in chronological and thematic terms on the one hand, and on the other in furthering his hope that the social and political aspects of naval history would be placed firmly in the mainstream of historical research. Howard Tomlinson provided me with many valuable ideas, particularly with regard to the use of the Pepys papers at Magdalene. At different times, other ideas and suggestions came from fellow participants in the seminars led by Keith Thomas and by Blair Worden and Anne Whiteman at Oxford, and by John Morrill and Mark Goldie at Cambridge, the Maritime History of Devon project colloquia at Exeter, and from my colleagues on the council of the Navy Records Society. However, the most direct influence on the work as a whole has come from the informal, ongoing Restoration navy team, comprising, *inter alia*, Sari Hornstein, Bob Glass, and above all Peter Le Fevre, whose photographic recall of manuscript references and book-titles, unrivalled knowledge of naval faction in the 1680s, and unerring ability to ask the most penetrating, awkward, but always necessary questions have made this book considerably better than it might have been otherwise. Where errors of fact or interpretation remain, they are probably at points where I have decided perversely to ignore Peter's advice.

Outside the realms of naval history, this study could not have been completed without the moral support and encouragement of many people, notably Chris Wilson; Martin Bentley, Colin King, and Peter Selwood; Michael Tillbrook, Ted and Dorothy Lanham, Christopher and Elizabeth Cox; Paul Liles; and above all, Joyce Davies and Alan Roderick. My colleagues at Bedford Modern School, and especially Peter Squire, the headmaster, have always been understanding of my attempts to balance my own research against the demands of teaching a full timetable, and (although they may not have realized it) the comments and questions of my sixth-form sets have forced me constantly to reassess my thoughts about many aspects of the early modern period, and indeed about the disciplines of history as a whole. However, the greatest debts are due to my parents, without whose unfailing support the original thesis could never have been contemplated, let alone completed and who also gave me the encouragement to complete the book. I dedicate this work to them with gratitude.

J. D. D.

Bedford
December 1989

CONTENTS

NOTE ON STYLE

The year has been taken as beginning on 1 January, with all dates given in the old style. The original spellings have been retained for quotations in English, though occasional modifications have been made to punctuation in order to enhance the clarity of meaning.

ABBREVIATIONS

Adm.	Public Record Office, Admiralty papers
Barlow's Journal	B. Lubbock (ed.), *Barlow's Journal of his Life at Sea in King's Ships, East and West Indiamen, and other Merchantmen from 1659 to 1703* (1934)
BIHR	*Bulletin of the Institute of Historical Research*
BL	British Library
Bod. Lib.	Bodleian Library, Oxford
CJ	*Journals of the House of Commons*
Coventry MSS	Manuscripts of the Coventry family in the possession of the Marquis of Bath, at Longleat House
CSP Col.	*Calendar of State Papers, Colonial*
CSPD	*Calendar of State Papers, Domestic*
CSP Ireland	*Calendar of State Papers, Ireland*
CSP Ven.	*Calendar of State Papers, Venetian*
DNB	*Dictionary of National Biography*
EHR	*English Historical Review*
HCA	High Court of Admiralty
Herbert Lbk	Yale University Library, James Marshall and Marie Louise Osborn Collection, shelf no. Fb 96: Letter-book of Arthur Herbert, 1678–83 (microfilm at the National Maritime Museum)
Hist. Parl.	B. D. Henning (ed.), *The Commons 1660–90* (History of Parliament Trust, 1983)
HMC	Reports of the Historical Manuscripts Commission
KAO	Kent Archives Office
MM	*The Mariner's Mirror*
Naval Minutes	J. R. Tanner (ed.), *Samuel Pepys's Naval Minutes* (Navy Records Society, 60; 1926)
NHL	Naval Historical Library, Ministry of Defence
NMM	National Maritime Museum, Greenwich
PC	Privy Council
Pepys's Diary	R. C. Latham and W. Matthews (eds.), *The Diary of Samuel Pepys* (1970–83)
Pepys MSS	Magdalene College, Cambridge, Pepys papers

PRO	Public Record Office
Prob.	PRO, Prerogative Court of Canterbury probate papers
Rawl. MSS	Bodleian Library, Oxford, Rawlinson MSS
RO	Record Office
SP	PRO, State Papers, domestic and foreign
Tangier Papers	E. Chappell (ed.), *The Tangier Papers of Samuel Pepys* (Navy Records Society, 73; 1935)
Tanner, *Catalogue*	J. R. Tanner (ed.), *A Descriptive Catalogue of the Naval Manuscripts in the Pepysian Library at Magdalene College, Cambridge* (Navy Records Society, 26–7, 36, 57; 1903–4, 1909, 1922)
TRHS	*Transactions of the Royal Historical Society*

INTRODUCTION

THE seventeenth-century Royal Navy has always seemed something of a poor relation beside its sixteenth- and eighteenth-century counterparts. It gained no immortal triumphs on the scale of the Armada fight or Trafalgar; it left no *Mary Rose* to raise and no *Victory* to preserve; even Robert Blake did not quite live on in the popular imagination as Drake or Nelson did. However, if the navy of the seventeenth century has been neglected by posterity, its true worth was always recognized by its own contemporaries. As one pamphlet put it, the fleet was 'the bulwark of our British dominions, the sole fence of our Country'.[1] Lists of ships and reports of battles survive in the papers of many gentlemen and aristocrats who lived far from the sea, and had no obvious connection with it. Naval issues were debated hotly in Parliament. The Anglo-Dutch wars of 1652–4, under the republic, and of 1664–7 and 1672–4 under the monarchy, were hard-fought affairs which saw significant advances in naval tactics and administration, and also helped to shape political developments in the nation as a whole. The navy also played a part in the two most significant political events of the later seventeenth century, the restoration of the Stuarts in 1660 and the revolution of 1688. In addition to these prominent appearances on the national stage, the often unsung navy played its part as an instrument of royal policy, convoying England's trade, guarding her fisheries, or fighting corsairs in the Mediterranean and buccaneers in the Caribbean.

The historiography of the Restoration navy reveals the same shift in priorities which characterizes studies of the force in the sixteenth, early seventeenth, and eighteenth centuries. The old emphasis on tactics and the minutiae of battles gave way gradually to a more wide-ranging treatment of the nature of naval administration: John Ehrman's masterly study of William III's navy, published in 1953, was a landmark in this change of priorities, though Michael Oppenheim and J. R. Tanner had pointed the way over half a century earlier.[2] Other historians have

---

[1] *Gloria Britannica: Or, The Boast of the British Seas* (1689), 1, echoing the formula in the preamble to the articles of war of 1661: N. A. M. Rodger (ed.), *Articles of War* (Havant, 1982), 13.

[2] M. Oppenheim, *A History of the Administration of the Royal Navy and of Merchant*

taken up and reinforced the point that a study of the fleet at sea and in action is meaningless without considering the measures taken to finance, administer, and support it.[3] However, this enthusiasm for administrative history also has its dangers. It is certainly true that the actions of the navy can only be understood in terms of the administrative measures necessary to get ships to sea; on the other hand, the administration's efforts would have been rendered futile without the skill, patriotism, and courage of the seagoing personnel, assets and attitudes which the administration did not and could not create.

The tendency to view the navy from the administrative angle has been particularly pronounced for the Restoration period, entirely because of the regard paid to the dominance of one man—Samuel Pepys. As clerk of the acts to the Navy Board and secretary to the Admiralty, Pepys held arguably the two key posts in the naval administration for all but five years of the reigns of Charles II and James II. His vast collections of naval papers have formed the starting-point for most studies of the navy during the period. Furthermore, his famous diary of the first nine years of Charles's reign provides a unique insight into his own thoughts on the problems of naval administration, and, indeed, about many other aspects of life at the time. Unfortunately, the very attractiveness of Pepys's character, with all its faults and foibles, has created problems of its own. There has been a tendency among historians to take Pepys's side, to accept many of his judgements uncritically, and to condemn those whom he condemned.[4] This has led, in turn, to an over-reliance on Pepys's collections of source material: both Tanner and Ehrman believed that it was possible to write the administrative history of the Restoration navy almost exclusively from the Pepys papers at Magdalene College, Cambridge.[5] This attitude has contributed to a serious neglect of other sources, and has increased the bias in favour of Pepys's attitudes.

The present study attempts to consider the navy of Charles II and

Shipping in Relation to the Navy from 1509 to 1660 (1896); Tanner, *Catalogue*, i. *passim*.

[3] e.g. D. A. Baugh, *British Naval Administration in the Age of Walpole* (Princeton, 1965), and *Naval Administration 1715–1750* (1977); A. Turnbull, 'The Administration of the Royal Navy from 1660 to 1673,' Ph.D. thesis (Hull, 1975); W. Cogar, 'The Politics of Naval Administration 1649–1660', D.Phil. thesis (Oxford, 1983).

[4] Richard Ollard's *Pepys: A Biography* (1974) is guilty of this to an extent, but on the whole is more even-handed and fair than Sir Arthur Bryant's trilogy, *Samuel Pepys* (1933, 1935, 1938).

[5] Tanner, *Catalogue*, i. 3; J. Ehrman, *The Navy in the War of William III* (Cambridge, 1953), 283.

James II from the viewpoint of the officers and men who served on its ships. It seeks to examine the reactions of the seagoing personnel to the demands of Pepys and the naval administration, and to explore their responses to some of the major events and developments, political, religious, and military, of the period. It seeks to consider to what extent officers and men were part of the 'political nation'; to establish how far the attitudes of the officers, in particular, were formed by their background and connections outside the navy; and to assess the nature of the relationship between the navy and the state it served. By considering the relationship between naval personnel and 'the shore', it might be possible to shed light on several other aspects of the history of the navy during this period. The reigns of Charles and James have long been regarded as the most important formative years in the evolution of a naval profession, and the central role in that evolution has long been attributed to Pepys. This study seeks to assess the extent to which this interpretation is justified, and to explore the ways in which the officers of the fleet themselves contributed to the development of their profession. In a broader context, it also seeks to examine the extent to which Pepys's interpretation of the relationship between the administration and the seagoing personnel—an interpretation generally favoured by subsequent historians—can be accepted. Therefore, this is not intended to be a comprehensive administrative or operational history of the Royal Navy between 1660 and 1689. Administrative aspects, such as the recruitment of seamen, and operational aspects, such as the course and outcome of battles, are touched on, but only where they are relevant to the study of the attitudes of the seagoing personnel.

Similarly, this study is not intended to be a comprehensive social history of the navy during this period, in the mould of Nicholas Rodger's seminal work on the mid-eighteenth century, *The Wooden World*.[6] This is due in part to the absence of anything like the same amount of Admiralty records that survive for Rodger's period, in part to the need to consider at length issues which were less relevant in the later period, such as the 'gentleman–tarpaulin' controversy and the influence of religion in the fleet. Moreover, the navy's central role in several of the major events of the period seemed to demand fuller treatment than could have been provided in a purely thematic social history. Consequently, the book combines elements of both thematic

[6] N. A. M. Rodger, *The Wooden World: An Anatomy of the Georgian Navy* (1986).

and narrative approaches. Part I, 'The Nature of the Sea Service', considers the origins and career patterns of the kind of men who served in the navy during this period, their conditions of service, and their attitudes both to the 'constants' of naval life, and to the various reforms and changes introduced into the navy during this period. Part II, 'The Navy in Peace, War, and Revolution', attempts to consider the ways in which the seagoing personnel responded to the major events of the period which affected them most directly, in which they played important parts in deciding the outcome. Geography and political circumstances dictated that the two wars which the restored Stuart monarchy fought against the Dutch would be almost exclusively naval wars; similarly, the failure of the navy to intervene actively against Charles II in 1660 and for James II in 1688 ensured the success of the Restoration and the Glorious Revolution.

The sources for studying the navy in this period present several problems of their own. A conscious effort has been made to break with the supposition that Pepys's papers must have pride of place in any study of the Restoration navy: many of the Admiralty papers for this period have been little used by other historians, and material from other national and provincial repositories has been used in an attempt to give this study as broad a perspective as possible. Nevertheless, these sources have their shortcomings. In particular, although the official documentation is often extensive, little of the private correspondence of naval officers and seamen survives. There is a danger, therefore, of extrapolating generalizations about 'the views of the officers' and 'the views of the seamen' from the views of perhaps only a very few men, who of course may be quite unrepresentative. This danger is particularly apparent when dealing with the seamen, who were less literate than their officers, and who left far less evidence of their lives and opinions. Consequently, much of this study is devoted to the officers of the fleet, partly because of the importance both of their position and of the various measures introduced during this period which affected them, but also because of the comparative lack of evidence about the men on the lower deck.

Several terms which have been used to refer to naval men require explanation. Strictly speaking, during this period the term 'officers of the navy' referred only to the principal officers of the Navy Board, namely the controller, surveyor, treasurer, and clerk of the acts. The contemporary term 'sea-officers' has therefore been used to describe the officers of the fleet as a body, except when dealing specifically with commissioned, warrant, or petty officers. The commissioned officers were generally regarded by contemporaries and later writers as being divided into several distinct groups, and the lack of clear definition of the terms used to characterize these groups has led several historians into error. For the purposes of classification in this study, the two principal groups, 'gentlemen' and 'tarpaulins', have been distinguished as far as possible by career structure and other professional, rather than social, criteria; these criteria are considered more fully in Chs. 2 and 3. In general, a commissioned officer has been classified as a tarpaulin if he had experience in the merchant service; if he had entered the navy as an officer's servant or able seaman, working his way up through petty and warrant-posts; or if contemporaries regarded him as a tarpaulin. The term 'gentleman officer' often refers to men who were 'gentlemen' in the sense of social status which would have been accepted on land, but it was also applied to men from a variety of other backgrounds. The criteria for classifying such officers, there-fore, are again essentially professional ones: entry into the navy, and progress towards a commission, as a 'volunteer' serving by royal appointment; promotion to a commission after little or no maritime experience, or after service in the army; and classification as a 'gentle-man officer' by contemporaries. The other two terms used in this study have been applied to sea-officers who generally had experience of naval service before 1660. 'Cavalier officers' were those who had served the Crown at sea or on land in the 1640s and 1650s, or who were classified as such when they entered the navy after 1660. The only term not employed by contemporaries, 'interregnum officers', has been used to describe those who held offices from the governments of the Commonwealth and Protectorate between 1649 and 1660. It is plainly unsatisfactory, even absurd, to classify all sea-officers who served the republic as 'tarpaulins', for such a definition would embrace men from aristocratic or military backgrounds—notably Edward Mountagu, later earl of Sandwich, and George Monck, later duke of Albemarle.[7]

Inevitably, these definitions are arbitrary and not entirely satis-factory. Several sea-officers do not fit conveniently into a category (several 'gentlemen' officers, for example, had some experience in the merchant service), and the categories were by no means mutually

---

[7] See Ollard in *Pepys's Diary*, x. 285; cf. B. Capp, *Cromwell's Navy: The Fleet and the English Revolution 1648–1660* (Oxford, 1989), 159–61, 172–7.

exclusive: in particular, many of the Cavalier and most of the interregnum officers came from tarpaulin backgrounds. Nevertheless, such categories do have some value. Contemporaries, notably Pepys, perceived the existence of a struggle between gentlemen and tarpaulins for posts in the fleet, and a realistic assessment of this struggle (and of this perception) can only be attempted if a rough idea exists of the numbers of men who belonged to each category. Ultimately, a cautious and qualified acceptance of these broad groupings is necessary if the most famous and abiding single remark about the seagoing personnel of the Restoration navy is to be either accepted or challenged: 'There were gentlemen and there were seamen in the navy of Charles the Second. But the seamen were not gentlemen; and the gentlemen were not seamen.'[8]

[8] T. B. Macaulay, *The History of England from the Accession of James the Second*, ed. C. H. Firth (Oxford, 1913), i. 294.

PART I

THE NATURE OF THE SEA SERVICE

1

THE KING'S NAVY

THE King, with the two Dukes [of York and Gloucester] . . . and Prince of Orange, came on board . . . After dinner, the King and Duke . . . altered the name of some of the Shipps, viz. the *Naseby* into *Charles*—The *Richard*, *James* . . . That done . . . the Duke of York went on board the *London* . . . which done, we weighed Ancre, and with a fresh gale and most happy weather we set sail for England . . . [1]

In this way, in his diary entry for 23 May 1660, the young clerk Samuel Pepys recorded the actions by which Charles II and his brother James took possession of their navy. For the next three decades, the royal brothers were to enjoy a unique relationship with their sea service. Its numerical strength was greatly augmented under their sponsorship. It fought their wars, and protected their trade; its internal systems and procedures were reformed under their auspices, and (at least in part) through the work of the same young clerk from the *Naseby*'s quarter-deck. The degree of personal interest which Charles and James took in the fleet, and in the careers of its officers and men, had no parallel between the reigns of Henry VIII and William IV.[2] Finally and ironically, the surviving brother and his naval minister, Pepys, were overthrown precisely because the navy they had done so much to nurture was unable to carry out its primary function, namely to prevent an invasion of England—an invasion carried out by the least remarked-upon 'royal' present at Scheveningen in May 1660, William III, prince of Orange. The navy brought the Stuarts back to England, and ultimately it was the outcome of a naval campaign which was to eject them from England once again.

Of course, such prospects were in no one's mind when Charles and James went aboard their fleet. More significant was the fact that the

---

[1] *Pepys's Diary*, i. 154–5.
[2] These general remarks are explicitly intended to contradict the seemingly fashionable 'counter-revisionism' which rejects the sincerity and significance of the Stuart brothers' commitment to the navy: see e.g. J. R. Jones, *Charles II, Royal Politician* (1987), 99. As I hope to show, the evidence for the 'revisionist' interpretation, and even a more emphatic version of it, is overwhelming.

royal brothers' first executive action on English territory was to order
the renaming of many of their ships, in an obvious attempt to oblit-
erate the memory of the interregnum.[3] The navy which Charles and
James inherited from the Commonwealth in this way was a formidable
fighting machine, which had been greatly expanded in the 1650s to
fight wars against the Dutch and Spanish. Using the system (adopted
in the reign of James I) of rating ships according to weight of ordnance embarked, the navy in 1660 possessed 4 first-rates of about
80–100 guns, of which 2 had been built since 1649; 11 second-rates
of about 60–80 guns (4 built since 1649); 15 thirds of about 54–64
guns (all built since 1649); 45 fourths of about 34–54 guns (26 built
since 1649); 35 fifths of about 26–34 guns, and 20 sixths of about
10–20 guns. However, the personal interest of the royal brothers,
Parliament's fears of England's continental naval rivals, and the effects
of two more Anglo-Dutch wars contributed to a significant change in
the balance of the fleet after 1660. When James fell in 1688, he passed
on to William 9 firsts, of which 8 had been built since 1660; 11
seconds (10 built since 1660); 39 thirds (30 built since 1660); 43
fourths (20 built since 1660); 12 fifths, and 8 sixths.[4] These figures
reflect the royal brothers' priorities. The fifth- and sixth-rates, use-
ful only in coastal waters and for trade protection, were practically
abandoned, and the Commonwealth's fourth-rates were allowed to
grow old, while still carrying the burden of scouting and convoy duties.
Charles and James wanted big ships. In part, this might have been a
consequence of the new naval tactic, the line-of-battle (considered
later in this chapter), in which only large ships could expect to survive;
in part, undoubtedly, it reflected their own desire for 'great ships'
which should be impressive symbols of their power and of the English
Crown's long-claimed sovereignty over the seas. The elaborate figureheads and stern-carvings which adorned the new royal ships were not
there simply for decoration; they were instruments of international
power politics.[5]

However, large ships also demanded large crews to man them. The
complement of a warship could vary according to the area in which it

---

[3] On ship-naming as a 'party political' process, see Capp, *Cromwell's Navy*, 5, 52–3,
134.
[4] F. Fox, *Great Ships: The Battlefleet of King Charles II* (1980), 185. On the expansion
of the navy during the interregnum, see Capp, *Cromwell's Navy*, 4–6, 52.
[5] B. Lavery, *The Ship of the Line*, ii. *Design, Construction and Fittings* (1984), 47. Cf. the
drawings and paintings reproduced in Fox, *Great Ships, passim*.

was deployed and the state of international affairs: official establishments therefore laid down distinct complements for 'peacetime' and war 'at home' and 'abroad'. In this way, the complement of the same fourth-rate could vary from 150 in peacetime to 280 for wartime service against the Dutch in the North Sea. A first-rate in wartime would require up to 800 men to man her; a third-rate, even in peacetime, would require 300.[6] To command such large bodies of men, a large officer corps was required, though this term implies a degree of homogeneity which was almost entirely lacking in the seventeenth-century navy. The officers of any ship exercised command by virtue of several different authorities. At the head of the regular hierarchy came the captain and lieutenant, holding commissions from the lord high admiral which permitted them to hold that post in a specified ship for as long as that ship was in service, a period which might be as brief as a few weeks or as long as several years. In general, the first-, second-, and third-rates carried two lieutenants and fourth- and fifth-rates one, though first-rates carried three lieutenants from 1678 and flagships had a second captain from 1672; sixth-rates and lesser craft carried no lieutenants, and the captain (though generally known by that title) held a commission as 'master and commander', a post which seems to have come into being in the 1640s or 1650s.[7] Warrants of various kinds were held by the master, the boatswain, the gunner, the carpenter, the purser, the cook, the chaplain, and the surgeon. Of these, the master, chaplain, and surgeon, like the commissioned officers, served only for the duration of the active service of the ship, while in the majority of cases the other five warrant-officers continued to serve when their ships were laid up in harbour. These 'standing officers' formed the basis of the skeleton crews which guarded and maintained the ships while they lay 'in ordinary', the dismasted, unarmed state which was, indeed, the ordinary condition of much of the fleet in peacetime. At the foot of the hierarchy came the many petty officers, such as the master's, boatswain's, gunner's, and carpenter's mates, the midshipmen, the quartermasters, the coxswain, and the swabber. Their numbers, duties, and means of appointment were regulated in 1662–3; thereafter, they were appointed on a purely internal basis by the captain in consultation with his warrant-officers.[8] The hierarchy of the

[6] Tanner, *Catalogue*, i. 266–95.
[7] Cf. Capp, *Cromwell's Navy*, 155. For an early usage of 'master and commander', see BL, Addit. MS 9305, fo. 165 (a commission of 1656).
[8] Adm. 106/7 fo. 159; NMM, ADL/A/4 (16th general instruction).

officer corps, therefore, always seemed rather lop-sided. In 1678, a first-rate in wartime carried 4 commissioned, 8 warrant-, and 89 petty officers; a fourth-rate in peacetime carried 2 commissioned, 8 warrant-, and 32 petty officers.[9] The contemporary term used to describe the officers of the fleet, 'sea-officers', could thus be applied to a remarkably diverse collection of individuals whose means of appointment were as varied as their duties.

Similarly, the very term 'fleet' could be used and misused in different ways. Applying it, as contemporaries often did, to the ships in active service during peacetime was always something of a misnomer. In general, only between twenty and forty ships of the fourth- to sixth-rates, carrying perhaps 3–4,000 men, were set out each summer, depending on circumstances and (more commonly) on how little money the government possessed. Rather fewer were set out in winter, though the old distinction between 'summer and winter guards', still common at the beginning of the period, fell increasingly into disuse and had all but disappeared by the 1680s. Throughout the period, the commitments of the peacetime navy changed little, though the number of vessels allocated to a particular station or duty would obviously vary according to circumstances. In September 1675, for example, three ships were attending the herring convoy and fishery, two were attending the Newfoundland fishery, three were in transit to or from the Mediterranean with convoys, two were on duty in the Caribbean, one was on the Channel Islands station, two were serving as guardships at Portsmouth and Sheerness, and the three frigates in the Downs, the navy's favoured operational anchorage (between the Godwin sands and the Kent coast), constituted the only 'fleet' in home waters. The bulk of the navy's strength was in the Mediterranean, fighting the seemingly interminable wars against the North African corsairs: 2 third-rates, 10 fourths, and 6 smaller craft formed the 'Straits fleet', the 'Sallee squadron', and the vessels on local service for the English colony at Tangier.[10] While these few ships attempted to undertake all the navy's peacetime commitments, the great majority of the king's ships remained in harbour, their masts and guns removed. The bulk of

---

[9] Bod. Lib., Tanner MS 39, fo. 7.

[10] Bod. Lib., Rawlinson MS A. 175, fo. 299. For other peacetime disposition lists, see BL., Addit. MS 9302, fos. 164–80 (1660–4); and Adm. 8/1 (1673–88). For a detailed survey of the commitments and deployment of English warships, see S. Hornstein, 'The Deployment of the English Navy in peacetime 1674–88', D.Litt. thesis (Leiden, 1985).

the 'ordinary' was moored in the Medway, though several of the larger units were laid up at Portsmouth and several of the smaller ones at Deptford and Woolwich. Apart from providing continuous naval employment for officers and men who would otherwise have had to sever their connections with the service, the ordinary's only other significant peacetime function was as a tourist attraction: Charles and James often went down to the Medway to view their great ships, or to show them off to important foreign visitors.[11]

The ordinary would only be mobilized in the event of war, or the expectation of war. The wartime fleet could be vast: in the Dutch wars it totalled well over a hundred vessels, manned by over 20,000 men. The great majority of these ships were specifically built as royal warships: although many merchantmen were taken up as auxiliaries, increasingly few were taken up, in Tudor fashion, for service as actual men-of-war, in part because (as contemporaries recognized) the differences in design and 'survivability' between warships and merchantmen were becoming ever greater, in part because of the consequent reluctance of shipowners to commit their vessels to conflicts in which they stood a very good chance of being destroyed by Dutch broadsides.[12] War also brought opportunities for the officers to advance to flag-rank, for the few ships set out in peacetime usually could not justify the appointment of flag-officers (except in the Mediterranean, where the commander-in-chief usually received an admiral's commission, and particularly large fleets there would also have a vice- and a rear-admiral). Flagmen were appointed afresh for each year's campaign, a system which was criticized for producing a lack of continuity.[13] The number of flags depended on the nature of the conflict, and the presence or otherwise of an allied squadron in the fleet. Normally, the fleet was divided into three squadrons, the red, white, and blue, each with an admiral, a vice-admiral, and a rear-admiral; the commander-in-chief (the lord high admiral himself in 1665 and 1672) served as admiral of the red; the blue was regarded as the most junior squadron. In the second Dutch war, all nine of the flag-posts were filled, but in the third war the white squadron was

---

[11] See e.g. L. Magalotti, *Travels of Cosmo III, Grand Duke of Tuscany, through England, during the Reign of King Charles II* (1821), 355–61. For the appearance of the Medway ordinary, see the endpapers in Fox, *Great Ships*.

[12] See *Naval Minutes*, 176–7; *The Journal of Edward Mountagu, First Earl of Sandwich*, ed. R. C. Anderson (1929), 222; Capp, *Cromwell's Navy*, 6–9.

[13] R. C. Anderson, 'English Flag Officers, 1688–1713', *MM* 35 (1949), 333–41.

given to the French, and in the smaller fleets mobilized in 1678 and 1688 only three flags were allocated in the fleet as a whole.[14] The division of the fleet into squadrons was one aspect of a recent and particularly important development in naval tactics, the introduction of the line-of-battle. Naval historians have spilt much ink in attempting to ascribe and date precisely the invention of this tactic, but it is now clear that it was introduced during the first Dutch war of 1652–4 (probably at the battle of the Gabbard in 1653), and it formed the basis, if not always enthusiastically or successfully implemented, of English fleet tactics in the second and third Dutch wars, and thereafter in the eighteenth-century wars against the French. The line was one of the most significant influences on the development of the navy in this period, tilting the scales in favour of the large, purpose-built warship, and helping to create the system of flag-posts which governed the fleet in wartime. Questions concerning its desirability and degree of success contributed to the jealousies and faction fights which were to blight the navy's performance during the second and third Dutch wars.[15]

History and the requirements of conflict with the Dutch ensured that the navy was concentrated on the Thames and Medway dockyards, which had been established in the sixteenth century. Chatham, the largest dockyard in Europe, was the major refitting yard, as well as being an important shipbuilding centre and the home of much of the ordinary. Lesser rates were refitted or laid up at the smaller Thames yards of Deptford and Woolwich, or at Chatham's outport, Sheerness. Portsmouth's distance from the theatre of war limited its usefulness as a repair base in the Dutch wars, but in peacetime it undertook a considerable amount of refitting work and could also build vessels of the largest rates. Smaller repairs and stores facilities were maintained at several ports, including Harwich, Dover, Deal, Plymouth, and Kinsale. The dockyards and outports were the points of contact between the seagoing personnel and the shore: they were the places where employment could be obtained, where seamen would need to be brought to man the fleet in wartime, and where men were discharged after their naval service.[16] Therefore, the location of the yards helped

[14] Tanner, *Catalogue*, i. 313–15.

[15] See *Pepys's Diary*, vii. 194; J. S. Corbett (ed.), *Fighting Instructions, 1530–1816* (1905), 81–172; J. Creswell, *British Admirals of the Eighteenth Century: Tactics in Battle* (1972), 17–18, 27; Lavery, *Ship of the Line*, i. 26–8; M. Baumber, *General-at-Sea: Robert Blake and the Seventeenth-Century Revolution in Naval Warfare* (1989), 111–20, 125, 168–70, 182–6.

[16] For the dockyards, and the administration of the navy in general, see D. C.

to determine several aspects of the relationship between seafarers, the navy, and the nation. Among other things, geography dictated that much of the navy was based close to London. This had obvious administrative advantages for the individuals or boards who exercised the powers of the Admiralty, and for the subordinate Navy Board, which handled routine administrative matters. However, the navy's proximity to London also caused problems. Captains intent on pursuing an active social life, or unpaid seamen intent on harassing the administration, had easy access to the capital. Moreover, in an age when the gunfire of naval battles in the North Sea could be heard in London,[17] and when wounded seamen were brought up the Thames to fill the city's hospitals, the outcome of naval warfare was almost literally on the doorstep of the capital and the institutions it contained, notably the royal court and the Parliament. The king's navy was not some alien force, out of sight and out of mind on distant seas. It was an immediate and noticeable presence, at once the largest spending department of the state,[18] the largest industrial concern in the country, a floating community that could be as large as many a town or county community, and, in the eyes of most Englishmen (thanks to a popular mythology which already encompassed Alfred the Great, the Spanish Armada, and Robert Blake), the only effective and desirable defence of the nation. As the marquis of Halifax observed, 'the Navy is of so great importance that it would be disparaged by calling it less than the life and soul of government'.[19] The officers and men of the Restoration navy had a great deal to live up to.

Coleman, 'Naval Dockyards under the Later Stuarts', *Economic History Review*, 2nd ser. 6 (1953–4); Ehrman, *Navy . . . of William III*, chs. 2, 3, 7; essays on 'Admiralty', 'Dockyards', and 'Navy Board' in *Pepys's Diary*, x; R. Saville: 'The Management of the Royal Dockyards, 1672–8', *The Naval Miscellany*, 5 (1985), and his forthcoming edition of documents on naval administration, 1660–88, for the Navy Records Society.

[17] See e.g. *Pepys's Diary*, vii. 217.

[18] The navy usually cost between £300,000 and £450,000 p.a. in peacetime, and between £800,000 and £1m. p.a. in wartime. It generally took up over 20% of the government's total expenditure in any given year: BL, Addit. MS 9302, fo. 186; Coleman, 'Naval Dockyards', 136; Capp, *Cromwell's Navy*, 9–10.

[19] Halifax, 'A Rough Draft of a New Model at Sea', *The Works of George Savile, Marquis of Halifax*, ed. M. N. Brown, 3 vols. (Oxford, 1989), i. 303.

2

THE OFFICERS: RECRUITMENT
AND PROMOTION

GIVEN the complex patchwork of ranks and posts held by officers of the Restoration navy, and the variety of authorities by which they held those offices, it was inevitable that the system for acquiring them and advancing through them would be an intricate one, with many loopholes and anomalies. There was no naval 'career pattern' *per se*. As far as the commissioned officers were concerned, there were two common routes by which to attain that status.[1] The older system involved entry into the service at an early age, often 9 or 10, as a captain's or other officer's servant, rising through various petty and warrant posts. This system was regulated in 1662–3, transforming such servants into apprentices indentured for seven years, rather than merely being covenanted for each voyage.[2] As such, the system continued to provide the navy with its quota of 'cabin boys' who rose to high rank: Admiral Sir John Norris, commander of the Channel fleet in the 1740s, had started his career as a captain's servant in 1680.[3] The alternative method, instituted in 1661, entailed spending several voyages as a volunteer '*per* order' by authority of a royal letter to the ship's captain, and serving with a midshipman's pay. This system was conceived originally as a means of getting young gentlemen to learn navigation, and thereby qualify for commissions. It was regulated by establishments of 1676 and 1686, which laid down an upper age limit of 16 for these 'king's letter boys'.[4] These types of career pattern were not mutually exclusive, but the social and professional distinctions implicit in them had important repercussions on the development of the officer corps during this period, and a fuller examination of these distinctions and the problems they created will be conducted later in this chapter, and in Ch. 3.

---

[1] Cf. Capp, *Cromwell's Navy*, 171–2; Rodger, *The Wooden World*, 263–72.
[2] Adm. 1/3546, pp. 487–93; NMM, AND/9, fo. 127.
[3] D. D. Aldridge, 'Admiral Sir John Norris, 1670–1749', *MM*, 51 (1965), 174.
[4] Adm. 2/1745, fos. 41ᵛ, 43, 44ᵛ, 45, etc.

Apart from the two main career patterns, few sea-officers gained commissions by other means. Even in wartime, merchant-ship masters were rarely given warship commands unless they had some previous naval experience. Men who had served continuously in the navy were generally given preference, unless a merchant skipper brought himself to the authorities' notice by particularly distinguished service.[5] The administration was wary of retaining the original merchant captains in command of vessels hired in wartime, as it was believed that captains with a stake in their ships would be unwilling to risk them in battle, and in the second and third Dutch wars such appointments were usually vetoed.[6] (The reluctance to employ merchant shipowners in the navy might well have been due, in part, to the association of such a policy with the interregnum regimes, notably the Rump Parliament.)[7] Success in privateering, or even piracy, could also bring a captain to the notice of the king and the Admiralty, and lead to the granting of a naval commission: in this way one of the period's most notorious Caribbean buccaneers, Bartholomew Sharpe, secured a naval command, from which he promptly absconded in search of richer pickings elsewhere.[8]

For the great majority of sea-officers whose careers were less spectacular, whether former officers' servants or former volunteers *per order*, the key to advancement in the service theoretically entailed securing certificates of good conduct from captains, dockyard officials, and flag-officers. Names of candidates for both commissioned and warrant-posts were then entered in list-books, and their certificates and recommenders noted. When vacancies occurred, the lord high admiral (1660–73), the king (1673–9, and 1684–8), or the lords commissioners of the Admiralty (1679–84) would select suitable appointees from the lists and certificates presented by their secretary.[9] Even without other distortions of the system, notably the many subtle intrusions of patronage and influence, this method of supposed promotion by merit had several shortcomings. It was seen as leading to

[5] SP 29/104, fo. 114; Pepys MS 2854, p. 77; Pepys MS 2862, p. 296; BL, Addit. MS 11602, fo. 87; Adm. 1/5139, fo. 30.
[6] W. G. Perrin (ed.), *Boteler's Dialogues* (1929), 7–8; Coventry MS 102, p. 10; SP 29/122, fo. 93; Adm. 1/5138, p. 53.
[7] Capp, *Cromwell's Navy*, 164–5.
[8] C. Lloyd, 'Bartholomew Sharpe, Buccaneer', *MM* 52 (1966), 291–6.
[9] SP 29/49, fo. 33; Bod. Lib., Rawlinson MS A. 174, fo. 491; Rawl. MS A. 181, fo. 213'; Tanner, *Catalogue*, ii. 282, 359–60; Pepys MS 2855, p. 200; Pepys MS 2858, pp. 394–5, 410–11; Pepys MS 2859, p. 490. The list-books for 1673–88 survive as Adm. 6/428.

an overdependence of men on their superior officers, to the advancement of men whose diligence in collecting certificates worked to the detriment of men who were diligent in remaining at their posts, and to the advancement of inferior men by certificates from captains who wanted to be rid of them. The whole system was inevitably based on the subjective judgement of the superior officer, and assessments of the same man by different officers could vary wildly.[10] Moreover, the system did not prevent sea-officers spending many months and large sums of money attending at Whitehall or the Admiralty, despite Pepys's many attempts to assure them that soliciting advancement directly was pointless, and that only the objective examination of certificates by the authorities would secure posts.[11]

The system could be distorted in several ways. Outstanding gallantry could lead to rapid promotion on the direct orders of the king or lord high admiral: the rise of William Davies, one of William III's flagmen in his French war, began when Davies's captain was slain in battle in 1665, and Lieutenant Davies's excellent conduct of the ship against superior Dutch forces so impressed the duke of York that he gave him his own command.[12] During the 1670s, when the administration was trying to enforce stricter adherence to the official instructions to captains, the promise of advancement was held out to those who performed these duties particularly well.[13] Charles also knighted several captains who distinguished themselves in combat, honours which were intended both to encourage other officers and to raise the status of the sea-officers in the nation.[14] Death of a captain usually led to the automatic elevation of the lieutenant to acting command, and of the master to the lieutenancy. This long-established rule of the navy caused some problems on foreign stations, notably the Caribbean, where colonial governors attempted to assert themselves by issuing their own commissions and elevating young volunteers, or even land-officers from their own garrisons—actions which the Admiralty vigor-

---

[10] Rawl. MS A. 173, fo. 5; Rawl. MS A. 194, fo. 195ᵛ; Tanner, *Catalogue*, ii. 237; Pepys MS 2854, pp. 381–2; Pepys MS 2856, pp. 34–5, 44, 63–4; Adm. 1/3545, p. 843; H. Maydman, *Naval Speculations, and Maritime Politicks* (1691), 182–3.

[11] See e.g. Tanner, *Catalogue*, ii. 359–60; Pepys MS 2858, pp. 482, 531–2.

[12] J. S. Clarke, *The Life of James the Second* (1816), i. 419–20.

[13] Rawl. MS A. 228, fo. 103ᵛ; Tanner, *Catalogue*, iv. 532.

[14] Leicestershire RO, Finch political papers 148, fo. 5; 'P. C.', *The Three Establishments Concerning the Pay of the Sea-Officers* (1714 edn.), p. xv; *CSPD*, 1670, p. 190.

ously condemned.[15] In 1671, for instance, the governor of Jamaica (Sir Thomas Lynch) turned out Captain Wilgress of the *Assistance* for drunkenness, and replaced him with Major William Beeston, an island landowner and member of the Jamaican assembly, as captain, and Lawrence Prince, a notorious Caribbean buccaneer, as lieutenant; it was said that the change of command was intended only to permit Lynch to use the frigate to enrich his circle of cronies.[16] Nevertheless, it was convenient for some delegated authorities to have powers to issue commissions. Above all, admirals or commanders-in-chief overseas had authority to fill vacancies and make promotions, and these appointments were usually given retrospective sanction by the Admiralty.[17] War constituted the greatest distortion of the method of appointment. The admiral of the fleet usually had the power to appoint and dismiss officers, and a dual authority could therefore exist, with both the admiral and the authorities in London issuing commissions and warrants. The sheer size of the wartime fleets made central control of all appointments, and adherence to peacetime procedures, unrealistic propositions. For example, captains in wartime were often given considerable licence to choose their own lieutenants and warrant-officers, though even in peacetime captains' nominees for these posts were sometimes accepted.[18]

Most of the warrant-posts also depended on a system of certificates. Masters were appointed by the Navy Board's warrants after they had been examined at Trinity House, which certified the rate of ship and the geographical area for which they were competent. They were re-examined occasionally, and the scope of their qualifications was extended if necessary.[19] This system was criticized at times, most notably in 1664 by William Coventry, secretary to the duke of York, who advocated its replacement by an examination before a panel

[15] Adm. 106/360, fo. 24; SP 104/177, fo. 74ᵛ; Tanner, *Catalogue*, iii. 45–6, 96; Pepys MS 2860, pp. 219–21; Pepys MS 2861, pp. 301–3; H. A. Kaufman (ed.), *Tangier at High Tide: The Journal of James Luke, 1670–3* (Paris, 1958), 131; HMC, *Finch MSS*, ii. 105–7; *CSP Col.*, 1681–5, p. 428; ibid., 1685–8, p. 530.

[16] *CSP Col.*, 1669–74, pp. 299, 323, 347, 386–7; BL, Addit. MS 12424, *passim*; *DNB*, s.n. 'Beeston, William'.

[17] For the powers granted to individual commanders-in-chief, see Adm. 2/1, *passim*.

[18] Rawl. MS A. 186, fo. 31; Pepys MS 2854, pp. 75, 82, 94, *et passim*; HMC, *Finch MSS*, iv. 244. Cf. Chs. 8 and 9.

[19] Pepys MS 2867, pp. 634–5; NHL, MS 121/9, p. 121; SP 46/136, fos. 213–14; Adm. 106/3539, pt. 1, 'Trinity House Certificates' folder; Adm. 106/2908, *passim*. Cf. Pepys MS 2581, p. 208.

of senior captains, but the method survived unchanged.[20] External agencies also influenced the selection of two of the 'civilian' officers who only served aboard a ship when it was actually in service, the chaplain and the surgeon, whose position as sea-officers was in any case debatable (as the naval officer and polemicist Nathaniel Butler had observed in the 1630s), 'partly in that their functions and charges are everywhere known, and partly because that these are not officers peculiar to the sea'.[21] Chaplains were appointed on an *ad hoc* basis by individual captains until 1665, when the scarcity and poor quality of recruits led to an attempt to secure their selection by the archbishop of Canterbury. This system also proved unsuccessful, and in 1677 it was reformed to provide for selection by the bishop of London, whose nominees were appointed by an Admiralty warrant directed to ships' captains.[22] Surgeons were examined at Barber-Surgeons' Hall and appointed by Navy Board warrants, but disputes between the two authorities over the extent of their respective jurisdictions occurred regularly, and captains were often able to take advantage of the lack of qualified surgeons to appoint their own, often unworthy, nominees.[23]

The standing officers were appointed by Admiralty warrants directed to the Navy Board, following an examination of candidates' competence by the latter board, and its recommendation of suitable names to the Admiralty; recommendations from others, notably flag-officers and dockyard officials, were also accepted.[24] From the beginning, the Restoration naval administration adopted the practice of preferring officers from lesser rates to greater in order to encourage deserving men, though this system was not always adhered to rigidly.[25] Reviews of the qualifications of officers were undertaken periodically, and long-serving officers were promoted.[26] Masters, boatswains, and

---

[20] Rawl. MS A. 174, fo. 478. A. W. Tedder, in *The Navy of the Restoration* (Cambridge, 1916), 60–1, misread the purpose and effect of this document.

[21] Perrin, *Boteler's Dialogues*, 64.

[22] Adm. 2/1745, fo. 117; Tanner, *Catalogue*, iv. 400–2; Pepys MS 2867, pp. 161–3; W. F. Scott, 'The Naval Chaplain in Stuart Times', D.Phil. thesis (Oxford, 1935), ch. 6; G. Taylor, *The Sea Chaplains* (Oxford, 1978), 86–96.

[23] NHL, MS 121/13, pp. 73–4, 77; J. J. Keevil, *Medicine and the Navy, 1200–1900*, ii (1958), 85, 100, 147–70.

[24] Adm. 106/6, fo. 337; Tanner, *Catalogue*, ii. 287; Pepys MS 2857, p. 76; Maydman, *Speculations*, 3.

[25] BL, Addit. MS 32094, fo. 40; Rawl. MS A. 174, fo. 468; Tanner, *Catalogue*, iii. 312; Pepys MS 2856, pp. 20, 153.

[26] Pepys MS 2853, pp. 43, 78, 120, 290, 366; Pepys MS 2858, pp. 394, 410, 478.

gunners generally rose through the ranks of mate and midshipman, perhaps gaining additional experience in the merchant service, before gaining their first warrant-posts.[27] Thereafter, although promotion to a higher rate was always possible, opportunities for further advancement were limited. Gaining a commission was a possibility, particularly in wartime, but these openings became more restricted in the long peace of the 1670s and 1680s. Senior boatswains, masters, and some captains were preferred for the posts of master-attendant in the dockyards, supervising the movements and maintenance of the ordinary. Carpenters had a more diverse career structure, often alternating between service aboard ship and employment as shipwrights in the yards, and several former ship carpenters reached the summit of their profession, the post of master shipwright in the building yards.[28] Pursers were usually former clerks from the dockyards, the Navy Board, or other government offices, and from 1662 onwards they had to pay substantial sureties, which varied according to the rate of ship, before entering into office. Promotion for pursers could take the form of appointment to a higher rate, to appropriate dockyard posts such as clerk of the cheque (responsible for mustering the men of the yard and the ordinary) or storekeeper, to more lucrative clerical posts ashore, or even, very occasionally, to commissioned posts at sea.[29] The cook, the lowest in the hierarchy of the standing officers, was invariably a badly maimed sailor, appointed to the office more out of compassion than any regard to his culinary ability; several were blind or had lost both hands, and therefore had to employ a mate to carry out their duties.[30]

Promotion through the rates, based on certificates of merit, was the general rule for the standing officers, but this system, like that for commissioned officers, was not incorruptible. Patrimony was not widespread, but the administration did occasionally tolerate the resignation of a father's office to his son if the latter was suitably qualified.[31] Covert purchase of office, or bribery of officials to secure an appointment, was probably more common, but it is difficult to establish the

[27] See e.g. Rawl. MS A. 181, fo. 230; Adm. 106/3539, pt. 2, *passim*.

[28] Rawl. MS A. 194, fo. 261; NMM, CHA/E/1A, *passim*; Adm. 106/3539, pt. 2, 'Carpenters' folder; C. Knight, 'Carpenter Master Shipwrights', *MM* 18 (1932), 411–16.

[29] Rawl. MS A. 179, fos. 53–5; Adm. 1/3547, p. 659; Adm. 1/3549, p. 423; Adm. 2/1749, p. 285; Tanner, *Catalogue*, iv. 570; NHL, MS 121/9, p. 133; Maydman, *Speculations*, 193; Capp, *Cromwell's Navy*, 207–9.

[30] e.g. Tanner, *Catalogue*, iv. 118, 351.

[31] e.g. Adm. 1/3546, p. 1007; Adm. 3/278, pt. 1, pp. 52, 104; Adm. 106/7, fo. 395.

extent of such corruption. Certainly, Edward Gregory, purser of the largest ship in the navy, the *Sovereign*, in the early 1660s, admitted that he had purchased the post from his predecessor.[32] The payment of fees to the secretaries of state and the Admiralty, and to their clerks, was an accepted part of the method of obtaining a commission or warrant, though it came under attack several times as part of wider political assaults on the naval administration.[33] Examples were made at times of sea-officers who had attempted to offer money for commissions or warrants,[34] but more subtle inducements were commonplace. Pepys regularly and loftily declared his disdain for financial or other inducements, and rebuked several men who attempted to offer him presents.[35] However, he happily accepted money for offices at the beginning of his naval career (a fact he conveniently forgot in later years), and as secretary to the Admiralty he was never averse to gifts of wine or more esoteric presents from sea-officers: in 1686, for example, he told one captain, 'For God's sake, instead of apologizeing for sending me noe more Birds, helpe me to some excuse . . . for robbing you of soe many'.[36] The dividing line between gifts given out of genuine respect and friendship, and those given with an ulterior motive in mind, is virtually impossible to draw.

The most important influence on the system of appointment was the working of patronage, though this was not necessarily a detrimental influence: as several recent studies have shown, patrons generally would want to prefer only deserving clients.[37] Much naval patronage was purely internal, particularly for those warrant posts which relied on considerable technical skill; carpenters, for example, depended chiefly on certificates from the master shipwrights of the dockyards and their assistants.[38] The reliance on the certificate system helped to create a

---

[32] BL, Addit. MS 11531, fos. 11–12.

[33] Between 1673 and 1679 the Admiralty received £14,600 in fees for 914 warrants: NMM, AGC/19/7. Cf. Rawl. MS A. 171, fo. 137.

[34] e.g. Pepys MS 2853, fos. 249ᵛ–50; HMC, *House of Lords MSS*, 1690–1, p. 430. Cf. BL, Addit. MS 60386, unfol., memo of 3 May 1679.

[35] Tanner, *Catalogue*, iii. 46–7; Rawl. MS A. 185, fos. 51, 64, 66, 70; NMM, LBK/8, p. 719.

[36] Pepys MS 2859, p. 268. For the 'gifts' Pepys received in 1660, see *Pepys's Diary*, i. 77–8, 90, 100, 101, 114, 121, 180, 232; in later years, see Rawl. MS A. 179, fos. 26, 28; Pepys MS 2857, pp. 252–3.

[37] Rodger, *Wooden World*, 273–314; Capp, *Cromwell's Navy*, 185–9.

[38] Adm. 6/428, *passim*.

dependence of junior officers on their superiors, and led to the creation of the 'shifting, amorphous' factions which permeated the officer corps.[39] Each commissioned officer, from flag-rank down to the lowest 'master and commander', had his own circle of clients; the captain's power to appoint petty officers gave him a body of men personally loyal to him, and if he rose in the service these clients could continue to rise under his patronage. The loyalties of patrons and clients were often very strong, with captains frequently requesting permission to take their lieutenants, their master, or some of their other officers and men with them when they changed ship. Captains and flag-officers naturally wished to have good men under them, and to retain subordinates who had proved their competence.[40] Flag-officers were usually able to officer their own ship, and often their whole division, with their own clients. These cliques competed ruthlessly for promotion, although the nature of the naval profession ensured that naval patronage was rarely immutable. Even the closest client of a senior sea-officer could find himself placed under the command of a different admiral, and preferment would depend on winning the favour of this new superior. A successful naval career, therefore, often depended on acquiring a series of influential patrons. Ralph Wrenn, for example, relied on the recommendation of Prince Rupert and Captain William Coleman in the early 1670s, but by 1679 he was being advanced by Admiral Sir Thomas Allin, controller of the navy, and the commander-in-chief in the Mediterranean, Sir John Narbrough. The lieutenancy in the Mediterranean fleet which resulted from their patronage put him under the command of Admiral Arthur Herbert, who gave Wrenn his own command in 1681.[41] Naval factions might have a hard core of men who were whole-heartedly committed to their patron, but they also contained a larger, more peripheral group of men who changed allegiance if circumstances seemed to require it,

---

[39] The phrase is Professor D. A. Baugh's: *British Naval Administration*, 126. As in this case, many elements which he considered characteristic of the 18th-c. officer corps were clearly present in the Restoration period, or even earlier.

[40] *Tangier Papers*, 153; KAO, U. 1515/O. 8, unfol., papers concerning Jacob Barber, 5 May 1679; *CSPD*, 1667–8, p. 279; ibid. 1671–2, pp. 85, 192; Capp, *Cromwell's Navy*, 181–2; Rodger, *Wooden World*, 275–8. At times, officers refused promotions out of loyalty to their patrons: *Sandwich Journal*, ed. Anderson, 234; *The Life of Captain Stephen Martin 1666–1740*, ed. C. R. Markham (1895), 9.

[41] Adm. 6/428, 1673–9 capts. list, no. 43; ibid., 1679–84 list, no. 8; Rawl. MS A. 234, fo. 3ᵛ; BL, Addit. MS 60386, unfol., Allin to Capel, 28 Oct. 1679; Tanner, *Catalogue*, i. 426–7.

or in the alarming but common eventualities of one's patron dying or falling from favour.[42] These transitions were made easier by the small size of the commissioned officer corps. In the course of a reasonably long career, a sea-officer could expect to serve or socialize with many of his fellows, and an officer posted to a different station or squadron would rarely find himself among complete strangers. Moreover, it was likely that his new admiral would already know something of him.[43]

The most tightly knit groups were those based on family or neighbourhood ties, and several naval 'dynasties' existed in the Restoration navy.[44] Admiral Sir Thomas Allin, from Lowestoft, was followed into the service by his three Ashby nephews, an Ashby great-nephew, an Utber brother-in-law, two Utber nephews, an Anguish (brother to his son-in-law), and several more distant relatives among the Mighells and Leake families.[45] Sir John Kempthorne's successful naval career provided the springboard by which his three sons all gained commissions.[46] However, the 'Cockthorpe admirals'—Sir Christopher Myngs, Sir John Narbrough, and Sir Cloudesley Shovell—were the most remarkable example of a 'dynasty' based on neighbourhood loyalties. Shovell began his career as captain's servant, then became midshipman and master's mate, under Narbrough, just as Narbrough had begun in the same way under Myngs; all came from the village of Cockthorpe on the north Norfolk coast.[47] Their connections were extensive, and indicate the way in which commercial and financial ties, as well as those of neighbourhood and kinship, helped to shape the character of naval factions. In 1669 Narbrough recommended Nathaniel Peckett for a lieutenancy on his voyage to the South Seas; Peckett later commanded a merchant ship which was part-owned by Shovell, who also had shares in the merchant ships commanded by the former naval captains John Maine (whom Shovell continued to promote when Maine returned to the navy in 1689), Peter Pickard,

[42] Capp, *Cromwell's Navy*, 187; Rodger, *Wooden World*, 280–1.

[43] In 1665 the duke of Albemarle knew, or knew of, all but a handful of captains in the fleet, as did Edward Russell in 1691: NMM, LBK/47, TRN/39.

[44] Cf. Capp, *Cromwell's Navy*, 182–4.

[45] *The Journals of Sir Thomas Allin 1660–78*, ed. R. C. Anderson, ii (1940), p. lii; E. Gillingwater, *An Historical Account of the Ancient Town of Lowestoft, in the County of Suffolk* (1791), 60, 221–45, 301–2, 401; J. Charnock, *Biographia Navalis: Or, Impartial Memoirs of the Lives and Characters of Officers of the Navy of Great Britain* (1794), iii. 74.

[46] G. A. Kempthorne, 'Sir John Kempthorne and his Sons', *MM* 12 (1926), 289–317.

[47] F. E. Dyer, *The Life of Admiral Sir John Narbrough* (1931), 1–14, 93; P. Le Fevre, 'Sir Cloudesley Shovell's Early Career', *MM* 70 (1984), 92.

and Francis Sanders, a fellow Norfolk man.[48] Narbrough's other lieutenant on the South Seas voyage was Thomas Armiger, a relative of Myngs; Sir John's nephew Edmund Loades became a naval captain in the 1690s; Seth Thurston, another captain who alternated between merchant and naval service, was probably a cousin of Shovell.[49]

Many naval careers were furthered exclusively by purely naval patronage, but external influences also affected the system. Ministers of state, royal mistresses, merchants, MPs, courtiers, mayors, and bishops, among others, all sought to recommend certain sea-officers for preferment. Such interventions were often based on concern to promote a relative, or perhaps to advance the son of an old servant, or simply because of local connections.[50] Captains living at Plymouth in the 1670s and 1680s, for example, could rely on the recommendation of Sir Richard Edgecumbe, and (in the case of Captain Stephen Ackerman) on that of Lords Bath and Arundel, Sir John Covington, and 'all the gentry in the West'.[51] Thomas Dilkes, later to become one of Queen Anne's admirals, owed his first commission to his relative Sir John Thynne, who reminded the Admiralty secretary, Pepys, of Dilkes's kinship to Pepys's old friend and predecessor, Sir William Coventry.[52] Another of Anne's flag-officers, Robert Fairfax, gained his first naval post by means of a letter of recommendation from Lord Belasyse, a distant kinsman, to Sir Roger Strickland, the admiral, a Yorkshire connection of both Belasyse and Fairfax. He sought further advancement by trying to cultivate Strickland's friendship and by obtaining the recommendation of another Yorkshire cousin, Lord Fairfax of Gilling.[53] Making an impression on ladies of the court, or on influential passengers aboard one's ship, might also advance an officer's career significantly: Captain Sir Robert Robinson was said to have obtained his commissions 'by the smock and by bribeing',

[48] KAO, U. 1515/O. 3, 1 Sept. 1669; U. 1515/O. 11, pp. 87, 101, *et passim*; Adm. 8/2, entry for Maine. Cf. HMC, *Finch MSS*, iv. 105–6.
[49] For Armiger, see Coventry MS 99, fo. 91; Dyer, *Narbrough*, 88. For Loades and Thurston, see NMM, MAT/17A.
[50] Adm. 2/1745, fos. 5–6; Adm. 3/277, pt. 2, p. 118; BL, Addit. MS 21948, fos. 94–5; Bod. Lib., Carte MS 49, fo. 323; Rawl. MS A. 185, fo. 281; Rawl. MS A. 191, fo. 48; Pepys MS 2854, p. 122; Pepys MS 2858, p. 306; Tanner, *Catalogue*, iii. 255; *CSPD*, 1664–5, p. 11; ibid., 1667, p. 19; ibid., 1680–1, p. 342; HMC, *Dartmouth MSS*, i. 23, 107, 123, 137, 139; Capp, *Cromwell's Navy*, 184.
[51] Pepys MS 2853, p. 341; Pepys MS 2857, pp. 214, 223; Adm. 6/428, 1679–84 capts.' list, no. 24.
[52] Rawl. MS A. 189, fo. 146; *DNB*, s.n. 'Dilkes, Thomas'.
[53] C. R. Markham, *The Life of Robert Fairfax of Steeton* (1885), 58–61, 67.

Captain Charles O'Brian by his ability to dance prettily at court.[54] Sea-officers who came from aristocratic or gentry families benefited from the efforts of their fathers or other relatives to further their careers: the promotion of Sir William Berkeley from lieutenant to vice-admiral in four years because of the influence of his brother Charles at court was the most spectacular instance of the importance of family ties,[55] but many other gentlemen officers were assisted by natural paternal or fraternal loyalty.[56] Sir George Rooke, the future conqueror of Gibraltar, owed much in the early days of his career to the dogged persistence with which his father pestered the Admiralty on his behalf.[57]

The single most important external influence on naval appointments was that of the royal brothers themselves. Even when the powers of the Admiralty were out of his hands, from 1660 to 1673 and 1679 to 1684, Charles II retained the prerogative to order the appointment of sea-officers to specific posts: on several occasions during the life of the much maligned Admiralty commission of 1679–84, Charles ordered it to appoint particular individuals to commands, or selected captains himself from an Admiralty shortlist.[58] Charles and James took a genuine interest in the careers of many sea-officers, and intervened either to save individuals from punishments imposed by courts-martial or the Admiralty, or to order that a particular officer be given the first available vacancy.[59] Even when in exile in 1680, James attempted to use his influence on behalf of officers he favoured, seeking a report on the conduct of a young officer so that he could then recommend him to the Admiralty, and recommending an old client, 'that he may be employed, he having now laid long out of Command, but, I hope, now it will not be long before I may solicit for him myself'.[60] The officer

---

[54] Adm. 106/311, fo. 368; Pepys MS 2581, p. 221. Cf. *CSPD*, 1661–2, p. 2; ibid., 1689–90, p. 173; Bod. Lib., Carte MS 219, fo. 133; Adm. 106/371, fo. 52; Pepys MS 2857, p. 481.

[55] KAO, U. 269/C. 298; Bod., Lib., Carte MS 75, fo. 147; *DNB*, s.n. 'Berkeley, William'.

[56] e.g. BL., Addit. MS 60386, unfol., Sir Henry Felton to Capel, 20 May 1679; Rawl. MS A. 173, fo. 55; R. D. Merriman, 'Sir John Ernle: A Confusion of Identities', *MM* 33 (1947), 97–105; M. F. Bond (ed.), *The Diaries and Papers of Sir Edward Dering, Second Baronet, 1644–84* (1976), 108, 116, 130. Cf. Appendix II, below.

[57] Pepys MS 2857, pp. 30, 103; Tanner, *Catalogue*, iii. 150.

[58] J. D. Davies, 'Pepys and the Admiralty Commission of 1679–84', *Historical Research*, 62 (1989), 42.

[59] *Further Correspondence of Samuel Pepys, 1662–79*, ed. J. R. Tanner (1929), 298; Adm. 6/428, 1673–9 lieuts.' list, nos. 18, 19; Pepys MS 2853, pp. 291, 352; Pepys MS 2854, fo. 13; Pepys MS 2860, p. 310; Davies, 'Admiralty Commission', 42.

[60] BL., Addit. MS 18447, fos. 37, 41ᵛ.

corps knew only too well that Charles and James were not just the figureheads of the naval administration, but the greatest naval patrons as well. Officers therefore competed to be noticed, and favoured, by the royal brothers, at sea and on land, and thronged the galleries of the royal palaces. In December 1670, Captain Thomas Guy wrote to inform Pepys that 'the Duke [of York] spyinge me as he went to dinner, call'd me to him & told me he had spoke with the Kinge & my business should be done'; exactly a week later Guy was commissioned captain of one of the royal yachts.[61] By far the most effective form of naval patronage, therefore, was often just a quiet word spoken in a gallery of Whitehall.[62]

The role of Charles and James in shaping the nature of the officer corps of the Restoration navy was particularly significant in the context of the controversy between 'gentlemen' and 'tarpaulin' officers. The years before 1660 had seen the evolution of two disparate kinds of commissioned-officer corps. Until 1642, and particularly in the ship-money fleets of the 1630s, the Crown had appointed captains and lieutenants largely from aristocratic or gentry backgrounds. Many of these officers had acquired a considerable amount of technical skill, but even so, there had been widespread criticism of their appointment by various commentators whose arguments were later recycled by critics in the Restoration period.[63] When the fleet adhered to Parliament in 1642, this high-born element was purged almost completely from the navy because of suspicions that such men might be inclined to royalism, and the nature of the officer corps changed radically, particularly after another extensive purge in 1649. The captains of the fleets which served the interregnum governments were drawn largely from the ranks of the warrant-officers or owner-masters of merchant ships.[64] At the restoration, therefore, Charles and James faced the task of integrating these two seemingly divergent lines of development, a

---

[61] Rawl. MS A. 174, fo. 191; Tanner, *Catalogue*, i. 358.

[62] Or even at Newmarket, where Charles signed many naval commissions: Adm. 6/426, pt. 2.

[63] See e.g. *The Naval Tracts of Sir William Monson*, ed. M. Oppenheim, iii (1912), 434–5; *The Life and Works of Sir Henry Manwaring*, ed. G. E. Manwaring and W. G. Perrin, ii (1922), 83–6, 279–81; N. P. Bard (ed.), 'The Earl of Warwick's Voyage of 1627', *The Naval Miscellany*, 5 (1985), 65, 79; D. E. Kennedy, 'Naval Captains at the Outbreak of the English Civil War', *MM* 46 (1960), 181–98. The current work on Charles I's navy by K. R. Andrews and Andrew Thrush should throw more light on the controversy during that period.

[64] Capp, *Cromwell's Navy*, 53–7, 162–79.

subject explored in Ch. 7 of this study. It was inevitable that a royalist element would be reintroduced into the fleet, but the proven fighting record of most of the Commonwealth's commanders and the continuing influence of their patrons, together with the administrations's desire not to alienate the interregnum veterans and drive them to disaffection, ensured the retention of a large number of these experienced officers.

The surviving interregnum officers were, socially, a very diverse group. Some of the most senior men, notably Edward Mountagu and Sir George Ayscue, came from backgrounds as distinguished as those of any royalist.[65] The majority, however, came from seafaring backgrounds: Captain, later Sir, Richard Haddock (whose father had been a vice-admiral in Parliament's fleets) came from a family which had been using the sea since the fourteenth century at least.[66] Several of the most prominent officers had owned or part-owned their own merchant ships, and only joined the state's navy when their ships were taken up for service. Some had been leading figures in the mercantile communities of their towns, for example Thomas Teddeman and Valentine Tatnell, mayors of Dover, and Roger Cuttance, mayor of Weymouth.[67] The tarpaulin officers who rose to command after 1660 were drawn less frequently from the merchant shipping industry, partly because of the royal policy not to have men commanding their own ships, but they were still drawn chiefly from the same communities. Many came from the east coast, partly because of the orientation of the Dutch wars, partly because of the tendency for many sea-officers of this sort to remain within the cosmopolitan seafaring suburbs of London, or in lodgings elsewhere in the capital, close to the sources of employment.[68] Socially, the tarpaulins, too, were a diverse group. Sir John Kempthorne was the son of an attorney who had been a royalist officer in the civil war, and was a relative of the earls of Marlborough; Sir John Berry was the son of an impecunious country

[65] F. R. Harris, *The Life of Edward Mountagu, K.G., First Earl of Sandwich* (1912), i. 1–23; P. Le Fevre, 'Sir George Ayscue, Commonwealth and Restoration Admiral', *MM* 68 (1982), 189–90; Capp, *Cromwell's Navy*, 175–7.

[66] E. M. Thompson (ed.), 'Correspondence of the Family of Haddock', *The Camden Miscellany*, 8 (1883), p. iii.

[67] For the social origins of the interregnum officers, see Capp, *Cromwell's Navy*, 164–79.

[68] The majority of masters, from whose ranks many tarpaulin captains were drawn, lived in the eastern suburbs of London: SP 29/232, fo. 183; SP 46/136, fos. 213–14; Adm. 106/2908, *passim*. Cf. Capp, *Cromwell's Navy*, 167–8.

vicar; and Captain Charles Royden was a younger son of a poor royalist family of minor gentry from north Wales.[69] The tarpaulins, therefore, were drawn from a variety of social groups, although those from seafaring backgrounds predominated. Even within the ranks of these seafarers, clear social distinctions could exist: Kempthorne, Zachary Browne, and others who owned or part-owned large merchant ships were very different from the likes of Captains John Crabb and William Hobbs, poor, socially obscure men who depended on naval service, in any capacity, for their livelihood.[70]

Socially, the Cavalier officers with previous seagoing experience who entered the navy after 1660 were almost indistinguishable from the interregnum officers and the tarpaulins. The large number of Cavalier warrant-officers placed in the fleet between 1660 and 1670 came from the same areas and backgrounds as those they joined; the criterion for describing them as 'Cavaliers' was usually a tenuous past link with royalism, often no more than a claim that an officer's father fought in an engagement or two for the king.[71] Of the more prominent Cavalier officers, Sir Thomas Allin and his relatives came from exactly the same kind of East Anglian mercantile community as the inter-regnum officers Vice-Admiral William Goodson, Captain Joseph Ames, and Captain Sir Robert Robinson, but they were all Yarmouth men, and Allin's allegiance had been determined by his roots in Yarmouth's great rival, Lowestoft.[72] Only the aggressive Irishmen who had served in royalist privateers in the 1650s, Robert Holmes and Edward Spragge, introduced a significantly new social element into the officer corps, though their minor gentry backgrounds were hardly superior to those of some of the tarpaulins.[73]

The introduction of the 'volunteer *per order*' system in 1661 in-creased the social diversity of the navy. In the early years of the system,

[69] Kempthorne, 'Sir John Kempthorne', 290–1; *DNB*, s.n. 'Berry, John'; J. D. Davies, 'Wales and Mr Pepys's Navy', *Maritime Wales*, 11 (1987), 109–10.

[70] Kempthorne: Prob. 11/361, fo. 152. Browne: Adm. 2/1746, fo. 14; Tanner, *Catalogue*, iii. 389. Crabb: Adm. 2/1750, p. 258. Hobbs: Adm. 106/3539, pt. 2, 'Masters' folder, his petition; BL, Harleian MS 7504, fos. 7–8. Cf. Capp, *Cromwell's Navy*, 169–70, 177–8, 199–201.

[71] Coventry MS 101, fos. 241–2; BL, Addit. MS 18986, fo. 364; Adm. 7/687, pt. 1, no. 369; Adm. 106/317, fo. 316; Adm. 106/345, fo. 9; Adm. 106/3539, pt. 2, 'Carpenters' folder, petition of Joseph Goodwin; *CSPD*, 1660–1, pp. 71, 102, 115; ibid., 1666–7, pp. 223, 382.

[72] *Journals of . . . Allin*, ed. Anderson, i, pp. x–xii.

[73] R. Ollard, *Man of War: Sir Robert Holmes and the Restoration Navy* (1969), 15–17; *Hist. Parl.*, iii. 468–9.

appointments followed a pattern which was to be largely maintained throughout the reigns of Charles and James: the first batches of young gentlemen-officers were generally younger sons of royalist aristocrats or gentlemen who had fought or suffered in the civil wars and interregnum, such as Hugh Seymour (third son of the Cavalier MP Sir Edward Seymour), Francis Digby (second son of the earl of Bristol), and Thomas Darcy (fourth son of John, Lord Darcy).[74] Later 'king's letter boys' included Daniel Dering (third son of Sir Edward Dering, MP), John Every (second son of Sir Henry Every of Eggington), and Francis Wheeler (younger son of Sir Charles Wheeler).[75] However, as the system became more firmly established, its social base broadened. Some first sons entered the service, notably the second Lord Berkeley of Stratton.[76] On the other hand, sons of the lesser gentry also joined, particularly if they had influential connections: George, fourth son of John St Loe of Little Fontmell, Dorset, owed his rise in the navy to a distant family connection with the Hydes, which led to the earl of Rochester becoming his patron.[77] The duke of York's liking for Irishmen was noted by Pepys at an early date, and well over a dozen Irish 'gentlemen' officers held commissions in the Restoration navy. Like their English counterparts, they came from a variety of social backgrounds, ranging from Charles O'Brian, second son to the earl of Inchiquin, to James Montgomery, who hailed from Newtownards merchant stock.[78] Several foreign officers, mainly Swedes, also served in the navy, reflecting a particularly close relationship between the English and Swedish navies. In 1665, three Swedish volunteers were admitted to serve in the royal navy, and others were borne aboard English ships at regular intervals.[79] Five Swedes gained commissions during the second and third Dutch wars, and of these Gustavus,

[74] Coventry MS 99, fo. 233; H. St Maur, *Annals of the Seymours* (1902), 291; HMC, *Lindsey Supplement*, 181–2; Charnock, *Biographia Navalis*, i. 95–6.

[75] Bond, *Dering*, 108, 116, 130; Charnock, *Biographia Navalis*, ii. 252; *CSPD*, 1678, pp. 456–7; *The Conduct of the Earl of Nottingham*, ed. W. A. Aiken (1941), 113n.

[76] G. E. C.[okayne et al.], *The Complete Peerage*, s.n. 'Berkeley of Stratton'. Cf. Dr Rodger's perceptive remarks on the lack of first sons in the Georgian navy: *Wooden World*, 258–9.

[77] R. D. Merriman, 'Captain George St Lo, R. N., 1658–1718', *MM* 31 (1945), 14–15; 32 (1946), 186; *CSPD*, 1682, 546.

[78] *Pepys's Diary*, v. 345; H. McDonnell, 'Irishmen in the Later Stuart Navy, 1660–90', *The Irish Sword*, 16 (1985–6), 87–104; J. D. Davies, 'More Light on Irishmen in the Stuart Navy, 1660–90', *The Irish Sword*, 16 (1985–6), 325–7.

[79] BL, Addit. MS 18986, fo. 385; Adm. 1/5139, fo. 184; Adm. 2/1745, fos. 139ᵛ, 152ᵛ; Adm. 2/1746, fo. 62; Rawl. MS A. 228, fo. 108; Pepys MS 2857, p. 28.

Count Horne, served as a vice-admiral in his own navy in 1677, while Erik Sjöblad became one of Sweden's leading admirals in the war with Denmark, eventually becoming governor of Gothenburg.[80] The only Dutch and French officers to be commissioned, Lauris van Heemskerck and Jean-Baptiste du Tiel, were exceptional cases, the one a renegade from the Dutch fleet in the second Dutch war, and the other a personal servant to the duke of York; one other French officer, a Huguenot lieutenant in Louis XIV's navy, served as a midshipman aboard English warships in the early 1680s after fleeing France for his religion.[81]

The most controversial distortion of the original objectives of the system for gentlemen volunteers was the practice of sending pages into the navy. During the second and third Dutch wars, a few former pages rose to prominent commands, notably Richard le Neve and Sir William Reeves, once pages to the duke of York and Prince Rupert respectively, and in later years this practice became even more common: in 1685, for example, the quota of four volunteers allowed to one frigate included pages to the king, the duke of Grafton, and the earl of Rochester.[82] Other gentlemen volunteers were the sons or relations of serving sea-officers, entered as volunteers and later promoted to gratify their fathers.[83] The diversity of the origins of so-called gentlemen officers, and the pretensions of former pages or low-born volunteers to gentility, drew a barrage of vitriolic and colourful abuse from critics of the system:

your Gentlemen Captains are Sons of Noblemen, Brothers or Kinsmen to Bedchamber Men, Kinsmen to Waiteing Gentlemen, Pages &c sent to sea . . . Butterfly Captaines . . . coachmen, footmen, and the relations and friends, and sometimes stallions and bastards of lewd women . . . some snotty-nosed Letter-man, the Product of some *quondam* Punk, or Alewife.[84]

Even so, for all the contemporary attacks on their ability, the gentlemen officers who came into the service under the 'volunteer *per* order'

[80] Adm. 2/1735, fo. 125ᵛ; *Naval Minutes*, 32. I am grateful to Försvarsstabens Bibliotek, Stockholm, for providing biographical material on Horne and Sjöblad.

[81] *Tangier Papers*, 8, 106; Adm. 3/278, pt. 3, p. 58.

[82] Pepys MS 2858, p. 147; cf. *Tangier Papers*, 121, 150, 206, 212.

[83] See e.g. Adm. 3/277, pt. 1, p. 232; Pepys MS 2856, p. 98; Pepys MS 2858, pp. 413, 429; *Tangier Papers*, 173.

[84] BL, Addit. MS 11602, fos. 87ᵛ, 92; 'An Enquiry into the Causes of Our Naval Miscarriages' (1707), *The Harleian Miscellany*, 1 (1808), 571; E. Ward, *The Wooden World Dissected*, ed. G. A. R. Callender (1929), 27.

system were at least meant to receive *some* training before qualifying for a commission. Unfortunately for their posthumous reputations, they were tarred with the same brush as the other gentlemen volunteers who flocked to the fleet in wartime—the crowds of high-born, courageous, and generally useless landsmen who volunteered to serve at sea in every campaign, seeking a chance of glory and honour. In 1666, for instance, Sir Robert Lynch obtained a place in the fleet only because he had dreamt of shooting the Dutch admiral de Ruyter, while the earl of Dorset's sole contribution to the navy in the second Dutch war seems to have been the composition of the archetypal patronizing ballad of the landsman gone to sea, 'To All you Ladies now at Land'.[85] Classifying such men as 'naval officers' is clearly stretching a point too far, as their only contribution to the life of a ship was usually to take up limited cabin space, but a few made a greater impact. Particularly prominent volunteers, like the duke of Buckingham and earl of Falmouth in the second Dutch war, could demand to play a part in decision-making, and a few (like Prince Rupert's illegitimate son Lord Bellamont in 1666, or the earl of Mulgrave in 1673) were even rewarded for good service with independent commissions of their own.[86] But in general such appointments served only to discredit those gentlemen who had genuinely acquired some technical skill, particularly if an aristocratic officer lost his ship. George Legge, later Lord Dartmouth, became captain of the *Pembroke* in 1667 after one summer's service at sea, and promptly lost her in collision with the *Fairfax*.[87]

In assessing the relative claims of gentlemen and tarpaulins to command in the navy, Charles and James had to take account of several considerations. First, particularly in the years immediately after 1660, the related issues of security and reconciliation were vitally important: a strong royalist element had to be introduced into the fleet to ensure its loyalty, but a significant number of the surviving interregnum officers had to be retained in order to prevent discouragement and

[85] Bod. Lib., Carte MS 222, fo. 108; C. H. Firth (ed.), *Naval Songs and Ballads* (1908), 56–8.

[86] On Buckingham and Falmouth see Ch. 8, on Mulgrave Ch. 9. For Bellamont see G. E. C., *Complete Peerage*, s.n. 'Bellamont'.

[87] *Pepys's Diary*, ix. 39–40; P. Le Fevre, 'Another False Misrepresentation', *MM* 69 (1983), 299–300.

disaffection.[88] Secondly, appointments in the navy could be one way of rewarding a father or a family for loyalty to the monarchy before the Restoration, particularly if the young sea-officer could make enough money out of his active service to recoup some of the money lost to the family by compounding or sequestration; this subject is considered more fully in the next chapter. The question of national honour was also important. Well-born, or at least well-spoken, captains were thought to be better able to handle the diplomatic functions which sea-officers often had to undertake on foreign visits,[89] and it was believed that such men would be more prepared to uphold the honour of the country in an emergency than those who had no fixed estate or interest in the nation.[90] On at least one occasion, a sea-officer's cowardice was considered to have been aggravated by his being a gentleman.[91] Finally, the personal preferences of Charles and James inclined them towards the appointment of gentlemen-commanders. Charles once stated that 'I am not for imploying of men meerly for quality, yett when men of quality are fitt for the trade they desire to enter into, I thinke tis reasonable they should be encouraged at least equally with others'.[92] The problem was whether the 'men of quality' were truly 'fitt for the trade', and whether they were being 'encouraged at least equally', or rather more equally, than others.

[88] *Pepys's Diary*, iv. 169; BL., Egerton MS 3383, fo. 117; Coventry MS 99, fos. 185, 234; Pepys MS 2581, pp. 216–17.
[89] *Monson Tracts*, ed. Oppenheim, iv. 16; Capp, *Cromwell's Navy*, 159–60.
[90] Leicestershire RO, Finch political papers 148, fo. 5; Pepys MS 2581, p. 217; HMC, *Dartmouth MSS*, i. 181; HMC, *Stuart Papers*, ii. 199, 243; *Tangier Papers*, 121.
[91] Tanner, *Catalogue*, iv. 466–7.
[92] HMC, *Finch MSS*, ii. 167. Cf. BL, Addit. MS 11602, fos. 76, 128.

3

THE 'GENTLEMAN–TARPAULIN' ISSUE AND THE REFORM OF THE OFFICER CORPS

THE officers of the Restoration navy in general, and the gentlemen captains in particular, have long been damned by the judgements in Pepys's diary, in his other writings, and in the works of other contemporary or near-contemporary writers, all of whom accuse them of having been indisciplined and incompetent. It is dangerous to rely almost exclusively for our view of the state of discipline in the officer corps on the opinions of administrators and polemicists, even one as persuasive as Pepys, for the administrators were often (and with some justification) the targets of the sea-officers' own censure. Even so, whereas the historiography of the eighteenth-century navy was once dominated by an image of gallant sea-officers struggling manfully against a corrupt administration,[1] the pre-eminence of Pepys has ensured the perpetuation of a diametrically opposite view of the service in the late seventeenth century. This view sees a band of rough, brave tarpaulin captains being supplanted by vicious, arrogant 'gentlemen' who brought into the fleet such vices as drinking, swearing, whoring, and effeminate clothing, corrupting the remaining tarpaulins and clashing in the process with enlightened administrators (or, more accurately, with one enlightened administrator).[2] Historians from Macaulay onwards have found this interpretation attractive and convincing, and have used it to fashion some vivid descriptions of a corrupt and inept fighting service. Unfortunately, this interpretation has always begged one crucial question. If the gentlemen captains really were so bad, and really so dominant numerically, how did the

[1] Baugh, *British Naval Administration*, 2, 500.
[2] For contemporary opinions of this sort, see e.g. BL., Addit. MS 11602, *passim*; BL., Egerton MS 3383, fo. 118; Bod. Lib., Rawlinson MS D. 147, fo. 36; Pepys MS 2581, p. 229; *The Diary of John Evelyn*, ed. E. S. de Beer (1956), v. 10–11. For the perpetuation of this attitude see, *inter alia*, Macaulay, *History of England*, i. 293–4; J. R. Tanner, *Samuel Pepys and the Royal Navy* (Cambridge, 1920), 68–71, 76; Ollard, *Pepys: A Biography*, 160, 221–2, 228.

royal navy manage to hold its own in two wars with arguably the best-commanded naval force of the age, the Dutch fleet, and manage in 1692 decisively to defeat arguably the best-designed naval force, Louis XIV's new French fleet? The glib answer, that Pepys put the navy to rights, simply will not do. The Restoration navy could not have been a clearly defined battleground of the forces of good and evil: the tradition which nurtured and inspired Nelson owed at least as much to the much-maligned gentlemen captains as it did to Samuel Pepys.

In the first place, the nature of the 'gentleman–tarpaulin' issue was not constant. As recounted in Chs. 7 and 8 of this study, at least until the end of the second Dutch war the majority of the commissioned officers were veterans of the interregnum navy; the experienced Cavalier officers were too few, and the first intake of gentlemen officers too inexperienced, to challenge their dominance significantly.[3] This situation changed in the years between 1667 and 1674, partly because of the deaths of many of the old captains and their patrons, Monck (duke of Albemarle), Mountagu (earl of Sandwich), and Sir William Penn, partly because Sir William Coventry, an opponent of the wholesale promotion of gentlemen officers, was replaced as secretary to the lord high admiral by Matthew Wren, who favoured their appointment.[4] By 1673, Coventry was aware that the nature of the officer corps had changed dramatically since he left office six years earlier, and the third Dutch war was fought largely by the new breed of gentlemen captains, as were the subsequent wars with the Barbary corsairs.[5] During the long period of peace from 1674 to 1689, the majority of commissions were granted to 'gentlemen'; the tarpaulins were a minority, restricted chiefly to the smaller ships of the fleet.

Before and during the second Dutch war, therefore, the 'gentleman–tarpaulin' issue was essentially political, a question of the relative balance of royalist and republican elements in the navy. Some of the newly appointed Cavalier and gentlemen officers resented the continued dominance of the interregnum officers and the presence of 'fanatics' in the service, while the future marquis of Halifax, reflecting in later years on this controversy, perceived profound implications for the whole nation in the issue:

---

[3] Unless otherwise stated, this paragraph is based on Appendix I, below.
[4] Capp, *Cromwell's Navy*, 389–90; cf. Ch. 9, below.
[5] Coventry MS 104, fo. 124. Cf. *Tangier Papers*, 235; Pepys MS 1534, p. 36.

In case the officers should bee all Tarpaulins, it would . . . bee in reality . . . too
great a tendency to a Commonwealth; such a part of the Constitution being
Democratically disposed, may bee suspected to endeavour to bring it into
that Shape . . . Gentlemen in a generall definition will bee suspected to ly
more than other men, under the temptations of being made Instruments of
Unlimited power . . . there must bee a mixture in the Navy of Gentlemen and
Tarpaulins, as there is in constitution of the Government of power and
liberty.[6]

Moreover, as suggested in Chs. 7 and 8 below, the issue was also
inextricably interwoven with the complex antagonisms and factional
disputes between the great naval patrons—the dukes of York and
Albemarle, Prince Rupert, Sandwich, Penn, and Sir John Lawson—
which blighted the English fleet's performance during the second war.
From the beginning, Sandwich and Sir William Coventry attacked the
supposed incompetence and indiscipline of the new gentlemen sea-
officers, and their prejudices were assimilated readily by the young
Pepys,[7] who maintained an almost obsessional antagonism towards
gentlemen officers until the end of his life, despite the fact that many
of the basic criteria of the 'gentleman–tarpaulin' dispute changed
considerably after the 1660s. Later in the Restoration period, for
instance, the controversy was based more clearly on social and professional criteria: one Admiralty commissioner of the 1690s assessed
the relative merits of the different kinds of officer on strictly professional grounds, stating that gentlemen would 'not keep the sea' and
were 'not obedient to orders', while drawing an interesting distinction
between true tarpaulins who had risen from warrant-posts ('their
accounts imperfect . . . great care of their ships . . . constant among
their men') and those who had come in from merchant service ('wil
trade . . . their accounts regular . . . can detect imbezellments').[8]
    The social criteria involved in the dispute were always rather
dubious: in fact, there might be little difference in social status
between a gentleman and a tarpaulin. When the 'tarpaulin' Captain
Charles Royden, younger son of a minor Welsh gentleman, fell out
with his 'gentleman' lieutenant, George Aylmer, younger son of an
impecunious Irish knight and once a page to the earl of Arlington, he
quoted Aylmer as saying that 'he was a better Gent then any of the

---

[6] *Works of Halifax*, ed. Brown, i. 303–4.
[7] *Pepys's Diary*, iii. 121–3, 129, iv. 169, 196, 423.
[8] Cumbria RO, Carlisle, MS D/Lons/L/Box 4, 'Book 5', p. 16.

Roydons, I said admitt it be true yet I never was a footman...'.[9] Gentlemen often objected more to the habits of the tarpaulins than their birth. They criticized the tarpaulin captain's supposed over-familiarity with his men, slovenly appearance, and slowness of mind, and accused him of not knowing the difference between the honour of merchant ships and warships—all generalizations which were as exaggerated and unfair as some of those levelled against the gentlemen by their critics.[10] However, like many of the criticisms of the gentlemen, they did contain some truth. Several tarpaulin captains were illiterate,[11] and others disgraced themselves on formal occasions abroad. A gentleman captain had to apologize for the drunken cavorting of his tarpaulin commodore to their Swedish guests by hoping 'that they would not judge of the behaviour of the English gentlemen by this of Captain Robinson, who was but so & so & better could not be expected of him', and one interregnum captain was so lacking in a sense of protocol that, instead of kissing the hand of the new queen of England, he playfully slapped her wrist.[12] Even 'gentlemen' admirals who were prepared to praise and encourage tarpaulins, notably Lord Dartmouth and Edward Russell, believed that their own kind were entitled to the great majority of commands in the navy.[13] For their part, the tarpaulins naturally resented the increasing domination of the navy by gentlemen officers who blocked their paths to promotion, even though tarpaulins (as they believed) possessed greater knowledge of the sea.[14] They objected to the gentlemen's near-monopoly of the most lucrative voyages, and to the greater ease with which the gentlemen could solicit favours at court;[15] and they mocked the fine clothes, manners, and desire for a modicum of comfort which characterized many gentlemen officers.[16]

One of the most significant differences between gentlemen and tarpaulins was also hinted at by Captain Royden when he exclaimed to Lieutenant Aylmer, 'Oh Sir, you are a young lieut[enant], I have

---

[9] Rawl. MS A. 181, fo. 357. For Aylmer, see Rawl. MS A. 190, fo. 236; for Royden, see Davies, 'Wales and Mr Pepys's Navy', 109–10. Cf. Capp, *Cromwell's Navy*, 175–9.

[10] BL, Egerton MS 3383, fos. 118–19; HMC, *Finch MSS*, iv. 290, 390; Pepys MS 2581, p. 228; Capp, *Cromwell's Navy*, 178–9.

[11] e.g. Tanner, *Catalogue*, iv. 464; Adm. 1/3545, pp. 419–20; Adm. 106/282, fo. 75.

[12] Pepys MS 2581, p. 229; BL, Sloane MS 505, fo. 34.

[13] *Tangier Papers*, 207; HMC, *Finch MSS*, iv. 154, 244.

[14] Pepys MS 2581, p. 216; *Tangier Papers*, 233–4. Cf. Rawl. MS A. 314, fo. 22ᵛ.

[15] *Tangier Papers*, 150.

[16] Ibid.

been an ould one.'[17] Several critics of the gentlemen officers objected implicitly or explicitly to the youth of such men, and many of the clashes between young gentlemen and older tarpaulins clearly originated in the age difference.[18] This was a natural result of the different career structures of the two types of officer: many warrant-officers did not attain that rank until their early thirties,[19] and could be rather older when they first received a commission. An analysis of the careers of 165 commissioned officers suggests that on average a gentleman officer could expect to gain a lieutenant's commission at 23 and a command at 25, whereas a tarpaulin would be 37 and 39 respectively.[20] The officer corps of the Restoration navy may have suffered less from a microcosm of the 'court and country' conflict,[21] than from a severe case of a generation gap. Moreover, it would be misleading to suggest that there was constant conflict and jealousy between all gentlemen and all tarpaulins. Conflict naturally tended to attract more attention from both contemporaries and historians, and the many cases of good relations tend to be overlooked. The mutual respect and loyalty between the earl of Ossory and his flag-captain, Sir John Narbrough, matched the equally cordial relationship between Sir Frescheville Holles and his tarpaulin lieutenant, Jeremy Roche, in the second Dutch war.[22] Shipboard dinner parties were often large, friendly social gatherings of officers from all backgrounds.[23] The most interesting manifestation of these cordial relations was the formation of a club for naval captains in 1674, which was to meet weekly 'for the improvement of a mutuall society, and an encrease of love and kindness among them'; its membership consisted of roughly equal numbers of gentlemen and tarpaulins under the stewardship of Sir John Kempthorne.[24] Nevertheless, the undoubted existence of excellent relations between many gentlemen and many tarpaulins, and the great number of conflicts—political, social, 'ageist'—which divided

[17] Rawl. MS A. 181, fo. 340.
[18] Coventry MS 99, fo. 234; Adm. 106/338, fo. 360; Tanner, *Catalogue*, ii. 207–8; *Tangier Papers*, 120, 153–4.
[19] Analysis based on the careers of the officers of the ordinary (notably at Deptford) in 1685: Adm. 106/3540, pt. 2, 'Musters' folder.
[20] Cf. Capp, *Cromwell's Navy*, 163–4.
[21] This view has been advanced by N. Elias, 'Studies in the Genesis of the Naval Profession', *British Journal of Sociology*, 1 (1950), 298–308; Ollard, *Pepys*, 225.
[22] *CSPD*, 1673, 443, 508; B. S. Ingram (ed.), *Three Sea Journals of Stuart Times* (1936), 54–5, 63, 74.
[23] e.g. *The Diary of Henry Teonge, 1675–9*, ed. G. E. Manwaring (1927), 63, 82, 126.
[24] NMM, SOC/21.

them, cannot conceal the fact that at the bottom of many of those conflicts was the issue of technical competence. Quite simply, tarpaulins
and their propagandists, especially Pepys, accused the new gentlemen
officers of being unfit to command at sea.

The charges of incompetence which were levelled at the gentlemen should be treated with caution. Many gentlemen officers were
undoubtedly promoted before their time, and in the 1660s in particular
criticism was directed at the short period spent as volunteers by some
men, and at the lack of application displayed both by the volunteers
and by those captains and under-officers intended to train them, who
preferred to pander to their well-connected young charges, and promoted them in a blatant attempt to increase their own influence at
court or in the service.[25] At least one gentleman officer who later rose
to prominence, George Legge, Lord Dartmouth, regretted his lack of
early training.[26] Even so, many officers quickly acquired some degree
of technical knowledge, and were enthusiastic to learn more; even a
land-officer like William Beeston, commanding a fourth-rate in the
West Indies in 1670, could acquire a reasonable command of navigation within a few weeks, and some progressed to a considerable degree
of technical skill.[27] Even one of the most aristocratic and severely
criticized of the first generation of gentlemen officers, Francis Digby,
is revealed in his private journals as a competent navigator who took
more than a passing interest in the technical side of ship command;
indeed, on one occasion only Digby's quick thinking prevented his
ship being wrecked in fog on the north African coast, and saved the
squadron following in his wake.[28] Moreover, few disputed the bravery
of most of the gentlemen commanders. They were young men in
search of glory, and their yearning for action could be obsessive:
'consider how unfortunate a Young Man I am to be at home in a
disabled ship when all the world is fighting,' 21-year-old Digby wrote
in 1666.[29]

---

[25] Leicestershire RO, Finch political papers 148, fo. 5; Rawl. MS A. 191, fo. 153;
Pepys MS 2853, fo. 200ᵛ, pp. 264–5; Pepys MS 2581, pp. 223–4; *Tangier Papers*, 145,
156, 163, 229.

[26] Tanner, *Catalogue*, iv. 544.

[27] BL, Addit. MS 12424, *passim*.

[28] BL, Addit. MS 17484, fos. 46–7 *et passim*.

[29] Coventry MS 95, fo. 409ᵛ. Cf. Adm. 106/308, fo. 161; BL, Sloane MS 1745, p. 2;
Rawl. MS A. 186, fo. 344.

The single most important measure taken to improve the overall
level of competence within the officer corps, and a measure which is
still generally regarded as one of the most important steps in the
evolution of the naval profession (as well as being one of the greatest
achievements of Samuel Pepys), was the introduction of a qualifying
examination for lieutenants in 1677. This regulation laid down a
minimum age of 20 and a probationary period of two years as a volunteer *per* order and one as a midshipman, followed by an examination
before a board of senior captains, before the aspiring sea-officer could
qualify for a commission.[30] The establishment grew out of a complaint
from Sir John Narbrough, admiral in the Mediterranean, about the
incompetence of his lieutenants, and Pepys played a major part in
shaping the new system.[31] Its provision of training in the petty rank of
midshipman simply codified a long-established practice; under the
Commonwealth, midshipmen, regarded as trainee officers, had been
over 21 and capable of taking a boatswain's or gunner's place.[32]
Compelling gentlemen volunteers to do a midshipman's duty was seen
as the centrepiece of the scheme; as one of its instigators observed: 'it
will unite the officers & destroy the distinction between gentleman &
tarpaulin, for as all tarpaulins are made gentlemen by accepting the
Kings Commission, so every gentleman haveing performed this duty
cannot be denied to be as capable of employment as any.'[33] Pepys was
delighted with the establishment, exulting that the 'bastard Breed' had
now been excluded from the service,[34] and it certainly raised the level
of technical competence among those gentlemen officers who gained
commissions after 1677. The examination itself took the form of a stiff
interview before a panel of senior captains, and the young officer
needed to be able, for example, to explain how he would take observa-
tions of the ship's position, how he would handle her when tacking or
in a storm, and to recount differentials in tide times from those at
London Bridge.[35] Young volunteers were forced to prepare diligently
for the ordeal. Pepys's nephew Samuel Jackson got the yeoman of the
Foresight's powder room to teach him navigation; another nephew,

[30] Tanner, *Catalogue*, i. 202–5.
[31] Pepys MS 2853, fos. 231ᵛ, 256, pp. 264–5; Tanner, *Catalogue*, iv. 493–4, 535–6,
543–5; Adm. 106/3537, pt. 4, 'Exams. of Officers' folder.
[32] C. G. Pitcairn Jones, 'Midshipmen', *MM* 40 (1954), 212–14.
[33] Rawl. MS A. 191, fo. 153. Cf. Pepys MS 2853, fo. 256.
[34] Pepys MS 2854, fo. 17ᵛ; Pepys MS 2855, pp. 206–7.
[35] NMM, LBK/8, pp. 810–12; *Tangier Papers*, 131.

John Pepys, was spurred on by his captain to learn 'those things that seeme likely to future preferment'; while the future admiral, Robert Fairfax, resorted to a respected navigation tutor at Wapping in the intervals between his sea service in order to 'cram' for the examination.[36] As a result of such rigorous training, by 1688 even such aristocratic young officers as Lord William Murray (a son of the marquis of Atholl) and John Granville (second son of the earl of Bath) were considered fit to command fire-ships, arguably the most technically demanding vessels in the navy and a traditional preserve of the 'tarpaulins'.[37]

Despite the definite improvement in the quality of the gentlemen officers between the 1660s and 1680s, critics continued to press the point that they were less fit to command than those with a lifetime's experience at sea, and a whole range of specific charges of incompetence continued to be brought against the gentlemen. One of the most significant of these was the charge that their comparative ignorance of the seaman's trade would prevent them keeping an adequate check on their subordinate officers, who would be able to persuade the incompetent captain to adopt a cowardly or unwise tactic, or to sign for unnecessary stores.[38] However, a more frequent occurrence was an attempt by a captain who had acquired a modicum of technical expertise to trespass on the territory of the master, who remained in theoretical charge of the navigation of the ship, and many disputes of this sort occurred.[39] Critics of the gentlemen, wary of the potential dangers of the certificate system, warned that such captains should not recommend masters or other warrant-officers, whose skills they did not fully understand.[40] However, such criticisms overlooked the fact that the level of competence among masters, or tarpaulins in general, was often alarmingly low. Many masters were of a poor standard; their hit-and-miss methods of navigation surprised passengers aboard warships, and even one of the longest-serving tarpaulin captains, Sir

---

[36] Rawl. MS A. 179, fos. 14, 70; Markham, *Life of Robert Fairfax*, 54–6. Cf. NMM, NVT/8, the 'navigational workbook' of a volunteer in the 1680s.

[37] Rawl. MS A. 186, fo. 429.

[38] BL, Addit. MS 11602, fo. 75; Addit. MS 32094, fos. 43–4; SP 29/152, fos. 70–1; SP 29/171, fo. 156; SP 29/211, fo. 218; Rawl. MS A. 195, fo. 68ᵛ; Pepys MS 2581, p. 229; *Tangier Papers*, 106, 117, 123–4; Adm. 106/3537, pt. 1, 'Masters' folder, charges against John Smith.

[39] See e.g. SP 29/330, fo. 63; Pepys MS 2581, pp. 241, 260; *Tangier Papers*, 116, 134.

[40] *Naval Minutes*, 256; *Tangier Papers*, 217.

Richard Munden, rarely got his ship's position right, and confused
some of the most prominent headlands in the English channel.[41] In
1672, another veteran tarpaulin complained that the navigator's trade
was being undermined by 'prateing popingais' who rose to become a
mate after just a voyage or two, despite having 'nothing either in art or
experience'.[42] The tarpaulins were not the uniformly competent collection of experts that their advocates claimed.

The most important charge brought against the gentlemen officers,
that they were above the rules of the navy, was in many ways the
obvious one for administrators to make. 'It is not hard to make good
rules, but to gett them executed is the difficulty,' Coventry once told
Pepys,[43] and sea-officers and administrators clashed on many occasions. Though the administrators' desire to enforce strict rules was
commendable, it created a considerable amount of resentment. In
addition to coping with a new set of administrative requirements, the
sea-officers were faced with stinging rebukes for taking unauthorized
leave, or for exploiting the various unofficial 'perquisites' available to
them, and had to contend with attempts by the administration to check
on their activities when overseas.[44] Although Pepys, in particular,
cloaked his rebukes with protestations of affection and occasional
humour, sea-officers (both gentlemen and tarpaulins) objected to the
notion that their word could be doubted, or that their statements might
be disproved by Pepys's rigorous research into the records of the
service.[45] Officers responded by attempting to cover for each other,
either by providing alibis for (or deliberately vague reports on) colleagues under investigation,[46] or by favouring colleagues at courts-
martial: senior naval men as diverse as Pepys and Prince Rupert
complained of the tendency of such courts to acquit captains in the
majority of cases, regardless of the evidence, or else to impose
disproportionately lenient sentences.[47]

This budding spirit of professional solidarity as a reaction against

[41] BL, Addit. MS 11606, fo. 53ᵛ; Rawl. MS D. 147, fo. 14; All Souls College,
Oxford, MS 317, fos. 55–6; Pepys MS 2350, pp. 92–4, 97, *et passim*.

[42] Rawl. MS A. 316, fos. 1–2.

[43] Rawl. MS A. 178, fo. 270ᵛ.

[44] See Tanner, *Catalogue*, iii. 39, 87–8; iv. 80–1, 85; Bod. Lib., Carte MS 47, fo.
442; BL, Addit. MS 19872, fo. 34; Adm. 2/1752, pp. 96–7.

[45] See e.g. Pepys MS 2858, pp. 543–4, 555–6; Pepys MS 2859, p. 459; Pepys MS
2860, pp. 440–1.

[46] Pepys MS 2853, p. 123; Pepys MS 2856, pp. 44, 56.

[47] NHL, MS 121/13, p. 121; BL, Addit. MS 11602, fo. 60ᵛ; Adm. 3/275, p. 68;
Pepys MS 2861, pp. 53, 121–2; *Naval Minutes*, 323.

the demands of the administration was a manifestation of a more fundamental attitude within the officer corps. Commissioned officers regarded themselves as being ultimately responsible only to the lord high admiral and the king, not to any of their subordinates.[48] Moreover, there was no clearly defined hierarchy to relate the respective authorities of administrators and sea-officers: it was never clear, for example, whether a resident commissioner of the navy in one of the dockyards was actually superior to the captains of the ships in his yard.[49] Both gentlemen and tarpaulins were often on bad terms with the Navy Board, the body which sought to enforce the administrative duties demanded of them. Both types of officer resented being reprimanded, or having their demands rejected, by what they regarded as a subordinate body,[50] and this resentment extended as far as the secretary of the Admiralty. Pepys knew that many captains disliked him because of his attempts to enforce stricter discipline,[51] and some gentlemen officers may also have resented him for social reasons: if a captain could object to Pepys's friend, the shipbuilder Sir Anthony Deane, as 'a tradesman', others could object to the secretary himself as a mere tailor's son (an easy jibe, and one which Pepys's many critics liked to stress).[52] Moreover, the sea-officers regarded much of the administration as corrupt and incompetent. Admiral Sir Edward Spragge's justification for pocketing men's pay and exploiting other 'windfalls' was that if he did not, 'some boddy or other hee was sure would prevent the Kings haveing the benifitt of them',[53] and this cynical remark probably contained more than a grain of truth. The Navy Board was often criticized for its tardiness in paying bills drawn by captains,[54] and the changes introduced into the Board's procedures during the Restoration period were censured for being too intricate and preventing the rapid despatch of business.[55]

---

[48] See e.g. Bod. Lib., Carte MS 47, fo. 482; Adm. 106/359, fos. 103, 114; *CSPD*, 1672, 369.

[49] BL, Addit. MS 11602, fo. 223; Cumbria RO, MS D/Lons/L/Box 1, 'Book containing information regarding the navy of various dates from 1587 to 1697 . . . ', p. 296; R. D. Merriman (ed.), *The Sergison Papers* (1950), 273; Ehrman, *Navy . . . of William III*, 101–2.

[50] See e.g. Adm. 1/3548, p. 483; *CSPD*, 1668–9, 396–7; *The Letters of Samuel Pepys and his Family Circle*, ed. H. T. Heath (1955), 219–21.

[51] NMM, LBK/8, p. 806.

[52] *CSPD*, 1666–7, 218; *A Hue and Cry After P. and H., and Plain Truth* [1680], 3.

[53] Pepys MS 2581, pp. 225–6.

[54] See e.g. Adm. 106/381, fos. 17, 274; Adm. 106/384, fo. 307; KAO, U. 1515/O. 8, unfol., Narbrough to Pepys, 6 Nov. 1678 (second fo. *verso*).

[55] Maydman, *Speculations*, 43–6.

Clashes occurred most frequently between sea-officers and the subordinate dockyard officials, the masters-attendant, the master ship-wrights, and their colleagues. The master-attendant's supervisory role over ships in his yard led to friction with captains, who accused him of usurping their authority; for their part, the masters-attendant (invariably long-serving tarpaulins) resented the pretensions and demands of young gentlemen captains.[56] Clashes with the shipwrights usually centred on differences of opinion about the nature and amount of decoration adorning a vessel, about the number and placing of cabins, and about measures necessary to improve the sailing and fighting qualities of the ship. Inseparable issues of vanity and honour shaped the sea-officers' attitudes: a ship's appearance and performance reflected on her captain, so a reputation could suffer if she sailed badly,[57] while decoration made the ship a more impressive symbol of the honour of king and country. Critics of the gentlemen argued that decoration was costly and pandered solely to the captains' vanity; master shipwrights objected to the 'whimsicall fancies' of captains; and administrators in general complained about the excessive and unreasonable demands of captains for more elaborate ornamentation.[58] For their part, captains could argue that shipwrights were ignorant of the importance of having a ship capable of upholding England's honour, and some were prepared to pay for improvements to the ship's decoration themselves.[59] Pride and vanity were certainly present in the sea-officers' demands on the dockyard officers, but so, too, was concern for the image of England which their ships would present to the world; a desire to prevent unnecessary expense was certainly present in the dockyard officers' attitudes, but so, too, was professional jealousy and a feeling that they knew best.

The administration could complain that the gentlemen, or sea-officers in general, were above the rules of the navy, but the officers could respond by attacking the rules themselves. From 1663 onwards, captains were governed by the duke of York's 'General Instructions . . . to Commanders', a set of over forty regulations which were supple-

---

[56] Adm. 1/3553, p. 5; Adm. 106/319, fo. 94; Adm. 106/343, fo. 326; Adm. 106/373, fo. 425; Adm. 106/379, fos. 433, 435.

[57] See e.g. Adm. 106/314, fo. 240; Adm. 106/345, fo. 94.

[58] Rawl. MS D. 147, fos. 36–7; Maydman, *Speculations*, 96–100; *Naval Minutes*, 26; Adm. 1/3556, pp. 678, 681; Adm. 106/319, fo. 153; Adm. 106/374, fos. 275–6; Pepys MS 2581, p. 106; Pepys MS 2862, p. 183; *CSPD*, 1666–7, 96; ibid., 1671, 15.

[59] Adm. 106/379, fo. 7; Herbert Lbk, 1.

mented by additional rules for shipboard discipline.[60] The general instructions imposed on commanders a series of tasks which, taken together, demanded a careful scrutiny of many aspects of shipboard activity: subordinate officers' accounts and disbursements had to be checked; at the end of a voyage, various account-books were to be submitted to the appropriate principal officers at the Navy Board; muster-books of the crew were to be sent to the Board at regular intervals during the voyage; and a journal had to be submitted at the voyage's end. Captains found these obligations onerous, particularly because they compelled them to investigate technicalities and to follow unfamiliar, bureaucratic procedures, with a penalty of suspension of wages for irregular compliance.[61] One captain, censured by the board for inadequate book-keeping, protested that he was not 'bred a Clerke',[62] and during the second Dutch war ships' books were not checked too rigorously for fear of provoking an outcry from the captains.[63] However, in 1672 so many captains failed to comply fully with the instructions that the administration had to create the new post of captain's clerk to cope with the problem.[64] This change had little immediate effect, and complaints of neglect on the part of captains continued. As a result, examination of their performance was put on a still more formal footing, with the Board examining captains on their performance of each instruction, and checking all books and papers carefully.[65]

Nevertheless, the problem of non-compliance persisted, and, if anything, got worse.[66] Many captains' explanations and excuses undoubtedly attempted to conceal their own neglect or corruption. A surprising number claimed to have lost all their books and papers owing to a variety of convenient natural disasters, while others shifted the blame on to their clerk or purser.[67] Many claimed that they had

---

[60] The number of instructions was increased piecemeal over the years. Several copies survive: hereafter, reference is made to NMM, ADL/A/4 (a printed copy issued to Sir Edward Spragge in 1669) and NMM, RUSI/NM/135. For a summary, see Tedder, *Navy of the Restoration*, 67–8.

[61] NMM, ADL/A/4, RUSI/NM/135.

[62] Pepys MS 2581, p. 167. Cf. Capp, *Cromwell's Navy*, 159.

[63] *CSPD*, 1667, 510.

[64] Adm. 106/24, fos. 138, 225; Adm. 106/28, fos. 260–1.

[65] Adm. 106/27, fos. 5, 147; NMM, SER/3, 10 Jan. 1676; BL, Addit. MS 9303, fos. 7, 10–12. Cf. Adm. 106/3537, pt. 3, 'Papers relating to Instructions'.

[66] See e.g. *CSPD*, 1676–7, 389.

[67] Adm. 1/3547, pp. 413, 989, 1223–4; Adm. 1/3548, p. 989; Adm. 1/3550, pp. 787–9, 997–8; Adm. 1/3552, pp. 113–14; Adm. 1/3556, p. 345; Adm. 106/382, fo. 213.

never received copies of the instructions or the necessary books,[68] and even captains who had served before claimed that failure to receive a copy of the instructions with each new commission absolved them from a duty to comply—one officer argued that 'it is unjust to condemne a man for the breach of a law where there is none made'.[69] Others excused their non-compliance by pleading that they could not read, though these pleas were invariably made retrospectively and not when the instructions were received.[70] However, the administration's insistence on the letter of each instruction raised several practical difficulties which brought the whole system into disrepute. One of the most common shortcomings of captains was a failure to comply with the thirteenth instruction, which insisted on a muster of the ship's company once a week and the despatch of two full muster-books to the Navy Board every two months. Captains of vessels employed on short voyages in home waters argued that as they were usually under a shore-based muster-master or clerk of the cheque, they should be exempt from this provision;[71] even so, the Board replied that the instructions had to be complied with in all cases.[72] Captains on long voyages, or on overseas stations, complained that it was difficult or impossible to send books at regular intervals, and that there was no point in mustering men once a week at sea, where they could not desert. Despite the obvious defects of the thirteenth instruction, the administration's attitude remained rigid: non-compliance constituted grounds for suspension of wages, even if it had been physically impossible for a captain to send muster-books to London or wholly unnecessary for him to conduct a weekly muster.[73] Gentlemen and tarpaulins were affected equally by, and responded with equal bemusement and annoyance at, these inflexible bureaucratic requirements. For instance, the attempt to impose a standard, tabular form of journal on all captains may have been designed to force 'ignorant' gentlemen officers to give full accounts of their voyages, but it also

[68] Adm. 1/3545, pp. 419–20; Adm. 1/3547, pp. 120–1, 1057, 1219; Adm. 1/3556, p. 345; Adm. 106/306, fo. 30; Adm. 106/381, fo. 276; Tanner, *Catalogue*, iv. 409, 454.
[69] Adm. 106/382, fo. 213.
[70] Adm. 1/3545, pp. 419–20; Adm. 1/3550, pp. 997–8; Tanner, *Catalogue*, iv. 464.
[71] Adm. 1/3547, pp. 120, 333, 413, 761; Adm. 1/3550, pp. 563–4; Adm. 1/3552, pp. 281–2; Adm. 106/338, fo. 194.
[72] NMM, SER/3, 23 Feb. 1676; BL, Egerton MS 928, fo. 254; *Sergison Papers*, 19.
[73] Adm. 1/3547, pp. 120, 317–18, 605, 961; Adm. 1/3550, pp. 787–9; Adm. 106/308, fo. 73; Adm. 106/317, fo. 366; Adm. 106/333, fo. 360; Adm. 106/340, fo. 288; Adm. 106/343, fo. 315; Adm. 106/352, fo. 634.

imposed a new method on veteran sea-officers who had been using their own systems for years.[74] The new requirements were drawn up by landsmen like Pepys and his clerk Richard Gibson, who analysed captains' journals in detail to see how far they complied with their 'ideal'; while some of their criticisms were sensible and valid, others scarcely rose above the level of nit-picking.[75] Captains resented having to comply so precisely with an alien form of journal, yet the administration again insisted on compliance in return for payment of wages.[76]

The general instructions were criticized bitterly for many years, both by the sea-officers and even by some of the administrators. In 1673 Prince Rupert warned that it was impossible to comply with some of the instructions, but the other members of the Admiralty commission overruled him. Pepys intended to revise them but never undertook the task, partly because of pressure of work, and partly because of his insistence on a substantial reimbursement for making the revision.[77] The main complaints against the instructions as a whole were that they had become too numerous and intricate, and that they omitted important matters, notably the nature of the relationship between sea-officers, yard officials, and the Navy Board.[78] The instructions were seen as imposing too much on 'Captaynes who know not very well how to use their Penns', and greater delegation of authority to the subordinate officers was suggested as a remedy.[79] Without revision, the Navy Board had little option other than to impose the instructions as they stood, despite the resentment which this course bred among the sea-officers. A gentleman-captain could protest that, although he had not complied fully with each instruction, he had not dishonoured the king's service; in the depths of winter, a tarpaulin captain could find his crew in desperate need of clothing and yet be unable to provide for them, because the instructions did not permit it.[80] Revision required time and money, neither of which materialized, and the captains serving in the French war after 1689 still found that they were

---

[74] See e.g. Adm. 1/3548, p. 150. For other 'non-standard' journals by prominent tarpaulins, see e.g. Adm. 51/3580, pt. 2; Adm. 51/4398, pt. 5.

[75] Pepys MS 2350, p. 91; Pepys MS 2351, *passim*; BL, Addit. MS 11602, fos. 62–3, 77, 385–404.

[76] See e.g. Adm. 3/278, pt. 1, p. 112.

[77] Adm. 3/275, pp. 71–2; Pepys MS 2856, pp. 191–2.

[78] Ibid.; BL, Addit. MS 11602, fos. 190, 223; *Tangier Papers*, 158–9.

[79] PRO, PRO 30/32/1, paper beginning 'That the Commanders Instructions be Reviewed'.

[80] Adm. 106/333, fo. 467; Adm. 106/337/2, fo. 370.

expected, even in the height of action, to send to London two muster-books once every two months.[81]

The one rule of the navy which was broken more often than any other, and the one which contemporaries and later writers could justly charge the gentlemen with breaking more often than the tarpaulins,[82] formed the basis of the seventh instruction: sea-officers had to give constant attendance on their ships while they were in pay. In reality, captains were often absent when a ship was fitting out, and came ashore as soon as the vessel came in. Gentlemen officers, who might possess pressing political, business, or social reasons for attending at Whitehall or strolling in Covent Garden, were particularly prone to this failing. A captain's absence could create many difficulties, including the danger of serious indiscipline aboard ship if his subordinates were inadequate, the risk that the ship might not be available for service in an emergency, and the setting of a bad example to others in the service.[83] In theory, a captain had to petition the king or lord high admiral in advance for leave of absence for a predetermined number of days, and then only for essential reasons; in practice, captains either left their ships without any form of authority, or claimed that they had received the permission of a local official such as the resident commissioner of the dockyard.[84] Pepys and his fellow administrators never coped satisfactorily with this problem. Occasional attempts were made to restrict grants of leave, but it was thought unreasonable to confine the captains too closely, and after a few months of rigorous scrutiny of requests for leave the authorities usually relaxed their grip.[85] Efforts were made to check on the movements of officers, with resident commissioners and clerks of the cheque (dockyard officials who mustered crews of ships in their yards) receiving instructions to report the departure of sea-officers from their ships.[86] Although the admin-

---

[81] *Sergison Papers*, 19. Exactly the same problems with the instructions were still being encountered forty years later: *Naval Administration*, ed. Baugh, 56–7, 62–3.

[82] Or perhaps, not wholly justly; for the incidence of this abuse in the 1650s, see Capp, *Cromwell's Navy*, 227–8.

[83] Pepys MS 2854, pp. 271–2, 290; Pepys MS 2855, pp. 126, 153–4, 239–40; Cumbria RO, MS D/Lons/L/Box 1, 'Book . . . regarding the navy . . .', pp. 296–8.

[84] Ibid.; Pepys MS 2858, p. 499; Pepys MS 2859, pp. 40, 93; Pepys MS 2860, p. 214.

[85] Adm. 2/1752, pp. 3, 31, 63; Adm. 3/275, p. 56; Pepys MS 2854, p. 296; Pepys MS 2855, p. 352; Pepys MS 2856, pp. 137, 219, 225–6, 236–7, 250–1, 255; Pepys MS 2858, pp. 278, 330, 340, 356, 448, 460–1; Pepys MS 2859, pp. 87, 93, 372; Tanner, *Catalogue*, iii. 55.

[86] Pepys MS 2855, pp. 245–6, 250, 262; Rawl. MS A. 172, fo. 1.

istration's intentions were commendable, its attempts to put its wishes into practice only served to increase the sea-officers' opposition. In 1673, the Admiralty responded to the absence of many captains from their ships by making them subject to the clerk of the cheque's summons. The outcry, from sea-officers who thought themselves dishonoured by being publicly summoned and noted for absence before their assembled ship's companies, was so violent that the system had to be immediately and substantially relaxed.[87] Sea-officers resented the inconsistency of the administration's attitude to leave. The periodic imposition of a stricter policy could work against those who had genuine and urgent business away from their ships, as well as against those who were inclined to take regular, prolonged, and unofficial leave; even captains returning home after several years overseas could find their natural expectations of immediate leave thwarted by a new mood of strictness at the Admiralty or Whitehall.[88]

The navy had many other rules which could be broken, side-stepped, or perverted by moderately unscrupulous sea-officers. Some abuses had more to do with morals than money: drunkenness, for instance, was endemic in the officer corps and, indeed, on the lower deck, and the Restoration naval administration struggled vainly to control it.[89] However, the charge that the gentlemen were responsible for the introduction of this vice into the service was unfair and exaggerated.[90] The bottle had been as much a characteristic of the late Tudor and early Stuart navy as it was of its Restoration counterpart,[91] and the middle-aged Pepys' condemnations of insobriety among the sea-officers ignored the fact of the youthful Pepys's day-long drinking sessions with prominent captains of the supposedly sober Commonwealth navy.[92] Drunkenness was simply too commonplace to be eradicated, and prominent figures in the navy were inclined to tolerate it, provided an intoxicated sea-officer did his duty in battle. Prince Rupert was not alone in believing that if all the drunken officers in the navy were cashiered, there would be none left.[93] The same could be

---

[87] Adm. 3/275, pp. 73, 82–3; Tanner, *Catalogue*, ii. 98–9, 102.

[88] See e.g. Pepys MS 2859, p. 372.

[89] See e.g. *Pepys's Diary*, i. 169; Adm. 3/275, p. 51; Pepys MS 2857, pp. 89, 136, 331.

[90] J. Charnock, *An History of Marine Architecture* (1800), i, p. lxxxviii; 'Enquiry into the Causes of our Naval Miscarriages', 571.

[91] *Naval Tracts of Sir William Monson*, iv. 153.

[92] See e.g. *Pepys' Diary*, i. 166–7; ii. 17, 23, 45, 66, 74. Cf. Capp, *Cromwell's Navy*, 220, 224, 228, 249, for the incidence of drunkenness in the interregnum.

[93] *Pepys's Diary*, ix. 5–6. Cf. HMC, *Seventh Report*, pt. 1, 197.

said of every sea-officer who exploited the various possibilities for enhancing his personal income. Sir Edward Spragge's 'windfalls' were regarded by many as perquisites of the job: false musters,[94] over-rating of crewmen, embezzlement, and other financial abuses, often carried out in collusion with the purser, were commonplace.[95] However, these were not new abuses brought into the navy by vicious gentlemen captains, as was sometimes claimed—false musters, for example, were regarded even by as prominent a naval administrator as the earl of Nottingham, first commissioner of the Admiralty from 1682 to 1684, as an abuse brought from the army by young gentlemen who held posts in both services.[96] In fact this, like most of the other irregularities committed by the restored monarchy's captains and lesser sea-officers (especially the pursers), predated the Restoration.[97] Similarly, the practice of rating non-combatants, landsmen, or servants as able seamen was not exclusively a vice brought into the service by gentlemen officers, as critics sometimes claimed.[98] Many sea-officers indulged in this fraud to a greater or lesser degree, for increasing and then pocketing the wages of a personal servant was a simple way of augmenting one's income.[99]

The greatest opportunity for personal enrichment available to the Restoration naval captain was the 'good voyage', a perquisite which uncomfortably straddled the dividing-line between legality and crime. Between 1663 and 1686 the carriage in warships of gold, silver, and other precious cargoes was permitted (albeit within strict guide-lines) by the general instructions, while the carriage of all other merchant goods was prohibited. These related but distinct problems have been confused by some historians.[100] The carriage of valuables and merchandise in warships was a practice which pre-dated the Restoration: it was particularly common in the Mediterranean fleet and became a central element of the factional jealousies within that force, as recounted in Ch. 10 of this study, but cases of unlawful carriage of

---

[94] The false muster entailed entering non-existent seamen on the ship's books; their wages could then be appropriated by the captain. See Rodger, *Wooden World*, 320–1.

[95] 'P. C.', *The Three Establishments*, pp. xv–xviii.

[96] Leicestershire RO, Finch political papers 148, fo. 4.

[97] Capp, *Cromwell's Navy*, 232–43.

[98] See e.g. Charnock, *Marine Architecture*, i, p. ɪxxxix.

[99] For some of the many examples of this abuse, committed by both gentlemen and tarpaulins, see Adm. 1/3547, pp. 121, 317, 353–4, 1224; Adm. 1/3548, pp. 41–2; Adm. 1/3550, pp. 619–20; Adm. 106/3539, pt. 2, 'Captains' folder, report by commissioners for past accounts, 8 Mar. 1686.

[100] e.g. by H. Horwitz, *Revolution Politicks: The Career of Daniel Finch, Second Earl of Nottingham, 1647–1730* (Cambridge, 1968), 27; Ollard, *Pepys*, 223–4.

prohibited goods also occurred on ships returning from the East Indies, from the plantations in the Caribbean, and even in the royal yachts in home waters.[101] Competition was intense for plum voyages which gave opportunities for plate-carriage or illicit trading, and a particularly fortunate captain could find himself several thousand pounds richer after one voyage.[102] Lesser, but still worthwhile, rewards could even be obtained from humdrum convoy duty. The commander of a convoy of Levant Company ships could expect to receive £200 and ten bales of silk as a gift from the company, while commanders of the Barbados convoy often received large amounts of sugar from the government of the island.[103]

Pepys and his fellow administrators regularly fulminated against the iniquities of the pursuit of wealth by sea-officers, and warned of the jealousies which resulted from seemingly partial allocations of 'good voyages' to captains in favour at court or with the local admiral, but the administrators were acutely aware of the dilemma which they faced. Quite simply, the rates of pay for sea-officers were inadequate, on their own, to provide a comfortable living for the great majority of officers, whether gentlemen or tarpaulins. The captain of a fourth-rate, the vessel most commonly employed, could expect to earn officially only £10. 10s. a month, and payment of this sum was often delayed by administrative problems, which could cause great hardship.[104] In 1667, for example, even such a high-ranking officer as Admiral Sir Thomas Allin complained of 'how handsomely Mr Treasurer of the Navy hath dealt with me' by not paying his wages and other sums due to him, giving him only a bill on the poll tax instead: 'I would never be accounted a mutineer but knowe too much of the ill management of the office,' Allin observed.[105] Naval service could also entail considerable expense for captains. 'Necessities', ranging from sea-beds, through bibles, to claret, might have to be purchased for a voyage—Lord Dartmouth's expenses on going to sea as admiral in 1683 totalled over £1,800.[106] Once at sea, a captain (particularly one

[101] e.g. Adm. 106/8, fo. 322; Tanner, *Catalogue*, iv. 184, 199–200, 206–7, 214, 217; Adm. 2/1747, p. 351. Cf. Capp, *Cromwell's Navy*, 233.

[102] Cf. Ch. 10. For the survival of this practice well into the next century, see Rodger, *Wooden World*, 314–20.

[103] Hornstein, 'The Deployment of the English Navy', 75; Tanner, *Catalogue*, iv. 294; *CSP Col.*, 1669–74, 189, 492; ibid., 1675–6, 167. Cf. Rodger, *Wooden World*, 258.

[104] Tanner, *Catalogue*, i. 150; Adm. 106/349, fo. 266; Adm. 106/381, fo. 76; Adm. 106/382, fo. 137; Capp, *Cromwell's Navy*, 242–3.

[105] Coventry MS 95, fo. 365.

[106] NMM, DAR/27, first sequence, p. 107.

serving overseas) could often find himself using his own money and credit to buy urgently needed provisions, in the hope that the administration at home would eventually reimburse him.[107] In the face of such expenses, many sea-officers would have agreed with one captain's assertion that the king's 'Pay without other Benefitts findes them not Bread',[108] and many were therefore forced to exploit any moderately dubious means of enhancing their income.

Moreover, all commissioned and many warrant-officers had to budget for long periods out of employment, for the wars of the period were only short interludes in what was otherwise an age of 'dead peace' for England.[109] In peacetime, there were never even remotely enough places available to satisfy all the qualified competitors for naval office: in September 1674, for example, the Admiralty had fifty-eight captains in service (itself an unusually high number) and 158 more out of employment.[110] The administration took several measures to deal with this problem. Between the second and third Dutch wars, unemployed captains were given preference in appointments to lieutenancies, and unemployed lieutenants were sent as midshipmen aboard the Mediterranean fleet.[111] In 1676 this policy was placed on a more formal footing by the regulation of the practice of appointing midshipmen extraordinary.[112] In future, this post was to be restricted to former commissioned officers who would be placed as supernumeraries aboard vessels in active service. The scheme had the advantage of keeping officers in naval pay and employment, and also provided an experienced officer in reserve in case of the death of the captain or lieutenant. Many sea-officers served in this capacity between 1676 and 1688, and some spent many years in such posts, so that the degree of continuity in the commissioned officer corps was greater than a simple list of commissions issued would suggest.[113] Another policy which enhanced this element of continuity was the preference frequently given to experienced officers in appointments in

---

[107] See e.g. Rawl. MS A. 186, fo. 288; Adm. 106/322, fo. 16; Adm. 2/1746, fos. 58–9; Adm. 2/1752, p. 73; Hornstein, 'Deployment', 65–8.

[108] Pepys MS 1534, p. 39.

[109] The phrase was used by one of the secretaries to the Admiralty: Adm. 2/1752, p. 18.

[110] Adm. 8/1, fos. 43–4. For contemporary comments on the extent of this problem, see Pepys MS 2857, p. 379; Pepys MS 2858, pp. 183, 531–2; Pepys MS 1534, p. 38.

[111] Adm. 106/16, fo. 269; Adm. 2/1734, fos. 59, 63ᵛ.

[112] W. E. May, 'Midshipmen Ordinary and Extraordinary', *MM* 59 (1973), 187–8.

[113] BL, Harleian MS 7504, fos. 3–24.

the 1670s and 1680s. Like the establishment for midshipmen extra-ordinary, this policy attempted to mitigate the effects of unemployment on those sea-officers who relied exclusively on naval service. However, by giving preference to men who had been impoverished by long periods out of service, the administration effectively blocked the road to advancement for some of its younger officers.[114] It soon became apparent that even the lieutenants' establishment was less of a success than had been thought. The few vacancies available ensured that many young sea-officers waited much longer than the nominal three years of the establishment before qualifying for a commission.[115] In all, 282 men served as volunteers between the institution of the system in 1677 and the mobilization of the fleet in the autumn of 1688; of these, only thirty-four had become lieutenants and six had gained commands before that mobilization began.[116] The commissioned officer corps of the 1680s, therefore, was dominated by a generation of gentlemen officers who had first gained commands in the 1660s and 1670s: Pepys and the 'young gentlemen' whom he had attacked for so long were growing old together. The only hope for younger men was another war: as one young volunteer wrote in 1678, 'peaceable times will never raise a young man, & in war it may be my good fortune in time to fare as well as others have done before me'.[117]

Another measure which had a bearing on the employment problem, the introduction of half pay for officers not in employment, occurred on a piecemeal basis. Half pay was granted to former flag-officers in 1668, to captains of first- and second-rates in 1674 (and to their masters in 1675), and to commodores of large detached squadrons in 1675.[118] At first, half pay was seen as a reward for former services, particularly for those officers who lacked the opportunities available to captains of smaller vessels in wartime, notably income from prizes and convoys. However, it soon came to be regarded by the administra-tion as a retainer to ensure that the most experienced sea-officers would always be available for service, although the officers themselves disputed this interpretation.[119] The introduction of superannuation

[114] Tanner, *Catalogue*, ii. 361; Pepys MS 2856, p. 14; Adm. 2/1752, p. 142.
[115] In Feb. 1682 admissions of volunteers were stopped for the rest of the year in an attempt to clear the 'backlog': Adm. 3/278, pt. 2, p. 19.
[116] BL, Harleian MS 7504, fos. 24–41.
[117] KAO, U. 1713/C. 1, fo. 49.
[118] Pepys MS 2867, pp. 164–8, 477–8. Cf. Tanner, *Catalogue*, iv. 129, 159–63, 172–3.
[119] Adm. 1/5138, p. 123.

regulations in 1672 also proved popular, though few grants were actually made. The ordinary had long been regarded virtually as a floating pensioners' hospital; when the oldest standing officers became incapable of duty, they simply took on less onerous posts.[120] The new regulations provided that standing officers who were too ill or old to continue could be superannuated after fifteen years' continuous service, masters and surgeons after eight years' intermittent service.[121] Nevertheless, the ordinary continued to contain many veteran officers, who had to be laid aside or exchanged when their ships went to sea: one boatswain, Giles Shelley, was at least 79 years old and had been a warrant- or commissioned officer since 1650 when he transferred to another ship in 1689.[122] Despite their later importance in the evolution of a naval profession, the half-pay and superannuation regulations actually benefited very few sea-officers during this period. By 1687, only two men were drawing half pay as rear-admirals, together with six captains and four masters, while only six masters, two gunners, and two surgeons were superannuated.[123] Half pay did not yet constitute a 'pool' of sea-officers in reserve; superannuation was not yet on a sufficiently extensive basis to permit a clear system of retirement and replacement.

Pepys admitted that not even the thriftiest captain could hope to make a living from his pay alone, particularly if he had a family to support,[124] and this problem affected both gentlemen and tarpaulins. For the latter, supporting one's family usually meant the immediate circle of wife, children, and close relatives.[125] For gentlemen, 'family' could be a broader concept. Substantial earnings from naval service could help to pay off the debts of an impoverished Cavalier dynasty, and this prospect may have helped to persuade gentry families to send their younger sons into the navy after 1660. Captain Francis Digby, who believed that not even 'good voyages' could provide adequately for a gentleman, gained a profitable cruise in lieu of a large debt owed by the Crown to his father, the earl of Bristol; similarly, Sir Roger Strickland and Sir John Chicheley used or intended to use their naval

---

[120] Adm. 1/3545, pp. 155–6; Perrin, *Boteler's Dialogues*, 9.

[121] Tanner, *Catalogue*, i. 148; iv. 24, 36.

[122] Adm. 106/3540, pt. 2, 'Musters' folder (Chatham ordinary, Feb. 1685); Adm. 3/279, p. 30.

[123] BL, Addit. MS 9302, fos. 206–7.

[124] Pepys MS 2853, fos. 183, 190, 235ᵛ; Pepys MS 2581, p. 216.

[125] See e.g. Adm. 1/5139, fos. 121, 233, 235; Adm. 106/3539, pt. 2, 'Masters' folder, petition of Capt. William Hobbs; Rawl. MS A. 189, fos. 105, 191.

earnings to pay off some of their families' debts.[126] The attitude of Captain Thomas Binning, who claimed that the king had given him his ship to make his own profit by, was certainly not unique.[127]

The degree to which a sea-officer could make a fortune from naval service depended to an extent on good connections (to obtain the best voyages, particularly those in the Mediterranean), and to an equal or greater extent on good luck: it was unfortunate if a captain who expected a profitable plate cargo arrived in port just a few days after another English frigate had sailed with most of the available riches.[128] In wartime, prospects for enrichment depended on the uncertain prospect of capturing prizes. A detailed study of prize and the workings of the Admiralty court during this period is needed, but it seems probable that prize-money was a less important contributory factor to the wealth of sea-officers than it became in the 1690s and the eighteenth century, or possibly than it had been in the 1650s, partly because of the short duration of the Dutch wars and partly because of the comparative lack of success in taking Dutch prizes.[129] During Charles II's reign, captains could usually expect half the value of a prize and its contents, though this allocation varied; any goods or valuables in the prize's great cabin were reserved for the captain, while the seamen were free to get what else they could between decks.[130] Captains of smaller ships were at a clear advantage, as their vessels were employed on cruising and convoy duties and were therefore far more likely to encounter enemy warships or merchantmen than those in the main fleet. Even a comparatively unsuccessful action, such as the attack on the Dutch Smyrna fleet in 1672, could profit individual commanders by over £200 apiece.[131] At a war's end, flag-officers and senior captains could expect to be granted prize-ships or fire-ships, which could then be sold or operated as merchantmen.[132] However, the chief drawback of the prize system was the delay in allocating

---

[126] Pepys MS 2581, p. 228; D. Ellison, 'Lend Me a Frigate', *MM* 68 (1982), 81–2; D. Scott, *The Stricklands of Sizergh Castle* (Kendal, 1908), 183–4; E. Legh, *Lyme Letters 1660–1760* (1925), 114.

[127] Adm. 106/3537, pt. 3, 'Affidavits' folder, papers relating to Binning.

[128] See e.g. SP 94/63, fo. 120; NHL, MS 169, p. 172.

[129] Capp, *Cromwell's Navy*, 168–9, 241, 260; Rodger, *Wooden World*, 256–8; A. McGowan, 'The Dutch Influence on British Shipbuilding', in C. Wilson and D. Proctor (eds.), *1688: The Seaborne Alliance and Diplomatic Revolution* (1989), 92, 95.

[130] SP 29/122, fo. 58; HMC, *Finch MSS*, iv. 387–8. Cf. Tedder, *Navy of the Restoration*, 70–1.

[131] Adm. 2/1735, fo. 125ᵛ.

[132] See e.g. Adm. 106/15, fos. 35, 108, 186; *CSPD*, 1667, 119.

rewards to individuals: the Smyrna convoy money was only paid two years after the event, and the belief that payment would be greatly delayed if the proper procedures were observed probably persuaded the earl of Sandwich to wreck his naval career by ordering an immediate distribution of the cargoes of several wealthy Dutch prizes in 1665.[133] The inadequacies of the official prize system also help to explain the incidences of plundering during this period. By 1672, according to the duke of York's acting secretary, this practice had 'growne soe extravagant, & customary that thence the Captains conclude it lawfull'.[134] Even so, the administration's reluctance to part with a brave, skilful captain limited the action taken against those who looted their prizes: Captain Jasper Grant was identified as 'a great plunderer' in the 1660s, but was only dismissed in 1673, for faults of 'a very foul sort'.[135]

Pepys believed that Charles II's captains either died poor, or else gained estates by indulging in various abuses.[136] It would be difficult, if not impossible, to establish how much of an individual officer's income derived from legitimate, as against illicit, sources, but Pepys's point contains some truth: the relative estates of sea-officers did vary dramatically. Among the more prominent officers, Sir Thomas Allin, Sir John Berry, Sir John Narbrough, and Sir Roger Strickland, all veterans of long years of service in the profitable Mediterranean fleet, benefited sufficiently to be able to purchase substantial landed estates.[137] In the 'second rank' of captains, those who left fairly considerable estates, with moveable goods and capital valued at over £1,000, also tended to be men with substantial peacetime service in the Mediterranean, such as Sir Richard Munden, Anthony Langston, and James Storey.[138] Both gentlemen and tarpaulins tried to buy land: for poorer tarpaulins, the acquisition was often a modest house in the eastern suburbs of London, together (for the slightly more affluent) with some tenements which could then be leased out.[139] More prominent sea-officers acquired land in the vicinity of their

---

[133] Harris, *Life of Edward Mountagu*, ii. 3–21; Capp, *Cromwell's Navy*, 276–7.
[134] Coventry MS 104, fos. 108, 115.
[135] Coventry MS 99, fo. 92; Tanner, *Catalogue*, ii. 93; Rawl. MS A. 314, fo. 5.
[136] *Tangier Papers*, 235.
[137] Allin: W. A. Copinger, *The Manors of Suffolk*, v (1909), 6; Berry: Prob. 11/391, fo. 291 *et seq.*; Narbrough: *Notes and Queries*, 7th ser. 6 (1888), 502–3; Strickland: *Hist. Parl.*, iii. 503–4.
[138] Prob. 4/14421, 5/4427, 4/17390.
[139] See e.g. NMM, LBK/8, p. 678; Prob. 4/15054; Prob. 11/317, fos. 131–2; *CSPD*, 1668–9, 590.

birthplaces,[140] or aimed to settle in a county close to London—Berry and Narbrough in Kent, Sir Joseph Jordan in Hertfordshire, Captain Matthew Tennant in Essex.[141] Sea-officers generally dispersed their assets. If some of their capital was tied up in land, another part of it might be aboard their ships in the form of gold or silver artefacts, or bonds. Many officers, particularly tarpaulins, held shares in merchant ships,[142] and several engaged in other forms of commercial enterprise: two senior gentlemen officers, Sir Frescheville Holles and Sir William Jennens, became concerned in, respectively, an Irish timber contract, and the erection of the first Turkish baths in London.[143]

Few captains, however, successfully bequeathed substantial estates to their heirs. Many sea-captains lived and died in an ocean of credit, owing money to traders, merchants, and landlords, owed money by naval colleagues, other merchants, and, above all, by the Crown in arrears of wages.[144] The impecunious captain, desperately avoiding creditors while seeking a lucrative voyage or a rich widow, was a familiar sight on the Restoration stage, while Sir William Jennens's plea for his arrears of half pay was characteristically colourful, but telling: 'except I have my Bills to get the money, I shall be turned out of dores before tenn days; my Bills are my blood, haveing lost severall pounds to make myself capable of His Majesty's Bounty, and the detaining of them will be worse then the wounds I received.'[145] Even gentlemen-captains who were said to have enriched themselves greatly through 'good voyages' left moveable estates valued at only a few hundred pounds: their money might have been diverted to their families, or, as Pepys implied, it might have been squandered on the social life of the capital.[146] Pepys also bemoaned the deaths in poverty of many brave sea-officers whose families were left destitute. One captain spent his entire estate of forty pounds in an attempt to get a command; one lieutenant, the son of a Durham baronet, ended his career by begging the Admiralty for charity. Even a sea-officer with the

[140] e.g. Prob. 5/4427; Prob. 11/317, fos. 327–8; Prob. 11/361, fo. 152.
[141] Berry and Narbrough: see n. 137 above. Jordan: Prob. 11/380, fo. 173ᵛ. Tennant: Prob. 11/402, fo. 171.
[142] Prob. 4/14421, 4/16723, 4/17390, 4/18455; Prob. 11/316, fo. 384; Prob. 11/361, fo. 152; KAO, U. 1515/O. 11, p. 101.
[143] *CSPD*, 1671, 76–7 *et seq.*; ibid., 1678, 51, 55.
[144] e.g. Prob. 5/112, 5/143, 5/1124, 5/5350; Prob. 4/17390; KAO, U. 1515/O. 11, *passim*.
[145] Adm. 106/371, fo. 481. Cf. W. Davenant, *News from Plymouth* (1673), Acts I, IV, V, *et passim*; W. Wycherley, *The Plain Dealer*, ed. L. Hughes (1968), Acts I, II, *et passim*; C. Shadwell, *The Fair Quaker of Deal* (1715 edn.), Act I.
[146] Prob. 4/19416; Prob. 5/514; *Tangier Papers*, 207.

very best connections and a Mediterranean command, Sir William Berkeley, could complain that the navy was 'so begerly a trade'; but then, Berkeley had resolved to 'serve truly & honestly'.[147]

The sea-officers responded to pay and employment problems in various ways. Those without substantial patrons spent months or years at Whitehall or the Admiralty, soliciting for posts or for the settlement of their arrears. Once they obtained a place, they wrote regularly to the Admiralty's secretary to remind him of their services and their desire for a better ship.[148] Rumours of the dismissal, illness, or death of an officer led to an immediate rush of requests for the post, and talk of the fitting-out of more ships led to the bombardment of the administrators by optimistic solicitants.[149] One officer, realizing that preference was being given to men who had held commissions previously, even resorted to forging the word 'lieutenant' on one of his certificates.[150] However, many were prepared to cut their losses and settle for lesser posts. The permanent nature of warrant posts in the ordinary was an attractive proposition for those commissioned officers (invariably tarpaulins) and masters who were prepared to accept the loss of status. Most became gunners or boatswains, though a few former lieutenants became pursers, and one particularly impoverished former captain became a shipwright in the royal dockyards.[151]

The most popular response to a lack of employment in the navy was service aboard merchant ships. Alternating between mercantile and naval employment was a fact of life for the seamen, and the interregnum and tarpaulin officers often took the same course, depending on the availability of openings in merchant service.[152] Even such

[147] Pepys MS 2853, fos. 183, 190, 235ᵛ; *CSPD*, 1666–7, 401; Adm. 106/3540, pt. 1, 'Lieutenants' folder, petition of William Lydall; KAO, U. 269/C. 298, unfol., William to Charles Berkeley, 7 June 1663.

[148] *Naval Minutes*, 272; Tanner, *Catalogue*, iii. 153, 396; Pepys MS 2854, fo. 3; Pepys MS 2857, p. 105; Pepys MS 2858, pp. 24, 101–2, 487; Pepys MS 2859, p. 20; BL, Addit. MS 29556, fos. 109, 121; Adm. 3/277, pt. 1, pp. 95, 154, 169, 188, and pts. 1–3 (and Adm. 3/278), *passim*.

[149] Rawl. MS A. 181, fo. 137; Tanner, *Catalogue*, iii. 269; Pepys MSS 2853–4, *passim*; Pepys MS 2857, pp. 212, 214; Pepys MS 2858, p. 98; Pepys MS 2816, p. 387; Adm. 3/278, pt. 1, p. 95; BL, Addit. MS 60386, unfol., William Stewart to Sir Henry Capel, 12 Aug. 1679.

[150] Pepys MS 2856, pp. 14, 22, 35, 63–4.

[151] Tanner, *Catalogue*, iii. 311–12; Pepys MS 2853, fo. 183ᵛ; *Naval Minutes*, 214; BL, Harleian MS 7504, fos. 4–23. Cf. *CSPD*, 1668–9, 173; Adm. 106/343, fo. 322; Capp, *Cromwell's Navy*, 180–1.

[152] Or on the extent of their existing mercantile ties: see Capp, *Cromwell's Navy*, 196–8.

a prominent officer as Sir John Wetwang, with half pay for rear-admiral's status and three decades' naval service behind him, left the navy in 1682 when he got the chance of lucrative employment with the East India Company.[153] More typical was the career of Sir Richard Haddock's brother Joseph, a merchant captain in the 1660s, a lieutenant in the third Dutch war, captain of a merchantman in the Mediterranean in the mid-1670s, commissioned to command a frigate during the 1678 mobilization, and a captain in the East India trade in the 1680s.[154] Masters, whose chances of continuous naval service were particularly limited, alternated regularly between naval and mercantile employment, and some standing officers took the same course.[155] Several tarpaulin officers who saw no immediate prospect of further naval service retired temporarily to their home towns to take posts in the customs, returning to the navy when an opportunity arose.[156] Although some gentlemen officers also served in merchantmen, most were unwilling or unable to take such a course, and for many of them the alternative to naval service was a commission in the army.[157] It is difficult to establish how far these officers thought of themselves as part of a larger profession of arms, in the old tradition of fighting men who alternated between land and sea service, or whether they regarded themselves as sea-officers who took land posts while out of naval employment. On the whole, however, naval service was regarded as being more profitable,[158] and by 1691, certainly, Sir Ralph Delaval (then a flag-officer, but a naval captain in earlier years, and an army officer from 1674 onwards) regarded military service as 'a means to introduce the seay officers that aire not tayken caire of into imployments...'.[159] George Rooke was a lieutenant in the duke of York's foot regiment in 1675, but he was soliciting for a naval

[153] *CSPD*, 1682, 96; ibid., July–Sept. 1683, 436.

[154] Tanner, *Catalogue*, i. 358; Adm. 7/630, fo. 37ᵛ; KAO, U. 1515/O. 6, 29 Sept. 1677; BL, Sloane MS 3671, fos. 2–3.

[155] Adm. 1/3555, pp. 641–9; Pepys MS 2862, pp. 50–1; *DNB*, s.n. 'Benbow, John'; S. Martin-Leake, *The Life of Admiral Sir John Leake*, ed. G. A. R. Callender (1920), i, pp. xvi, 11; Capp, *Cromwell's Navy*, 204–5.

[156] *CSPD*, 1679–80, 287; ibid., 1683–4, 182; ibid., 1685, 218; Pepys MS 2853, p. 92.

[157] Leicestershire RO, Finch political papers 148, fos. 4–5; J. K. Laughton (ed.), *Memoirs Relating to the Lord Torrington* (Camden Society, NS 46; 1889), 17; P. Le Fevre, 'John Tyrrell (1646–92): A Restoration Naval Captain', *MM* 70 (1984), 149; C. Dalton, *English Army Lists and Commission Registers, 1661–1714* (1892), i. 156 *et passim*.

[158] Laughton, *Torrington Memoirs*, 36; for attitudes in the earlier period, see Capp, *Cromwell's Navy*, 173–5.

[159] HMC, *Finch MSS*, iii. 1. Cf. HMC, *Ormonde MSS*, NS 8, 13–14.

command at the same time; promotion in the army (to captain in 1687) had to await another period out of naval employment.[160] Special dispensations were usually given for these officers to be borne on the musters of their regiments, and to receive their army pay, while serving at sea.[161] Service abroad was a more drastic response to the employment problem, and one which was not usually encouraged by the administration. Nevertheless, Sir Frescheville Holles and Sir William Jennens gained dispensations to serve in the French navy (both men had dubious reputations, and the French rejected them), one officer captained a Portuguese warship, while at least three others captained ships in the Swedish and Danish navies during the 1670s and 1680s.[162]

One other development of the Restoration period, which was partly a response to the lack of employment, partly an innovation by the administration, and partly an expression of the sea-officers' own mood, was the evolution of the concept of seniority. The granting of commissions was a prerogative of the lord high admiral or the king and, in theory, it could be an entirely arbitrary process, as it was in the third Dutch war when the earl of Ossory became a flag-officer and the earl of Mulgrave the captain of a second-rate without any regard to their almost complete lack of experience.[163] Nevertheless, there were certain accepted norms, particularly the right of an admiral's flag-captain to the first vacancy in the flag-list, and in the third Dutch war the precedence of former flag-posts was used to determine promotions within the flag-list.[164] The sailing instructions which James issued in 1672 specified that a younger captain should give way to an elder if they were in ships of equal size, but no criteria for defining 'younger' and 'elder' were provided.[165] In peacetime, with fewer posts available, a less arbitrary system, encouraging merit and long service, was desirable. The administration's stated preference for experienced officers, and the long-established concept of promotion by a *de facto* system of seniority in the warrant-posts, also encouraged the establishment of a more formal procedure for commissioned posts. In the

---

[160] Adm. 10/15, p. 109; Dalton, *Army Lists*, i. 187, 321; ii. 26, 77, 103; Tanner, *Catalogue*, iii. 150, 285; NMM, LBK/8, p. 725.

[161] e.g. *CSPD*, 1677–8, 84, 264, 403, 453, 550, 649.

[162] *Naval Minutes*, 35, 356; *Hist. Parl.*, iii. 564–5; SP 89/5, fo. 18; *CSPD*, 1676–7, 119, 188; Adm. 7/687, pt. 3, no. 29; Rawl. MS A. 189, fo. 251.

[163] Anderson, 'English Flag Officers', 334; Capp, *Cromwell's Navy*, 179–81.

[164] See Ch. 9. For another case of seniority being ignored, see Adm. 2/1736, pp. 147–8.

[165] Pepys MS 2873, pp. 110–11.

1670s, disputes over precedence were frequent, and the administration was unclear about the rules to be followed. Should a captain whose career had been interrupted claim seniority from the date of his first commission?[166] Should a captain who had commanded small ships for many years be under a younger captain who had commanded great ones? Should a captain of a third-rate be under the command of the captain of a fourth-rate, if the latter had served for longer?[167] These questions were particularly important because so many captains who had commanded great ships in war had to settle for small ships in peace: Henry Carverth, captain of a first-rate in 1673, spent the years between 1674 and 1678 cruising the Channel in sloops and sixth-rates.[168] A clearly confused Pepys struggled to establish some firm rules. Seniority depended, he wrote, on the precedence of commissions, 'unless worth was lacking'; yet seniority of commissions alone could not establish precedence, only superiority of former ships, or seniority in a like command.[169]

In this atmosphere of confusion, the disputes continued, and added another dimension to the friction already existing between factions, or between gentlemen and tarpaulins more generally. In 1681, for example, the tarpaulin William Coleman—a captain since 1666, and commander of third-rates in 1673 and 1678—objected to being put under the command of the gentleman Edward Russell, a captain since 1672 and commander of a third-rate in 1677.[170] Tarpaulins often commanded fire-ships, yachts, and other small craft, and attempted to claim seniority on the basis of these commissions. Charles II ruled that such posts could not give rights to precedence, but further confusion was introduced in 1681 when sixth-rate commissions were changed from 'master and commander' to captain, to preserve the status of those who had stepped down from great ships to small craft.[171] The first serious attempt to solve the problem came in 1683, when Lord Dartmouth, commanding the fleet sent to demolish Tangier, drew up a system of rules governing precedence and seniority. These established that precedence should stem from the captain's first commis-

[166] Pepys MS 2856, pp. 210, 223, 278–9; Adm. 3/277, pt. 1, pp. 1, 4–6.

[167] Rawl. MS A. 185, fos. 305–7.

[168] BL, Addit. MS 29554, fo. 426; Addit. MS 29556, fo. 109; Pepys MS 2853, pp. 172, 175, fo. 181.

[169] Pepys MS 2853, p. 93, fo. 181; Pepys MS 2854, pp. 176–7; Pepys MS 2855, p. 430; Pepys MS 2856, pp. 39–40.

[170] Appendix II, below; Tanner, *Catalogue*, i. 337, 400–1.

[171] Adm. 3/278, pt. 1, pp. 140, 158; NMM, JOD/173, p. 3; Pepys MS 2860, pp. 55–6. 'Master and commander' was soon restored.

sion, not the rate of his ship, and these rules were immediately accepted by Charles and James.[172] By 1688 the situation had been resolved to the extent that Pepys and other naval administrators already thought in terms of 'holding post rank', the concept which was to dominate the eighteenth-century navy;[173] when the fleet was mobilized to meet the threatened Dutch invasion, Pepys drew up a list of all serving captains in order of seniority for the use of the admiral, Dartmouth.[174] Although the various attempts to clarify seniority had been concerned initially with establishing the precedence of captains in company with each other, it was already being seen as a device to secure advancement: in December 1688, George Rooke argued that he should have a command ahead of the three men who were being considered for it on the grounds that he was senior to all of them, and by 1692 seniority of post-rank, rather than any other criterion, was being put forward as an argument for advancement to flag-rank.[175] Seniority, 'that commendable Order . . . which takes off the powerful Sollicitations of great men for Commands, for their Creatures, greatly to the Prejudice of the Service', but which was to turn the quest for advancement in the next century into 'an almost indecent scramble to remain alive longer than one's neighbours in the list', was born.[176]

The perils of the various lotteries which seemed to dictate employment, advancement, and enrichment in the navy's officer corps constituted substantial disincentives to any man, especially any young gentleman, seeking a career at sea. However, if gentlemen could not be guaranteed a fortune in the navy, Admiral the duke of Grafton observed in 1690, they would serve only for reasons of honour.[177] Notions of personal and national honour pervaded the commissioned officer corps of the Restoration navy, serving, in varying degrees, both to unite and divide the gentlemen and tarpaulins. It was argued on the one hand that acceptance of the king's commission automatically

---

[172] Rawl, MS A. 190, fos. 152–3; Pepys MS 2877, p. 268. Cf. *Tangier Papers*, 135, 215.
[173] Pepys MS 2860, pp. 55–6; Pepys MS 2861, p. 246.
[174] HMC, *Dartmouth MSS*, i. 162–3, 174; Pepys MS 2862, pp. 236, 274–5, 374. Cf. Pepys MS 2861, pp. 252–3, for an earlier draft.
[175] HMC, *Dartmouth MSS*, i. 237; HMC, *Finch MSS*, iv. 305.
[176] *Memoirs of the Secret Services of John Macky, Esq.* (1733), 108; M. Lewis, *The Navy of Britain: A Historical Portrait* (1948), 264–5. Cf. Rodger, *Wooden World*, 297–302, 308–9.
[177] HMC, *Finch MSS*, ii. 386. Cf. BL, Addit. MS 32094, fo. 43; *Tangier Papers*, 207.

elevated a tarpaulin to a position of honour, even, perhaps, to the status of a gentleman. However, it was also argued that only true-bred gentlemen were really men of honour, capable of defending the realm with the innate courage of their kind, and several gentlemen captains held this opinion.[178] Regard for considerations of honour could be manifested in many ways. The appearance of an officer's ship was important, but so was the appearance of the officer himself: senior commanders argued that they needed regular half pay to maintain a style of dress and living which would reflect their own status and the king's honour.[179] Any suggestion of misconduct in battle was an affront to the honour of the accused captain, and had to be answered with a retraction or result in a duel; captains often deliberately requested courts-martial in order to clear their names.[180] Flag-officers were obsessed with the minutiae of receiving the appropriate ensign, establishing their jurisdiction over subordinates, and asserting themselves in relation to colonial or foreign authorities,[181] while individual captains clashed regularly, bitterly, and sometimes violently with colonial governors over disputed jurisdictions.[182] Above all, a sea-officer's word was his bond. English naval captains were angered by any suggestion from foreigners that they should give undertakings in writing: one admiral in the Mediterranean observed that 'the Honnour of my place is above giving any other testimony than my owne word'.[183]

Both gentlemen and tarpaulins were concerned equally to uphold the honour of their nation when overseas, particularly when enforcing the 'salute to the flag' demanded by tradition, national pride, and the general instructions to commanders. The correct number of guns to be fired in salute, or return of salute, when encountering foreign ships or entering foreign ports, was an issue with which the entire officer corps was obsessed. Admirals as diverse as the old republican Sir John Lawson, the old cavalier Sir Thomas Allin, and the archetypal,

---

[178] Rawl. MS A. 191, fo. 153; Pepys MS 2581, pp. 213–18, 228; HMC, *Finch MSS*, iv. 244, 290. Cf. *Tangier Papers*, 122.

[179] Adm. 1/5139, fo. 170.

[180] See Chs. 8 and 9.

[181] See Herbert Lbk, *passim*; Pepys MS 2877, pp. 336–54; Pepys MS 2858, pp. 208–9, 227, 368, 379, 406–7, 420; Pepys MS 2859, pp. 173, 178; Pepys MS 2860, pp. 274–9; Pepys MS 2861, pp. 310–11, 340–1, 374–6.

[182] See *CSP Col.*, 1675–6, 306–8; ibid., 1681–5, 252–3, 262, 264–5, 292–3, 316, 358, 401, 415–17, 483, 491–3, 533–4, 596–7; ibid., 1685–8, 262, 308, 311–12, 372–4, 465–7, 471–2, 494–6, 621, 657; A. P. Thornton, *West India Policy under the Restoration* (Oxford, 1956), 234–6.

[183] Herbert Lbk, 172.

'ignorant' young gentleman officer Arthur Herbert all insisted on the exact observance of the punctilios of the salute: every sea-officer would have agreed readily with Herbert's assertion that in these matters he would uphold the king's honour, 'sink or swim'.[184] Particularly enthusiastic captains were prepared to defend this principle even to the extent of exchanging shots with foreign ships, or threatening to bombard foreign ports.[185] Though this aggressive patriotism was due in part to the captains' natural inclinations, it was also inspired by an acute awareness that officers' behaviour in these matters was closely watched at home. Charles II himself insisted on the maintenance of the correct salute due to his flag (or so the sea-officers were told),[186] and examples were made of commanders who failed to observe the expected procedures: the most potent case was that of Captain Joseph Harris, sentenced to death for striking his colours to a Spanish warship, and reprieved only when the muskets were at his head.[187] Captains were expected to resist even if faced with overwhelming odds. When Cloudesley Shovell was forced to salute the Spanish fleet, the local English consul protested that 'if hee & all had bin lost by Maintaineinge our Kings honor, hee had don his Deutye & left a famous Name behynde hime'.[188] Other captains, too, had sound reasons for shunning the prospect of posthumous glory. On several occasions, incorrect salutes from foreigners were ignored, or demands for a salute from the English ship were complied with, on the grounds that English merchants and shipping would suffer from retaliation if an international incident occurred.[189] The demands of honour did not necessarily take precedence over the demands of commerce.

Critics of the gentlemen officers contrasted their insistence on matters of honour with their 'slavish' adherence to patrons. The key to the criticisms made by Pepys, Nottingham, and others was the belief

[184] NMM, AGC/L/1; *Journals of Sir Thomas Allin*, i. 30, 61, 102, 107, 117; ii, p. xii *et passim*; SP 101/80, newsletter, 28 July 1682; Herbert Lbk, 25–9, 30–1, 54 (quotation from p. 27); Rawl. MS A. 228, fos. 38–42.

[185] See e.g. BL., Sloane MS 2439, fo. 31; SP 89/10, fo. 152; Pepys MS 2877, pp. 197–8; *CSPD*, 1668–9, 292.

[186] Pepys MS 2855, p. 63. Cf. Adm. 2/1750, p. 82.

[187] Rawl. MS A. 314, fo. 14; Tanner, *Catalogue*, iv. 278–9, 282–3; Lincolnshire Archives Office, Jarvis MS IX/1/A4, 7 and 14 Feb. 1677.

[188] All Souls College, Oxford, MS 240, fo. 471. Cf. Rawl. MS A. 190, fos. 248–57; Pepys MS 2877, pp. 199–234. It was suggested that Shovell, a tarpaulin, did not have the manners and judgement to make the right decision in this incident: *Tangier Papers*, 167.

[189] See e.g. SP 71/2, fo. 144; SP 93/1, fo. 214; SP 101/80, newsletter, 8 Feb. 1683; National Library of Wales, MS Deposit 38B, 20 May 1680.

that gentlemen captains were able to rely on their patrons and their interest at court to safeguard them against punishment and guarantee their promotion. When Lieutenant Aylmer quarrelled with Captain Royden, he was able to threaten Royden with his 'interest', to petition the duke of Ormonde, and to rely on the protection of his patrons, Ormonde's son the earl of Ossory and Colonel George Legge, governor of Portsmouth. Similarly, the tarpaulin Captain Wright lost a long-promised opportunity for preferment because of the intercession of the earl of Rochester for a gentleman captain.[190] However, the attitudes of Pepys and Nottingham were not above reproach. Their proposed solution to the 'gentleman–tarpaulin' problem, the training of well-born officers to the sea from an early age, was undoubtedly the correct one,[191] but they were inconsistent in their own immediate responses to the problem. Despite Pepys's protestations that he never advanced sea-officers out of partiality, he was always willing to advance well-born protégés of his old friends;[192] when Nottingham criticized the fact that sea-officers 'take more care to keep their patrons favour, than of their duty, depending upon his protection even against his superior officer (under whose command he happens to be)', he overlooked his own defence of his cousin Captain Daniel Dering, who had relied on Nottingham's protection against a superior officer, under whose command he happened to be.[193] The dependence of gentlemen captains on court patronage, and their close associations with Charles and James, provoked considerable disquiet. A link between the introduction of gentlemen officers and a tendency towards arbitrary government was first suggested publicly in the 'exclusion' Parliaments of 1679–80, and was taken up by many writers at that time and in the 1690s, when even Halifax took up the subject.[194] After the revolution of 1688, these writers developed the thesis that Charles and James had sought to bring in gentlemen officers to undermine the natural affections of the seamen to Protestantism and liberty; these charges were exaggerated, as were the claims that the 'vices' of the gentlemen were

[190] Rawl. MS A. 181, fos. 346, 357ᵛ, 381, 387; SP 29/421, fo. 86. Cf. *Pepys's Diary*, ix. 563; *Tangier Papers*, 125, 139–40; Pepys MS 2856, p. 214; Pepys MS 2861, p. 333.
[191] Leicestershire RO, Finch political papers 148, fo. 5; Rawl. MS D. 147, fo. 38ᵛ; Pepys MS 2581, pp. 218, 243; Tanner, *Catalogue*, ii. 232; *Further Correspondence of Samuel Pepys*, 356–7; *Tangier Papers*, 109, 122; *Works of Halifax*, ed. Brown, i. 296–314.
[192] e.g. Tanner, *Catalogue*, ii. 320, 391; iii. 185; Pepys MS 2854, p. 39; NMM LBK/8, p. 711. Cf. Rawl. MS A. 178, *passim*.
[193] Leicestershire RO, Finch political papers 148, fo. 4; *Tangier Papers*, 132.
[194] J. D. Davies, 'The Navy, Parliament, and Political Crisis in the Reign of Charles II', *Historical Journal* (forthcoming). For an important recent discussion of Halifax's view of the controversy, see *Works of Halifax*, ed. Brown, i. 122–39.

an inevitable consequence of the 'lewdness' of the court or the nation in general, but they were natural country or whig distortions of the motives of Charles and James in seeking an officer corps loyal to the monarchy.[195]

Both gentlemen and tarpaulins were indeed loyal to their kings, and in return their kings were loyal to them. The administrators soon learnt that their efforts to impose stricter discipline on a recalcitrant officer corps might be thwarted by tolerance, leniency, or inconsistency from above. Attempts to enforce the general instructions had little long-term success because 'the King wont not [*sic*] easily part with a good fighting captain for a neglect of keeping a good Checque upon his Purser'.[196] Charles and James often intervened to secure payment of captains whose wages had been suspended for failing to comply fully with the instructions: they usually took the view that past good service excused administrative shortcomings.[197] Charles was warned by his Admiralty board that forgiveness only encouraged captains to break the instructions,[198] but he never consistently applied a strict standard. Even the sterner, less flexible James, a king who regularly stated his desire for greater sobriety and discipline in the navy, often intervened to reprieve or lessen the sentences of officers and men sentenced at courts-martial.[199] Both monarchs tolerated and even encouraged the 'good voyage' as a means for their sea-officers to enrich themselves. The administrators might complain about the inconstancy of their kings—indeed, even Sir Edward Spragge accused Charles and James of being too inconstant to support their subordinates[200]—but the Pepyses, Coventrys, and Nottinghams of the world were in a comparatively weak position. At the end of the day it was the sea-officers, not the administrators, who would win the nation's battles.

[195] Leicestershire RO, Finch political papers 148, fo. 5; BL, Addit. MS 11602, fos. 58, 66, 69, 127ᵛ; BL., Egerton MS 3383, fos. 120, 134; G. Burnet, *Bishop Burnet's History of his Own Time*, ed. M. J. Routh (Oxford, 1823), i. 290; Maydman, *Speculations*, 220; E. Stephens, *A Plain Relation of the Late Action at Sea* (1690), 17–19. Moreover, 'interest' in naval promotions had also been a burning issue under the republic: Capp, *Cromwell's Navy*, 186–9.

[196] Rawl. MS A. 178, fo. 270ᵛ.

[197] See e.g. Adm. 106/17, fo. 206; Adm. 106/18, fo. 403; Adm. 3/277, pt. 2, p. 73; Adm. 3/278, pt. 1, pp. 88, 136; Tanner, *Catalogue*, iv. 31, 83–4, 199, 278–9.

[198] Ibid. 403–4.

[199] See e.g. Pepys MS 2858, pp. 89, 303, 330; Pepys MS 2859, p. 458; Pepys MS 2861, pp. 41, 358.

[200] *Tangier Papers*, 221.

4

THE SEAMEN

IN many respects, the manning of the navy was one of the most difficult administrative tasks which a seventeenth-century government could undertake: as Sir William Coventry once noted, 'the greatest difficulty & vexation in a warre is the manning of ships'.[1] In wartime, up to 25,000 men had to be brought into naval service within a matter of a few weeks, got to the fleet, and retained for the duration of the campaign, all without disrupting the trade of the nation to an unacceptable degree. Restoration naval administrators, like all their counterparts from the sixteenth to the nineteenth centuries, struggled to reconcile these objectives. In doing so, they were hindered by the absence of any accurate information about the actual size of the seafaring community from which they were expected to gain their recruits. Attempts were made at the start of the second and third Dutch wars to use the JPs and parish constables to draw up accurate lists of the seafarers in their areas, but the sheer scale of the operation ensured its failure.[2] Similarly, in the 1690s attempts to establish accurate figures with a view to establishing a national register of seamen, similar to that used by the French navy, also came to nothing.[3] However, both contemporary and later estimates suggest that there must have been some forty to fifty thousand men in the deep-sea and coasting trades, and in the various fisheries, and about ten thousand more in other activities which could be interpreted as satisfying the usual criterion of naval recruitment, that of 'using the sea'.[4] Even allowing for the very tentative nature of the figures, therefore, the Restoration navy in wartime would seem to have been calling on

[1] Coventry MS 102, fo. 10.
[2] NHL, MS 121/10, p. 59. For attempts to implement this scheme in the counties, see Devon RO, DQS 1/11, sessions of Apr. and July 1672, Jan. 1673; Norfolk RO, C/52/3, July 1672 Norwich sessions.
[3] Ehrman, *Navy . . . of William III*, 112. For the French system see G. Symcox, *The Crisis of French Sea Power 1688–97: From the Guerre d'Escadre to the Guerre de Course* (The Hague, 1974), 14–17.
[4] Ehrman, *Navy . . . of William III*, 110–11; J. A. Johnston, 'Parliament and the Navy, 1688–1714', Ph.D. thesis (Sheffield, 1968), 310–28.

between one-third and one-half of the maritime community of the nation.[5]

Geography played its part in determining the distribution of this burden within the maritime community. The late Tudor and early Stuart navy seems to have been manned largely from the west of England, partly because of the presence there of a large body of mariners skilled in deep-sea voyages, and partly because English foreign policy was generally directed against Spain. However, this pattern of recruitment changed during the seventeenth century: the development of Chatham as the main fleet base created the obvious logistical problem of getting west country seamen from their homes to their ships, while the growing antagonism between England and the Netherlands created a need for seamen from the east coast who knew the North Sea well.[6] By the time of the Restoration and the second and third Dutch wars, the majority of seamen, both volunteers and pressed men, were being drawn from the east coast, and more particularly from the towns and villages along the Thames and Medway. Aboard the great ships in the third war, for instance, Thames mariners constituted anything between 60 and 80 per cent of the entire crew, and the east coast as a whole provided 80 to 90 per cent.[7] However, several qualifications have to be made to these generalizations. In the first place, the nature of the evidence for the composition of crews is not ideal: Admiralty muster-books giving full residence information do not survive for this period, and the pay-books which contain such information are confined largely to the third Dutch war, and to the first- to third-rates. Secondly, residence in London did not by any means imply birth, family background, or upbringing in the capital. Since Elizabeth's reign at least, seamen had been moving to the Thames from all parts of the country, staying in lodging houses close to the river.[8] By the late seventeenth century, men who lived outside London were finding it difficult to get employment, as most of the opportunities were concentrated there.[9] Edward Barlow, a Lancashire man who

---

[5] Cf. Capp, *Cromwell's Navy*, 258.

[6] K. R. Andrews, 'The Elizabethan Seaman', *MM* 68 (1982), 254; *Boteler's Dialogues*, 263; J. R. Powell and E. K. Timings (eds.), *The Rupert and Monck Letter Book, 1666* (1969), 117–18.

[7] Sample of ships' pay-books from 1673: Adm. 33/96, *Edgar*; Adm. 33/98, *Henry*; Adm. 33/101, *Royal Katherine*; Adm. 33/104, *St Michael*; Adm. 33/106, *London*; Adm. 33/107, *Sovereign*; Adm. 33/111, *Rainbow*; Adm. 33/113, *Unicorn*, *Victory*; Adm. 33/114, *Warspite*; Adm. 33/115, *St Andrew*.

[8] Andrews, 'Elizabethan Seaman', 248–9.

[9] See e.g. Adm. 106/3539, pt. 1, 'Mariners' folder, petition of Thomas Powell.

moved to London in his teens to get a place at sea, was typical of a large class of migrant seamen who formed a unique community along the Thames, lodging there in the intervals between employment and paying only occasional visits back to their homes.[10] Away from London, generalized remarks about the importance of certain 'maritime counties' like Devon and Norfolk only distort the complex picture of naval recruitment. In Norfolk in 1664, 53.5 per cent of the county's estimated 2,425 seamen were drawn from the two ports of Yarmouth and Lynn, 40.2 per cent of the total being from Yarmouth alone. Two coastal hundreds, North Erpingham and North Greenhoe, provided another 23 per cent of the county's mariners. Thirty-two of Norfolk's thirty-six hundreds provided less than a quarter of its seamen.[11]

Recruitment from these communities and the seafaring population as a whole was undertaken in several ways. In peacetime, there were usually enough volunteers to man the three or four thousand berths available, but in a war other means had to be employed.[12] Nevertheless, volunteers continued to form the backbone of the fleet, and substantial bounties were promised in attempts to encourage them.[13] At the start of a campaign, just as at the beginning of a peacetime voyage, a captain might go to his home area in person, or send word to his friends that he was raising men, or send down one of his subordinate officers to encourage recruits. The traditional method of beating drums to attract volunteers at seamen's inns or at the waterside could supplement their efforts.[14] A captain's reputation was vital to the success or failure of voluntary recruitment, for men volunteered to join individual ships, not the navy *per se*.[15] Seamen were always more willing to serve under a local man, well respected in their community,

[10] *Barlow's Journal*, i. 15 *et seq.* Many other examples of migration are given in Adm. 106/3023, *passim*; PRO, HCA 13/73–9, *passim*. For a study of one of the seamen's communities, see M. Power, 'Shadwell: The Development of a London Suburban Community in the Seventeenth Century', *The London Journal*, 4 (1978), 29–43.

[11] Holkham Hall, Norfolk, Townshend MSS: list of seamen within the county of Norfolk, Dec. 1664 (consulted through Norfolk RO). For the demography of naval recruitment in Devon, see J. D. Davies, 'Devon and the Navy in the Civil War and the Dutch Wars, 1642–88', in S. Fisher, B. Greenhill, and J. Youings (eds.), *A New Maritime History of Devon* (forthcoming).

[12] *Pepys's Diary*, vi. 11.

[13] NHL, MS 121/10, pp. 1, 3.

[14] BL, Egerton MS 928, fo. 215; Bod. Lib., Carte MS 34, fo. 228ᵛ; Adm. 106/336, fos. 393, 396, 399; HMC, *Downshire MSS*, I. i. 298; N. Luttrell, *A Brief Historical Relation of State Affairs, from September 1678 to April 1714* (Oxford, 1857), i. 457; J. Dennis, *An Essay on the Navy* (1702), 6. Cf. Rodger, *Wooden World*, 155–7.

[15] NMM, CHA/E/1/A, fo. 157; Pepys MS 2581, p. 222.

than under a stranger.[16] Plymouth captains were notably successful in attracting local men, and some were able to man their vessels almost entirely with their countrymen.[17] Sir John Kempthorne was particularly popular among Devonian seamen. In 1673 he recruited 173 men from his home county (at the same time his second captain, John Archer of Yarmouth, was recruiting another 92 volunteers in *his* home town); in the 1678 'war scare' Kempthorne was able to man his large first-rate almost entirely with volunteers, many of them from Plymouth, whereas the East Anglian Sir Thomas Allin, raising men in Plymouth at the same time, found that practically no one came forward for him.[18] Family ties might also assist a tarpaulin captain: when Sir John Lawson's flagship *London* was accidentally blown up in 1665, twenty-one crewmen of his 'kindred and name' perished with her.[19] This ability of tarpaulin officers to attract seamen who knew them was seen by some as an advantage of the tarpaulins over the gentlemen. It was argued that interregnum and tarpaulin officers found it easier to attract men because they came from the same communities as the seamen, whereas the gentlemen were often unknown men from inland counties.[20] This interpretation is plausible, but it draws too fine a distinction. A gentleman-officer could make himself popular by good usage of his crew,[21] seamen's preferences could be unpredictable (for all his influence in the East Anglian maritime community, Allin was almost universally hated),[22] and gentlemen could attract followers of their own, though not necessarily skilled seamen. Many Huntingdon men died with their local magnate, the earl of Sandwich, on his *Royal James* at the battle of Solebay, and men from the Sidmouth area of Devon volunteered to serve under Captain Francis Courtenay, a son of the great Powderham Castle family. In both cases, the 'volunteers' may have been tenants or servants, following their master to the wars.[23]

---

[16] Pepys MS 2581, p. 218; *CSPD*, 1664–5, 217, 243–4; ibid., 1673, 42, 49; ibid., 1678, 86; *Barlow's Journal*, ii. 413. Cf. Capp, *Cromwell's Navy*, 217–18, 260–1; Rodger, *Wooden World*, 119–24.

[17] Pepys MS 2854, p. 78; Pepys MS 2858, p. 191; Adm. 3/279, p. 34; Ingram, *Three Sea Journals of Stuart Times* (1936), 112, 117, 131–2.

[18] Adm. 33/115, *St Andrew* pay-book, 1673; *CSPD*, 1672–3, 543, 621; ibid., 1678, 125; Pepys MS 2854, p. 59. Cf. Davies, 'Devon and the Navy'.

[19] BL, Addit. MS 10117, fos. 134–5. Cf. Capp, *Cromwell's Navy*, 217–18.

[20] Pepys MS 2581, p. 218.

[21] See below, pp. 99–100.

[22] *CSPD*, 1670, 255. Cf. ibid., 1678, 62.

[23] Adm. 106/3026, fo. 26; PRO, PRO 30/24/5, fos. 88–95; E. Cleaveland, *A Genealogical History of the Noble and Illustrious Family of Courtenay* (1735), 102.

The needs of the fleet in wartime exceeded the number of volunteers available, and the naval administration was forced to resort to compulsion. An embargo on shipping could be imposed in an attempt to force merchant seamen into the navy, but this course usually met with little success and raised storms of protest from trading interests.[24] The chartered companies of watermen and fishermen were supposed to provide quotas of men for naval service, but throughout the reigns of Charles and James administrators and sea-officers complained about the prevarication of the companies, the inadequacy of the men they provided, and the success with which genuine watermen or fishermen bribed unqualified substitutes to take their places. In January 1689, for instance, Captain Frederick Frowde of the *Ruby* informed the Navy Board that

the new prest men are as bare of Clothes, as the *Swans*, and those sent by Watermens hall, & the free fisher men, barer than the rest of the Shipps company: being most of them servants, and badly fitted out by their masters, haveing noe more clothes than Backs.[25]

The right to press was claimed by the Crown as part of its prerogative, and, although there were frequent attacks on its arbitrariness, its legality (or at least, the necessity for it) was generally accepted, and it was even suggested that many seamen looked on it indifferently, as an occupational hazard.[26] Pressing was carried out in several ways. Homeward-bound merchantmen were a prime target for warships' boats or specially hired tenders operating in the Medway, the Downs, or Spithead: seamen pressed in this way naturally resented being kept from their families and their pay, but the goverment considered it more acceptable to impose hardships on them than to disrupt outward-bound trade, and examples were made of sea-officers who pressed from ships leaving England.[27] Experienced seamen could also be obtained from the herring fisheries of the east coast, the Newfoundland and Icelandic fisheries, and the colliers of the east

[24] NHL, MS 121/10, pp. 33–8; Ehrman, *Navy . . . of William III*, 113–14.

[25] Adm. 106/389, fo. 49. Cf. Adm. 2/1734, fos. 4, 18ᵛ; Adm. 106/282, fo. 104; SP 29/105, fo. 18; SP 29/115, fo. 71; Rawl. MS A. 186, fo. 364; Pepys MS 2862, pp. 89–90, 94, 115–16, 135–6, 204–5, 221, 359–60, 384.

[26] Ehrman, *Navy . . . of William III*, 115–16; 'An Enquiry into . . . our Naval Miscarriages', 566; B. Slush, *The Navy Royal: Or, A Sea-Cook turn'd Projector* (1709), 88–90. Cf. *Barlow's Journal, passim*.

[27] BL, Addit. MS 32094, fo. 40; Pepys MS 2854, pp. 379–80; Pepys MS 2855, pp. 104, 233; *Barlow's Journal*, i. 146. On the pressing process as a whole, cf. also Capp, *Cromwell's Navy*, 262–72.

coast. The Newfoundland fishery and the collier fleets, in particular, already had long-standing (if debatable) reputations as 'nurseries of seamen', as it was believed that just a few voyages could turn a 'green' landlubber into a capable seaman; in 1693, one naval captain, in a proposed reform of the recruiting system, believed that a fifth of the wartime navy's entire manpower requirement could be met from the colliers alone.[28] However, in practice few warships could supply the whole of their needs from merchantmen or fishing boats, and sea-officers or specially appointed press-officers (often retired sea-officers) were sent ashore in charge of press-gangs to gather more seamen from among able-bodied men aged between 18 and 60 in the maritime counties. Press-officers gained a *per capita* allowance for the men they pressed, and, in turn, the men themselves received a shilling and a certificate, with instructions to proceed to a dockyard. 'Conductors' were specially appointed to oversee the journey of the pressed men, in a (not always successful) attempt to ensure that they actually reached their ships.[29]

The journal of John Westcott, lieutenant of the second-rate *Unicorn* in 1678, provides a rare, if not unique, insight into the mechanics of the pressing process.[30] On 1 May he was ordered to press men at London and send them to his ship, using a ketch hired for use as a tender. In four days he pressed fifteen men in such localities as Wapping and Billingsgate, but another three managed to run away. Westcott then sailed in the ketch with orders from his captain to 'goe either to the Norward or to the westward, as I should think fitt for my best advantage'. He pressed nine men out of merchant ships at the Nore and then sailed for the Downs, entering one volunteer at Dover and pressing eleven men out of several Topsham merchantmen bound from Rotterdam. On 12 May, the ketch closed two shallops which escaped by running close inshore in bad weather, despite a couple of shots from Westcott's craft. On returning to London for provisions, he found the Navy Board unable to supply the ketch because he did not possess the necessary paperwork, and because of a two-day holiday

[28] BL, Addit. MS 11602, fos. 76, 127; NHL, MS 121/10, p. 47; G. St Loe, 'England's Safety, or, a Bridle to the French King' (1693), *Lord Somers Tracts*, 11 (1814), 64–6; R. G. Lounsbury, *The British Fishery at Newfoundland 1634–1763* (New Haven, 1934), 116, 139, 171, 174.
[29] NHL, MS 121/10, pp. 27, 71, 75.
[30] Cf. R. Hutton, *The Restoration: A Political and Religious History of England and Wales*, 1660–7 (Oxford, 1985), 361 n. 116.

which effectively prevented any business. The master of the ketch then went missing for a day, further delaying their departure. When Westcott finally got back to sea, he managed to press six men on the night of 1 June and delivered them to the *Unicorn*, only to find on the following day that the Admiralty had ordered a halt to all pressing. The 'French war' for which he had been recruiting men was not going to happen, and all Westcott's efforts had been in vain.[31]

Not surprisingly, pressing was an unpopular and tedious task for those entrusted with it. Apart from the sort of tribulations which befell Westcott, it could lead to a sea-officer's dismissal if he pressed men who were exempt; over-enthusiastic officers who pursued men into inns or private houses also found themselves in trouble with the administration.[32] The authorities always had to balance the needs of the navy and trade, keeping one eye on the prospect of a hostile reaction to excessive pressing from mercantile interests in Parliament.[33] Protections from the press were granted on a widespread basis, either to large groups (for example, employees of the navy, victualling, and ordnance offices, mackerel fishermen during their season, and certain entire collier fleets) or to individuals. An individual protection often depended on influence; a fortuitous connection with a minister or MP, or even marriage to the nurse of one of the king's bastards, could secure a seaman an exemption from the press.[34] The attentions of the press-officers could be avoided in other ways. Bribery was commonplace: in 1668, a 'gift' of two salmon was said to be an acceptable alternative to pressing a man, while captains of press-boats could extort large sums from merchant captains in return for leaving their men alone. Merchant shipowners conspired to hide their men, or landed them before they came within range of the press-boats (in order to collect them later). Seamen hid in barns and woods, or took back lanes to avoid the press-gangs who roamed the main roads between maritime towns.[35] At the start of the 1689 campaign, hun-

[31] Adm. 51/4380, pt. 2, *Unicorn* log.

[32] Pepys MS 2853, p. 435; Pepys MS 2854, pp. 170–1; BL, Egerton MS 928, fos. 72–3; Adm. 3/275, pp. 76, 85; St Loe, 'England's Safety', 57.

[33] Tanner, *Catalogue*, ii. 234–5; Pepys MS 2853, p. 52; Pepys MS 2854, p. 213; Pepys MS 2862, p. 327.

[34] NHL, MS 121/10, p. 46; Pepys MS 2853, pp. 48, 91, 377; Pepys MS 2854, p. 227; Pepys MS 2856, p. 145; Adm. 2/1733, fo. 154.

[35] SP 29/107, fo. 41; SP 29/153, fo. 22; SP 29/160, fos. 142, 160; Adm. 106/281, fos. 40, 196–8; Adm. 106/284, fo. 74; Adm. 106/290, fo. 87; E. Coxere, *Adventures by Sea*, ed. E. H. W. Meyerstein (Oxford, 1945), 22–4; Powell and Timings, *Rupert and Monck*, 87.

dreds of mariners left London *en masse*, heading for East Anglian ports where they believed they would be less likely to encounter the press.[36] More violent evasion was also common. Press-officers were often attacked by seamen's mobs, and entire coastal towns could turn against the press-gangs, often with the connivance of the mayor or magistrates.[37]

Another method of forced recruitment, conducted simultaneously with the activities of the press-officers and often causing problems of disputed jurisdiction with them, was the raising of fixed quotas of seamen by the vice-admirals of the maritime counties. This method was of considerable antiquity, and was used in all the major mobilizations of Charles II's reign: in the second and third Dutch wars, 5,300 men were demanded from the vice-admirals, and the amount was increased to 10,100 in 1678.[38] The counties were assessed according to the strength of their seafaring communities. In 1678, Devon was to provide 1,300 men, Bristol and Norfolk 950 apiece, but only 160 were required from Lincolnshire and 150 from Cheshire; in all, 4,460 were required from the east coast, 3,560 from the south-west, 1,520 from the south coast, and 620 from the north-west.[39] This system was supplemented by direct appeals to the civil authorities. In 1664, for example, the mayor of Bristol was asked to raise five hundred men, while his counterparts at Dartmouth and Yarmouth were asked to obtain 150 apiece, and the lord-lieutenants were also expected to assist in the pressing process.[40] In fact, the physical process of pressing at the local level often devolved upon the parish constable. When the JPs were asked to draw up lists of the seamen in their counties, it was the constables who had to undertake the task; when the vice-admirals tried to raise their quotas, it was invariably the constables who carried out their orders.[41] Not surprisingly, the opportunities for collusion between the constable and his neighbours were legion. The rejects of a village community could be off-loaded into the navy: throughout the Dutch wars, captains protested at the inadequacy of the specimens

[36] Adm. 106/392, pt. 2, fo. 71.
[37] Tanner, *Catalogue*, ii. 205; iv. 3; Pepys MS 2854, p. 126; Adm. 106/311, fo. 185; J. Baltharpe, *The Straights Voyage*, ed. J. S. Bromley (Luttrell Society; 20; Oxford, 1959), 17.
[38] NHL, MS 121/10, p. 67; BL, Addit. MS 9316, fos. 21–2; Adm. 2/1, fo. 1; Adm. 2/1735, fo. 123ᵛ; Adm. 1/5138, pp. 906–16.
[39] Adm. 1/5138, p. 916. London was not included in the assessment.
[40] NHL, MS 121/10, pp. 53, 73.
[41] See the sources cited in n. 2 above, and cf. Capp, *Cromwell's Navy*, 265.

being pressed by the vice-admirals, and the vice-admirals, in turn, protested at the failure of the constables to obtain good men. In one ten-day period of 1673, for instance, the navy's new recruits included butchers, cordwainers, ribbon-weavers, bakers, a 'Country lad', 'an old man blind', and a one-armed apprentice to an innkeeper.[42]

Some men were recruited from peripheral sources. Scots seamen were pressed in some numbers during the second and third Dutch wars, continuing a practice begun in 1626, but the administration was reluctant to follow this course, and on the rare occasions when pressing was contemplated in peacetime Scots were specifically exempted.[43] In 1665, the possibility of recruitment from Ireland was considered, but the remoteness of the country and the depopulation of its maritime areas as a result of the civil wars made the scheme impractical (though it was revived in 1678, equally unsuccessfully).[44] However, small numbers of Irish seamen served in the fleet throughout the period, and the two or three small warships usually assigned to guard the Irish coast were often manned locally.[45] Small numbers of foreigners were also pressed into service, generally overseas in peacetime, and were retained until released by their ambassadors;[46] merchantmen taken up for service as tenders or auxiliaries in home waters in wartime often had a significant foreign element in their crews.[47] The Restoration navy therefore numbered among its personnel small numbers of Frenchmen, Dutchmen, Italians, Swedes, and even Russians and American Indians.[48] More common was the recruitment of English seamen overseas: the Crown claimed a right to search foreign ships for

[42] Adm. 106/282, fos. 12, 104, 210, 211–12, 245, 266–9. Cf. Powell and Timings, *Rupert and Monck*, 65, 67–8; *CSPD*, 1664–5, 1665–6, 1666–7, 1671–2, 1672, 1672–3, 1673, *passim*; Davies, 'Wales and Mr Pepys's Navy', 103–6. For the constables at work in one maritime county, see Devon RO, Q/S 128/12/1, 128/105/1.

[43] J. Grant (ed.), *The Old Scots Navy from 1689–1710* (Navy Records Society, 44; 1914), p. xix; Adm. 1/5138, p. 266.

[44] *CSP Ireland*, 1663–5, 524–5; Bod. Lib., Carte MS 47, fo. 446ᵛ; HMC, *Ormonde MSS*, NS, iv. 421.

[45] e.g. Adm. 106/311, fo. 454.

[46] *Naval Minutes*, 373; Rawl. MS A. 181, fo. 146ᵛ. Cf. Adm. 33/106, *Leopard* pay-book, 1677–8, tickets 289, 299, 304–6.

[47] See e.g. Adm. 33/96, *Elizabeth Victualler* pay-book, 1673; Adm. 33/105, *Batchelor* pay-book, 1673.

[48] Rawl. MS A. 181, fo. 146ᵛ; Pepys MS 2854, p. 174; Pepys MS 2857, p. 465; Pepys MS 2858, p. 70; Adm. 2/1749, p. 132; Adm. 106/311, fos. 154, 167; Adm. 106/360, fo. 473. The Indians were oarsmen for the *Margaret Galley* at Tangier, a vessel built in Italy and manned and officered largely by foreigners. Cf. Rodger, *Wooden World*, 158–61.

English mariners (a claim which was naturally and bitterly resented by other states), and also permitted its captains to exchange men with English merchant ships overseas.[49] Warships in the Mediterranean, in particular, often entered men from English merchant vessels, or picked up any seamen waiting in ports from Cadiz to Smyrna, and discharged other crewmen who wanted to try for a berth on a merchantman.[50] Local recruitment also took place on other stations: vessels guarding the Newfoundland fishery often entered some men at St John's, while ships assigned to New England, Virginia, or the West Indies usually recruited some proportion of their crews among local seamen.[51]

The ideal of manning the navy entirely with men who possessed some nautical training was never attainable in wartime, and the administration had to resort to more desperate measures. During both the second and third Dutch wars, a large but indeterminate number of unqualified landsmen were deliberately pressed, in addition to those palmed off on to the navy by unscrupulous local officials; these were supposed to be drawn from the ranks of the common labourers, but particularly desperate press-officers often provoked storms of protest by pressing farmers or other substantial men, and the drag-net of the press might even be extended to inland counties—an action admitted even by the Admiralty to be a sign of particular desperation.[52] On the whole, however, fewer landsmen seem to have been recruited in this period than in later years. The other last resort was the filling-up of ships' companies with soldiers, though there was a fine line between this and the maintenance of the old tradition of having fighting men aboard ships in case of close action. In the first Dutch war under the republic, up to one-third of each crew had consisted of soldiers; in 1664 the administration settled on one-eighth, and the complements of undermanned ships were regularly completed by this means in wartime.[53] However, the administrators regarded the use of soldiers as

[49] NMM, ADL/A/4 (38th general instruction); Pepys MS 2879, pp. 53 ff; Rawl. MS A. 191, fo. 217; SP 29/398, fo. 16.

[50] Adm. 106/314, fo. 242; Adm. 106/319, fo. 340. Cf. e.g. Adm. 33/92, *Assurance* pay-book, 1680; Adm. 33/100, *James Galley* pay-book, 1676–9; Adm. 33/103, *Plymouth* pay-book, 1677–9.

[51] See e.g. Adm. 33/106, *Leopard* pay-book, 1677–8; Adm. 33/119, *Dartmouth* pay-book, 1682–5; Adm. 33/108, *Falcon* pay-book, 1682–4.

[52] BL, Sloane MS 1745, p. 4; BL, Addit. MS 10117, fo. 167; SP 29/163, fo. 11; SP 29/331, fo. 275; NHL, MS. 121/10, p. 67; Hutton, *Restoration*, 221, 243–4.

[53] Coventry MS 95, fo. 65; *CSPD*, 1665–6, 456, 458, 463, 464, 465; Powell and Timings, *Rupert and Monck*, 43, 46, 55, 61, 76, 79; J. Childs, *The Army of Charles II* (1976), 72; Capp, *Cromwell's Navy*, 272–5.

something of an admission of defeat, and a suggestion that it should be used in peacetime was decisively rejected by the Admiralty in 1682.[54] Captains were naturally reluctant to have unskilled landsmen and soldiers in their crews, and the administration was constantly troubled by captains pressing above their official complements in attempts to exchange inadequate men for good ones.[55]

One of the most deeply rooted beliefs concerning the sailing navy is the notion that the great majority of its men were pressed.[56] However, as has been seen, the peacetime navy under the later Stuarts was overwhelmingly a volunteer force, resorting to pressing only occasionally—notably in 1675 and 1677, when ships bound for the Mediterranean were seriously undermanned.[57] Even in wartime the genuine attractions of naval service ensured that there was always a substantial volunteer element among ships' companies, alongside the three other elements—soldiers, pressed men, and those 'turned over' from other ships, who might, of course, include a mixture of men who had originally been volunteers or pressed. The relative proportions of these groups aboard any ship would depend on many factors, notably the popularity of the captain and officers, but the available evidence suggests that during the third Dutch war, at least (again the only period for which sufficient evidence survives), volunteers could account for between one-quarter and three-quarters of a ship's company. In 1672, for example, over 60 per cent of the men of the first-rate *Sovereign* and the fourth-rate *Leopard* were pressed, while only 29 per cent of the crew of the second-rate *Old James* had been recruited in this way; but then, another 18 per cent of the *Old James*'s men were soldiers. On the third-rate *Fairfax*, the proportions of volunteers, pressed men, turnovers, and soldiers, were, respectively, 27, 48, 17 and 8 per cent.[58] Perhaps surprisingly, there is no evidence in the relevant pay-books of greater enthusiasm for the lesser rates, which would have had more opportunities for taking prizes and, therefore, should have been more popular; indeed, proportions of volunteers aboard the great

---

[54] *Pepys's Diary*, viii. 147; Adm. 3/278, pt. 2, p. 99.

[55] e.g. BL, Addit. MS 34727, fos. 117–18; Pepys MS 2855, p. 437; Powell and Timings, *Rupert and Monck*, 51.

[56] See e.g. Merriman, *Sergison Papers*, 164; Ehrman, *Navy . . . of William III*, 119.

[57] Tanner, *Catalogue*, ii. 234–5; iii. 58–9, 68, 72–3, 413–15; iv. 187–8, 412.

[58] Adm. 33/91, *Fairfax*; Adm. 33/100, *Old James*; Adm. 33/106, *Leopard*; Adm. 33/107, *Sovereign*. A similar picture emerges from the other pay-books which contain this information. These figures should be compared with those of N. A. M. Rodger for the mid-18th-c. navy: the comparison seems to confirm that the proportion of pressed men was greater, and the rate of turnover much less, in the Stuart Navy (Rodger, *Wooden World*, 153–63, 353, 359).

ships were sometimes much higher than on the fourth-rates.[59] As Sir William Coventry well knew, naval recruitment was nothing if not unpredictable.

Whether volunteers or pressed, the seamen were generally numbered among the lowest orders of society, for (in Pepys's view) the unpleasant nature of their trade restricted it to 'poor illiterate hands'.[60] Many probably came from long lines of seamen, but sons of husbandmen, boys left to the care of the parish, or the children of tradesmen also entered the service; whatever its shortcomings, the navy could provide employment for those who found few opportunities for work in their own areas, or who sought a chance to travel and see something of the world.[61] The navy also had a reputation as a refuge for runaway husbands and drunks, and there were several attempts to join the service by escaped prisoners and failed tradesmen seeking to evade their creditors.[62] Most seamen had very few possessions, often bequeathing only a handful of household goods and the expectation of wages due for their naval service.[63] Many died in debt, for those who lived along the Thames usually lived on credit from local tradesmen and landladies; indeed, pressure from creditors was often given as a reason for seamen's petitions for payment, and landladies were believed to be the instigators of much of the sporadic discontent among mariners.[64] Those pressed into service in wartime included the very poorest members of society, but the lower decks of warships could also contain men who were comparatively well off. The seamen pressed for service in 1673 from coastal villages in Kent and Sussex were largely fishermen who used the Yarmouth fishery, but many of them were small householders who probably followed trades in their communities in

[59] This contradicts Dr Capp's findings for the 1650s: *Cromwell's Navy*, 261.

[60] *Tangier Papers*, 120–1.

[61] *Barlow's Journal*, i. 15 *et seq.*; Adm. 106/3539, pt. 1, 'Mariners' folder, petitions of William Hale and Matthew Keynell; R. Davis, *The Rise of the English Shipping Industry* (1962), 114–15; C. Lloyd, *The British Seaman* (1968), 54–5; M. Rediker, *Between the Devil and the Deep Blue Sea: Merchant Seamen, Pirates, and the Anglo-American Maritime World, 1700–50* (Cambridge, 1987), 12–14.

[62] *Barlow's Journal*, i. 28; Pepys MS 2853, pp. 6, 436; *Naval Minutes*, 62.

[63] Sample of seamen's inventories in Prob. 4 and 5, and of wills in Prob. 11. Cf. Rediker, *Devil and Deep Blue Sea*, 146–9, for the 'non-accumulative' ethos of seamen.

[64] Bod. Lib., Carte MS 73, fo. 510; Adm. 1/3553, p. 635; Adm. 106/3539, pt. 1, 'Seamen' folder, petitions of Elizabeth Reamer and Elaine Morris; Adm. 106/3540, pt. 2, 'Petitions' folder, petition of crew of *Cleveland Yacht*, 1682; HMC, *Finch MSS*, iv. 490, 500.

the intervals between voyages.[65] One Dorset seaman, pressed in 1672, owned three houses in his home town; several others left the service on inheriting estates from relatives.[66] The level of personal wealth among the seamen, therefore, was by no means as uniformly low as Pepys assumed.

Many seamen alternated between naval and mercantile employment. Some served in the navy only in wartime, and only as a result of being pressed, while others chose any employment which seemed likely to secure them preferment and higher pay. Seamen wanted to be able to experience a variety of voyages; in fact, opportunities for merchant voyages were often unpredictable, with the seasonal pattern of many trades forcing seamen to take temporary jobs ashore during the winter, and many attempted to seek fresh employment only when their pay from the previous voyage ran out.[67] The peacetime navy, therefore, should have been able to compete with merchant shipping for the services of the large pool of seamen who were always 'between jobs'. Indeed, the service could already depend on a hard core of seamen who preferred the navy and remained in it for many years. Few could match the seaman who sought a place ashore in 1680 after about sixty years of almost continuous service, but there were other cases of men serving between thirty and fifty years.[68]

Several factors attracted these men to naval service, and made them prefer it to mercantile employment.[69] Many entered the navy in search of advancement.[70] In 1652, the system of rating seamen as 'able' and 'ordinary' was introduced, with the former earning 24s. a month and the latter 19s. The general instructions to commanders laid down that an able seaman had to be at least twenty years old, with five years' experience at sea, and that the rating of seamen should be conducted

[65] KAO, U. 269/O. 29. Cf. J. H. Farrant, 'The Rise and Decline of a South Coast Seafaring Town: Brighton 1550–1750', *MM* 71 (1985), 63.
[66] Adm. 106/3023, fo. 20; Adm. 106/368, fo. 515; Adm. 106/3540, pt. 2, 'Petitions' folder, petition of John Wyatt.
[67] Pepys MS 2581, p. 223; *Barlow's Journal*, i. 38–9, 252 *et passim*; Davis, *Shipping Industry*, 116; Ehrman, *Navy ... of William III*, 111; Rediker, *Devil and Deep Blue Sea*, 79–83.
[68] NMM, ADL/L/3; Adm. 106/3539, pt. 1, 'Seamen' folder, certificate by Lawrence Wright, 14 Apr. 1686; Tanner, *Catalogue*, iii. 22.
[69] For one seaman's view of these factors see *Barlow's Journal*, ii. 426. Cf. Rodger, *Wooden World*, 114–18, 125–6, 135–7.
[70] See e.g. R. C. Anderson (ed.), *Journals and Narratives of the Third Dutch War* (Navy Records Society, 86; 1946) 59; Adm. 106/330, fo. 135; KAO, U. 1515/O. 12, unfol., Cloudesley Shovell to Pepys, Apr. 1688.

by the captain, in consultation with the master and boatswain.[71] In fact, the system had several shortcomings. Men could only be rated effectively when a ship was at sea, so captains of vessels spending long periods at anchor complained that they were unable to assess their men.[72] More significant was the dependence of the system on the personal choice of the captain and his deputies: critics warned that captains would rate their own servants and retinue as able seamen in order to draw their wages, and this abuse was certainly commonplace.[73] Men who sought further preferment as petty officers generally volunteered for great ships, where more posts were available, but advancement still depended to a great extent on gaining friends and patrons among the ship's officers.[74]

The second great advantage of the navy was the provision of substantial victuals, including meat, peas, oatmeal, and a gallon of beer a day. The allowance was better than anything available in merchant ships and superior to the normal diet of the seamen's social equals ashore, though modern opinion would consider it too heavily calorific and lacking in vitamins.[75] Pepys's famous remark about seamen loving their bellies contained a great deal of truth, but the appalling quality of some of the victuals provided for the fleet persuaded some seamen that it was almost better to starve.[76] The chance of plunder and prize money was another attraction which drew seamen to the smaller ships of the fleet, though many of those who considered this incentive important preferred to serve in privateers, where discipline was looser, the chances of taking prizes greater, and the distribution of the booty less heavily weighted towards the officers.[77] Those who served in the navy could also hope for rewards from the Crown for gallant service;

---

[71] NMM, ADL/A/4. For the proportions of able and ordinary seamen allowed to different rates, see Pepys MS 2266, p. 148.

[72] Adm. 106/324, fo. 354; Adm. 106/338, fos. 196, 502.

[73] NHL, MS 121/11, p. 103; Pepys MS 2581, pp. 108, 198; Adm. 106/294, fo. 341; BL., Egerton MS 928, fo. 191.

[74] Rawl. MS A. 314, fo. 20; *Barlow's Journal*, ii. 425.

[75] Slush, *Navy Royal*, 71–2, 75–7. Cf. J. R. Bruijn's analysis of the similar diet of Dutch seamen: 'Dutch Men-of-War—Those on Board, c. 1700–50', *Acta Historiae Neerlandicae*, 7 (1974), 107. For the detailed allowance of victuals and exceptions to it (petty-warrant and short-allowance victuals), see Lloyd, *British Seaman*, 95–6.

[76] *Naval Minutes*, 250; *Barlow's Journal*, i, *passim*. There are many colourful tales of bad victuals: see e.g. Adm. 1/3552, p. 79; Adm. 106/314, fo. 103; Adm. 106/340, fo. 171.

[77] Pepys MS 2581, p. 255; Slush, *Navy Royal*, 23–4, 93–111; Capp, *Cromwell's Navy*, 260–3.

awards were made regularly, partly for their own sake but chiefly to encourage others. In 1668, £100 was shared between a midshipman and ten seamen for bravery in the West Indies, while in 1673 a sailor received £6 for repelling a Dutch vessel which was attacking an English first-rate.[78]

Probably the most important attraction of the navy for seamen with families was the provision of pensions and bounties. In 1673, following a more limited effort in 1665, an attempt was made to encourage volunteering by instituting a system of bounties to widows and orphans, together with an award of one year's wages for the loss of a limb in combat.[79] Payments were also made by counties out of their funds for the relief of 'maimed soldiers'.[80] However, the main source of charitable provision for wounded seamen continued to be the Chatham Chest, an institution originally established under Elizabeth I. The Chest paid fixed rates for different injuries, although it also made an inequitable distinction between wounds sustained in wartime and in peacetime in order to save costs. Nevertheless, the wars of the Restoration period put the Chest under great strain: 817 pensioners were created by the second Dutch war and 493 by the third, and by 1676 the total value of all pensions was over £5,000. The Chest's problems were compounded by a fall in the rents from the five farms it owned, and from the Restoration onwards the administration tried to buy off pensions in an attempt to lessen the financial burden. Even so, the Chest kept many pensioners of very long standing. In 1676 one man had been receiving aid for fifty-six years, and many others had been benefiting from the Chest for between twenty-five and fifty years.[81] The pension alone was inadequate to support seamen with large families, and many crippled mariners sought to augment their income by getting further employment at sea. The merchant service refused to take any physically disabled men, and in 1674 Charles II and his Admiralty board introduced a quota of berths for crippled seamen aboard seagoing warships (usually one cripple to every fifty able men). Demand for places soon outstripped supply, and the

[78] Adm. 106/17, fo. 242; Adm. 2/1746, fo. 135ᵛ. Cf. Powell and Timings, *Rupert and Monck*, 85, 102, 107, 128–9, 131, 135.
[79] NHL., MS 121/12, p. 149; Adm. 106/285, fo. 140; Adm. 2/1746, fo. 114; Adm. 106/3023, *passim*; Pepys MS 2874, pp. 59–65, 67–8; Keevil, *Medicine and the Navy*, ii. 134–7, and pp. 80–170 *passim*.
[80] Davies, 'Devon and the Navy'.
[81] Rawl. MS A. 299, fos. 67ᵛ, 68ᵛ, 69, 70 *et passim*; Rawl. MSS A. 230, C. 199, *passim*; Adm. 82/3, 82/12, *passim*; Adm. 82/128, pp. 15, 20, 22–3, 24–5, 26–8.

Admiralty made periodic attempts to persuade governors of hospitals to give preference to seamen.[82]

Ranged against the attractions of naval service was a formidable array of disincentives, which changed little over the years.[83] The supposed harshness of naval discipline, explored in the next chapter, was considered by some observers to be a major cause of seamen's resentment, but to most, the uncertainty of payment was the main reason for the widespread antipathy to the navy: ''tis nothing but badd Pay does it nor any thing necessary but good Pay to remedy it', one of Pepys's friends believed.[84] In theory, a ship's company should have been paid at the end of each expedition or each summer's campaign, but the naval administration rarely had the funds to permit such prompt payment, and delays, together with the accumulation of substantial arrears of pay, became commonplace. During the second Dutch war the administration resorted to payment by tickets, effectively promissory notes from the treasurer of the navy, in an attempt to reduce the demands for ready money. The method was not new, but it had always been detested by seamen: going to London to get tickets exchanged could be an expensive and time-consuming process, and seamen often sold out to ticket-brokers at a substantial loss to themselves.[85] By 1667, many ships had two, three, or even four years' arrears due to them,[86] mutinies were endemic, and seamen's mobs were attacking the Navy Board's offices in London.[87] The disastrous collapse of the naval pay system in the second Dutch war created a store of resentment which endured for many years. In 1668–9, several crews refused to go out without money, and payment by ticket was said to have so alienated the seamen that they would rather have served an enemy than their own country.[88] At the start of the third war, the

---

[82] Adm. 106/3539, pt. 1, 'Seamen' folder, petitions of Felix Magnus, Edward Simpson, and Evan Williams; Adm. 1/3545, p. 1098; Tanner, *Catalogue*, ii. 275, 409–10; iv. 17, 91–2, 332.

[83] See e.g. Perrin, *Boteler's Dialogues*, 35; BL, Addit. MS 11602, fo. 76; Dennis, *Essay on the Navy*, 7–26.

[84] Pepys MS 2581, p. 254. Cf. Capp, *Cromwell's Navy*, 277–80.

[85] D. E. Kennedy, 'The Crown and the Common Seamen in Early Stuart England', *Historical Studies, Australia and New Zealand*, 11 (1964), 173; W. N. Hammond, 'The Administration of the English Navy, 1649–60', Ph.D. thesis (British Columbia, 1974), 111–14; Turnbull, 'The Administration of the Royal Navy', 408–25.

[86] *CSPD*, 1667, 46, 75 *et seq.*; Coventry MS 96, fo. 266.

[87] M. P. Schoenfeld, 'The Restoration Seaman and his Wages', *The American Neptune*, 25 (1965), 278–85.

[88] Rawl. MS A. 191, fo. 229; Pepys MS 2581, p. 199; Bod. Lib., Tanner MS 44, fo. 53; BL, Addit. MS 9311, fo. 194'; SP 29/262, fo. 108.

administration attempted to regain the seamen's affections by paying arrears and offering a substantial bounty to volunteers, but these measures failed to counteract the suspicion and mistrust which persisted among the seamen.[89] As late as 1692, the memory of the use of tickets in the second Dutch war, and a fear that this system would be reintroduced on a large scale, were still being given as reasons for the seamen's unwillingness to serve.[90]

Another bitterly resented aspect of the pay problem was the use of the turnover. The notion that turning over crews *en masse* from ship to ship was largely an innovation of William III's war is misleading,[91] for the turnover was often used during the second and third Dutch wars (and in 1678), and had also been common in the interregnum.[92] Turning over was seen by the administration as a means of transferring men from ships due to be laid up into ships going to sea, thereby avoiding the need to press more extensively—and avoiding the need to pay those men immediately.[93] The seamen objected to it on several grounds. Turning over kept men from their families, and made them lose any interest they had gained with their captains; a man rated as a petty officer on one ship could find himself demoted to able seaman on another, with a consequent loss of pay.[94] Above all, turning over was seen as a means of cheating the men of their pay. At best, a 'turned-over' seaman could expect a difficult hunt for his wages from several former ships, and crews often petitioned for all or part of their back pay before they would consent to being turned over. As a last, desperate resort, many seamen were prepared to desert and lose several months' wages, rather than submit to the turnover.[95]

Unless in response to the threat of the turnover, seamen who decided to desert the service were usually men who had recently joined, as loss of wages was a deterrent to many who had served for some time; a man deserting with seven or eight months' pay due was considered worthy of comment, but few cases were recorded of men

[89] SP 29/309, fo. 71; SP 29/325, fo. 53; *CSPD*, Addenda 1660–85, 350, 368 *et seq.*
[90] HMC, *Finch MSS*, iv. 392.
[91] Ehrman, *Navy . . . of William III*, 133; Baugh, *British Naval Administration*, 192.
[92] Hammond, 'Administration', 179.
[93] Adm. 106/13, fos. 448–50; Adm. 2/1752, pp. 1, 18, 44–5; Pepys MS 2854, pp. 337–8.
[94] Adm. 106/3539, pt. 1, 'Mariners' folder, petition from *Mountague*, 16 June 1684; NHL, MS 121/10, pp. 98–9, 114.
[95] Pepys MS 2581, pp. 199–200; Pepys MS 2855, pp. 38, 94–5, 130–1; Adm. 106/11, fos. 13, 146; Adm. 106/337, pt. 2, fo. 425; Adm. 106/345, fo. 507; SP 29/148, fos. 47, 78; *Barlow's Journal*, i. 173.

deserting when owed money for longer service.[96] Both in war and peace, the main incentive for deserters was the prospect of gaining higher wages in the merchant service. During the second and third Dutch wars, the navy's demand for seamen led to a rise in the wages offered by merchant ship owners to between 35s. and 40s. a month on average for able seamen, 50 per cent more than they could earn in the navy, and the Newcastle colliers paid up to 55s. a month in the second war.[97] Sea-officers and administrators complained that the attraction of these high wages made it impossible to keep seamen, with some naval recruits being willing to lose several months' pay and run the risk of being pressed again in order to serve in the colliers.[98] Merchant ship wages remained high in the 1670s, when England was able to take advantage of her position as a neutral carrier in the continuing European war, and desertion from the navy, or unwillingness to join, caused a severe shortage of manpower and forced the administration to resort to the extremity of pressing in peacetime.[99] The prospect of higher pay and the inadequacy of wage-rates in their own navy tempted many other English seamen into the service of foreign states. Many served in the enemy fleet throughout the second and third Dutch wars; in 1672, 1,000 Englishmen and 1,500 Scots were said to be present in the Dutch fleet.[100] At the end of the second war, the French attempted to exploit the discontent with the ticket system by offering attractive financial inducements to English seamen, and others sought to join Mediterranean navies which would pay them more regularly.[101] When the third war ended and the active fleet was greatly reduced in size, foreign service became an even more attractive proposition. Navies at war could offer more pay, more plunder, and more opportunities for preferment than a navy at peace, and English seamen flocked to join the French and Dutch services (or even lesser fleets, such as that of Tuscany), despite half-hearted attempts by the administration to stop the exodus.[102]

---

[96] SP 29/197, fo. 135. Cf. Rodger, *Wooden World*, 196–9; Capp, *Cromwell's Navy*, 282–6.

[97] Pepys MS 2581, p. 200; Davis, *Shipping Industry*, 135–6, 324–5; Capp, *Cromwell's Navy*, 259; Rodger, *Wooden World*, 126–7.

[98] Pepys MS 2581, pp. 196, 200; Adm. 2/1745, fo. 123; SP 29/122, fo. 21; SP 29/194, fo. 89; Bod. Lib., Carte MS 34, fos. 228–9.

[99] Pepys MS 2853, fo. 178; Adm. 106/322, fo. 110; Tanner, *Catalogue*, ii. 240; iii. 58–9.

[100] SP 29/305, fos. 18, 198; SP 29/331, fo. 219.

[101] *Pepys's Diary*, viii. 601; SP 29/225, fo. 181; SP 29/255, fo. 164.

[102] Tanner, *Catalogue*, iv. 20; *CSPD*, 1677–8, 25, 45, 47–8; PRO, E/M/21/58, no.

The widespread willingness to serve an enemy power in wartime suggests that many seamen were not concerned with political issues: their main concerns were material, particularly the provision of good pay and victuals. The seamen had deserted Charles I when he failed to provide adequately for them; throughout the civil wars, and under the republic, their attitudes continued to be dominated by material considerations.[103] Throughout the reigns of Charles II and James II, material issues continued to preoccupy the seamen. Almost all cases of protest and mutiny, and most of the serious cases of desertion, which were recorded in this period were concerned with pay, victuals, or conditions of service.[104] The few recorded instances of seamen supposedly speaking treason were usually dismissed as the rantings of the simple-minded, ignorant, and useless.[105] On other occasions, 'original' protests by seamen turned out, after investigation, to have been instigated by ringleaders among the officers.[106] The seamen were considered to be outside the 'political nation', characterized both by outsiders and their own kind as men concerned overwhelmingly with food, drink, and sex—'a people that will say one thing today and another to morrow'.[107]

However, it would be misleading to suggest that seamen were wholly apolitical. Many possessed a simple but strong patriotism, characterized by xenophobia and distaste for all administrators and ministers of state. The xenophobia often found an outlet in the form of drunken brawls with foreign seamen in Mediterranean ports,[108] while the 'country' attitude to politicians also reflected a more general suspicion of landsmen, with Edward Barlow, for instance, regarding ministers and gentry alike as corrupt, treacherous, and ignorant of the needs of the seamen and ordinary people of England.[109] Other seamen dis-

---

113; *Naval Minutes*, 36.

[103] Kennedy, 'Crown and the Common Seamen', 170–7; J. R. Powell, *The Navy in the English Civil War* (1962), 10–11; Hammond, 'Administration', 365–6; Cogar, 'The Politics of Naval Administration', 283 *et passim*.

[104] Cf. Capp, *Cromwell's Navy*, 228–30.

[105] *CSPD*, 1675–6, 464–5, 466, 487–7, 493, 510; Rawl. MS A. 314, fo. 2ᵛ; Adm. 106/381, fo. 43.

[106] See e.g. Rawl. MS A. 314, fos. 7–8; Adm. 1/5253, fos. 42, 44–6.

[107] HMC, *Finch MSS*, iv. 494. Cf. Baltharpe, *Straights Voyage, passim*; *Barlow's Journal, passim*; Ward, *Wooden World Dissected*, 89–99; Capp, *Cromwell's Navy*, 243–5, 249.

[108] e.g. SP 79/3, fo. 64; SP 101/80, newsletter, 13 July 1683.

[109] *Barlow's Journal*, i. 116, 119, 134–5, 148, 165–6. Cf. Rediker, *Devil and Deep Blue Sea*, 244–5.

played an equally passionate, unsophisticated love of country, critical of any tactics which smacked of caution, and of any suggestion of ending a war with a dishonourable peace.[110] Seamen were not untouched by political issues. They debated them in coffee-houses and inns, and, despite the lack of evidence, it would be naïve to assume that such debates never took place aboard ship, though freedom of speech at sea would have been limited by the constraints of the articles of war and the risk of being taken to a court-martial on an informer's word.[111] Similarly, the lack of evidence should not lead to an assumption that all seamen shared a common political standpoint. During the exclusion crisis, the seamen of London seem to have been divided in the same way as other social and occupational groups; moreover, the paternalistic nature of naval recruitment and promotion might have created a divide between those, generally volunteers, who were loyal to and dependent upon the system, and 'anti-authoritarian' pressed men or newcomers from the merchant service.[112] Some men might have hated the ship in which they served, and the officers who commanded them; others might have contemplated desertion because of uncertain payment, turnovers, or stinking victuals; many might have hated the ministers who ordered them to sea; but in the heat of a battle, other loyalties and enmities became more important.

---

[110] Bod. Lib., Carte MS 34, fo. 516; *Pepys's Diary*, vii. 158; SP 29/211, fo. 106; *Barlow's Journal*, i. 233. Cf. Baltharpe, *Straights Voyage, passim*; Kennedy, 'Crown and Common Seamen', *passim*.

[111] T. Harris, *London Crowds in the Reign of Charles II* (Cambridge, 1987), 29.

[112] Ibid. 214–15; Rediker, *Devil and Deep Blue Sea*, 244–5, and Ch. 5 *passim*.

5

THE ELEMENTS OF NAVAL LIFE

[THE officers] dressed as if for a gala at Versailles, ate off plate, drank the richest wines, and kept harems on board, while hunger and scurvy raged among the crews, and while corpses were daily flung out of the portholes.[1]

After a century and a half, Macaulay's melodramatic vision remains the single most memorable description of daily life in the Restoration navy. Unfortunately, it bears little resemblance to historical truth, begging as it does such obvious questions as how did a ship in such a state manage to get to sea at all, let alone fight, and why did so many seamen perversely volunteer for a service in which they were most likely to be starved to death by a crowd of lecherous and gluttonous aristocratic sadists? In reality, the navy of Charles II and James II was a far more prosaic world than Macaulay would have had it: more prosaic, and infinitely more professional.

The internal organization of a Restoration warship was governed by a set of long-established, traditional forms, which remained essentially the same well into the eighteenth century,[2] and which in some cases still govern the working life of the modern Royal Navy. Captain John Smith's *The Seaman's Grammar*, first published in 1627 and reprinted several times during the course of the century, set down the method by which the crew was to be divided and the daily routine run. On first assembling, the crew was divided into two watches, the starboard under the master and the larboard under his chief mate. The watches then worked a rota system, changing over every four hours—a system usually controlled by the ringing of the ship's bell, with one additional stroke for every half hour that passed. The duty watch then worked the ship, taking the helm, trimming the sails, and working the pumps, only calling on the assistance of all hands in an emergency.[3] The general instructions of 1663 laid down an appropriate number of men for each

---

[1] Macaulay, *History of England*, i. 293.

[2] Rodger, *Wooden World*, 25–7.

[3] On the similar system in merchant shipping, see Rediker, *Devil and Deep Blue Sea*, 88–9. While I would agree with Professor Rediker that 'it is impossible to separate the work experiences and the cultural life' of the merchant and naval services, I would take issue with his assumption that the 'class warfare' he identifies (however correctly) in the

gun, for the sails, and for the other tasks aboard ship, and specified
that a list giving each man's name and station should be hung in the
steerage, supplemented by additional lists in every quarter of the men
allocated to stations there.[4] The watch system also reduced pressure
on accommodation. Between four and eight men from both watches
formed a mess, accommodated between the guns and focused around
its mess table, so that the constant presence of half the members of the
mess on watch gave the others more room in which to relax.[5] With
space at a premium, the general acceptance of the hammock into the
navy at the end of the sixteenth century had come as a considerable
boon, though as yet it was regarded chiefly as a receptacle for the
crewman's other bedding, usually a mattress and pillow, which could
be rolled up within the hammock and stored during the day.[6]

   One of the most constant and bitter bones of contention in the
Restoration navy was the allocation of cabins. The influx into the
service of officers' servants, gentlemen volunteers, midshipmen extraordinary, and other supernumerary officers, created a serious problem
of space, and this could lead to considerable discontent within a ship.
Great ships in wartime could be inundated by such outsiders: the duke
of York's retinue on the flagship *Prince* in 1672 totalled 150 men,
many of whom would have expected a cabin as being due to their rank
in society.[7] The Admiralty attempted to deal with this problem in
October 1673, when it promulgated an establishment setting down the
allowance of cabins to different rates of ship, so that, for example, a
first-rate would have 55 cabins, a fourth-rate 21, and a sixth-rate 7.[8]
The great majority of these cabins were in fact temporary hanging
canvas structures set up on wooden frames between gunports, and the
1673 establishment laid down that these were generally to measure no
more than 6 ft. × 4 ft. Even most of the larger cabins for the senior

merchant service also pervaded the navy: as I hope to show in this study, the vital bases
of authority, payment, recruitment, promotion, and (very often) length of service were
entirely different in the navy, creating a very different 'maritime world'. See *Devil and
Deep Blue Sea*, 154 n., 161, 207–43, 243 n.
   [4] NMM, ADL/A/4 (17th general instruction). Cf. J. Harland, *Seamanship in the Age
of Sail* (1984), 91–3.
   [5] J. Smith, *The Seaman's Grammar* (1652 edn.), 38–9; B. Lavery, *The Arming and
Fitting of English Ships of War 1600–1815* (1987), 182–5, 252–3.
   [6] Lavery, *Arming and Fitting*, 179–82; Rediker, *Devil and Deep Blue Sea*, 160; Rodger,
Wooden World, 61.
   [7] Adm. 33/103, *Prince* pay-book; J. Jusserand, *A French Ambassador at the Court of
Charles the Second* (1892), 135.
   [8] Lavery, *Arming and Fitting*, 155–6; Fox, *Great Ships*, 196.

officers, situated aft, were temporary structures, the bulkheads of which had to be demolished when the ship cleared its decks for action. The size and location of one's cabin was therefore a telling indication of one's status aboard the ship, and the 1673 establishment attempted to leave little room for captains to manipulate the situation in favour of their protégés. On a third-rate, for example, the master and lieutenant were to divide the roundhouse (at the very stern, beneath the poop) between them, the boatswain and carpenters were to have cabins opposite each other at the quarterdeck bulkhead, several of the mates would be accommodated in the forecastle, while the gunner, the surgeon, and their crews were accommodated in the gunroom, the after part of the lowest gundeck. Gentlemen volunteers were to be confined exclusively to first- and second-rates, where they would have the 'lower great cabin', right aft on the middle deck, while the trumpeters, who were needed to sound orders to the crew or for ceremonial greetings, were allocated minute, exposed cabins at the highest point on the poop.[9] The establishment of 1673 was only partly successful in preventing the peevish jealousies and quarrels which the matter of cabins could cause: it simply changed the basis for such disputes. From being purely internal arguments over precedence and favouritism, they became subjects for discord between captains and the Navy Board, which now had to be consulted whenever any change, no matter how small, was made to the cabin establishment.[10]

While the ringing of the ship's bell and the ever-present tyranny of the watch-keeping rota dictated working life on the ship, and the physical circumstances of one's mess, hammock, or cabin dictated the degree of comfort which could be enjoyed during much of the time spent off duty, most of the opportunities for socializing and communal life centred around mealtimes. The crewmen, who generally ate their main meal at about seven p.m., took their meals on pewter plates at their mess tables after getting their food from the galley, usually situated in the forecastle, and (in smaller ships at least) probably obtained their ale with a common ladle from an open barrel.[11] For the

---

[9] Lavery, *Arming and Fitting*, 155–76; Fox, *Great Ships*, 196; Rodger, *Wooden World*, 65–8.

[10] See e.g. Adm. 1/3556, pp. 405–10; Adm. 106/322, fo. 295; Adm. 106/374, fo. 225.

[11] Smith, *Seaman's Grammar*, 38–9; Slush, *Navy Royal*, 115; R. G. Holman, 'The *Dartmouth*, a British Frigate Wrecked off Mull, 1690: 2. Culinary and Related Items', *International Journal of Nautical Archaeology and Underwater Exploration*, 4 (1975), 264.

officers, dining became something of an obsession, with the quality of a ship's fare contributing to the reputation of the ship itself. The chaplain Henry Teonge recorded with relish the meals provided for the officers of the ships on which he served in the mid-1670s: a meal of hens, pork, mutton, beef, geese, turnips, and cheese, washed down with four types of wine, sherry, cider, ale, and beer, for the officers of their squadron; beef, plum puddings, and mince pies for Christmas Day; veal, mackerel, lobster, salad, and eggs for the king's birthday. An ordinary day's dinner could still consist of pork, cauliflower, and baked pudding.[12] Despite the lavishness of the fare, even the officers generally had to put up with eating conditions rather less sumptuous than those envisaged by Macaulay. Silver-dipped dishes were the exception, with the ubiquitous pewter dominating the officers' meal-times too.[13] Stormy weather forced the abandonment of the table, with officers having to brace themselves against anything they could in order to eat their meals off the deck.[14]

Dinner was also the focal point of another constant factor in shipboard life, the day's drinking. For the officers, any excuse, no matter how flimsy, could justify a frantic evening's toasting. Saturday was already traditionally the day for toasting wives and absent friends with bowls of punch, though they could just as easily provide an excuse for a toast on any other day of the week, as could the other perennial favourite, the health of the king. When Teonge served on the *Assistance*, two bowls of punch was the norm on weekdays, but this was frequently exceeded on 'special occasions', and the liberality of the *Bristol*'s officers surpassed even this standard: 'punch and brandy since I came on board have run as freely as dishwater', Teonge observed. Arriving in a foreign port, or meeting a friendly ship or squadron was usually the signal for several days' uninterrupted merriment. Particularly prolonged drinking sessions might degenerate into party games, while the occasional practice of smashing a glass after each toast led on one occasion to the destruction of a whole crate of Venetian glasses.[15] Given the consumption of food and drink aboard the Restoration warship, it may be no coincidence that the period saw several refinements to the sanitary arrangements of the vessel.

---

[12] *Teonge Diary*, 44, 55, 117, 126, 208.

[13] Holman, 'The *Dartmouth*', 264.

[14] *Teonge Diary*, 82.

[15] Ibid. 17, 40, 42, 49, 94, 97, 117, 120, 121, 206 et *passim*; Rodger, *Wooden World*, 72–4.

'Roundhouses' at the stern, for the use of the warrant-officers, and seats in the heads (albeit often at a ratio of one for over 100 men) were both innovations of the 1670s and 1680s, while the common urinal or 'pissdale' on the upper deck was already a standard fitting.[16] Officers benefited from the relative seclusion of quarter-galleries at the stern, though Teonge put great store on his ability to get hold of a second-hand chamber pot. For an excess of punch, or even to relieve the seaman's daily ration of eight pints of beer, however, the ship's rail on the lee side remained the quickest and easiest option.[17]

Fortunately for the efficient running of the service, the time spent off duty also had its quieter moments. Officers generally ensured that they had a variety of pastimes to occupy their time. Some took musical instruments aboard ship (or even musicians, in the guise of officers' servants)—impromptu concerts seem to have been a popular diversion within the officer corps—while the better educated spent much of their spare time reading anything from navigational textbooks to philosophical discourses.[18] On the lower deck, probably the favourite pastime was smoking. In an attempt to combat the obvious implications of this habit aboard a wooden ship, the general instructions of 1663 codified what was already a long-standing tradition of the navy, namely that smoking should take place only over a tub of water in the forecastle, or on the upper deck if the ship lacked a forecastle. The large number of clay pipes found in the wrecks of Restoration warships suggests that, despite these restrictions, smoking was one of the most commonplace activities on the ship.[19] As they smoked, the seamen sang, danced, told tales to each other, or gambled—the 'rituals of sociability' characteristic of the seafaring world.[20] Fishing was another pastime which was popular among all ranks, providing an opportunity to supplement the official victuals quickly and cheaply. Aboard the *Adventure* off Portugal in 1661, the crew went fishing for dolphin: after

[16] C. J. M. Martin, 'The *Dartmouth*, a British Frigate Wrecked off Mull, 1690: 5. The Ship', *International Journal of Nautical Archaeology and Underwater Exploration*, 7 (1978), 53.

[17] *Teonge Diary*, 31; Lavery, *Arming and Fitting*, 201–3.

[18] BL, Sloane MS 505, fo. 6; Sloane MS 1745, p. 3; *Pepys's Diary*, i. 119, 153; *Teonge Diary*, 208; Holman, 'The *Dartmouth*', 264; Capp, *Cromwell's Navy*, 247–8.

[19] NMM, ADL/A/4 (34th general instruction); P. Marsden and D. Lyon, 'A Wreck Believed to be the Warship *Anne*, Lost in 1690', *International Journal of Nautical Archaeology and Underwater Exploration*, 6 (1977), 16; P. F. de C. Martin, 'The *Dartmouth* . . . 4. The Clay Pipes', ibid. 219–23; V. C. Barber, 'The *Sapphire*, a British Frigate, Sunk in Action in Bay Bulls, Newfoundland, in 1696', ibid. 310.

[20] Rediker, *Devil and Deep Blue Sea*, 189–91; Capp, *Cromwell's Navy*, 245–6.

the master's mate had struck one on the head, it was hauled into the ship's boat and killed with an axe, then fried for supper.[21]

Despite Macaulay's pointed remarks about harems at sea, the sex-lives of naval personnel were, in the main, confined to the shore.[22] Traditionally, wives and girl-friends were allowed to remain aboard a ship setting off on a long voyage for the first part of its passage. Teonge, serving in the *Assistance* in 1675, observed with bemusement the antics aboard the ship as it sailed round from the Thames to the Downs, with the women keeping pace with the men's heavy drinking before adjourning to the hammocks for activities at which Teonge only hints. However, the women were all disembarked at Dover in a tearful leave-taking, and the ship then sailed for the Mediterranean.[23] On arriving in foreign ports after such a voyage, the seamen's first destination was often the brothel; as a result, at Lisbon in 1661 thirty-seven members of the *Mountague*'s crew of 300 went down with VD.[24] Few Restoration seafarers seem to have been tempted to incur the authorities' displeasure by smuggling women aboard for the duration of voyages. Even the notoriously immoral Admiral Arthur Herbert confined himself to the whores of Tangier, and not even his arch-enemy Pepys accused him of keeping women aboard his ship.[25] However, Captain Charles O'Brian passed a woman off as a kinsman of his, dressing her in man's clothes and keeping her in his cabin; he even entered her on the ship's books, and attempted to obtain pay for her from the Navy Board.[26] Having been refused permission to take his wife with him on a Mediterranean voyage in 1671, Sir William Jennens installed her on one of the merchantmen in the convoy, and was consequently dismissed the service on his return to England.[27] Jennens soon returned to the navy, only to be accused in later years of keeping his mistress aboard, and of supposedly boasting that he had been buggered by a fellow captain.[28] Such a boast would have been a dangerous one to make, for the articles of war of 1661 laid down a mandatory death penalty for the 'unnatural and detestable sin of

[21] BL, Sloane MS 505, fos. 72–4. Cf. Rediker, *Devil and Deep Blue Sea*, 128.

[22] Cf. Capp, *Cromwell's Navy*, 254–6.

[23] *Teonge Diary*, 29–30, 32–3, 36–7. Cf. Capp, *Cromwell's Navy*, 249.

[24] *The Journal of James Yonge (1647–1721), Plymouth Surgeon*, ed. F. N. L. Poynter (1963), 48–9.

[25] *Tangier Papers*, 90, 138, 152, 216.

[26] Pepys MS 2581, p. 241.

[27] SP 29/301, fo. 95.

[28] HMC, *Dartmouth MSS*, i. 245–6; BL, Addit. MS 51511, fo. 10.

buggery or sodomy with man or beast'.[29] In fact, although the surviving evidence of courts-martial in the Restoration period is incomplete, there is virtually no evidence of homosexual activity in the navy, though such activity must certainly have taken place. The only clear-cut case was the exception which proves the rule, for the only officer known to have been dismissed for sodomy was the notorious Titus Oates, chaplain of the *Adventure*, and therefore not a true sea-officer in any sense of the term.[30]

The possible consequences of illicit sex were just a few of the hazards which confronted the naval men of the Restoration period. Even laying aside the obvious perils from war or weather, service at sea was exceptionally dangerous, with the possibility of fatal or serious accidents accompanying many of the activities attendant upon it. The regulations to restrict smoking are one indication of an awareness of the danger from fire, and other attempts were made to prevent the destruction of warships in accidental conflagrations. The general instructions specified that after the night-watch had been set, an officer should tour the ship to check that all fires had been put out, and that no private candles were in use, except in lanterns.[31] Such precautions were not always enough. The second-rate *Henry* was burned and destroyed in the Medway in 1682 when an elderly seaman knocked over a candle when going to bed, and a total of seven other warships were accidentally burnt or blown up between 1660 and 1688.[32] There must have been many other narrow escapes, only a few of which have been recorded: for instance, the master of Teonge's ship in 1678 left a candle burning in his cabin, which fired a bunch of rosemary and almost destroyed the ship.[33] Death and injury could come in many other ways aboard a warship. Teonge observed that one man broke a leg, and another fell from the mainyard on to a gun, while lowering the yards in a gale in August 1677; two months later, a seaman trying to disentangle the ship's pendant from the mizzen-chains fell into the sea and drowned.[34] During exactly the same period, aboard the flagship *Plymouth* in another part of the Mediterranean,

---

[29] Rodger (ed.), *Articles of War*, 18.

[30] J. P. Kenyon, *The Popish Plot* (1972), 54–5. However, there are several recorded sodomy courts-martial in the wars of 1689–1713.

[31] NMM, ADL/A/4 (34th general instruction); Adm. 106/359, fos. 19–20.

[32] Adm. 1/5253, pp. 25–6; Fox, *Great Ships*, 174–83.

[33] *Teonge Diary*, 228. Cf. BL, Addit. MS 10117, fo. 160; *Yonge Journal*, 44, 50.

[34] *Teonge Diary*, 182, 194.

one man lost a hand when a gun being loaded for a salute went off accidentally, 'the vent not being stop't whilst spunging', and another accident occurred when, on 8 September, 'att 4 this morning the Gunn to discharge the Watch being fired, and the Shott through forgetfulness not drawne, unluckily killed a man as hee was easing himselfe aboard the [*Portsmouth*] . . .'.[35]

In one respect, at least, Macaulay's fanciful portrayal of the later Stuart navy does contain an element of truth: accidents apart, hunger and disease were far more likely to kill mariners than enemy guns. Epidemics could spread quickly in the cramped conditions aboard ship, and scurvy was commonplace. The later stages of Sir John Narbrough's expedition to the South Seas in 1669–71 were marred by several outbreaks of scurvy among the crew, at a time when the allowance of victuals per man per week was only 3½ lb. of flour, 8 lb. of beef, 13 oz. of cheese, and 112 pts. of oatmeal.[36] On the West African coast in 1685, the *Mordaunt* lost 65 men to disease and scurvy in twenty days, though this death-rate was considered exceptional at the time.[37] Ships in the Mediterranean were better off, as there were usually many opportunities to 'top up' with fresh provisions. Teonge's ship stocked up with beans and peas at Malta, fresh meat, fruit, and bread at Tripoli, and also kept poultry in coops on the upper decks.[38] However, seamen could carry their enthusiasm for fresh provisions to extremes: on one ship at Lisbon in 1661, the cheapness and pleasant-ness of melons led to a spate of over-indulgence which laid many men low with the flux.[39]

Even in battle, splinters from their own ship were more likely to maim or kill seamen than direct enemy fire. Off Algiers in 1661, the surgeon's mate of the *Mountague*, James Yonge, noted two deaths and three serious wounds caused by splinters, and only two wounds caused by shots; one man, whose knee had been 'torn by a bullet', died the next day after the surgeon had refused to amputate, simply dressing the wound instead.[40] For those who fell victim to disease, the fortunes

---

[35] Bod. Lib., MS Eng. Hist. C. 236, fos. 7ᵛ, 8. On other types of accident common in sailing warships, see Harland, *Seamanship*, 294–312; Rediker, *Devil and Deep Blue Sea*, 92–4.

[36] KAO, U. 1515/O. 3, unfol. journal, 11 Aug. 1670, 7 Apr., 15 May, 17 May 1671. Cf. *Yonge Journal*, 44.

[37] Rawl. MS C. 255, *Mordaunt* journal, 23 Jan.–13 Feb. 1685.

[38] *Teonge Diary*, 129, 132, 189.

[39] BL, Sloane MS 505, fo. 41.

[40] *Yonge Journal*, 41–2.

of war, or accidents, the procedures for burial were already well established. When the trumpeter of the *Adventure* died in 1661, he was 'sewed up in canvas, with a culverin shott at his head & another att his feet', and heaved overboard at daybreak.[41] Officers had grander committals, and were buried ashore whenever possible: the coffin of Teonge's boatswain was covered with a Union Jack, on which his whistle and crossed pistols were placed, and escorted to the graveside by an honour-guard of sailors shouldering muskets.[42] The burials of some of the captains and flag-officers who perished in the Dutch wars, including Sir Edward Spragge, Sir Frescheville Holles, and the earl of Sandwich, were transformed into spectacular state funerals for heroes of the nation.[43]

In addition to the ever-present hazards of death and injury, the men of the Restoration navy also ran the risk of falling foul of the complex disciplinary code which governed the service. Until 1661, naval discipline was based on an uncertain legal foundation: capital cases were to be tried ashore according to the common law, lesser ones 'according to the known Orders and Customs of the Seas'. A set of Articles of War had been introduced in 1652, and these formed the basis of the so-called Naval Discipline Act of 1661, which provided thirty-five articles 'for the regulating and better Government of his Majesty's Navies'.[44] The articles empowered the lord high admiral to summon courts-martial to hear serious cases. In home waters, the usual procedure was to issue a summons to a senior captain to act as president of the court, and additional summonses to as many serving captains as could be got together; the trial was then usually held aboard a royal yacht moored in the Thames, or occasionally on one of the great ships in ordinary. On foreign stations, the admiral would usually hold the trial aboard his flagship, with the captains of his squadron present (and lieutenants, if too few captains were available). In either case, a judge-advocate or a deputy, appointed by the High Court of Admiralty, would be in attendance, and commissioners of the Navy Board might

---

[41] BL, Sloane MS 505, fo. 71. Cf. Rediker, *Devil and Deep Blue Sea*, 195–8.

[42] *Teonge Diary*, 97–8.

[43] This was not always the case: see the description of Sir John Lawson's funeral in *Pepys's Diary*, vi. 145.

[44] 13 Chas. II, st. 1, c. 9. NHL, MS 121/13, pp. 121–2, 125; Rodger, *Articles of War*, 7–8, 13–19; *CJ*, viii. 302, 307–8.

also attend for cases relating to ships in harbour.[45] However, the articles of 1661 left a great many grey areas in respect of court-martial jurisdiction, for example the lack of authority for the judge-advocate to subpoena witnesses, the inability of the court to disbar men from further employment in the navy (thereby infringing the lord high admiral's prerogative to appoint whomsoever he pleased), the accept-ability of registering dissenting minority opinions, and uncertainty over how far a court could deviate from the punishments specified in the articles of war.[46] The articles provided mandatory or optional death sentences for desertion, mutiny, embezzlement, striking an officer, sleeping on watch, murder, theft, and sodomy, and laid down that fines or imprisonment should punish swearing, drunkenness, and quarrelling aboard ship. In 1663 ten additional orders, appended to the general instructions, provided punishments for non-capital crimes and gave captains discretion to give lesser punishments in some cases of theft or sleeping on watch. Swearing and drunkenness would lead to the loss of one day's pay, telling lies to being hoisted from the mainstay for half an hour with a broom and shovel tied to the offender's back and the whole crew crying 'a liar, a liar'; the liar would then spend a week scrubbing the ship's sides directly beneath the heads. The lash was specified as a punishment only for one crime, that of seamen relieving themselves below decks, but it became the standard punish-ment in most cases where a capital punishment was not involved.[47] The effect of all punishments was intended to be exemplary. In 1677, one court-martial declared that the seamen before it should 'learne (wee hope) by those few stripes they are to receive the better how to doe their duty for the future & give an example to others', while men reprieved from death sentences were not to learn of their good fortune until the ropes were actually around their necks, in order to provide a suitably terrifying example.[48]

The severity of punishments, measured in the number of lashes given, increased steadily in the Restoration period, exceeding the

---

[45] Lincolnshire Archives Office, Jarvis MS IX/1/A/4, 1, 4, 5 Feb. 1675; *Pepys's Diary*, ix. 488–9, 497–8, 505, 508; NHL, MS 121/13, pp. 157–8, 162. Cf. Rodger, *Wooden World*, 222–4.

[46] NHL, MS 121/13, pp. 122, 123; Pepys MS 2860, p. 400. Many examples of court-martial verdicts, and in some cases of the depositions laid before the courts, are given in Adm. 1/5253; Rawl. MSS A. 314, C. 972. Others are scattered among the State Papers and High Court of Admiralty records.

[47] Rodger, *Articles of War*, 7–8, 13–19; NMM, ADL/A/4. On the long history of the punishment for liars, see Smith, *Seaman's Grammar*, 36; Maydman, *Naval Speculations*, 219.

[48] Rawl. MS A. 314, fo. 19ᵛ; Pepys MS 2859, p. 458.

comparative leniency of the interregnum, but never approaching the Draconian levels of the eighteenth century (for example, nothing approximated to the 500 lashes given for mutiny in 1746).[49] Whipping around the fleet or squadron was already a well-established practice by the time of the Restoration, and the available evidence suggests a degree of harshness greater than that employed in the 1650s. In 1673, a mutiny case produced five lashes at the sides of each of seven ships; in 1675, abetting an assault on a senior officer led to nineteen lashes at each of six ships; while desertion cases in 1684 and 1687 produced, respectively, nine strokes at each of six ships (together with thirty-one more on the flagship), and twenty-one strokes at each of four ships.[50] Other punishments were tailored to fit crimes. Seamen who stole some beef were tied to the mainmast with a piece of beef around their necks, with the rest of the crew taking turns rubbing the meat over their mouths; in 1676, a seaman who stole and then pawned his captain's wig was sentenced to have his hair cut off.[51] However, this image of harshness, even barbarity, was not entirely unmitigated. At least one court-martial made a powerful plea for mercy in a case where it had no option other than to deliver a mandatory death sentence, reprieves were often issued, care was taken of the widows and orphans of executed offenders, and mulcts of single days' pay were preferred in lesser cases, because the alternative was waiting for a man's crimes to become so frequent that he would have to lose all his wages at a court-martial.[52]

The surviving evidence of court-martial records—in other words, of official action—conceals the full extent of crime and punishment in the Restoration navy. Some captains, naturally, were harsher than others, and on every ship the boatswain could use the cat and the cudgel to impose immediate and arbitrary punishment. The articles of war and the additional instructions did not preclude the possibility of other punishments at the captain's discretion: on Teonge's ship, three swearers had marlin-spikes clapped into their mouths and tied behind their heads, so that they stood for an hour 'till their mouths were very bloody'.[53] Even cases as serious as desertion could be handled infor-

[49] D. Hannay, *Naval Courts-Martial* (1914), 68–9; Capp, *Cromwell's Navy*, 220–1; D. A. Baugh (ed.), *Naval Administration 1715–50* (Navy Records Society, 120; 1977), 139; Rodger, *Wooden World*, 218–29.
[50] Rawl. MS A. 314, fos. 7–8; Rawl. MS C. 972, fo. 5; Adm. 1/5253, fos. 27, 37. Cf. Capp, *Cromwell's Navy*, 220–1.
[51] *Teonge Diary*, 39; Rawl. MS C. 972, fos. 31–2.
[52] Rawl. MS A. 314, fos. 17–18; Pepys MS 2858, p. 381.
[53] *Teonge Diary*, 124–5.

mally. One captain rounded up some youths who had run from his ship at an alehouse twenty miles inland, but after giving them a sound whipping, he told his admiral that he did not want them brought to trial.[54] For virtually any offence, but especially for drunkenness, a spell in the bilboes (the naval equivalent of the stocks) was a quick and easy punishment.[55] The ship's boys met their nemesis every Monday, when the boatswain or his mate whipped them for all misdemeanours committed in the previous week.[56]

The main problem for seamen living under such a regime was not necessarily the actual level of punishment, but the lack of a channel of complaint to higher authority: indeed, in 1683 some seamen took the most direct channel of all and beat up the boatswains of the ships in which they had served.[57] The only procedure for making complaints was that laid down in the twenty-second article of war for cases of bad victuals, which stated that a seaman should raise the matter 'quietly' with his superiors on the ship.[58] Despite the privately sympathetic attitude of individual administrators, notably Pepys, the Restoration naval administration was markedly less sympathetic towards seamen's complaints than its predecessors in the 1650s had been, or, indeed, than some of its successors were to be.[59] Seamen who attempted to petition against their captain found themselves whipped around the fleet, ducked from the yard-arm, or sentenced to forfeit their pay; in any case, seamen suspected with some justification that their officers' words would be taken before theirs. A few even tried to bypass the naval administration completely, by appealing directly to the king.[60] The administrators were in a dilemma, believing that the seamen should have some means of making complaints, but not wishing to encourage mutinous practices. Nothing was done, and in 1689 a new Admiralty Board could even take the view that the articles of war provided adequate procedures for expressing grievances.[61]

With no effective means of appeal to higher authorities, seamen could either desert or hope that they would not receive ill-treatment

---

[54] Bod. Lib., Tanner MS 39, fo. 77.
[55] See e.g. KAO, U. 1515/O. 3, 10 June 1667; BL, Sloane MS 505, fo. 40.
[56] Smith, *Seaman's Grammar*, 35; *Teonge Diary*, 55.
[57] Adm. 1/3553, p. 497; Adm. 106/364, fos. 191, 193, 196, 200.
[58] Rodger, *Articles of War*, 17.
[59] Capp, *Cromwell's Navy*, 223–5; Rodger, *Wooden World*, 229–35.
[60] Rawl. MS A. 314, fos. 7–9; *Barlow's Journal*, i. 162–3; Adm. 106/337, pt. 2, fo. 425.
[61] Pepys MS 2855, pp. 327–8, 469; Adm. 2/169, pp. 37, 44; Adm. 2/1752, p. 229; Adm. 3/279, p. 31. Cf. Slush, *Navy Royal*, 60–6.

from their officers. Several commentators believed that they were more likely to receive such treatment from gentlemen captains, ignorant of the ways of the sea; moreover, seamen were believed to prefer being commanded by their own kind, and were thought to be resentful of the rating of gentlemen officers' servants and friends as able seamen and petty officers.[62] There were indeed a few complaints by seamen against the presence of aristocratic volunteers and servants aboard ship, but these were probably inspired by the need for qualified men to work harder to compensate for the presence of unskilled men among the ship's company.[63] All captains, regardless of their background, promoted their own friends and protégés, and tarpaulins were often harsher than any gentleman.[64] For most seamen, the social background of their captain was irrelevant: they wanted, above all, a captain who would care for his crew.[65] Many gentlemen captains got on very well with their men, and a captain with good connections at court or in the administration could be a positive boon for a ship's company when the time came to secure payment of wages.[66] Many captains appreciated the maxim that if men were not well served, they would not serve well, and it made sense for any officer to cultivate the affections of his crew. Many already had strong neighbourhood ties with the men they commanded, and all tried to retain good men who had proved their ability and loyalty. On gaining a commission for a new ship, a captain would seek to take many of his men with him: in March 1689, for example, Cloudesley Shovell sought permission to transfer between 100 and 150 men from his old crew, many of whom had served under him for up to ten years.[67] Conversely, the men themselves were often enthusiastic to follow particular officers and would desert from unpopular captains in order to serve popular ones.[68] The

---

[62] BL., Addit. MS 32094, fo. 44; Pepys MS 2581, pp. 214–15, 218; Charnock, *History of Marine Architecture*, i, pp. xliv, lxxxix.

[63] See e.g. SP 29/53, fo. 50; *Barlow's Journal*, i. 134–5.

[64] Slush, *Navy Royal*, 17, 27–8. For examples of seamen's disputes with supposedly cruel tarpaulin captains, see Rawl. MS A. 314, fos. 7–9; SP 29/236, fo. 60; *CSP Col.*, 1677–80, 281–2; Capp, *Cromwell's Navy*, 221–3.

[65] *Tangier Papers*, 109.

[66] See e.g. Adm. 106/285, fos. 135, 140; Adm. 106/294, fo. 92; Adm. 106/346, fo. 158; Adm. 106/373, fos. 47, 51, 63; Adm. 106/383, fo. 94.

[67] KAO, U. 1515/O. 12, unfol., Shovell to Phineas Bowles, 14 Mar. 1689; Adm. 2/377, fo. 10ᵛ. Cf. Pepys MS 2861, p. 216; Adm. 2/1752, p. 169; Adm. 3/277, pt. 1, pp. 232, 246.

[68] NMM, LBK/8, p. 228; Pepys MS 2581, pp. 206–7, 218, 222; Capp, *Cromwell's Navy*, 213–17.

men who offered, with tears in their eyes, to avenge their dead admiral, Christopher Myngs, by making a suicide attack on the Dutch fleet—a gesture which greatly moved Pepys—were probably not atypical.[69]

Good relations between captains and men took several forms. Captains were naturally concerned for the health of their crew, and were often vigorous in supporting seamen's complaints over victuals or pay.[70] The appearance of a crew reflected on both the captain's and the nation's honour, so it was in a captain's interest to ensure that his crew was well-clothed and clean.[71] It was also important to keep a crew contented by granting leave whenever possible. Captains had to use considerable discretion in this, particularly in wartime when newly pressed men might be tempted to escape, but by 1673 the usual practice was for captains to grant four or five days' leave at a ship's fitting out and ten days at its coming in; the administration thought this too lenient, and by 1680 four or five days' leave at the end of a voyage was the accepted norm.[72] Leave was granted regularly in foreign ports, but both abroad and at home the seamen's priorities when ashore (drink and women) were the same. In peacetime, concern not to lose back pay and loyalty to the captain must have deterred many attempts to extend leave-periods indefinitely and unofficially. Even if a man did overstay his leave accidentally, the navy had a sufficiently flexible attitude to excuse him from the harsh penalties for desertion: a sliding scale of mulcts of pay covered the first three cases of absence without leave, with a man being regarded as 'run' only on the fourth offence.[73] There was, therefore, a considerable divide between the theoretically Draconian attitude to desertion expressed in the articles of war and the more lenient attitudes in practice of a service which needed every man it could get.[74]

One other way in which a sense of solidarity was built up within a ship was through the survival of a system of communal decision-making. Traditionally, most major tactical decisions were not taken by the captain alone, but were made in consultation with the ship's

[69] *Pepys's Diary*, vii. 165.
[70] See e.g. Rawl. MS A. 174, fo. 372; Capp, *Cromwell's Navy*, 214–15, 280–2.
[71] See e.g. BL, Addit. MS 19399, fo. 119.
[72] NMM, CHA/E/1/A, fo. 110; Adm. 2/1752, pp. 301, 305; Adm. 106/342, fo. 179. But cf. Capp, *Cromwell's Navy*, 248–9.
[73] NMM, ADL/A/4 (fifth order for govt. of ships); NMM, CHA/E/1/A, Capt. John Cox to Chatham clerk of cheque, 28 Mar. 1672. For wartime regulations, see Powell and Timings, *Rupert and Monck*, 46–7.
[74] Capp, *Cromwell's Navy*, 284.

warrant-officers. Before going into battle against an Algerine squadron in 1681, Captain Morgan Kempthorne of the *Kingfisher* called all his officers together to discuss what he should do, and found a unanimous verdict in favour of a defensive running fight.[75] Such discussions could also involve the crew. When the *Sapphire* had found herself in a similar predicament in 1670, the officers were divided, with the master favouring an engagement and the captain and lieutenant favouring flight. The crew, who seem to have been informed of every stage of the discussion, took the master's side, and even asked him to take over command, crying 'God blesse you Master, let us fight them.'[76] However, this practice of consultation seems to have become progressively less common in the Restoration period; by the 1690s, certainly, the naval purser and polemicist Henry Maydman could state that it had almost completely died out, not because (interestingly enough) of an attitude of social superiority on the part of gentlemen captains, but because of the unwillingness of subordinate officers to give unwelcome advice to captains on whose recommendations and certificates they would depend for promotion.[77] Even so, one element of the system of consultation did survive, namely the council of war. The admiral of a wartime fleet took advice from two bodies, a council of his subordinate flag-officers, and a general council of all captains. In practice, the general council was often simply a means of ratifying the decisions of the council of flagmen, which tended to meet more often: in the last ten days of April 1672, for example, the flagmen met eight times, the general council only once.[78] A decisive admiral could overrule the advice even of his flagmen, as the duke of Albemarle did in 1666 when he decided to attack the Dutch with inferior numbers; but, significantly, it suited Albemarle's purpose after the battle to imply, disingenuously, that the decision he had foisted on the divided flagmen was, in fact, their unanimous opinion.[79]

The officers and men of the Restoration navy were the defenders of the society they served, but they were also a part of that society. In

[75] NMM, JOD/173, pp. 28–31.

[76] PRO, HCA 1/9, fo. 155.

[77] Maydman, *Naval Speculations*, 188–90; but cf. Rodger, *Wooden World*, 235–7, for the survival (or revival?) of the practice in the 18th century.

[78] Anderson, *Journals and Narratives of the Third Dutch War*, 76–80. Cf. J. D. Davies, 'James II, William of Orange, and the Admirals', in E. Cruikshanks (ed.), *By Force or by Default? The Revolution of 1688–9* (1989), 94; Baumber, *General-at-Sea*, 161, 169.

[79] Powell and Timings, *Rupert and Monck*, 231, 238, 244, 248. Cf. Capp, *Cromwell's Navy*, 190–2.

some respects, certainly, the navy was an alien environment with a
way of life and language all its own, but its men were still recogniz-
ably seventeenth-century Englishmen: they were certainly not a race
apart.[80] Many ties continued to bind them to the shore, even when
they found themselves on distant stations or in a war. It was usually still
possible to communicate with home, albeit haphazardly; ships serving
in the Mediterranean would often meet a merchantman bound for
England, and officers and men would hastily write letters to family and
friends. Return mail could be directed to ports where English warships
invariably called, notably Tangier, Cadiz, and Leghorn.[81] In this way,
naval men could keep in touch with family affairs, or, indeed, with
more public matters. Family gossip, courtship by long-distance correspondence, problems with rentals on estates at home, business
transactions, attempts to solicit advancement in the service, political
intrigue, and attempts to secure parliamentary seats all feature in the
private correspondence from sea of commissioned officers of the
Restoration navy.[82] The manifold concerns of the Restoration naval
officer are well illustrated by the letter of Francis Wheeler, then
captain of the *Nonsuch*, to his father, a letter given as Appendix II
to this study; Wheeler was a young gentleman captain in his first
command, and a typical product of the 'volunteer *per* order' system and
the early days of the lieutenants' examination. Apart from contacts
maintained from sea, the intermittent nature of naval employment,
which ensured that the majority of commissioned officers would spend
long periods ashore awaiting a new post, provided them with many
opportunities to renew their connections on land. Warrant-officers
and seamen, whose service was of a rather different nature and whose
employment could be more continuous, were more nearly a different
race, with distinctive dress, speech, and mannerisms; but even they
were influenced by ties ashore, sending the occasional letter from
foreign parts, transmitting money to their families, visiting them
whenever possible (even if only once in seven years, as was the case

---

[80] On the distinctive language of the sea in this period, see Rediker, *Devil and Deep
Blue Sea*, 162–9.
[81] *Teonge Diary*, 120, 123, 180; Capp, *Cromwell's Navy*, 249–50.
[82] See e.g. BL, Sloane MS 1745, *passim*; NMM, CLU/7, unfol., letters of Sir John
Narbrough to Lady Elizabeth Calmody, Feb. and Apr. 1676; KAO, U. 269/C. 298, U.
1713/C. 1–4, *passim*; National Library of Wales, MS 9346B; Staffordshire RO, MS
D(W) 1778/Ii/319–74.

with one naval cook in the 1680s), or endeavouring to deal with their creditors.[83]

In turn, these links provided a point of contact between English society and the navy. The entry into the service of gentlemen officers, in particular, gave many aristocratic and gentry families a direct personal interest in naval matters which they might not have possessed before. Correspondence from sons or brothers at sea provided an insight into the running of the service. Charles II's favourite of the early 1660s, the earl of Falmouth, gained his extensive knowledge of naval affairs from the letters of his younger brother, William Berkeley.[84] Lord Alington, holder of an Irish barony and MP for Cambridge, took pride in the exploits and finally the gallant death of his younger brother Argenton, even though he knew that Argenton's total commitment to a career at sea, and lack of interest in marriage, might mean the end of the male line of his family.[85] The rush of aristocratic volunteers to the fleet during the Dutch wars provided even more opportunities for the 'political nation' to obtain first-hand information on naval matters. Future ministers, such as Sir Thomas Clifford, several MPs, and an assortment of prominent and not-so-prominent figures of the Restoration period, ranging from the dukes of Buckingham and Monmouth, via the poets Dorset and Rochester, to the likes of the young John Churchill, saw naval warfare at first hand. Others, like the marquis of Halifax and Sir John Reresby, obtained detailed information from relatives in the fleet.[86] Far from being wholly ignorant of naval affairs, as is often claimed, the aristocracy and gentry of the Restoration period were probably better informed of, and certainly more directly concerned with, naval matters than any of their predecessors and many of their successors. For many Englishmen, the life of the navy might have been out of the ordinary, but it certainly was not wholly unknown.

[83] Adm. 106/3539, pt. 2, 'Cooks' folder, petition of Robert Wilde. Cf. *Barlow's Journal*, i. 139, 174–6; Adm. 106/345, fo. 276.
[84] KAO, U. 269/C. 298; C. H. Hartmann, *The King's Friend* (Kingswood, 1951), 91–2, 107, 121, 164.
[85] Rawl. MS D. 861, fos. 2, 4, 6–7.
[86] See e.g. W. D. Cooper (ed.), *Savile Correspondence* (Camden Society, 71; 1858), 6–7, 13–14, 16; M. K. Geiter and W. A. Speck, 'The Reliability of Sir John Reresby's "Memoirs" and his Account of the Oxford Parliament of 1681', *Historical Research*, 62 (1989), 106. For Clifford's service at sea, see C. H. Hartmann, *Clifford of the Cabal* (Kingswood, 1937), chs. 2, 3, 4, 6 *passim* (cf. ibid., 138–41, 222–3, 230, 239, for Clifford's subsequent interest in the navy and its administration).

6

RELIGION

AUGUSTAN polemicists, seeking the origins of what they perceived as the moral shortcomings of the navy of their own day, often contrasted the state of religious observance in the interregnum and Restoration navies, believing that the infectious libertinism of the court had transformed the latter into something 'more like the suburbs of Hell than a Christian navy'.[1] Whether the interregnum navy was really the bulwark of godliness which later pamphleteers claimed it to be is debatable;[2] even so, it seems likely that the Restoration naval seaman was little more or less immoral, drunken, blasphemous, and ignorant in religious matters than his predecessors or successors.

The conditions of naval service did little to encourage devotion. By the terms of the first article of war of 1661, the liturgy of the church of England was to be performed in every ship, and the first general instruction to commanders of 1663 specified that the entire crew should participate in public worship twice a day.[3] The single most revealing source about shipboard life in the Restoration navy, the diary of the chaplain Henry Teonge, suggests that these provisions were generally complied with. Daily prayers were evidently so routine that they make virtually no appearance in the diary, but ships in harbour and at sea do seem to have held some form of perfunctory service in the morning and late in the evening, though the exact timing was left to the captain's discretion.[4] Arranging a formal Sunday service was heavily dependent on the ship's operational commitments. Preparations to sail, or the sighting of another vessel, or even drying the crew's clothes and bedding after a storm could all cause the cancellation of the service, while the absence of the captain invariably led to the abandonment of a sermon, confining the service to prayers alone.[5]

---

[1] 'Enquiry into the Causes of our Naval Miscarriages', 517.
[2] See Capp, *Cromwell's Navy*, ch. 9 *et passim*.
[3] Rodger, *Articles of War*, 13; NMM, ADL/A/4. For interregnum practice see Capp, *Cromwell's Navy*, 307–8.
[4] *Teonge Diary, passim*; Rawl. MS A. 171, fos. 2–3.
[5] *Teonge Diary*, 75, 86, 111, 121, 133, 139, 215, 222, 231, 234, 253.

The physical arrangements for a gathering of the crew for divine worship also posed problems. Teonge had to preach his first sermon to the crew of the *Assistance* in the ship's steerage, holding on to both the 'pillars' of the cabin in order to steady himself; better weather permitted him to preach from the quarterdeck.[6] Services were held on the feast-days of the church, and additional prayers might be said on special occasions—especially when about to engage in battle.[7] Teonge's diary, and the enquiries of 1678 into the religious affections of the fleet, made in the aftermath of the popish plot, reveal no evidence of the taking of the sacrament aboard ship, though aboard the *Crown*, taking Sir William Trumbull to Constantinople in 1686, it was taken monthly and on feast-days.[8]

Interpretation of the first article of war and first general instruction therefore depended heavily on the attitude of the individual captain and chaplain. Many critics blamed the supposedly appalling spiritual state of the seamen on the chaplains: Teonge, who paid more attention to the quality of shipboard meals than to his sermons, and who had joined the navy largely to extricate himself from financial difficulties, was certainly not unique, and much has been made of the fact that one of his contemporaries in the naval chaplaincy was a certain Titus Oates.[9] Their other contemporaries included several young men, newly graduated from the universities and in search of employment before gaining a living (or in some cases before being ordained), for example William Frankland and John Wynne from Cambridge, Robert Gunnis and Thomas Sandys from Oxford.[10] The several Welshmen who served, such as Gunnis, Francis Llewellyn, David Nicholls, and John Morris, together with others from similar areas, might have sought to augment their incomes from poor parishes.[11] Moreover, under the *ad hoc* system of appointment by individual captains, which

[6] Ibid. 32, 223.
[7] Ibid. 117, 139, 169, 233, 248; Smith, *Seaman's Grammar*, 60–1.
[8] All Souls College, Oxford, MS 317, fo. 55.
[9] Rawl. MS A. 171, fos. 2–3.
[10] Taylor, *Sea Chaplains*, 489–90; J. and J. A. Venn (eds.), *Alumni Cantabrigienses . . . Part 1, From the Earliest Times to 1751* (Cambridge, 1922), ii. 174; iv. 483; J. Foster (ed.), *Alumni Oxonienses . . . 1500–1714* (Oxford, 1891–2), ii. 620; iv. 1310. Cf. Capp, *Cromwell's Navy*, 312–13, 314–15.
[11] Taylor, *Sea Chaplains*, 489–90; Foster, *Alumni Oxonienses*, iii. 921, 1035, 1067. Several others, such as Ferdinand Booth, William Edwards, Robert Bostock, and Benjamin Williams, came from or had livings in coastal areas, and might have looked on naval service as 'a natural way of making a living': Capp, *Cromwell's Navy*, 312; Venn, *Alumni Cantabrigienses*, i. 179; ii. 90; Foster, *Alumni Oxonienses*, i. 152; iv. 1636.

survived until 1677, there was no guarantee of moral suitability or theological orthodoxy: several chaplains who had served in the inter-regnum navy survived unscathed in the 1660s.[12] The introduction of a more centralized system of appointment by senior churchmen had little real effect. In practice, captains could still request chaplains who had served with them before, and the bishop of London often gave in to persistent demands from sea-officers. Teonge backed up his captain's demand by following the bishop wherever he went for over a week, until the harassed prelate finally gave in.[13] Thomas Turner, one of the first chaplains to be approved by the bishop under the new regulations, was responsible within months for a drinking session in his cabin for all his namesakes in the *Newcastle* to celebrate St Thomas's day, as a result of which one particularly inebriated Thomas later fell to his death from the yard-arm.[14] One of Turner's contemporaries, Richard Bradford, was dismissed for drinking, swearing, and cavorting in the nude with his wife.[15] By 1688, eleven years after the establish-ment of the new system, Pepys could write of the new and supposedly improved generation of chaplains that 'unless they be Men of exemp-lary Sobriety in their lives, as well as Doctrine, I must confess . . . I am of opinion . . . that they doe more harme then good by hardening a hundred in their Vices, sooner than reforming one'.[16]

However, there are obvious dangers in accepting this picture of a thoroughly degenerate naval chaplaincy: as with the gentlemen captains, the bad have attracted all the attention. The genuine piety, sense of pastoral duty, and devotion to their flocks which must have characterized many naval chaplains have been neglected by contem-poraries and historians alike. Youth and financial problems did not necessarily make a bad chaplain, and the list of naval chaplains includes several men who went on to high rank in the church, including Thomas Ken, Benjamin Woodruffe (chaplain to Charles II, and later principal of Gloucester Hall, Oxford), and possibly John Williams, later chaplain to William and Mary, and bishop of Chichester.[17] Even so, they had much to contend with. One com-mentator during the second Dutch war thought that seamen said their

[12] Capp, *Cromwell's Navy*, 374.
[13] Adm. 1/5138, pp. 780–1; *Teonge Diary*, 202–3.
[14] Pepys MS 2853, p. 19; Bod. Lib., MS Eng. Hist. C. 236, fo. 11.
[15] Rawl. MS A. 181, fos. 365–8.
[16] Pepys MS 2861, p. 210. Cf. Maydman, *Naval Speculations*, 146.
[17] *DNB*, s.nn. 'Ken, Thomas'; 'Williams, John'; 'Woodruffe, Benjamin'.

prayers backwards, and one chaplain decided to abandon the navy after one voyage because of 'the profane disrespectfull irregularities of most seamen'.[18] For crews of ships in harbour, attending church on Sunday might be an act concerned less with spiritual salvation than with avoiding extra duties.[19] Above all, like their brethren ashore, the Anglican chaplains who served in the Restoration navy had to contend with the problems of dissent and recusancy.

There certainly were dissenters aboard Restoration warships, but evidence for the existence of organized forms of dissent is largely circumstantial. On the rare occasions when they touched on the matter, naval administrators and sea-officers used the blanket terms 'dissenters' or 'fanatics', and made little attempt to classify them more exactly. However, the demography of naval recruitment helps to shed light on the issue. The seamen's communities along the Thames and Medway were areas of extensive, organized dissenting activity, and it was suggested to Pepys that one reason for the seamen's lack of regard for chaplains was that 'being bred up in factious towns [they] have no great fondness for clergymen'.[20] In the years after the Restoration, the Baptists were strong in Southwark, Bermondsey, and the dockyard towns of Chatham and Deptford, while there were significant numbers of Presbyterians at Rochester and Congregationalists at Deptford.[21] In the 1660s, mariners constituted one of the largest single occupational groups presented at the Middlesex sessions for attending conventicles, though no distinction was drawn between men in the naval and mercantile services.[22] During wartime, the expansion of the fleet by the widespread use of the press brought in men with a variety of religious views. Henry Lilburne, a seaman pressed during the second Dutch war, was captured by the enemy, decided to stay with them, and later wrote a virulent letter to Charles II demanding the introduction of full liberty of conscience.[23] Thomas Lurting, a Quaker, was pressed

---

[18] SP 29/116, fo. 40.

[19] See e.g. Lincolnshire Archives Office, Jarvis MS IX/1/A/4, 10 Mar. 1678. On irreligion at sea, and the problems facing naval chaplains, see Rediker, *Devil and Deep Blue Sea*, 169–79; Capp, *Cromwell's Navy*, 308–10, 321–3.

[20] Rawl. MS A. 171, fo. 2ᵛ.

[21] *CSPD*, 1672–3, 1673, passim; W. T. Whitley, *The Baptists of London, 1612–1928* (1928), 103, 105, 110, 116, 118–19; G. F. Nuttall, 'Dissenting Churches in Kent Before 1700', *Journal of Ecclesiastical History*, 14 (1963), 182, 186; C. W. Chalklin, *Seventeenth-Century Kent: A Social and Economic History* (1965), 224–9; Harris, *London Crowds*, 66–70.

[22] J. C. Jeaffreson (ed.), *Middlesex County Records*, iii (1888), 340–2.

[23] SP 29/235, fo. 26.

during the same war. The captain made every effort to accommodate him, offering him various non-combatant tasks, including hauling up ropes and assisting the surgeon, but Lurting refused them all. The crewmen were kind to him, offering him some of their food and drink when he refused on principle to partake of the king's provisions, but other Quakers in other ships met with less sympathetic treatment from the seamen.[24] Many Quakers served in merchantmen and were therefore eligible for the press,[25] but sea-officers found them more trouble than they were worth: Lurting's captain eventually put him ashore, where he was pressed again, only to be discharged almost immediately by another exasperated officer.[26]

A discussion of dissent in the officer corps is similarly hampered by a lack of precision in many of the contemporary accounts. The senior naval figures after 1660, notably Edward Mountagu, earl of Sandwich, generally labelled officers and men of doubtful persuasions as 'Anabaptists', and sought to remove them from their posts.[27] Many of the sea-officers removed in 1660 were certainly active conventiclers, and came from a variety of denominational backgrounds.[28] Of those who survived the Restoration, some were clients of General George Monck and may have shared their patron's Presbyterianism;[29] others who had once displayed radical tendencies in religion survived in spite of their links with the sects. The workings of patronage, or some other form of influence with the new royal authorities, could excuse past nonconformity. Thus Captain William Pestell, a renegade Fifth Monarchist, informed on his former co-religionists after the Restoration and gained a command through the recommendation of the bishop of London.[30] Those officers who had served the interregnum navy and had no past record of conformity to the church of England had to compete after the Restoration for a limited number of naval posts with men of certain loyalty and conformity, and many sought to consolidate their positions by playing down their past associations. Such high-ranking interregnum officers as Sir John Lawson and Sir

---

[24] T. Lurting, *The Fighting Sailor Turn'd Peaceable Christian* (1710).
[25] See e.g. Adm. 2/1735, fo. 61ᵛ.
[26] Lurting, *Fighting Sailor*.
[27] Bod. Lib., Carte MS 73, fos. 222, 402–4; Coventry MS 98, fos. 66–72; *Pepys's Diary*, i. 101, 109.
[28] Capp, *Cromwell's Navy*, 302–7.
[29] *CSPD*, 1659–60, 536; *Thurloe State Papers* (1742), vii. 387–8.
[30] Capp, *Cromwell's Navy*, 307.

John Harman conformed publicly to the established church,[31] and others, too, were at least occasional conformists. Sir Richard Haddock was reported on at least one occasion for attendance at a conventicle, but he was also a parishioner of Allhallows, Barking, and took charge of the enquiry into conventiclers at Woolwich yard in 1681.[32] In general, the Restoration naval administration expected some degree of conformity from the commissioned officers of its ships. The duke of York and his subordinates were concerned that promotion of overtly Nonconformist officers would be censured in Parliament, a concern which was amply borne out by Parliament's enquiry into the condition of religion in the fleet in 1673,[33] though in general the question of the commissioned officers' affections became less important as time went on and the older generation of men who had served the republic died out.

Dissent was a more important and abiding issue in relation to the noncommissioned officers of the fleet. Few refused to take the oaths of allegiance and supremacy in 1660–1, and the oaths were later administered to all warrant-officers entering into new employments.[34] Candidates for even the most minor post soon learned the value of producing certificates from their local minister and churchwardens, testifying to their conformity to the established church and their loyalty to the state, in addition to the usual certificates of technical competence from former captains.[35] From time to time the Admiralty updated its lists of officers eligible for employment and noted their loyalty and conformity: in 1686, for example, ninety-seven warrant-officers on the ships at Deptford and Woolwich were examined, and only one was listed as 'not conformable'.[36] However, the administration was aware that this satisfying picture of a conformist officer corps was seriously flawed. In the debates on the test bill in 1673, Sir

---

[31] E. Hyde, *The Life of Edward Earl of Clarendon . . . in which is included a Continuation of his History of the Grand Rebellion* (Oxford, 1827), ii. 391–3; A. Grey, *Debates of the House of Commons from the Year 1667 to the Year 1694* (1763), ii. 79–80. For their earlier affiliations, see Capp, *Cromwell's Navy*, 302–3, 305.

[32] SP 29/418, fo. 10; *Hist. Parl.*, i. 51; ii. 460–1; Rawl. MS A. 191, fo. 91; Adm. 3/278, pt. 2, p. 10.

[33] *Pepys's Diary*, viii. 485–6.

[34] *Further Correspondence of Samuel Pepys*, 257; Capp, *Cromwell's Navy*, 373.

[35] See e.g. BL, Addit. MS 18986, fo. 352 *et seq.*; Addit. MS 32094, fo. 1; Adm. 1/3552, p. 541; Adm. 1/3554, p. 220; Adm. 106/3539, pt. 2, 'Carpenters' folder, petition of John Brooker.

[36] Adm. 106/3540, pt. 2, 'Musters' folder.

Thomas Osborne (then treasurer of the navy), pointed out that many
of the warrant-officers were 'fanatics', and Pepys held the same
opinion in later years,[37] suggesting that the 'conformity' revealed by
the official records was, at best, of the occasional variety. During the
1673 debates it was implied that it would have been very difficult to
man and officer the fleet if stricter conformity was enforced, and
Parliament accepted this in the final form of the Test Act: warrant-
officers were exempted from the requirement to take the oaths and
sacrament before taking up their posts, and it was recognized that no
restriction of any kind could be applied to the seamen.[38]

Even so, both the administration and the sea-officers were lax in
their attitudes to these new legal requirements. When Pepys investi-
gated the religious affections of the officer corps in 1678, in response
to parliamentary fears that the popish plot had spilt over into the navy,
he found that most officers had last taken the sacrament, the oaths, and
the test, in the summer and autumn of 1673, though some had not
taken the oaths for fifteen or eighteen years and a few had never taken
the sacrament.[39] Pepys took a charitable view of the sea-officers'
irregular compliance with the law, believing that the mariners' general
ignorance of 'matters that relate to the shore' had led them to believe
that complying with the requirements once was sufficient for the whole
of their careers, rather than satisfying the law on entering each new
employment.[40] A similar story emerged in 1681–2, when an investigation was conducted into reports that officers and men had been
frequenting conventicles. It was found that several officers had still not
taken the test, but all who came under suspicion were able eventually
to convince the authorities of their conformity.[41] When James II
ordered another review of the officers' conformity in 1685, it was again
found, as noted earlier about the officers at Woolwich and Deptford,
that the whole corps was at least nominally 'conformable'.[42] The
discrepancy between the official reports and the opinion, held even by
such perceptive observers as Osborne and Pepys, that most of the
warrant-officers were dissenters suggests that the naval administration

---

[37] Grey, *Debates*, ii. 86; Pepys MS 2855, p. 378.
[38] Grey, *Debates*, ii. 79–90; *The Statutes of the Realm* (1819), v. 785.
[39] Rawl. MS A. 181, fos. 130–76, 352–5; Davies, 'The Navy, Parliament, and Political Crisis'.
[40] Pepys MS 2855, pp. 336, 355, 356.
[41] Davies, 'Political Crisis'.
[42] Adm. 106/3540, pt. 2, 'Musters' folder; Davies, 'Political Crisis'.

was deliberately presenting a false picture of religious belief in the fleet, one which concealed its own apparent laxity in enforcing the legal requirements.

There was also another kind of ambivalence towards religion in the officer corps. Some of the most senior sea-officers were genuinely sceptical in religious matters: Pepys was surprised to learn of the earl of Sandwich's indifference to matters of faith, while in a letter which was circulated widely in the 'political nation', James Ley, earl of Marlborough (a captain of great ships for both Charles I and his son), confessed to having cared little for religion until the prospect of battle turned his thoughts towards God.[43] When the abrasive Admiral Arthur Herbert refused on a point of conscience to support James II's proposed repeal of the Test Act, both the king and Herbert's own family were surprised to learn that he actually possessed a conscience.[44] Nevertheless, many of the Cavalier and gentlemen captains who entered the navy after 1660 were staunchly conformist in religion: they were the younger sons of royalist aristocrats and gentlemen, and were influenced by the same attitudes and prejudices that motivated their kinsmen ashore. In the years immediately after 1660, the tensions between these officers and those who had served the republic were based largely on professional, social, or political criteria, but there were a few cases of new sea-officers upbraiding colleagues for holding 'fanatic' views.[45] In later years, several sea-officers publicly displayed an intolerant attitude towards the nonconformist element in their ships. Sir William Jennens provided information on the prevalence of dissenter noncommissioned officers in the fleet during the 'tory reaction'; Sir Ralph Delaval objected to the presence of 'peaping conventicklers' in his squadron; and in 1691 one pamphleteer pleaded for captains to follow the example of the nation and tolerate different persuasions aboard their ships, implying that many were not doing so.[46] However, satisfactory working relationships must have existed on many ships of the fleet. Even the staunchly Anglican earl of Mulgrave, who captained a ship in the third Dutch war, could describe his boatswain as 'a Nonconformist, always sober, meek & quiet . . . & very often gave me an image of those enthusiastic people who did such

---

[43] *Pepys's Diary*, i. 141, 201, 261; G. Penn, *Memorials of the Professional Life and Times of Sir William Penn, Knt* (1833), ii. 340–1.

[44] PRO, PRO 30/53/8, fos. 42, 47.

[45] e.g. BL., Sloane MS 505, fo. 40.

[46] *CSPD*, 1682, 106; HMC, *Finch MSS*, iii. 284; Maydman, *Speculations*, 216–17.

brave things in our late Civill War: for he seem'd rather a Shepherd
than a Soldier; & was a kind of heroe in the shape of a saint'.[47] It may
be too extreme to suggest that a *de facto* state of religious toleration
existed in the Restoration navy, but the separate, dangerous nature of
shipboard life did much to encourage coexistence.

The dangers of the seafarers' trade also ensured that the formal
religion of officers and men was supplemented by a deeply rooted
sense of superstition. The porpoise was already regarded as a har-
binger of doom, and more particularly as the forerunner of dangerous
storms; Edward Barlow attributed the loss of his ship on the Goodwin
sands both to the will of God and to the bewitchment of the vessel by
some old women of Bergen, with whom the crew had quarrelled; gunners relied heavily on the intercession of their patron saint, Barbara;
while one ship's company, particularly desperate to get a cable to
break, resorted to a rite of exorcism.[48]

A more curious element in the seamen's religion was a remarkably
ambivalent attitude towards Catholicism. Unlike their social equals on
land, seamen had the opportunity to see Catholic countries at first-
hand, and this contact brought mixed reactions. During the civil war,
one pamphlet had argued that, as seamen could see the true nature of
popery and arbitrary government in foreign states, they would be more
determined to prevent their introduction into England, and this sentiment does seem to have influenced some of the men of the fleet.[49] On
the other hand, the most common reaction of officers and seamen
in foreign ports was actually rather different. Though they were
influenced by the usual anti-Catholic, xenophobic attitudes of the age,
they often found these received opinions under threat from natural
curiosity when they arrived in a Catholic port. Even Barlow, ever
willing to launch into tirades against supposedly crypto-Catholic ministers at Whitehall, found himself watching Catholic rituals and services
in fascination.[50] Lisbon, a regular port of call for English warships,
brought officers and men into contact with English monks and nuns,

[47] *The Works of John Sheffield, Earl of Mulgrave, Marquis of Normanby, and Duke of Buckingham* (1740 edn.), ii. 15.

[48] National Library of Wales, Powis papers, 14/7a; *Barlow's Journal*, i. 261; Ehrman, *Navy... of William III*, 24; Rawl. MS A. 316, fo. 5ᵛ. On superstition among seamen, cf. also Rediker, *Devil and Deep Blue Sea*, 179–89; Capp, *Cromwell's Navy*, 326–8.

[49] Kennedy, 'Crown and the Common Seamen', 175; *Life of Captain Stephen Martin*, ed. Markham, 183.

[50] *Barlow's Journal*, i. 63–4, 116, 168. Certainly, the virulent anti-Catholicism of the interregnum is often absent from Restoration sources: cf. Capp, *Cromwell's Navy*, 300.

whose modesty, openness, and hospitality greatly impressed their guests.[51] Indeed, some observers worried that seamen might be so impressed by the contrast between the strict-living, apparently sincere Catholic priests and their own chaplains that they might even turn Catholic themselves.[52] Though this may have been an exaggerated fear, there were certainly cases of desertion in foreign ports by seamen who then turned Catholic—but there were also a number of cases of seamen deserting to join the Barbary corsairs and turning to Muhammad in the process. Such 'conversions' were generally inspired by lack of pay or a desire to avoid discipline, rather than by sudden changes of religious conviction.[53]

Taking an ambivalent line towards Catholicism abroad was one thing; accepting a Catholic presence in the navy was another. Cromwell's chaplain, Hugh Peters, had once observed that there might have been atheists in the navy, but never any Catholics,[54] and even when the Stuarts returned from the exile which had formed their own inclinations towards Rome, they made no immediate attempt to introduce a Catholic element into the fleet. This was due in part to the lack of qualified Catholic candidates for naval offices, but also because of the vigorous opposition of Sir William Coventry, the duke of York's secretary from 1660 to 1667, to the appointment of Catholic sea-officers. An Irish Catholic who had commanded a privateer in the 1650s was turned away from naval employment by Coventry and subsequently went abroad, while Sir William dismissed the pretensions of another Irishman who claimed to have undergone a conversion to Anglicanism with the laconic remark, 'I am apter to believe him a convert to the Navy then the Church.'[55]

The navy did not remain free of Catholics for long. During the debates on the test bill in 1673, MPs were consumed by exaggerated fears of the hold exerted by Catholicism on the officer corps, and Sir Thomas Osborne sought to reassure them by stating that 'there were but two Captains Roman Catholics in the whole fleet, and they young Gentlemen and no notice taken of them'.[56] This remark seems to have

---

[51] BL, Sloane MS 505, fos. 13–14, 17, 19, 23–5, 32; Rawl. MS A. 316, fo. 17 *et passim*.

[52] See e.g. Maydman, *Speculations*, 148–9.

[53] e.g. Rawl. MS A. 189, fos. 78–9; Rawl. MS C. 972, fo. 27ᵛ; Bod. Lib., MS Eng. Hist. C. 236, fos. 41–2; Adm. 106/311, fo. 154.

[54] BL, Addit. MS 11602, fo. 77.

[55] *Naval Minutes*, 34–5; Bod. Lib., Carte MS 47, fo. 405ᵛ.

[56] Grey, *Debates*, ii. 74–90 (Osborne's speech quoted on p. 86).

been an accurate assessment of the state of the fleet. Two captains were forced to resign because of the passing of the Test Act: Thomas Chamberlaine is a shadowy figure who held only one command before being forced out of the service,[57] but Captain John Tyrwhitt is a more intriguing character. A member of the noted Lincolnshire family of recusant gentry, Tyrwhitt had been first commissioned five months after the Restoration and served almost continuously between 1660 and 1673, holding several important commands.[58] He served, there-fore, throughout Coventry's period of office, but Coventry's annotated lists of sea-officers suggest that he did not suspect Tyrwhitt of Catholicism, and there is no evidence to prove whether Tyrwhitt was a secretive Catholic of long standing or a recent convert when he left the service in August 1673.[59] Moreover, the resignations of Tyrwhitt and Chamberlaine were not entirely straightforward cases of disqualifica-tion for recusancy: in both cases, serious charges of incompetence and neglect of duty stood against the officers' names. Resignation because of inability to comply with the test was a face-saving way of avoiding dismissal in disgrace, and a convenient means of providing the admin-istration with its sacrifice to Parliament.[60]

The next and most searching enquiry into the extent of Catholicism in the fleet came in the immediate aftermath of the popish plot. The navy was a natural object of Protestant concern, because many of its commissioned officers had risen under the patronage of the duke of York: by mid-November 1678, MPs were beginning to express concern about the infiltration of Catholic officers into the fleet, and within days Pepys had ordered an exhaustive enquiry into the religious affections of the officer corps.[61] This inquisition received a fresh impetus in the spring of 1679, when the first exclusion Parliament met and Charles formed a new Admiralty commission containing a number of opposition parliamentarians.[62] Throughout, the most intensive scrutiny was applied to one group of officers in particular—

[57] Adm. 10/15, p. 26. Cf. Adm. 106/27, fo. 204.
[58] Tanner, *Catalogue*, i. 417; *Notices and Remains of the Family of Tyrwhitt* (1858), 60; L. C. Gooch, 'Catholic Officers in the Navy of James II', *Recusant History*, 14 (1977–8), 279.
[59] Coventry MS 98, fo. 53.
[60] Adm. 3/275, pp. 21, 23, 26, 36; Tanner, *Catalogue*, ii. 23, 28–30, 48; iv. 7; Rawl. MS A. 191, fo. 52.
[61] Pepys MS 2855, pp. 292–4 *et seq.*; Pepys MS 2856, pp. 243–4; Grey, *Debates*, vi. 195, 207; Davies, 'Political Crisis'.
[62] Ibid.; Davies, 'Pepys and the Admiralty Commission', 35.

the Irishmen, several of whom were Protestant converts from staunch Catholic families. Despite being such obvious targets, they were all able eventually to convince the authorities of their conformity, and only one of them (Randall MacDonnell) did eventually become a Catholic in James II's reign.[63] Indeed, the only officer to be suspended on suspicion of recusancy as a result of the enquiries was the gunner of the sixth-rate *Holmes*: his removal, and that of the handful of foreign Catholic seamen serving in the fleet, hardly constitutes an impressive purge of naval papists.[64] However, the one publicly voiced suspicion which was *not* directly followed up was arguably the most significant: in Parliament in 1679, Sir Roger Strickland, rear-admiral of the Mediterranean fleet, was accused of being a Catholic.[65] A first cousin of the recusant MP for Westmorland, Sir Thomas Strickland of Sizergh, he had entered the navy in 1661 and gained major commands and a knighthood in the third Dutch war, rising to flag-rank in the Mediterranean in 1678.[66] Strickland was a great personal favourite of the duke of York, partly because of his bravery under James's command in 1672, partly because he had a brother in James's household, and he was also a close friend of another naval favourite of the duke's, Colonel George Legge.[67] There is no evidence to support the view that Strickland was a covert Catholic during this period,[68] but his connections inevitably made him suspect. He had close ties to his Catholic cousins at Sizergh, and used some of the income from his naval service to pay off their debts; when Sir Thomas ran into further financial trouble in 1682, Sir Roger bought the Thornton Bridge estate in Yorkshire and the farm of the salt duties from him. Throughout his naval career, Strickland displayed, as he put it, 'my zeal and kindness to my blood family and name'—a family and name which were almost exclusively Catholic.[69] Nevertheless, his faith was not queried within the navy itself during the enquiries of 1678–9. His public conversion to the religion of his ancestors came later, under

---

[63] Davies, 'Political Crisis'; McDonnell, 'Irishmen in the Later Stuart Navy'.

[64] Davies, 'Political Crisis'.

[65] Grey, *Debates*, vii. 112–13.

[66] Tanner, *Catalogue*, i. 315, 410; H. Hornyold, *Genealogical Memoirs of the Family of Strickland of Sizergh* (Kendal, 1928), 264–7.

[67] BL, Addit. MS 18447, fo. 41ᵛ; HMC, *Dartmouth MSS*, i. 132–3.

[68] For this view, see J. C. H. Aveling, *The Handle and the Axe: The Catholic Recusants in England from Reformation to Emancipation* (1976), 183.

[69] Scott, *The Stricklands of Sizergh Castle*, 183–4, 185–6 (quotation from p. 185); Hornyold, *Strickland Memoirs*, 130, 251, 265.

James II, and helped to make him one of the dominant figures in naval affairs during that reign.

In the heated atmosphere of the popish plot and its aftermath, it was natural that at least some of the charges brought against individuals should contain more than a hint of malice and the settling of old scores. Captain Henry Priestman's name may have made him a target for the credulous: for six months he had to fend off accusations from his crew to the effect, among other things, that he had been drunk or playing cards on Sunday, or else singing or whistling while the ship's company was at prayer—all irrefutable proofs of papist leanings.[70] Similarly, the resident commissioner of the navy at Chatham, Sir Richard Beach, accused the gunners of two of the largest warships in his yard of Catholicism: Beach had been trying to get rid of at least one of the gunners on grounds of idleness for some time, and Pepys reacted coolly to his charges, permitting both officers to keep their posts.[71] Tacking a charge of Catholicism on to a range of more plausible accusations against a sea-officer had been known in the navy before 1678,[72] but in the frantic atmosphere of that year it must have seemed a convenient short-cut for men nursing grievances.

Despite all the anxieties of MPs and Protestant polemicists through-out the 'political nation', then, Catholicism was not a significant element in the complexion of the fleet during Charles II's reign. Despite the influence of the duke of York, overt adherence to the Roman faith was not a sensible course for any ambitious sea-officer to take: the highest founts of patronage were in too many different hands, with Sir William Coventry and other staunchly anti-papist figures like Albemarle and Sandwich influencing appointments before about 1670, and large Admiralty commissions containing men of varied but equally conventional backgrounds and beliefs holding sway after 1673. When a Catholic king governed naval affairs in person, with very few other influential patrons providing alternative avenues to promotion and with many examples of opportunist 'conversions' taking place in other professions ashore, the temptation to join the church of Rome became more enticing.

---

[70] Pepys MS 2855, pp. 293–4, 319, 327–8, 466–70, 472; Adm. 3/277, pt. 1, pp. 44, 55–6. In fact, Priestman went on to become a whig politician and an Admiralty commissioner.

[71] Adm. 106/330, fo. 487; Adm. 106/340, fo. 61; Pepys MS 2855, pp. 40, 383, 387, 396–7.

[72] See e.g. Adm. 106/5, fos. 320–1.

PART II

THE NAVY IN PEACE, WAR, AND REVOLUTION

7

THE RESTORATION

DURING the 1650s, the navy seemed to have become one of the bastions of the republican state. Many of its officers and men held advanced religious or political views, and were therefore well qualified to carry out the primary task of the unprecedentedly powerful fleet, namely the defence of the regime against the Stuarts and their potential foreign backers.[1] Yet by May 1660, the same fleet was prepared to bring the Stuarts back to England with every outward show of compliance, and even enthusiasm, 'with pendants loose, guns roaring, caps flying, and the loud Vive le Roy's echoed from one ship's company to another...'.[2] Moreover, many of its formerly 'radical' officers went on to serve the monarchy loyally, with several (like Vice-Admiral John Lawson, the fleet's commander during the crucial months of 1659–60) gaining knighthoods and the command of fleets or squadrons. These changes of heart and the motives which brought them about have recently been examined searchingly by Bernard Capp, who concludes that 'the charge of tame conformism...is at most a half-truth...Lawson, the leading republican still in service, was misled and outmanœuvred'.[3] There is no need here to duplicate Dr Capp's narrative of the navy's role in the Restoration; rather, I shall take up several of his contentions and ideas, and examine the remodelling of the navy in 1660 in the light of its royalist future, not its republican past.

By the middle of August 1659, the Rump Parliament had two major naval forces in northern waters: a fleet in the Baltic under Edward Mountagu, general-at-sea, and a squadron in home waters under Vice-Admiral John Lawson.[4] However, the Rump was deeply suspic-

---

[1] Capp, *Cromwell's Navy*, ch. 3 *et passim*.
[2] *Pepys's Diary*, i. 126.
[3] Capp, *Cromwell's Navy*, 397, 398, and ch. 10 *passim*.
[4] Unless otherwise stated, the narrative of the fleet's activities between Aug. 1659 and May 1660, contained in this and the following paragraph, is based on Capp, *Cromwell's Navy*, ch. 10.

ious of Mountagu, who had strong loyalties to the fallen protectorate of
his kinsmen, the Cromwells; Parliament had already despatched commissioners, who were intended to undermine Mountagu's influence in
the fleet.[5] Its suspicions were reinforced when Mountagu abruptly
brought the fleet back to England at the end of August. Royalists and
rumpers alike believed that he had planned to intervene on the side of
Sir George Booth's rebels in Cheshire, and after the Restoration
Mountagu claimed that this had been his true intention. However, he
had been very careful to cover his tracks: his ostensible reason for
leaving the Baltic, the shortage of victuals for his fleet, had been closely
argued and was plausible enough to be accepted by the Rump and its
commissioners.[6] Even so, the political gulf between Mountagu and the
Rump drove the general-at-sea into an enforced retirement. The
command of the fleet then devolved upon Lawson, who was aboard his
flagship in the Downs when, on 13 October 1659, the army grandees
ejected the Rump, which had peremptorily cancelled their commissions. Lawson was bitterly opposed to this change of regime and
remained so even after some of his subordinates had moved towards 'a
grudging acceptance' of the military government as the only means of
preserving the unity of the republicans. Instead, Lawson favoured
the pro-Rump stance of the former general-at-sea George Monck,
then commanding the army in Scotland,[7] and when the Portsmouth
garrison declared for the Rump early in December, Lawson decided to
act. On 14 December, the fleet left the Downs for the Thames, where
it proceeded to blockade London's trade. Rejecting all the army's
frantic overtures, Lawson held out for a restoration of the Rump, and
his pressure finally bore fruit on 26 December, when the grandees
capitulated and the Rump resumed its sitting.[8]

The rapid changes of government, and of the allegiance of the navy,
had greatly excited the exiled royalists throughout 1659. If the whole
fleet, or even a squadron, could be won over, the royalists might be
able to effect a landing, or blockade London into submission, so for
many months Charles II's agents had been engaged in the 'business of
seamen', sporadic attempts to buy the allegiance of naval officers
and men.[9] Strenuous efforts had been made to win over Mountagu in

[5] Capp, *Cromwell's Navy*, 336–7.
[6] Rawl. MS A. 468, fo. 6; Cogar, 'Politics of Naval Administration', 229–35; Capp,
Cromwell's Navy, 340–1.
[7] Ibid. 342–5 (quotation from p. 344).
[8] Ibid. 345–50.
[9] F. J. Routledge (ed.), *Calendar of the Clarendon State Papers Preserved in the Bodleian*

the Baltic, but his retirement from naval affairs temporarily stymied the royalists. Agents also made contact with Lawson, a far less promising potential convert because of his long track record as a political and religious radical; these overtures, and those to other commanders, had borne no fruit by the beginning of February 1660, when Monck's Scottish army arrived in London.[10] Subsequently, both Lawson and the royalists were taken by surprise when Monck declared for a free parliament and readmitted the MPs purged in 1648. The restructured parliament rapidly appointed Monck and Mountagu as joint generals-at-sea, thereby displacing Lawson from the command of the fleet. The vice-admiral seemed to have ample cause, both in terms of his past attitudes and the treatment meted out to him, for opposing the changes in nation and navy, but, surprisingly, Lawson acquiesced meekly, even when the new generals began to purge his clients and other radicals from the fleet in March and April 1660.[11] By mid-April both Mountagu and Lawson were in receipt of correspondence from the king, and the navy as a whole had come (albeit reluctantly, in many cases) to accept the growing inevitability of a restoration of the monarchy. Samuel Pepys, Mountagu's secretary, shrewdly summed up the difference between the seagoing personnel's public and private faces when he noted the reaction of the captains to Charles's declaration of Breda and Parliament's subsequent declaration in favour of monarchy: 'not one man seemed to say no to it, though I am confident many in their hearts were against it'.[12] Even so, the public face triumphed. By 14 May the fleet was off Scheveningen, ready to wait on its king and lord high admiral, and to transport them back to England.

Of all the leading national figures in the months before May 1660, John Lawson's conversion to the notion of a restored monarchy was probably the most unexpected, and his motives (after the enigmatic Monck's) the most 'mysterious'.[13] Bernard Capp presents a Lawson moving 'unwillingly and in part unwittingly' towards support for the Restoration,[14] his actions governed above all by a deep hatred of

Library, iv (Oxford, 1932), 164, 208, 244, 437, 469, 506–7, 520; *The Letter Book of John, Viscount Mordaunt, 1658–60*, ed. M. Coate (Camden Society, 3rd ser., 69; 1945), 76, 100, 151.
[10] Capp, *Cromwell's Navy*, 337–40, 352.
[11] *Pepys's Diary*, i. 123–4.
[12] Ibid.
[13] Hutton, *The Restoration*, 110.
[14] Capp, *Cromwell's Navy*, 356.

military rule and a firm belief that only Parliament possessed true, legal authority: as he stated in 1659, the country should be 'happy under a succession of parliamentary authority, derived from a civil rather than a military fountain, from whence floweth nothing but absoluteness, pride and unlimited arbitrary and tyrannical streams'.[15] Outmanœuvred by Monck's unexpected declaration for a free parliament and the return of the secluded members, Lawson adopted a policy of self-preservation, realizing that any resistance would be futile, hoping for the survival of the republic, but prepared to accept, as a last resort, the return of the Stuarts as a marginally lesser evil than the return of the army.[16] As Dr Capp observes, 'At some point soon after 21 February Lawson clearly decided to acquiesce in Monck's plans, wherever they should lead—hoping this would not mean monarchy but aware that it might . . . He probably saw no realistic alternative.'[17] This interpretation of Lawson's motives is convincing, but not necessarily comprehensive. Certainly, Lawson might have preferred monarchy to military rule on legal and practical grounds, but several other factors might have helped to push him towards the political solution most likely to deliver stable, lasting government.

The first of these concerns was trade. In December 1659 the merchant seamen of the Thames presented a petition to the city of London, calling for the restoration of 'merchandize, trade and navigation', which had been damaged (in their view) by the many political changes.[18] Though Lawson was not yet ready to accept their conclusion, namely that a free parliament would be the best way of achieving these ends, he did place much emphasis on the trade problem in two letters of the same month to the lord mayor and common council.[19] As with many of his fellow sea-officers, Lawson's roots lay in the coastal mercantile communities: he had gained his nautical expertise in the east coast coal trade, joining the navy only when his ship was taken up from trade, and several of his relatives were still engaged in commerce as grocers or merchants. Lawson himself continued to hold shares in several merchant ships until his death.[20] As he knew, trade

[15] Penn, *Memorials*, ii. 191; Capp, *Cromwell's Navy*, 347–50.
[16] Ibid. 352–6.
[17] Ibid. 356.
[18] Cogar, 'Naval Administration', 248.
[19] Penn, *Memorials*, ii. 192–4; Cogar, 'Naval Administration', 249–50; Capp, *Cromwell's Navy*, 347–8, 349–50.
[20] Bod. Lib., Clarendon MS 68, fo. 129; Prob. 11/317, fos. 327–8; Capp, *Cromwell's Navy*, 164, 167.

could prosper only if political stability were restored, and the agent chosen by Charles II to attempt the conversion of the republican vice-admiral was ideally qualified to emphasize that point to Lawson. On 3 November 1659, the king had given Arnold Braems authority to negotiate with Lawson, and to offer him virtually any terms.[21] Braems, an ageing Dover merchant who had fitted out ships for the royalists, implied that he had known Lawson for some time before 1659, and the vice-admiral himself wrote of Braems in terms of past friendship rather than of new acquaintance.[22] This relationship may have dated from the years before the civil war, when Lawson had been active in the coal trade and Braems's commercial bases, Dover and Sandwich, had traded regularly in coal with Newcastle and Lawson's home town, Scarborough.[23] In addition, Braems had many naval connections: the future controller of the navy, Captain John Mennes, was a neighbour and friend, while in the months and years which followed the Restoration Braems's commercial and social contacts included Edward Mountagu, his fellow MP for Dover in 1660, and the former general-at-sea William Penn. Both relationships seem to have predated the Restoration.[24] Whatever the origins of his relationship with Lawson, Braems was a shrewd choice as an intermediary: as a merchant, he was ideally qualified to play on the vice-admiral's preoccupation with the restoration of trade. It is possible that he made contact with Lawson before the latter's fleet made its momentous voyage from the Downs to the Thames in mid-December, but he was certainly in touch with the vice-admiral by the end of that month.[25]

The second great practical concern influencing Lawson over the winter of 1659–60 was the state of the navy itself. The financial position of the service had been deteriorating steadily since 1658 at least: by the end of 1659 some crews were owed up to four years' wages, and the supply of victuals to the fleet was in similarly dire straits.[26] During January and February 1660 the council of state had debated the needs of the fleet, but their deliberations brought

[21] *Mordaunt Letter Book*, 89–90.

[22] Bod. Lib., Clarendon MS 71, fo. 185; Clar. MS 72, fos. 229, 347; SP 29/9, fo. 14; *Hist. Parl.*, i. 707.

[23] J. H. Andrews, 'The Thanet Seaports 1650–1750', *Archaeologia Cantiana*, 66 (1954), 37–44 (esp. p. 42).

[24] SP 29/9, fo. 14; SP 89/5, fo. 60; Bod. Lib., Carte MS 73, fos. 450, 531; *Pepys's Diary*, i. 293, 323; ii. 192; ix. 57.

[25] *Mordaunt Letter Book*, 150.

[26] Capp, *Cromwell's Navy*, 341–2, 364–5.

no positive results, and by 13 February the Navy Board itself was forecasting the imminent collapse of the victualling system.[27] The Admiralty had been virtually moribund since the previous December, and little money had been paid to the treasurer of the navy since September.[28] By February, the crews of many ships were refusing to go to sea unless their arrears were paid; Lawson went down to the fleet in the middle of the month and saw the extent of the problem at first hand.[29] Lawson's concern for the material condition of his men was genuine, and was displayed on many occasions both before and after the Restoration—most notably in October 1654, when he had supported a seamen's petition demanding the end of impressment and more regular payment of wages.[30] However, the navy was competing with the politically more influential army for a share of the declining public revenue, and in the middle of February the Rump made a desperate attempt to placate some elements of the army by paying units in and around London (though not enough money could be raised even for this gesture).[31] The sailors had been grumbling for months that the army's arrears were getting preference;[32] the events of mid-February demonstrated that the Rump was unable and unwilling to deal with the problems of the fleet, and that it preferred to satisfy the force which Lawson resented so much as an absolute, arbitrary, and tyrannical authority—the army. This preference, together with the collapse of the naval administration, his desire to restore trade, and anger at the expulsion from the House of his old friend Sir Henry Vane,[33] helped to turn Lawson against the Rump. Viewed in this context, Lawson's decision not to oppose Monck in February 1660 would seem to have been born at least in part from a conviction that

[27] BL., Addit. MS 9302, fos. 94–8; *CSPD*, 1659–60, 315, 342, 520; HMC, *Portland MSS*, i. 695–6.

[28] Hammond, 'Administration of the English Navy', 105; Cogar, 'Naval Administration', 237, 247, 251–4. On naval finance in the period 1649–60 as a whole, cf. also H.-C. Junge, *Flottenpolitik und Revolution: Die Entstehung der englischen Seemacht während der Herrschaft Cromwells* (Stuttgart, 1980), 314–30.

[29] Bod. Lib., Clarendon MS 69, fos. 64–5, 159; Clar. MS 70, fo. 30.

[30] For examples, see *CSPD*, 1659–60, 509, 530, 535; Bod. Lib., Carte MS 73, fo. 353; Adm. 2/1745, fo. 27ᵛ; Capp, *Cromwell's Navy*, 135–6. The consistency of Lawson's concern for the seamen over a decade or more makes it seem unlikely that his machinations in 1654 were simply a cover for broader political ends.

[31] Hammond, 'Administration', 358–9.

[32] See Bod. Lib., Clarendon MS 67, fo. 34ᵛ; C. H. Firth (ed.), *The Clarke Papers*, iv (Camden NS 62; 1901), 102–3.

[33] Capp, *Cromwell's Navy*, 351.

the Rump had failed, rather than simply out of resigned acceptance of Monck's coup. Moreover, this view of Lawson's behaviour would seem to suggest that the crucial turning-point for him came in the middle, not at the end, of February.[34] On 7 February, Braems had mixed feelings about his chances of winning the vice-admiral: 'with all his utmost endeavours with Lawson hee can not yet worke on his rigid opinion for a comonwealth and this Parliament but yet with such personal kindness to him, as encourageth him still to ply him, in hope to finde him of a better temper as occasions alter'.[35] Lawson's temper had evidently improved within ten days, for on the 17th Charles II's minister, Hyde, was informed that Lawson had promised to follow the declarations of Monck and London for the restoration of the secluded members of the Long Parliament, and for a free parliament to succeed it, and that through Braems's zeal the royalists could have good hope of him.[36]

However, it may be misleading to suggest that Lawson's 'conversion' was based on entirely altruistic motives. The vice-admiral had always been careful to assert his rights to his own arrears of pay and to emphasize his wish to provide for his family; in 1649–50 he had busily acquired debentures in Crown lands.[37] In later years, his attempts to improve his standing at court by ingratiating himself wtih young gentlemen volunteers on his ships would lead Pepys to call him 'the greatest courtier of all the tarpaulins'.[38] Braems had been given authority to allow Lawson to name his own price, and perhaps, at the end, the vice-admiral named it. On 20 April 1660 Braems wrote to Hyde,

I had with the Vice Admirall good op[por]tunetye to discource his Ma[jesty']s affaers and found him so mutch Complyinge, *that I then tould him hee should finde all what I had formerly asshured him to follow.* Upon which I gave him his Ma[jesty']s letter the which hee did so Cordially receve with so mutch affexsion as would place it next his haert as a perpetuall honour to bee so mutch in his princes favor.[39]

---

[34] Ibid. 356.
[35] Bod. Lib., Clarendon MS 69, fo. 89.
[36] Ibid., fo. 164ᵛ. Cf. Clar. MS 71, fos. 185–6.
[37] BL, Addit. MS 21417, fo. 13; Addit. MS 21418, fo. 248; Addit. MS 21427, fos. 38, 48; SP 18/47, fo. 63; *CSPD*, 1641–3, 562; 1644–5, 223. Cf. Clarendon, *Life*, ii. 393–5.
[38] *Tangier Papers*, 229. Cf. Clarendon, *Life*, ii. 354–5, 391–3; *Pepys's Diary*, vii. 195.
[39] Bod. Lib., Clarendon MS 71, fo. 185ᵛ (my italics).

During March, Monck had considered offering Lawson a lump sum of £10,000 in lieu of his pension; Mountagu was instrumental in gaining an increase in Lawson's wages and securing the payment of the £500 voted by the Rump for his part in its restoration—gestures for which Lawson was suitably grateful.[40] Lawson also obtained a guarantee of protection from Monck and a promise of his right to personal liberty of conscience from the king.[41] Whether his new allegiance was bought or won, Lawson remained true to it. By the end of March, despite the continuing doubts of some royalist agents, it was generally believed that Lawson would follow the lead of Monck and Mountagu, and would act for the king.[42] This change of allegiance was cemented on 7 May when Lawson wrote to the king to assure him of his loyalty: on the same day, the man the royalists had regarded as a Rumper and Anabaptist barely five months earlier ostentatiously drank Charles II's health in Pepys's company.[43] Militant republicans nursed vain hopes that he would rejoin the old cause, and he died of wounds received in battle in 1665, a knight of the realm and a hero of his nation.[44]

The complexity of Lawson's position in the months leading up to the Restoration reflects a similar story in the officer corps as a whole. Ironically, probably the most straightforward conversion was that of the other key figure in naval affairs, Edward Mountagu, the general-at-sea, a known conservative who had advocated Oliver Cromwell's elevation to the kingship in 1657. By February 1660 he had realized that the most superficially attractive political settlement, the return of his kinsman Richard Cromwell as lord protector, was now unrealistic, and during March he listened with increasing favour to overtures from the royalists. A correspondence between the admiral and Charles II in early April, using the royalist naval officer Robert Holmes as an intermediary, cemented Mountagu's new loyalty to the Stuarts, a conversion which he backdated (probably in order to ingratiate himself still further with the new regime) to the events in the Baltic in August

[40] Bod. Lib., Carte MS 73, fo. 355; Penn, *Memorials*, ii. 253; Hammond, 'Administration', 363; Cogar, 'Naval Administration', 264.
[41] Bod. Lib., Clarendon MS 71, fo. 185ᵛ; E. Ludlow, *Ludlow's Memoirs*, ed. C. H. Firth (Oxford, 1894), ii. 278.
[42] Bod. Lib., Clarendon MS 71, fos. 41ᵛ, 105ᵛ.
[43] Bod. Lib., Clarendon MS 72, fo. 229; *Pepys's Diary*, i. 130–1.
[44] SP 89/5, fo. 13ᵛ; SP 29/84, fo. 64; *DNB* s, n, 'Lawson, John'; Capp, *Cromwell's Navy*, 382–3.

1659.[45] Other senior officers had been converted to royalism even earlier, though these were men who were not in commission during the crucial six-month period from October 1659 to March 1660. William Penn, the former general-at-sea, had been living in retirement since the ignominious failure of Cromwell's 'western design' in 1655, and had been in contact with the royalists since the middle of 1659. However, many of his wide circle of clients from Bristol and Ireland were still in the service, and in March 1660 his friend Monck brought him back into the navy—perhaps as a means of guaranteeing the loyalty of Penn's clients, perhaps as a way of giving Monck (who had to stay in London, despite being joint general-at-sea) a greater say in a fleet which was dominated by Mountagu and Lawson.[46] Another former flag-officer, Sir George Ayscue, might have been converted to royalism even earlier than Penn, but he had been in retirement for longer and had far less influence on patronage in the fleet.[47]

Elsewhere in the navy, 'a sense of defeat and demoralization' was certainly apparent in February to May 1660, as even some of the most radical officers faced the increasingly inevitable prospect of the king's return.[48] Yet the same blend of alarm at the state of navy and nation, and of a desire to preserve one's own career, that helped to motivate Lawson, also governed the behaviour of others in the fleet. For those with no close ties of family, friendship, or previous patronage to a flag-officer or other high naval dignitary, the prospects of future employment seemed slim, and such officers went out of their way to impress the authorities. Thomas Sparling attempted to keep his command by drinking the king's health at Flushing over a week before Parliament officially proclaimed him, and by giving Mountagu's secretary, Pepys, a present of blue silk stockings; Sparling told a naval colleague to get a friend in the king's party, for he could expect nothing from the previous generation of naval patrons, Mountagu, Monck, and Penn.[49] Another captain returned from the Iceland fishery to find the monarchy restored, and reacted with suitably public enthusiasm; others wrote to the generals-at-sea to assure them of their whole-

[45] Cogar, 'Naval Administration', 267–8; Hutton, *The Restoration*, 106; Capp, *Cromwell's Navy*, 356. For Holmes's role, see Bod. Lib., Clarendon MS 71, fo. 366; Clar. MS 72, fo. 129; BL, Addit. MS 9307, fo. 12.

[46] NMM, WYN/1/1; Bod. Lib., Clarendon MS 72, fo. 408; BL, Addit. MS 70100, fo. 291; Capp, *Cromwell's Navy*, 363.

[47] Ibid. 132, 148.

[48] Ibid. 365.

[49] Bod. Lib., Clarendon MS 72, fo. 9; *Pepys's Diary*, i. 164.

hearted acceptance of the change of government, or relied on the intercession of friends to assure the authorities of their loyalty.[50]

These rapid changes of allegiance were not founded on any sudden discovery of the merits of monarchical government. By the beginning of March 1660 the pay of every ship in the fleet was in arrears, many by over twenty months, several by over forty, and one by fifty-two months.[51] The royalists recognized the importance of assuring the seamen that they would not lose their arrears by serving the king, and that a restoration would bring a new age of good pay. Certainly, the enthusiastic reception given to Charles by the ordinary seamen can be attributed to an expectation of reward; the men on the ships which brought the king to England immediately received pieces of gold worth almost ten shillings, and shortly afterwards each ship received a month's pay.[52] By the beginning of June, the Admiralty was able to allocate £8,000 to pay some seamen's wages, which, the duke of York observed, 'they suppose will satisfy the common menn, the officers they judge will not be less hasty for theirs'.[53] The paying off of the fleet proved a long, fraught affair which dragged on well into 1661, but the new royal authorities had done enough in the short term to buy the allegiance of the seamen. Only later, as the delays in payment worsened, did the seamen become as 'highly incensed against them' as they had been against the republic's naval administrators.[54]

For the sea-officers, securing their money was one concern; securing their careers was another. The active foreign policy of the Commonwealth and Protectorate had led to the virtually continuous employment of the fleet and its officers, many of whom had weathered the rapid changes of government in the years before the Restoration with apparent ease—perhaps because they believed that 'faction-fighting among the parliamentarians would be a fatal self-indulgence',[55] but also because they were prepared to follow the lead of their senior officers, and to support whichever party was in the ascendant. Five

[50] SP 29/14, fos. 79, 88; BL, Addit. MS 22546, fo. 235; Bod. Lib., Carte MS 73, fo. 499; Carte MS 223, fo. 198.

[51] Bod. Lib., Carte MS 73, fos. 227–8; SP 18/223, fo. 85. The summary in Carte MS 73 of the state of the fleet has been erroneously attributed to March 1659 by Tedder, *Navy of the Restoration*, 12–14; Junge, *Flottenpolitik*, 325–6; Cogar, 'Naval Administration', 220.

[52] Routledge, *Calendar of Clarendon State Papers*, iv. 638; Pepys MS 2581, p. 254; *Barlow's Journal*, i. 42–5; *Pepys's Diary*, i. 123–4; Capp, *Cromwell's Navy*, 368.

[53] Adm. 2/1745, fo. 1.

[54] *Pepys's Diary*, ii. 45. Cf. Bod. Lib., Carte MS 73, fos. 510–11.

[55] Capp, *Cromwell's Navy*, 398.

captains signed both a letter of 4 November 1659 to Monck, which justified the army's dissolution of the Rump, and Lawson's letter to the lord mayor of London of 21 December, which supported the restoration of the Rump.[56] Despite its extreme pro-army and anti-royalist nature, several signatories of the first of these letters had distinguished careers after the Restoration: Richard Stayner and Christopher Myngs gained flag-posts and knighthoods, while others received important commissions between the Restoration and the second Dutch war. Richard Haddock, who signed both letters, could be regarded almost as a naval equivalent of the vicar of Bray: a captain under Protectorate, Rump, and committee of safety, he went on to serve every English monarch from Charles II to George I, finally dying six months after the accession of the house of Hanover.[57] This breed of naval 'survivors' was recognized by some contemporaries. Captain Charles Wager, father of the famous eighteenth-century admiral, signed the letter of 4 November 1659, received a royal commission in 1660, served with distinction before and during the second Dutch war, and was described in 1661 as the 'greatest safety man of a thousand'.[58] For sea-officers from low or middling social backgrounds, the navy had become a way of life from which they were reluctant to part. Moreover, Captain Sparling's remarks indicate an awareness of the importance of patronage in determining the attitudes of officers in 1660, and this factor certainly influenced many who were otherwise very closely associated with the republic. The Teddemans of Dover had a long history of religious radicalism, but Thomas Teddeman became a client of Mountagu, acted as his election agent at Dover in 1660, and went on to flag-rank after the Restoration.[59] When the new lord high admiral, James, duke of York, and Mountagu proceeded to name officers for the ships which were to be employed for the rest of 1660, giving commissions to 'such of the commanders as shall be thought fit to be continued', their choices reflected the pervasive influence of the leading flag-officers.[60] The captains included clients of Mountagu (for example, Roger and Henry Cuttance, Teddeman, Hayward, Tearne), Monck (Sackler, Nixon), Lawson (Harrison), and

[56] Penn, *Memorials*, ii. 183, 194. Cf. Cogar, 'Naval Administration', 246.
[57] E. M. Thompson (ed.), 'Correspondence of the Family of Haddock', *The Camden Miscellany*, 8 (Camden NS 31; 1883), pp. iv–v.
[58] Coventry MS 98, fo. 68.
[59] Capp, *Cromwell's Navy*, 304, 361.
[60] *Sandwich Journal*, ed. Anderson, 79; Bod. Lib., Carte MS 223, fo. 212; *Pepys's Diary*, i. 167; Coventry MS 98, fos. 50, 52–3.

Penn (Rooth, Sparling, Poole).[61] The notes of the lord high admiral's secretary, William Coventry, reveal that in the early 1660s several captains were given commands on the recommendation of such influential patrons, although to the administration their affections were unknown or doubtful.[62] Sparling's prediction that the great naval patrons of the interregnum would exert no influence under the monarchy was well wide of the mark.

Despite the fact that the administration carefully purged the officer corps in the twelve months after May 1660 through such devices as the tendering of the oaths of allegiance and supremacy, and by getting dockyard officials to report on the affections of the sea-officers,[63] the prospects of interregnum officers surviving under the new regime were greatly enhanced by the absence of qualified Cavalier candidates for naval office. Charles and James naturally wanted to introduce as quickly as possible as large a Cavalier element as possible, both to guarantee the fleet's loyalty to the monarchy and to satisfy the insatiable Cavalier demand for places. The few surviving captains who had been displaced in 1642 for remaining loyal to Charles I returned to high office, Sir Robert Slyngsbie becoming controller of the navy, Sir George Carteret treasurer of the navy, and Sir John Mennes commander-in-chief in the Channel before succeeding Slyngsbie in October 1661. Sir William Batten, the vice-admiral who had defected to the royalists in 1648, became surveyor of the navy.[64] As far as the seagoing officer corps was concerned, fifteen Cavaliers gained captain's commissions in the first year of the new naval administration, between the beginning of June 1660 and the end of May 1661.[65] These men were drawn from three main sources. Several veterans of the royalist privateering effort of the 1650s gained commissions, notably Thomas Allin and his Lowestoft kinsman Riches Utber, the Irishmen Robert Holmes and Edward Spragge, and the most notorious royalist privateer of all, Richard Beach. James Smith, who had

[61] Coventry MS 98, fos. 84–5.

[62] Ibid. fos. 52–3.

[63] BL, Addit. MS 15857, fo. 190; Coventry MS 98, fos. 66–72, 82–3; Capp, *Cromwell's Navy*, 372–4. For the 'survival rate' of interregnum officers in the period 1660–4, see ibid. 376.

[64] Kennedy, 'Naval Captains', 181–98; G. A. R. Callender, 'Sir John Mennes', *MM* 26 (1940), 276–82; G. R. Balleine, *All for the King: The Life Story of Sir George Carteret (1609–80)* (Jersey, 1976), ch. 12 *et passim*.

[65] As opposed to between 50 and 60 interregnum officers: Coventry MS 98, fos. 84–5, on which the following remarks about commissioned officers are based, unless otherwise stated.

fought for the royalists on the Isle of Man and the Scillies, subsequently built the *Hector* for the king at Brest in 1657 and was then imprisoned at Plymouth for three years; he gained three impressive commands after the Restoration, dying as commander-in-chief in the Mediterranean.[66] The second group of Cavalier officers were men who had served in the navy during the 1630s and 1640s. Richard Greene, gunner of the *Second Whelp* in 1645, gained the command of a frigate in 1660, and in later years John Johnson, captain of one of the marquis of Newcastle's privateers in the civil wars, and Richard Poole, who had commanded two ships for Charles I against the Irish rebels, both gained commands.[67]

The third category contained men whose qualifications to command at sea were, at best, very dubious. Lucas Walsh, an ensign in the duke of York's company of the tiny royalist army in 1657, became a naval lieutenant in 1660, but then returned to Ireland to join the duke of Ormonde's horse guards, and commanded a privateer in the second Dutch war.[68] Major John Fletcher, another Ormonde client who had served in the royal army under Lord Berkeley of Stratton, gained the command of the *Eagle* in 1660, while the Devonian William Pomeroy, a captain of horse under Charles I, took command of the *Dolphin* in October 1661.[69] The backgrounds of these men suggest another factor which Charles and James took into account when appointing Cavalier officers: in several cases, the officers had been ruined financially because of their loyalty to the king, and a naval commission was an obvious way of giving them some means of support.[70] The most apparent, and at the same time most eccentric, example of this policy was the commissioning of Nicholas Tettersall, the Brighton fisherman who had carried Charles II across the Channel in 1651, after his defeat at Worcester. Tettersall was commissioned to the frigate *Sorlings* in 1660 and the third-rate *Monck* in 1661, and, although he later went back to the coasting trade in his *Happy Entrance* (before becoming a noted persecutor of dissenters as high constable of Brighton), his son

---

[66] *CSPD*, 1665–6, 492–3; *CSPD*, 1673, 164–5.

[67] Greene: Coventry MS 118, fo. 140; Tanner, *Catalogue*, i. 356. Johnson: *A List of Officers Claiming to the £60,000, &c., Granted by his Sacred Majesty for the Relief of his Truly-loyal and Indigent Party* (1663), col. 155; *CSPD*, 1666–7, 401. Poole: H. Cheale, *The History of Shoreham* (1921), 172–4.

[68] *CSP Ireland*, 1669–70, 615–16.

[69] Fletcher: Coventry MS 98, fo. 53; Bod. Lib., Carte MS 49, fo. 323. Pomeroy: Devon RO, QS 128/99/1.

[70] e.g. the cases of Johnson and Pomeroy. Cf. *A List of Officers . . .*, col. 155.

continued to receive a pension from the navy until after the revolution of 1688.[71]

At a lower level, too, a substantial Cavalier element was introduced into the navy. Between 1660 and 1663, sea-officers with vaguely royalist antecedents were introduced into about a third of the warrant posts in the fleet, replacing those whose loyalty was more doubtful. However, this was not an entirely smooth process. James and Coventry admitted that the competence of the new men was often uncertain, due in part to their own inexperience and inability accurately to assess men's ability.[72] Similarly, the competence of the Cavalier commissioned officers was also soon under fire, though the opposition to them from the likes of Edward Mountagu, now earl of Sandwich, sounds suspiciously like sour grapes against men who were displacing interregnum officers (often Mountagu's own clients) from the service.[73] Even so, there was no sensible alternative to the royal policy of balancing the two disparate elements among the sea-officers—a policy carefully maintained in the early 1660s. Thus, in Sandwich's fleet sent in May 1661 to bring Catherine of Braganza to England, nine interregnum captains sailed alongside five Cavaliers, while the lieutenancies were predominantly in the hands of younger sons of Cavalier families such as the Berkeleys, Mohuns, and Hydes.[74] In that month, too, James instituted the system for training gentlemen volunteers, thereby beginning the process of breeding a new generation of Cavalier officers. A less renowned, but equally significant, step was the commissioning in that month of the first of the new breed of 'gentlemen captains' to command in the Restoration navy: on 18 May Hugh Hide, a kinsman to the lord chancellor, took command of the *Adventure*, and on the 25th William Finch, third son to the earl of Winchilsea, took command of the *Forrester*.[75] The direction in which the navy of the later Stuarts was to go was already clearly signposted, just a year after Charles II's return.

[71] Gillingwater, *Historical Account of the Ancient Town of Lowestoft*, 159 n.; Tanner, *Catalogue*, i. 412; Adm. 2/1734, fo. 69ᵛ; Adm. 2/1750, pp. 68–9; Adm. 1/3558, pp. 206–7.
[72] Coventry MS 101, fos. 241–2; Penn, *Memorials*, ii. 267; Adm. 106/6, fo. 337.
[73] *Pepys's Diary*, iii. 122; iv. 169–70, 196; Capp, *Cromwell's Navy*, 379–80. As Dr Capp rightly points out, the Cavaliers were equally scathing about the interregnum officers, though on ideological rather than professional grounds.
[74] Bod. Lib., Carte MS 73, fo. 512.
[75] Hyde: Coventry MS 98, fos. 52–3, Finch: Charnock, *Biographia Navalis*, i. 56. Commission dates are given in Coventry MS 98, fos. 84–5.

8

THE SECOND DUTCH WAR
AND ITS AFTERMATH

AFTER his resignation as secretary to the duke of York, Sir William Coventry summarized the causes of the war of 1664–7 with his usual perception: 'the truth is the Dutch warre arose by strange accidentall things . . . from severall parts & parties without any intent to helpe each other.'[1] The 'parts & parties' included those rising ministers and courtiers opposed to the ministry of the earl of Clarendon, and mercantile interests, particularly those involved in the Guinea trade, which had seen almost constant conflict with the Dutch since the Restoration.[2] These groups found support among the highest echelons of the navy. Those who had fought in the war of 1652–4 confidently believed that they could repeat their earlier successes in order to inflict a final, crushing defeat on the Dutch. The duke of Albemarle's contempt for the old enemy was almost a byword, and this attitude was shared by other veteran sea-officers: Sir John Lawson believed that 'if God says amen to it, the Dutch are not able to deale with our master the King of England'.[3] The belligerence of his subordinates reinforced the lord high admiral's own inclinations. James, 'having bin bred in armes was willing to have an occasion to show his Courage in the Sea as much as at land . . . this vigour of his R[oyal] H[ighness] broke the measure of those Ministers who would otherwise have preserved the peace at any rate'.[4] The duke's attitude was representative of more widespread feelings among the Cavalier officers who had entered the service after 1660. A Dutch war would provide many more opportunities for employment than had been available in the years of retrenchment since the Restoration, and employment in turn would create opportunities for building reputations and fortunes. The Cavalier

---

[1] Coventry MS 102, fo. 5.
[2] Ibid., fos. 4–5; Clarendon, *Life*, ii. 231–8; C. Wilson, *Profit and Power* (1957), ch. 7 *passim*.
[3] Coventry MS 102, fo. 7; PRO, PRO 31/3/113, fo. 336; *The Diary of John Evelyn*, ed. E. S. De Beer (Oxford, 1955), iii. 440; T. Gumble, *The Life of General Monck, Duke of Albemarle* (1671), 434; E. M. Thompson (ed.), *Correspondence of the Family of Hatton* (Camden Society, NS 22; 1878), i. 40; *CSP Ven.*, 1664–6, 105.
[4] Coventry MS 102, fo. 7. Cf. Clarendon, *Life*, ii. 238; Hutton, *The Restoration*, 215.

officers, like their lord high admiral, were largely untried in battle and therefore suffered in comparison with the experienced survivors of the republic's wars.[5] Equally important for many was the possibility of exploiting a war for private profit: Pepys's friend, the shipbuilder Sir Anthony Deane, believed that the throng of solicitants for naval office sought only to enrich themselves by taking prizes, rather than seeking to fight the nation's enemies.[6] The navy therefore suffered from the same over-confidence and arrogance which also manifested itself in the courtiers' optimistic assumptions that the king would be able to save a substantial amount out of the £2,500,000 voted by Parliament for the running of the war, and that an even greater profit would accrue from Dutch prize-ships.[7]

By the autumn of 1664 preparations for war were well advanced. Fleets were being made ready for service under the duke of York in home waters and under Prince Rupert at Guinea, though in the event the latter never set out.[8] From mid-October onwards an informal committee of senior commanders and administrators met to advise the duke: regular attenders were Albemarle, Sandwich, the navy treasurer Sir George Carteret, and Lawson, with other senior sea-officers attending on an *ad hoc* basis. The committee's posture was whole-heartedly belligerent and relied heavily on the experience of the previous Dutch war, with a general abandoning of commitments overseas in favour of a main fleet strategy. A fleet of one hundred ships, manned by up to 30,000 men, with thirty more vessels on convoy and coastguard duties, was approved for the 1665 campaign.[9] With his lack of experience of naval warfare, it was natural for James to rely heavily on advice from his subordinates, and Lawson and Sir William Penn came to be regarded as his chief advisers.[10]

The choice of captains for the fleet crystallized the arguments which had been aired since 1660 over the relative merits of Cavalier and interregnum officers. Strong pressure was exerted at court to give

[5] Coventry MS 99, fos. 185, 234.

[6] Rawl. MS A. 195, fo. 68.

[7] Pepys MS 2581, p. 213. Cf. P. Seaward, 'The House of Commons Committee of Trade and the Origins of the Second Anglo-Dutch War', *Historical Journal*, 30 (1987), 437–52.

[8] Tedder, *Navy of the Restoration*, 102–12.

[9] Coventry MS 95, fos. 60–1, 65, 75–6, 78–9. Cf. *Pepys's Diary*, vi. 11. A similar stance was adopted by the privy council's committee of the navy, which was to take charge of naval affairs in London while James was at sea (BL, Egerton MS 2543, pp. 145–53).

[10] Clarendon, *Life*, ii. 354–5; *Pepys's Diary*, v. 293.

commands to royalists of high social rank, notably the duke of Buckingham and Lord Berkeley of Stratton, on the grounds that such men were of known courage, that the fleets of Elizabeth and James I had been officered by the gentry and aristocracy, and above all on the grounds of domestic security, namely that the gentry had more obligations to the Crown than those of lower birth, whose loyalty might be bought by the disaffected.[11] The advocates of the appointment of aristocrats proposed that second captains, who would be experienced seamen, should be placed under the nominal commanders. The king supported the project, at least as far as Buckingham's appointment was concerned, but when the duke attempted to get a command and a place in the fleet's councils in 1665, James frustrated his designs.[12] Coventry vigorously opposed the whole scheme, believing that it would discourage the professional seamen, though even he had reservations about the loyalty of sea-officers of low social rank.[13] In the event, the strategy finally adopted involved the recall of many officers who had served the republic, but had not been employed since the Restoration. James asked Penn to present a list of captains who could be invited to serve, and Penn responded by basing his list on ability alone, regardless of political and religious attitudes.[14] However, although the recalled officers were believed to include Baptists and Presbyterians, on the whole the administration was suspicious of promoting 'fanaticks' and about ten captains were left on shore because of doubts about their conformity.[15] Coventry hoped that any thoughts of disloyalty among those recalled would be suppressed by the chance of making money out of the war, while the king observed with his usual wit that the recalled officers had all been cured of the plague, and would be less susceptible to infection than others.[16]

The fleet assembled in the Gunfleet anchorage off Harwich at the beginning of April 1665. James commanded the red squadron with Penn as his flag-captain, Lawson as his vice-admiral, and Sir William

[11] Pepys MS 2581, pp. 213–18.
[12] Ibid. 214; SP 29/117, fo. 96; SP 29/118, fo. 95; SP 84/175, fo. 229; Clarendon, *Life*, ii. 356–7; *Sandwich Journal*, 179; P. Seaward, *The Cavalier Parliament and the Reconstruction of the Old Regime, 1661–7* (Cambridge, 1989), 247.
[13] Pepys MS 2581, pp. 213–18; Coventry MS 99, fo. 185; BL, Addit. MS 32094, fos. 43–5.
[14] Penn, *Memorials*, ii. 293; Capp, *Cromwell's Navy*, 387. Albemarle later castigated Penn for bringing 'all these roguish fanatic captains into the fleet': *Pepys's Diary*, vi. 291.
[15] SP 84/171, fos. 186–7; SP 29/122, fo. 93; Rawl. MS A. 174, fos. 478, 489; Penn, *Memorials*, ii. 293; Capp, *Cromwell's Navy*, 387–8.
[16] SP 29/104, fo. 104; PRO, PRO 31/3/113, fo. 384. Cf. *CSP Ven.*, 1664–6, 61.

Berkeley, 26-year-old brother of the king's favourite, the earl of Falmouth, as his rear-admiral. Prince Rupert commanded the white, with the interregnum officers Christopher Myngs and Robert Sansum as his vice- and rear-admirals, while Sandwich commanded the blue, with Sir George Ayscue and Thomas Teddeman, fellow veterans of the republic's fleets, in the subordinate flag posts. The dominance of the interregnum officers was also reflected in the appointments to lesser posts. Of 107 captains in the main fleet, forty-seven were interregnum officers (twenty-seven of whom had been recalled to service in 1664–5); twenty-eight were tarpaulins, ten Cavaliers, and thirteen gentlemen. In the great ships, the first- to third-rates, the interregnum officers and tarpaulins held twenty-one commands, the Cavaliers and gentlemen only seven. The fleet therefore depended above all on the experience of those who had served the republic.[17]

At a lower level, the fleet depended on impressment to provide its personnel. Pressing began, initially on a small scale, in June 1664, but by the autumn the effort both to the press and to attract volunteers was running into serious difficulties. There were too few men, and many of those who came in were too young, too old, or too sick.[18] Desertion was endemic, with many seamen taking their press and conduct money but failing to report to their ships; by February 1665 the ships at Portsmouth were said to be each between 20 and 120 men short, and desperate captains resorted to stealing each other's men.[19] Even senior admirals, including the lord high admiral himself, contemplated over-riding the protections from the press which had been granted to the collier fleets.[20] Several reasons were put forward for the seamen's reluctance to serve. At first it was believed that men were unwilling to go to Guinea, but might be more prepared to fight in home waters. Other explanations put forward for the failure of the press included the corruption of the press-officers, clandestine attempts by merchant-ship owners and mayors of coastal towns to conceal their best men, and

---

[17] Based on the fleet list in *Sandwich Journal*, 174–7. Captains of detached units, such as those in the Mediterranean and the West Indies, have been omitted from this analysis; I have not been able to ascertain the career patterns of the other nine captains, all of whom commanded small ships. Cf. Appendix I, below; Capp, *Cromwell's Navy*, 383–4.

[18] *CSPD*, 1663–4, 607–8, 614; *CSPD*, 1664–5, 15, 29, 34–6, 38, 62, 66, 92, 99, 100, 103, 105–6, 236, 240, 273, 435.

[19] Ibid., 1664–5, 18, 62, 67, 70–1, 86, 109, 192, 269; *Barlow's Journal*, i. 95; Hutton, *Restoration*, 221.

[20] KAO, U. 269/C. 320, unfol., James to Falmouth, 22 May 1665; *Sandwich Journal*, 212–13, 222–3.

the level of merchant-ship wages.[21] Even so, reports reaching London from the coastal areas indicated that resistance to the service was by no means uniform: although west country ports reported the greatest reluctance to serve, the most optimistic reports of successful recruitment, and (in some cases) of genuine enthusiasm for the war, came from East Anglia and the north-east, the areas closest to the theatre of war, with local men like Lawson, Myngs, and other, older officers finding little difficulty in attracting men.[22]

The administration's reaction to the manning problem fell between the two stools of coercion and leniency. The need to encourage the seamen was fully recognized, and proclamations were issued promising bounties to volunteers; again, however, the consideration of domestic security was paramount, with James stressing the importance of keeping the seamen in a good temper by providing them with advances of pay, 'least their necessities prompt them to such tumultuary courses as ill people may encourage and take advantage of'.[23] The admirals, particularly the popular Myngs and (to a lesser extent) Sandwich, were criticized for failing to hang deserters from the very beginning, and this lack of a convincing deterrent was blamed by some for much of the endemic desertion.[24] Whatever the causes, the consequences of the disorderly recruitment effort of 1664–5 were clear enough. The fleet suffered from a dangerous shortage of men, while the methods of pressing and the mishandling of the whole effort created mistrust and resentment of the naval administration among the seamen; these feelings were to be reinforced as the war progressed.[25] By the late summer of 1665 it was clear that the administration's attempts to keep the men placated had failed. Mutinies began in the dockyards in June and quickly spread to the fleet, where the situation was exacerbated by the poor quality and quantity of victuals. Unpaid seamen starved in the streets or resorted to violence, and Pepys and his fellow administrators, though sympathetic to the men's needs, could do little.[26]

---

[21] SP 84/173, fo. 160ᵛ; *CSPD*, 1664–5, pp. 40, 45, 108, 123, 191, 240, 265.
[22] *CSPD*, 1664–5, 36, 44, 217, 243–4, 253; Pepys MS 2581, p. 198; Adm. 106/10, fo. 514.
[23] Adm. 106/10, fo. 301; Coventry MS 95, fo. 65; SP 29/103, fo. 145.
[24] Coventry MS 102, fo. 13; SP 29/104; fo. 104; SP 29/112, fo. 25.
[25] Adm. 106/11, fo. 68; Adm. 106/12, fo. 146; Pepys MS 2581, pp. 195–200; *Barlow's Journal*, i. 146.
[26] *CSPD*, 1664–5, 443, 454, 460, 462–5, 532, 569; *CSPD*, 1665–6, 3, 47, 61; *Pepys's Diary*, vi. 255, 284, 288; NMM, LBK/8, p. 279; Pepys, *Further Correspondence*, 70; Tedder, *Navy of the Restoration*, 112–15, 146–9.

The practice of turning men over from ship to ship contributed to the discontent. As in later years, this was a convenient device for avoiding the need to pay the seamen, but in the autumn of 1665 an equally important reason for turning over crews was fear of the plague. It was believed that if seamen were discharged they would go to London for their pay, or their wives would go down to them, and the likely result would be the spread of infection to the remarkably plague-free fleet.[27] The seamen saw turning-over simply as an attempt to deprive them of their pay and they reacted to it predictably, petitioning the authorities for their wages or, if all else failed, deserting.[28] The administration's other methods of retaining seamen for the next campaign in 1666 continued to display a blend of encouragement and coercion. Attempts were made to introduce more stringent checks on desertion, but even those who went absent without leave over the winter were promised their pay if they returned to their ships by 20 February 1666. The much-resented expedient of paying men only part of their wages was also used, with the balance held back as an incentive to further service and a deterrent to desertion.[29] If ever there had been a honeymoon period between the restored monarchy and its seamen, it ended abruptly and irrevocably in 1665.

Among the sea-officers, too, the 1665 campaign was a turning-point, for their surprisingly poor performance exploded the myth of the expertise and omnicompetence of the interregnum officers. A foretaste came even before the main fleets engaged, when Captain Edward Nixon, who had fought in the first Dutch war and whose courage had been highly commended by Albemarle himself, was sentenced to death for cowardice.[30] One lieutenant of Cavalier antecedents taunted his captain for having been a rebel, but the duke of York acted quickly to prevent the recounting of past differences.[31] The main engagement of the campaign was the battle of Lowestoft on 3 June, a convincing English victory marred only by a failure to pursue and destroy the retreating Dutch fleet. Even so, the conduct of some of the captains was severely censured and gave rise to the rumour that many of the old

[27] *CSPD*, 1665–6, 23, 24, 29, 117; NMM, LBK/8, p. 284; BL, Addit. MS 18986, fo. 379; Tedder, *Navy of the Restoration*, 144–6.

[28] Pepys MS 2581, p. 199; Adm. 106/11, fos. 146, 153; *CSPD*, 1665–6, 253, 257.

[29] Ibid. 195; Adm. 106/11, fo. 362; *Barlow's Journal*, i. 115.

[30] BL, Addit. MS 32094, fo. 56; Rawl. MS A. 174, fo. 460; Bod. Lib., Carte MS 73, fo. 410; Capp, *Cromwell's Navy*, 385.

[31] *Sandwich Journal*, 173.

republican officers had sought an opportunity to switch to the enemy's side in the middle of the action.[32] The true cause of the accusations of misconduct, however, was the beginning of the factional feuding which was to characterize every campaign fought by the English navy during the second and third Dutch wars,[33] feuds which embraced both disputes over tactics and personal jealousies (particularly over the question of who had the duke of York's ear), and which at once reflected and helped to shape factions ashore. At the very beginning of the 1665 campaign, Coventry had warned that court factions would seek to denigrate the duke's performance as admiral in an attempt to undermine his and Clarendon's influence; James and Coventry sought to insure themselves against censure by requesting detailed and explicit instructions, believing that certain (unnamed) ministers were 'unwilling to burne their fingers' and were trying to 'wash their handes of the business' by sending very vague orders to the duke.[34] Others in the fleet and at court sought to denigrate the performance of the earl of Sandwich because of his past ties to Cromwell, for his elevation above what some saw as his proper station, and for his close links with Clarendon.[35] Sandwich, in turn, was wary of Penn's influence in the fleet and on James: at the important council of war on 25 April, for example, James had shown himself more willing to listen to Penn and Lawson than to Sandwich.[36] Before his untimely death in the battle of Lowestoft, the earl of Falmouth, who was serving as a volunteer on the flagship, attempted to undermine Coventry's 'soveranity in the bisnes of the sea' and sought to advance Lawson, his brother's patron.[37] This advance was to be made largely at the expense of Penn, whom Falmouth condemned as 'a fellow of no sense' and 'a sot', though James later reported that just before his death Falmouth had retracted his censure after witnessing Penn's performance in the battle.[38] Penn had also been the chief advocate of the adoption of the line-of-battle for the 1665 campaign, and was therefore the target for those who

---

[32] SP 29/123, fo. 41; SP 29/124, fo. 61; PRO, PRO 31/3/113, fo. 54; SP 84/176, fo. 191; *Pepys's Diary*, vi. 129; *CSP Ven.*, 1664–6, 151; Capp, *Cromwell's Navy*, 388–9.

[33] But not the first, nor the 1650s as a whole: Capp, *Cromwell's Navy*, 190–4.

[34] BL., Addit. MS 32094, fo. 46. Coventry was probably referring to the secretary of state, Sir Henry Bennet, with whom he disagreed on war policy; for the relevant court factions in this period, see Seaward, *Cavalier Parliament*, 85–6, 233–4.

[35] Clarendon, *Life*, ii. 465–7, 475; *Pepys's Diary*, ii. 170; iii. 121–3; iv. 115.

[36] BL., Addit. MS 32094, fo. 46; Coventry MS 105, fo. 26; *Pepys's Diary*, vi. 50, 127, 134–5.

[37] Bod. Lib., Carte MS 215, fo. 187.

[38] Clarendon, *Life*, ii. 385–6; SP 29/123, fo. 41.

believed that such a tactic was somehow 'un-English'.[39] Sir William
Berkeley, whose influence at court declined after Falmouth's death,
was one of those singled out for poor conduct at Lowestoft, as was
Jonas Poole, Penn's brother-in-law. The first captain to be 'turned
out' after the battle was Henry Hide, a relative of Clarendon.[40] Other
'turned-out' sea-officers tried to redeem their courage and conduct by
going to sea again as volunteers or by seeking courts-martial to clear
their names.[41] Apart from the complex intrigues connected with court
politics or tactics, the senior officers were also engaged in a struggle
for preferment. The death of Robert Sansum in the battle created a
vacant flag post, and Sir Robert Holmes (the leading naval client of
Prince Rupert) sought the place. Influenced, perhaps, by Coventry's
dislike of Holmes, James gave the post to his own flag-captain, John
Harman, and Holmes resigned his commission in disgust.[42]

   After Lowestoft James gave in to pressure from the court, alarmed at
the danger to the life of the heir to the throne, and laid down his
command of the fleet. The two candidates to succeed him were Rupert
and Sandwich, with the latter having the advantages of seniority and
the duke's confidence.[43] The king favoured the idea of a joint command, but Rupert objected and the scheme had to be dropped in
favour of Sandwich commanding alone for the rest of the 1665
campaign.[44] Sandwich's position was undermined by a combination of
bad luck, bad tactics by his subordinates, and, ultimately, by an
astonishing error of judgement on his own part. The attempt to
intercept the Dutch East India fleet in the neutral harbour of Bergen
turned into a fiasco, with the English squadron pounded by Dutch and
Danish guns, and English seamen plundering Norwegian churches
for vestments and chalices.[45] The lack of success of Sir Thomas
Teddeman, the commander at Bergen and an interregnum officer

[39] *Pepys's Diary*, vii. 194–5; Bod. Lib., Carte MS 34, fo. 516. Cf. L. Streete, *An Uncommon Sailor: A Portrait of Admiral Sir William Penn* (Bourne End, 1986), 113–18—the only modern biography, but of limited value due to the absence of scholarly apparatus and understanding of naval warfare.

[40] *Pepys's Diary*, vi. 129; SP 29/124, fo. 135.

[41] Adm. 106/13, fo. 157; Adm. 2/1, fo. 5. Cf. BL, Addit. MS 14286, fos. 13–15; Powell and Timings, *Rupert and Monck*, 38, 199–200.

[42] SP 29/124, fo. 47; SP 84/176, fo. 191; Ollard, *Man of War*, 136.

[43] Clarendon, *Life*, ii. 399–400; *Pepys's Diary*, vi. 134–5. Sandwich held the honor-ific post of vice-admiral of England (effectively deputy to the lord high admiral).

[44] Coventry MS 105, fo. 25ᵛ; *Sandwich Journal*, 236; *CSPD*, 1664–5, 460–1; Clarendon, *Life*, ii. 401–3. Clarendon's account is distorted by personal prejudice, and is wholly inaccurate on Rupert's response to the proposal.

[45] Coventry MS 95, fos. 99–104, 107–57; Tedder, *Navy of the Restoration*, 126–39.

closely tied to Sandwich, was the cause of bitter comment among the Cavaliers at court, notably the earl of Peterborough: 'if a lord of the Kings party should have had noe better a success than this old sea man, or in deed should have taken his measures noe otherwise what a clamor we should have had; infine if I had commanded there betwixt you & I, I could not have done wors.'[46] Sandwich's choice of officers was also censured, with Coventry in particular objecting to some of the earl's promotions.[47] In September Sandwich's fleet captured two fully laden Dutch East Indiamen, and on their return to port the earl (acting largely on Penn's advice) ordered an immediate distribution of the plunder, without waiting for authorization from the king.[48] His irregular conduct was passed over by Charles, but not by Albemarle and other senior officers, notably Sir Christopher Myngs and Sir George Ayscue, who openly attacked Sandwich's actions. Myngs and Ayscue, as flag-officers, resented Sandwich's preferential treatment of lesser captains in the distribution of the prize-goods, but also saw an opportunity for their own advancement. Sandwich, his flag-captain Sir Roger Cuttance, and Penn were all heavily implicated in the prize-goods scandal, and with Teddeman in eclipse after Bergen it was possible that several leading rivals for flag-posts in the 1666 campaign might be eliminated from contention. Pressure from Albemarle, the flagmen, the court, and public opinion increased throughout October and November 1665, and culminated in Sandwich being sent into temporary exile as ambassador to Spain, while neither Cuttance nor Penn held posts during the 1666 campaign.[49]

The attack on Sandwich was accompanied by a more general inquest on those sea-officers whose conduct in the 1665 campaign had been questioned. A list was prepared, possibly by Albemarle, and sent to the court at Oxford. Of the eleven commanders named, eight had served in the interregnum fleets, one (John Ayliffe) had risen from a gunner's post, and another (Hugh Hide) was related to Clarendon.[50]

[46] SP 29/129, fo. 59.

[47] Coventry MS 95, fo. 157; Rawl. MS A. 468, fo. 6ᵛ.

[48] Tedder, *Navy of the Restoration*, 140; Bryant, *Samuel Pepys: The Man in the Making*, 265–74; Harris, *Life of Edward Mountagu*, ii. 3–21.

[49] *Evelyn's Diary*, iii. 423–5; Bod. Lib., Carte MS 215, fo. 214; *Pepys's Diary*, vi. 265–6; *Shorthand Letters from Samuel Pepys's Official Correspondence, 1662–79*, ed. E. Chappell (Cambridge, 1933), 62–4, 69; Harris, *Life of Edward Mountagu*, ii. 3–21.

[50] NMM, LBK/47, unfol.; Coventry MS 101, fo. 235ᵛ. The other officer, Richard Poole, had served in the 1630s and 1640s, but his later career and connections are obscure.

The list seems to have been compiled on a fairly impartial basis, for it included men who had risen under the patronage of Lawson, Sandwich, and Albemarle himself. However, whether it was intended as a deterrent to faction or to misconduct, it had markedly little effect. Seven of the named officers continued in uninterrupted service, two others regained commission posts in the 1666 campaign, Ayliffe went back to being a gunner, and only Hide never saw naval service again.[51] The failure to remove sea-officers despite the many accusations of misconduct was to be a conspicuous feature of the war as a whole. One of the officers on the 1665 list immediately went to the court at Oxford to learn the reasons for his dismissal, and subsequently gained a new command in the 1666 fleet. Influence at court could excuse even blatant shortcomings,[52] and the lord high admiral himself always took a lenient view of reported misconduct: James liked to believe that lack of success in battle 'did not arise from Want of Ability or Good Will, but from some other Fault or Misfortune'.[53] Above all, in naval battles which involved several hundred ships fighting each other over a sea area of perhaps dozens of square miles, amid smoke, noise, and confusion, it was almost impossible to obtain objective accounts of the behaviour of individual ships and captains. There were at once too many witnesses and too many alibis.

Albemarle's campaign against Sandwich was one manifestation of his new position as the leader of Cavalier and court opinion against the dominance of interregnum officers in the fleet. The duke railed against his erstwhile friend Penn and the sea-officers who had been recalled to service under Penn's auspices, and advocated the rapid promotion of gentlemen volunteers to commands in an attempt to diminish the crown's dependence on 'tarpaulins'.[54] This, in turn, could also be interpreted as an attack on Sandwich, who was associated with the promotion of interregnum officers and tarpaulins; their continued domination of appointments in the fleet, and Sandwich's role as their patron, had been a cause of Cavalier resentment since soon after the Restoration.[55]

Albemarle's position was an ambiguous one, however. His opposi-

---

[51] Adm. 10/15, pp. 6, 61, 62–3, 64, 83, 97, 102, 106, 111, 125; Adm. 2/1746, fo. 124ᵛ.

[52] SP 29/144, fo. 30; Coventry MS 98, fo. 189.

[53] Pepys MS 1490, p. 29.

[54] Bod. Lib., Carte MS 34, fo. 488; *Pepys's Diary*, vi. 291.

[55] BL, Egerton MS 3383, fo. 117; *Pepys's Diary*, ii. 216–17; iii. 121–3.

tion to interregnum officers stopped short of his own clients, and his private lists of officers in the fleet noted and praised those who were 'seamen'.[56] In fact, the duke's remarks were one element in the intrigues which surrounded the appointment of the commander-in-chief for the 1666 campaign. Albemarle may have sought a more active role in the fleet because of the lack of involvement in the war of the small standing army which he commanded, or simply because of jealousy: the duke may have believed that he could gain the decisive victory over the Dutch which had evaded his old subordinates Sandwich, Penn, and Lawson. He remained supremely confident of victory, even advocating an immediate declaration of war on both France and Denmark in the belief that a delay of even a few weeks would lose many valuable prizes.[57] Albemarle was determined to keep Penn out of the chief command, and with James and Sandwich also out of contention his chances of commanding the fleet appeared to be good. However, Charles decided early in December on a joint command by Rupert and Albemarle, a measure which may have been designed in part to reconcile opposing factions at court.[58] Clarendon approached the two men and put the proposal for them to go to sea together; characteristically, Rupert was reluctant and wanted to go alone, but Albemarle accepted the suggestion placidly enough and, indeed, he was soon said to be 'so gay & good Humourd as if hee weer all ready returned from victory'.[59] Against this backdrop, the English fleet prepared for its next campaign.

Rupert and Albemarle were commissioned as joint admirals on 22 February 1666, with powers to remove and appoint officers as they saw fit.[60] The appointments to the other posts in the fleet reflected the influence of the new admirals: in their own division of the red squadron, the first- and second-rates were commanded by John Kempthorne and Edward Spragge, respectively the son and nephew of officers who had served Rupert in the civil war,[61] the vice-admiral of the red was Myngs, 'the great favourite of the Prince', while the

---

[56] NMM, LBK/47, unfol.
[57] Bod. Lib., Carte MS 34, fo. 553.
[58] Ibid., fos. 488, 498, 506, 512, 516; Carte MS 46, fo. 227ᵛ; *Evelyn's Diary*, iii. 424–5; Gumble, *Life of Monck*, 424; *Pepys's Diary*, vi. 291.
[59] Clarendon, *Life*, ii. 482–8; Bod. Lib., Carte MS 215, fo. 248.
[60] Powell and Timings, *Rupert and Monck*, 15–16.
[61] Kempthorne, 'Sir John Kempthorne and his Sons', 291; *Hist. Parl.*, iii. 468–9.

rear-admiral, the aged Sir Joseph Jordan, had been Albemarle's
flag-captain in 1653.[62] The admiral of the white, Sir Thomas Allin,
had served in Rupert's squadron in the 1650s; his vice-admiral, Sir
Jeremy Smith, was an old friend and colleague of Albemarle, while Sir
Thomas Teddeman had weathered his misfortunes of the previous
year to serve as rear-admiral.[63] Sir George Ayscue, Sir William
Berkeley, and Sir John Harman occupied the three flag-posts in the
blue. The other commissioned officers looked forward to the new
campaign enthusiastically, and a 'multitude' sought posts in the fleet.[64]
Several of the captains who had served under Rupert in 1665 invited
him to dinner and declared their eagerness for the new campaign,
while the younger Cavalier and gentlemen officers were keen (at
times, too keen) to engage the enemy in an attempt to win a decisive
victory. Some, notably Berkeley, were determined to remove the
queries against their conduct which remained from the previous
year.[65] Despite the confidence of the sea-officers, the fleet encountered the same manning problems as the year before, with complaints
of incapable men being pressed, desertion, and reluctance on the parts
of merchant ship owners and civil authorities.[66]

The campaign of 1666 began with a saga of inaccurate intelligence,
strategic errors, and unfortunate timing, which produced the division
of the fleet into two squadrons under Rupert and Albemarle, the
former sailing west to meet an imaginary French threat and the latter
engaging the Dutch under de Ruyter with only two-thirds of the
enemy admiral's numbers.[67] The 'four days' battle' which followed
was in effect a fighting retreat in which the English fleet was badly
mauled, and the defeat produced the inevitable crescendo of recrimi-
nation. The account sent to the secretary of state, Arlington, by his

[62] *Pepys's Diary*, vii. 180; R. C. Anderson, *List of English Naval Captains, 1642–60*
(1964), 14, 16.
[63] *DNB*, s.nn. 'Allin, Thomas', 'Smith, Jeremy'.
[64] Adm. 2/1745, fo. 138ᵛ.
[65] *CSPD*, 1665–6, 252; Coventry MS 95, fo. 409; BL, Sloane MS 1745, p. 2; Powell
and Timings, *Rupert and Monck*, 213. Berkeley met his death by sailing too far into the
enemy fleet: ibid. 238.
[66] Ibid. 21, 51–4, 64–5, 88–9, 104; *CSPD*, 1665–6, 217, 227, 335; BL, Sloane MS
1745, p. 4.
[67] R. J. A. Shelley, 'The Division of the English Fleet in 1666', *MM* 25 (1939),
178–96; J. R. Powell, 'Talbot and the Division of the Fleet in 1666', *MM* 53 (1967),
136; Powell and Timings, *Rupert and Monck*, 185–9; H. A. van Foreest and R. E. J.
Weber, *De vierdaagse zeeslag, 11–14 Juni 1666* (The Hague, 1984), *passim*. Most of the
relevant documents are published in Powell and Timings, *Rupert and Monck*, 196–260.

protégé Thomas Clifford, who had served on the flagship *Royal Charles*, noted the common seamen's anger at the division of the fleet and the sending away of Rupert; one of the more articulate seamen, Edward Barlow, blamed the division on 'English papists and traitors . . . intending to sell the Mother of all Lands as a New Year's gift . . . for the love of the Devil and the Pope'.[68] In the immediate aftermath of the battle, though, most of the blame was attached to the performance of the sea-officers. 'If the King do not cause some of the captains to be hanged, he will never be well served,' Clifford observed, while Barlow believed that 'we had some cowardly commanders . . . who were more fit to go commanders in some dung-boats than in a good King's ship'.[69] Albemarle was livid, proclaiming loudly that only a score of captains had supported him in the fight and that he wanted many of the others removed, though this analysis conveniently ignored the widespread criticism among the captains of his decision to give battle with inferior numbers.[70] In the event, only five captains were removed: John Aylett, Henry Cuttance, Thomas Ewens, Henry Teddeman, and Jean-Baptiste du Tiel. Cuttance and Teddeman were, respectively, the son and brother of Sandwich's two closest naval colleagues, while Aylett and du Tiel had close ties to the duke of York. James and Coventry naturally regarded the dismissals as biased, particularly when Albemarle singled out his own and Rupert's nominees for praise for their parts in the battle, and in their place the duke of York and his secretary accused some of the joint admirals' appointees of being even worse than those removed.[71]

The subordinate sea-officers had their own battles to fight, and throughout the summer and autumn of 1666 Pepys recorded the antagonisms and jealousies which wracked the fleet. The older officers were said to be offended at the domination of the joint admirals by their clients, Holmes and Spragge in Rupert's case, Smith in Albemarle's, while indiscipline, swearing, and drinking were said to be rampant in the fleet. Young, arrogant gentlemen were reportedly being promoted at the expense of the experienced interregnum officers, and threatening to drive the tarpaulins out of the fleet.[72] However,

[68] Ibid. 253; *Barlow's Journal*, i. 116.

[69] Powell and Timings, *Rupert and Monck*, 256; *Barlow's Journal*, i. 123.

[70] Powell and Timings, *Rupert and Monck*, 212–13, 257, 259; *Pepys's Diary*, vii. 154, 158, 161, 194.

[71] Coventry MS 98, fo. 189; Coventry MS 101, fo. 235ᵛ; Powell and Timings, *Rupert and Monck*, 250; *Pepys's Diary*, vii. 163, 174, 180, 221–2; viii. 147; ix. 39–40.

[72] Ibid. vii. 158, 177, 194, 212, 221–2, 323, 332–3, 344, 345, 409.

Pepys's comments must be treated with some caution: his judgements on the supposedly chaotic situation in the fleet were seldom his own, and his informants were rarely detached, objective observers. He received little first-hand information from sources in the fleet itself. The few sea-officers to whom he spoke were the likes of Sir Thomas Teddeman, resentful of the influence of younger captains and of the dismissal of his brother; Sir William Penn, who had already been deprived of command by Albemarle's intrigues; and Captain Thomas Guy, who may have been aggrieved by his failure to obtain anything larger than a fourth-rate from the joint admirals.[73] Pepys's other sources of information were administrators who resented the joint admirals' and their subordinates' criticisms of their efforts. Sir William Coventry and Denis Gauden, the victualler of the navy, made vitriolic attacks on the state of the fleet, but they in turn were bearing the brunt of the admirals' criticisms for failing to send adequate provisions; Coventry was accused of sending accounts rather than supplies, and during August the admirals had to suspend operations because of the lack of victuals. Coventry also resented the ejection of his and James's appointees from commands.[74] Peter Pett, the resident commissioner of the navy at Chatham, and Thomas Middleton, his counterpart at Portsmouth, had been on the receiving end of the joint admirals' criticisms of the dockyards and the Navy Board.[75] The administrators' accusations concerning the appointment of gentlemen officers were largely unfounded. Most of the Cavalier and gentlemen officers in the fleet in 1666 had entered the navy under the auspices of Charles and James, not Rupert and Albemarle, and the impression given by Pepys and his colleagues of a wholesale promotion of gentlemen officers by the joint admirals is also misleading. Between 14 May and 21 September the joint admirals issued a total of eighty-four captains' commissions. Of these, fourteen went to interregnum officers, six to Cavaliers, nineteen to gentlemen, and thirty-six to tarpaulins.[76] Commissions to the four highest rates were divided almost equally

---

[73] Ibid. vii. 158, 163, 194, 344, 345. Guy was later closely identified with the interest of Pepys and the duke of York: Rawl. MS A. 174, fo. 191.

[74] *Pepys's Diary*, vii. 163, 174, 180, 221–2, 332–3, 351, 409; Rawl. MS A. 174, fos. 209–33; Coventry MS 95, fos. 241–63, 387; BL, Addit. MS 70100, fos. 341–3. Cf. Powell and Timings, *Rupert and Monck*, 137–8, 142–3 *et passim*.

[75] *Pepys's Diary*, vii. 186, 212, 311–13, 332–4; *CJ*, ix. 11–14; SP 29/170, fos. 70, 71; SP 29/171, fo. 156.

[76] Powell and Timings, *Rupert and Monck*, 179–81. No information has come to light on the other nine officers.

between the four groups. The relative positions of the old and new officers had certainly altered in favour of the younger 'gentlemen' since the gathering of the fleet for the 1665 campaign, but not to an extent which would justify the exaggerated claims of Pepys and his associates.

Nevertheless, there were considerable problems in the fleet in the 1666 campaign. After the engagement with the Dutch on St James's Day, Sir Robert Holmes publicly accused Sir Jeremy Smith of cowardice, and the bitter argument between the two men dragged on into the autumn and well beyond, despite Albemarle's attempts to exonerate Smith.[77] Sir Thomas Allin was antagonized by the dominance of Holmes and Spragge, and, possibly, by the dismissal of his brother-in-law Riches Utber after the St James's Day fight.[78] The quarrels of the flag-officers contributed to what Rupert called 'a very strange remissnesse in the fleet, as to the strict obeying of orders',[79] and on the lower deck the 1666 campaign degenerated into chaos. Sailors beat up sentries posted to keep them on their ships and leapt overboard to desert, despite having arrears of pay due to them.[80] Officers overlooked the 'licentiousnesse' of their men because of the constant likelihood of meeting the enemy, and because some of them sympathized with their men's claims. In September 1666, one lieutenant wrote

Certaine it is that they are in a sad & pitifull condition, & no small trouble it is unto us who are to command a company of mutinous unpayd men . . . I cannot butt wonder at this unreasonable and unpolitick course to disoblige the seamen who have behaved themselves so stoutly, & discontent the whole land, who have so largely disbursed for their pays.[81]

Several executions of deserters had a limited effect, but a chronic shortage of men continued to afflict the fleet throughout the campaign. Even when payment began, the men reacted violently to what they saw as its tardiness, and to the payment of only three months' wages to those on ships going out in the winter guard.[82] The decision to pay the

---

[77] *CSPD*, 1665–6, 596; *CSPD*, 1666–7, 1, 14–15, 40, 222, 231, 236; *Pepys's Diary*, vii. 339–40, 344, 348.

[78] Ibid. vii. 177, 332; *CSPD*, 1666–7, 2.

[79] BL, Addit. MS 12097, fo. 26. Cf. Capp, *Cromwell's Navy*, 386.

[80] Pepys MS 2581, p. 113. Cf. *CSPD*, 1665–6, 453–4, 455.

[81] BL, Sloane MS 1745, pp. 7–8. Cf. Pepys, *Further Correspondence*, 151–2; Hutton, *The Restoration*, 243–4.

[82] *CSPD*, 1665–6, 494, 500, 501, 506, 512–13, 536, 543; *CSPD*, 1666–7, 218, 248, 340, 351, 426; Adm. 2/1745, fo. 148ᵛ.

men gradually, rather than all at once, was not due entirely to lack of money: James ordered a gradual payment in October 1666 in the vain hope that it would be attended by less disorder than one large-scale payment.[83]

By September 1666 the navy's deficit totalled £930,496, while the estimate of wages and victuals alone for the projected 1667 campaign totalled over £1,700,000.[84] With Parliament refractory and the court hopeful of an early peace treaty, orders were issued during February 1667 to prepare a fleet which omitted the two highest rates, though even some third-rates were later ordered to stay in port.[85] However, the decision to set out commerce-raiding squadrons for a *guerre de course*, rather than a main fleet, could be justified on strategic grounds, as well as those of financial stringency: indeed, Sir John Lawson and Sir George Carteret had advocated such a policy earlier in the war.[86] Even so, the administration feared the reaction to its decision and elaborate cosmetic gestures were made 'to quiett the Seamen, Comfort the Exch[ange], bring down the price of Insurance & furnish matter for forraigne tr[ade]', while the true course of action was kept secret until well into March. The king himself went down to Chatham at the end of February to view the great ships, and a false rumour was circulated to the effect that Allin, Smith, and Spragge had gone to the Navy Board with orders to fit out the first- and second-rates.[87] The men of the fleet were amazed at the decision to lay it up. Lieutenant Thomas Browne, returning from a convoy to Cadiz, observed that

Wee came in with full expectation that wee should have found our fleet readie for this summers Action butt to the great greif of ourselves & all honest publick spirited souldiers & seamen, wee find all contrarie to our desires . . . I confesse as yet I understand not this counsell at land, butt I dare confidently say wee shall sadly repent of it. The Duch would never have given us this advantage . . . To treat for peace thus unprovided without a cessation of armes or Acts of hostilitie is not pleasing unto us but wee are readie to embrace a peace which should bee made with our swords in our hands.[88]

---

[83] Adm. 106/13, fos. 448–50; NMM, LBK/8, p. 407.

[84] BL, Addit. MS 9302, fo. 162.

[85] Adm. 106/14, fos. 337, 366. On the political, diplomatic, and administrative background to this decision, see Hutton, *The Restoration*, 243–4; Seaward, *Cavalier Parliament*, 304–5.

[86] Bod. Lib., Carte MS 35, fo. 356ᵛ.

[87] Ibid., fos. 323, 356ᵛ; Carte MS 36, fo. 244ᵛ; Carte MS. 47, fo. 476; Carte MS 215, fo. 341.

[88] BL, Sloane MS 1745, p. 17.

Edward Barlow fulminated against the treachery of those ministers who had advised the laying-up of the fleet.[89] For most of the seamen, however, material considerations were more important than questions of strategy or treachery. The discontent which had been barely held in check during the previous two years erupted in 1667, and a series of mutinies occurred. Seamen who had come to London for their pay used violence against officials, while others refused to take their ships to sea or deserted.[90] Some English prisoners of war had joined the Dutch in a desperate attempt to provide for their families, and Pepys sadly recorded the spectacle of Englishmen aboard Dutch ships as they attacked the laid-up English fleet in the Medway, shouting 'We did heretofore fight for tickets; now we fight for Dollers!'[91] It was an appropriately dismal end to a dismal naval war.

After the war had finally ended, a number of groups and interests in Parliament were prepared to attack the ministry of Clarendon in general, and the naval administration in particular. In the House of Commons, many members were outraged at the disasters of the war and at the mismanagement of what they regarded as a more than adequate supply, and their 'country' attitudes assisted the ambitions of a group of office-seeking politicians, many of them associated with the duke of Buckingham, who wished to overthrow Clarendon in order to further their own careers.[92] When Parliament met in October 1667, its first concern was the assault on Clarendon himself. Several ministers, including Coventry, had supported the dismissal of the lord chancellor in the hope that he would serve as a scapegoat, and the Commons did, indeed, attempt to blame him for the major naval miscarriages of the war.[93] However, it soon became clear that the inquest would not end by assigning all the blame to Clarendon, as the other members of the administration probably hoped.[94] A committee of miscarriages was set up on 17 October, supplementing the committee to study the accounts

[89] *Barlow's Journal*, i. 134–5, 148.

[90] Pepys, *Further Correspondence*, 163, 165; *Pepys's Diary*, viii. 28, 62–3, 251, 304; SP 29/198, fo. 3; SP 29/200, fo. 113; Bod. Lib., Carte MS 215, fo. 351.

[91] *Pepys's Diary*, viii. 267. The best account of the Medway affair is P. G. Rogers, *The Dutch in the Medway* (1970).

[92] C. Roberts, 'The Impeachment of the Earl of Clarendon', *Cambridge Historical Journal*, 13 (1957), 6–7; D. T. Witcombe, *Charles II and the Cavalier House of Commons 1663–74* (Manchester, 1966), chs. 6 and 7, *passim*; Hutton, *Restoration*, 270–84.

[93] *CJ*, ix. 15–16; Grey, *Debates*, i. 15, 35; Roberts, 'Impeachment', 5 *et passim*.

[94] BL, Egerton MS 2539, fo. 129.

of the navy, the ordnance, and the stores, which had been set up a year earlier.[95] On 22 October the new committee drew up fourteen heads of miscarriages, which included operational matters (including the failure to pursue the Dutch after the battle of Lowestoft, and the division of the fleet) and the administrative failures of the war (notably the payment of seamen by tickets, and the failure to set out a fleet in 1667).[96]

The committee and the whole House debated a number of the miscarriages between 19 and 25 October, and several sea-officers and others were examined. The bitter personal rivalries of the war surfaced once more, with officers attempting to exonerate themselves and settle old scores. Coventry attempted to absolve himself of blame for the division of the fleet by hinting that Spragge's inaccurate intelligence was responsible, and cast what were regarded as unseemly reflections on Albemarle's conduct in the Chatham disaster.[97] Holmes, who was becoming identified with the 'anti-Clarendonians' Buckingham, Arlington, and Sir Robert Howard,[98] blamed the failure to prosecute the victory at Lowestoft on Sir John Harman and Henry Brouncker (a confidant and senior member of the household of the duke of York, and a solicitant for a commissioner's place on the Navy Board), and obliquely denigrated James himself by suggesting that the Dutch would have been destroyed if Rupert had been allowed to continue the pursuit.[99] Brouncker 'modestly' excused his part in the shortening of sail after the battle, and for the time being the House accepted his explanation. Harman's close ties to the duke of York and his appointment to a flag post over Holmes's head in 1665 made him an obvious target, and, moreover, one who could not fight back—Harman had been at sea for some months as commander-in-chief of a squadron in the West Indies.[100] Coventry's target, Spragge, was in a less fortunate

[95] *CJ*, viii. 628; ix. 4.

[96] Rawl. MS A. 195, fo. 6.

[97] BL, Egerton MS 2539, fo. 129ᵛ; *CJ*, ix. 5–8; *The Diary of John Milward*, ed. C. Robbins (Cambridge, 1938), 91–4.

[98] Clarke, *Life of James the Second*, i. 445; *Evelyn's Diary*, iii. 528–9; A. Browning, *Thomas Osborne, Earl of Danby* (Glasgow, 1951), iii. 33–44.

[99] *Milward Diary*, 91–2.

[100] Bod. Lib., Carte MS 35, fos. 740, 779; BL, Egerton MS 2539, fo. 129. On the night after the battle, Brouncker had passed on orders (ostensibly from the duke of York) to Harman to shorten sail, thereby allowing the Dutch to outdistance the English fleet. The true origin of the order remains obscure: Clarendon suggested that his daughter, the duchess of York, had ordered Brouncker to guard the duke from danger: Clarendon, *Life*, ii. 396–9.

position. As well as being implicated in the division of the fleet, he had been widely blamed for the Medway débâcle, while his Irish background made him unpopular and led to rumours of papism. Rather than attempting directly to defend himself, he shrewdly turned the attack against his accuser by blaming Coventry for the inadequate manning of the fleet, and provided an alternative scapegoat for the Medway affair in the shape of the resident commissioner at Chatham, Peter Pett, who was already in the Tower for his part in the fiasco.[101]

For over a week, the House's attention was chiefly focused on the impeachment of Clarendon, but on 31 October a decisive turning-point in the examination of naval miscarriages took place when the House heard the narratives of Rupert and Albemarle on the events of 1666 and 1667. Rupert's account was partly a defence of his part in the division of the fleet, and partly a violent indictment of the naval administration's failure to provide properly for the fleet in 1666. He complained of the 'intolerable neglect' in supplying his ships, neglect which he attributed largely to Coventry, and of major shortcomings at the Navy Board and the dockyards, all contributing to 'the extraordinary prejudice of His Majesty's service in that whole summer'.[102] Albemarle's narrative, though it also mentioned 'the great negligence of the Commissioners of the Navy, in not providing for our supply', devoted much less attention to this topic. Albemarle had been *de facto* head of the naval administration in 1665, and had been responsible, therefore, for naval supplies and victuals for a large part of the war; not surprisingly, he was reluctant to emphasize a matter which eventually might have reflected badly on himself. Instead, the duke concentrated on the inadequate defences and poor preparations at Chatham, and again singled out Pett as the guilty man.[103] The House was delighted with the narratives. Rupert's, it was said, 'layes open many miscariages which some great ones will be called to account for', while it was 'like to goe very hard' with Pett.[104] Both Spragge and Albemarle might have blamed Pett to divert attention from their own roles at Chatham, but their versions of events struck a chord in the House of Commons. Pett was an ideal scapegoat, both for the government and the MPs: an official who had served the republic and had retained his

---

[101] *Pepys's Diary*, viii. 308; SP 29/206, fo. 43; BL, Egerton MS 2539, fo. 129; *Milward Diary*, 92–4.
[102] *CJ*, ix. 11–12. For Coventry's response, see BL, Addit. MS 32094, fos. 206–9.
[103] *CJ*, ix. 12–14.
[104] BL., Addit. MS 36916, fos. 11–14.

post after the Restoration, he was an obvious target for Cavalier resentment.[105] Impeachment proceedings against him began within a fortnight.[106] The narratives of the two former admirals gave the initiative to the opponents of the naval administration. Spragge, who in just a few weeks had moved from being a potential victim of the Commons' wrath to a respected witness, was chosen by the promoters of Clarendon's impeachment to prove one of the charges against the disgraced earl—that of bearing responsibility for dividing the fleet.[107]

Before the House adjourned in December, another important development occurred: at a by-election for Great Grimsby in October, Sir Frescheville Holles was returned to Parliament. The only son of Gervase Holles, the royalist antiquary and master of requests, Holles had served as a major of militia and as captain of a privateer before entering the navy in September 1665 on Albemarle's recommendation, immediately gaining command of a frigate and rising rapidly to the command of a third-rate.[108] Holles, a gentleman of the privy chamber since 1664, had been a friend and business colleague of the leading London merchant and future whig lord mayor, Robert Clayton, for some years, and he quickly became associated with Buckingham, Howard, and Lord St John.[109] He soon became an active member of the House, and was appointed to six committees within three weeks, one of them, significantly, being the committee of miscarriages.[110] Conceited but also brave in the view even of his friends, arrogant and corrupt in the view of his enemies, Holles could provide the committee and the 'anti-Clarendonians' with professional expertise and personal experience of the war at sea, though a man who implausibly blamed the administration for the loss of his arm in the four days' battle was hardly likely to be an objective witness.[111] Moreover, Holles believed that Coventry had been responsible for his failure to gain another command.[112] Coventry and Pepys found it

---

[105] When he was examined, one MP noted that 'the sectaries do very much favour Pett': *Milward Diary*, 127. Cf. Cooper, *Savile Correspondence*, 16.
[106] *CJ*, ix. 20; BL, Egerton MS 2539, fo. 140.
[107] *Milward Diary*, 116.
[108] *Hist. Parl.*, ii. 564–5; W. L. Clowes, *The Royal Navy: A History*, ii (1898), 426; NMM, LBK/47, unfol., Albemarle to Coventry, 28 Sept. 1665, Sandwich to Albemarle, 1 Oct. 1665; Adm. 10/15, p. 67.
[109] NMM, AGC/6/3; HMC, *Portland MSS*, iii. 317; *Hist. Parl.*, ii. 564–5.
[110] *CJ*, ix. 24, 29, 36, 38.
[111] Ingram, *Three Sea Journals*, 30–2, 54–5; *Pepys's Diary*, viii. 275, 304; ix. 75.
[112] Coventry MS 97, fo. 87; Coventry MS 101, fo. 232.

alarming and ironic that such men as Holmes, Holles, and Spragge should be attacking their conduct: 'the commanders, the gentlemen that could never be brought to order, but undid all, are now the men that find fault and accuse others.'[113]

When Parliament reconvened in February 1668, the discussion of miscarriages became more systematic. On the 14th, Sir Robert Brooke reported from the committee and presented the heads of miscarriages, which relied heavily on the evidence of Holles and Holmes. Their position was reflected most clearly in the article which criticized the 'ill choice of officers in the fleet', a point which Coventry interpreted correctly as an attack on the selection of sea-officers by himself and James.[114] The Commons debated, in turn, the more immediately controversial issues: the delayed recall of Rupert's squadron in 1666, the failure to fortify Sheerness in 1667, the failure to follow up the battle of Lowestoft, and the payment of seamen by tickets. The debates went on with 'heat and animositye', with the debate on the division of the fleet alone lasting for seven hours and 'strangely' dividing the house, while for the first time implicit criticisms of the duke of York and even of the king himself began to emerge.[115] The debate on tickets seriously implicated another close associate of James, the navy commissioner Viscount Brouncker; Holles, who had provided some of the committee's original evidence against him, defended Broucker in open debate out of personal friendship.[116] The naval administration finally fended off the ticket issue with Pepys's comprehensive three-hour speech to the Commons on 5 March, which justified the practice and implied that the fault lay partly with the Commons themselves for voting an inadequate supply.[117]

Holles, however, had already adopted another strategy by that time, one which singled out Coventry as his main target. Though Coventry had relinquished the post of secretary to the lord high admiral, Holles and another member of Buckingham's faction, Sir Richard Temple, sought to destroy his remaining influence by charging him with the sale of naval offices, an offence guaranteed to excite the anger of

[113] *Pepys's Diary*, viii. 571.
[114] *CJ*, ix. 49–51; *Milward Diary*, 184; Rawl. MS A. 191, fo. 229; *Pepys's Diary*, ix. 75.
[115] *CJ*, ix. 51–5; *Milward Diary*, 185–9; Bod. Lib., Carte MS 36, fo. 165; Witcombe, *Cavalier House of Commons*, 80.
[116] Rawl. MS A. 191, fos. 229–47; *CJ*, ix. 50; *Milward Diary*, 196–7.
[117] Ibid. 207–9; E. S. de Beer, 'Reports of Pepys' Speech in the House of Commons, March 5th 1668', *MM* 14 (1928), 55–8.

Parliament.[118] Holles employed a number of his fellow unemployed sea-officers to visit the Thamesside inns during February, March, and April 1668 to persuade officers to sign a petition which stated that Coventry had forced them to pay exorbitant fees for posts in the fleet. The chief agent was Valentine Tatnell, a former mayor of Dover and captain in the interregnum navy, who had been dismissed soon after the Restoration and had been reported at the time as 'most violent against H. M.'. Tatnell served as a press-master during the war, became implicated in ticket frauds and irregular pressing, and failed in his attempts to gain the command of a frigate.[119] He used a combination of bribery and promises of employment in his attempts to get sea-officers to sign, but had only limited success. Coventry was kept informed by several *agents provocateurs*, notably the former sea-officers Edmund Chillenden[120] and Gilbert Cornelius, who provided him with regular reports of Tatnell's visits to the inns and of his boasts that 'hee would have Sir Wms Periwigg from his head ere long'; Coventry also learnt from them of the involvement of Holles and Temple (the so-called 'good patriots') and others, including Temple's relative Captain John Temple, another unemployed sea-officer.[121]

On 24 February 1668 a paper was brought into the Commons, accusing an anonymous person (generally assumed to be Coventry) of selling offices, and during March Holles produced witnesses before the committee of miscarriages. Finally, on 29 April Holles presented 'The Humble Petition of Divers Officers belonging to his Majesties Navy, and of severall widdowes and orphans of other officers', who were supposedly discouraged by having to pay 'bribes, bargaiñs or gratuities' to Coventry.[122] With his ample advance warning, Coventry found it easy to deal with the threat. The petition itself was a pathetic affair containing a mere twenty-one names, and the only commissioned officer to sign it was Coventry's own agent, Cornelius; furthermore, it contained a fundamental mistake concerning the method of

---

[118] V. Vale, 'Clarendon, Coventry, and the Sale of Naval Offices, 1660–8', *Cambridge Historical Journal*, 12 (1956), 107–22; C. Roberts, 'Sir Richard Temple: "The Pickthank Undertaker"', *Huntington Library Quarterly*, 41 (1977–8), 149.

[119] Adm. 106/1, fo. 370; Adm. 106/2, fo. 3; Coventry MS 98, fo. 68; *CSPD*, 1664–5, 296, 533–4; Capp, *Cromwell's Navy*, 260, 304.

[120] The noted agitator and radical of the 1640s and 1650s, who had served as a purser in the second Dutch war; Capp, *Cromwell's Navy*, 389.

[121] Coventry MS 101, fos. 104–235; Vale, 'Sale of Naval Offices', 107–22.

[122] *Milward Diary*, 197; Coventry MS 101, fos. 107–8; Vale, 'Sale of Naval Offices', 116.

payment for sea-officers, which made its refutation even easier.[123] Coventry had ample evidence to prove that he had always been uneasy about the payment of fees for naval places, and that he had sought and procured a rationalization of the system in 1664 which gave him a salary of £500 a year in lieu of fees. He was also able to prove that between 1660 and 1663, 287 naval posts had been given *gratis* to Cavalier warrant-officers, and that any gratuities given to him since 1664 had been entirely voluntary.[124] The contrast between Coventry's generosity towards Cavaliers and the employment of men of doubtful political and religious beliefs by Holles and Temple helped to ensure that Parliament ignored the petition.

By March 1668, the naval debates in Parliament were being conducted in the knowledge that Charles II intended to set out a large fleet that summer, to fulfil his obligations under the 'triple alliance'.[125] The sea-officers' chief concern became the allocation of flag-posts and commands in the new fleet, and long-standing feuds were revived in attempts to eliminate potential rivals. Sir Robert Holmes and Sir Jeremy Smith renewed their mutual accusations of cowardice, and Holles also joined in the attack on Smith. Sir William Penn was suggested as an alternative to the younger, feuding commanders, but this suggestion angered Rupert, Albemarle, and many MPs.[126] In the midst of this bitter atmosphere, and partly because of the suggestion that the heavily censured Penn should go to sea that summer, the Commons proposed on 26 March that the committee of miscarriages should attempt to discover which individual sea-officers were guilty of miscarriages, 'that being found out they may be laid aside and others put in their place'. There was already strong pressure on Sir John Harman, who, it was suggested, was being kept at sea deliberately to prevent him giving evidence about the battle of Lowestoft.[127] Harman's continued absence forced the committee of miscarriages to consider another issue, the abuse of the prize-goods regulations by Sandwich and other sea-officers in 1665. The House debated the matter on 14 April, and the immediate target was Penn: in his defence

---

[123] Coventry MS 101, fos. 212, 232[v].
[124] Coventry MS 98, fos. 78, 103–4, 109, 119–21, 127–8; Coventry MS 101, fos. 225–42.
[125] *CJ*, ix. 62.
[126] BL, Addit. MS 36916, fo. 87; H. M. Margoliouth (ed.), *The Poems and Letters of Andrew Marvell* (2nd edn., Oxford, 1952), 67–9; *Pepys's Diary*, ix. 118, 125–6, 131, 138.
[127] *Milward Diary*, 234; BL, Egerton MS 2539, fos. 180, 182, 184[v].

he stated that he had only been following the orders of his superior officer, Sandwich. Holles seized the opportunity to remove several rivals for command at a stroke, and his indictment of Penn and Sandwich together on the 16th closely followed the House's summons to Sir Roger Cuttance and Sir Thomas Teddeman, two other flag-officers implicated in the prize-goods scandal, to attend it.[128] The nature of the supposed offences made a strong impression on the MPs, with 'great reflections on Lord Sandwich both for cowardice and giving away and distributing of the goods and afterwards gaining the King's hand and seal to confirm and justify the disposing of them'.[129] Articles of impeachment were ordered to be prepared against Penn, and Sandwich was only spared a similar fate because it was felt that such a move would damage his position as ambassador to Spain.[130]

In the meantime Harman's fleet had returned, and on 17 April the House returned to the issue of Lowestoft by examining the three principal witnesses, Harman, John Cox (the master of the flagship), and Henry Brouncker. Holles was determined to place Harman in as difficult a position as possible, declaring that, as James's immediate subordinate, Harman should have seen that the duke's orders were obeyed.[131] Harman, who later claimed that he knew little of the background to his examination, made an indecisive defence which cast some reflections on Brouncker but by no means scotched the rumours that he bore most of the responsibility himself or, indeed, 'that he had been tampered with from Whitehall'. Harman's confusion reflected badly on him, and it seemed that he, too, might be committed.[132] However, by the time of his re-examination on 21 April Brouncker had panicked and fled, and Harman tried to save himself by throwing all the blame onto Brouncker. Harman's appearance as 'a very gallant man, and very humble and modest' contrasted sharply with the abject behaviour of Brouncker, whose desertion of the House outraged his fellow MPs, and Harman was released.[133] Discussions over Penn's impeachment dragged on inconclusively until the prorogation in May,

---

[128] Grey, *Debates*, i. 136–7; *CJ*, ix. 80; BL, Egerton MS 2539, fo. 195ᵛ.

[129] *Milward Diary*, 257.

[130] Ibid. 269; BL, Egerton MS 2539, fos. 200ᵛ, 204ᵛ; Witcombe, *Cavalier House of Commons*, 88.

[131] *Milward Diary*, 261–3; *CJ*, ix. 85–6.

[132] BL, Egerton MS 2539, fos. 202ᵛ, 204ᵛ (quotation from fo. 202ᵛ); *Milward Diary*, 261–3; Grey, *Debates*, i. 143–4; BL, Addit. MS 36916, fo. 93; Margoliouth, *Marvell*, 72.

[133] *Milward Diary*, 268–70 (quotation from p. 270); BL, Egerton MS 2539, fo. 204ᵛ.

but by then the members of the House were 'not so hott as they were'.[134] Holles had lost much of his influence by making 'a very long and impertinent speech in order to a toleration to all dissenters', while the attempt to attack Sandwich and his clients was stillborn because of the earl's absence from the country and because the serjeant-at-arms forgot to carry out his orders to send for Cuttance.[135] The commission of public accounts maintained pressure on the naval administration throughout 1668 and 1669, and the parliamentary session in the autumn of 1669 attacked the former navy treasurer Carteret, but the attack on the administration by sea-officers working through the House of Commons had failed by the time of the May prorogation. Sir Frescheville Holles offered his services to the king of France in 1669, but became reconciled to the court in 1670, and died at the battle of Solebay in May 1672.[136]

Throughout their campaign against the administration, the chief motive of Holles and his colleagues had been clear: they sought to gain employment for themselves, both by placing the machinery of the naval administration in different hands and by settling old scores with rivals whom they hoped to remove from contention. The first of these objectives proved too ambitious. A project to replace James with Albemarle as lord high admiral came to nothing, and the only significant change was the installation of Buckingham's clients Osborne and Littleton as joint treasurers of the navy.[137] Coventry, Brouncker, and Pepys were able to weather the storm, not necessarily because their own cases were impregnable, but because their opponents' cases were poorly prepared or presented, and because, in any case, the Commons' investigation of miscarriages was conducted on an erratic, piecemeal basis. A two-month adjournment was enough to save Pett from impeachment, and it took three weeks for anyone to notice that Sir Roger Cuttance had not actually been sent for, despite a resolution of the House. For their part, the sea-officers had used Parliament as a means of working out the jealousies which had developed during the war: the discrediting of many interregnum officers, and the deaths in battle of other senior men, such as Lawson and Myngs, brought to the

---

[134] BL, Addit. MS 36916, fo. 96. On Penn's impeachment, see Streete, *Uncommon Sailor*, 140–8.
[135] *Milward Diary*, 248; Grey, *Debates*, i. 126; *CJ*, ix. 93.
[136] Turnbull, 'Administration of the Royal Navy', ch. 5 *passim*; Witcombe, *Cavalier House of Commons*, 92–7; *Hist. Parl.*, ii. 564–5.
[137] Roberts, 'Impeachment of the Earl of Clarendon', 10.

fore a younger generation of commanders, notably Holmes, Spragge, and Holles, whose chief concern was self-advancement. Among the sea-officers and among the unpaid, resentful seamen, the second Dutch war created or exacerbated a range of problems which would continue to blight the navy; a strong case can be made for seeing in the war the end of the atmosphere of 'harmony, mutual trust, and co-operation' which had characterized the interregnum navy,[138] and the beginnings of a service in which administrators, officers, and men were rather less tolerant of each other.

[138] Capp, *Cromwell's Navy*, 400.

9

THE THIRD DUTCH WAR

THE war of 1664–7 had been supported, at least at its outset, by a broad consensus of opinion, which embraced the belligerent attitudes of the most influential sea-officers. The disasters of that war deflated the optimism even of some of the anti-Dutch 'hawks', however, and less unanimity was apparent at the outbreak of the third war in 1672. Deep divisions in public opinion, and widespread opposition to the French alliance created by the treaty of Dover of 1670, were evident, and these sentiments were reflected in the navy.[1] For the more junior commissioned officers, a war again provided opportunities for employment (particularly after the severe retrenchment of 1668–71) with all its concomitant benefits, but the attitudes of some of the more senior sea-officers were ambivalent. The earl of Ossory, who took command of a third-rate early in 1672 despite only a few months' previous seagoing experience as a volunteer, spoke about the war to his friend John Evelyn, 'deploring his being ingaged in it to me, and he had more justice and honour than in the least to approve of it, though he had been persuaded to the expedition . . .'. The earl of Sandwich, the most experienced commander serving in 1672, held similar views.[2] Prince Rupert was reported to be opposed to the French alliance, an attitude consistent with his barely concealed contempt for his French subordinates in 1673.[3] Below the ranks of the officer corps, ominous rumblings were apparent even before the war broke out; the seamen of Deal, the main servicing base for the Downs anchorage and an important recruiting centre, were reported in the summer of 1671 to be opposed to the idea of war with the Dutch, and there were rumours of more widespread disaffection.[4]

---

[1] C. R. Boxer, 'Some Second Thoughts on the Third Anglo-Dutch War, 1672–4', *TRHS*, 5th ser., 19 (1969), 71–90.

[2] *Evelyn's Diary*, iii. 606, 617–18.

[3] Staffordshire RO, MS D(W)1778/Ii/355, 'A Full Answer', p. 2 (for this source, see below, n. 50); L. C. O'Malley, 'The Whig Prince: Prince Rupert and the Court vs Country Factions during the Reign of Charles II', *Albion*, 8 (1976), 337.

[4] SP 29/282, fo. 81; SP 29/293, fo. 121; SP 29/294, fo. 15.

Nevertheless, the king and duke of York, both totally committed to their war policy, hoped to avoid the mistakes of the previous conflict: in addition to the administrative problems of manning and victualling, these had included the development of bitter factional conflicts among the sea-officers. James himself therefore took command of the fleet for the 1672 campaign, an appointment intended to preserve unity among the captains, to provide a commander-in-chief of sufficiently high social rank to be acceptable to the French, and, perhaps, to enhance the duke's flagging popularity in England.[5] As in 1665, the presence of the heir to the throne attracted a flood of volunteers to the fleet, a flood encouraged by a proclamation of November 1671 which improved the arrangements for the entertainment of such volunteers aboard warships.[6] The enthusiasm of the nobility and gentry to serve impressed observers: 'I thinke a fourth part [of] the nobles of England [are] in the fleett', one captain wrote, while the Venetian ambassador estimated the total at five Knights of the Garter, ten peers, and over 400 other aristocrats or gentlemen.[7]

The allocation of the flags was a potential bone of contention, as it had been in the previous war, and could easily have been exacerbated by the decision to employ a French force as the white squadron, thereby reducing the number of flags available to Englishmen from nine to six. Several of the more experienced and influential gentlemen officers, notably Sir Frescheville Holles and Francis Digby, expected or were said to be expecting flag-posts.[8] The jealousies which might have resulted from such appointments were prevented by the allocation of the flags on a strict basis of seniority. A number of the most experienced candidates were out of contention for a variety of reasons: Rupert took charge of Admiralty business in London while James was at sea, and Sir Thomas Allin and Sir Jeremy Smith had recently joined the Navy Board. Once such exceptions had been made, the flags were allocated on the basis of the seniority of such posts held in the second war or afterwards. In the senior red squadron, James himself served as admiral, with two veterans of both the previous wars, Sir George

[5] *CSP Ven.*, 1671–2, 218.

[6] HMC, *Le Fleming MSS*, 84; *CSPD*, 1671, 503. Cf. *Works of Sheffield, Earl of Mulgrave*, ii. 12.

[7] Thompson, 'Haddock Correspondence', 13; *CSP Ven.*, 1671–2, 218. Cf. Adm. 2/1735, fos. 1–28; Adm. 2/1746, fos. 126, 127^v, 136^v, 137^v.

[8] *Flagellum Parliamentarium: Being Sarcastic Notices of Nearly Two Hundred Members of the First Parliament after the Restoration* (1881 edn.), 15; HMC, *Sixth Report*, 369.

Ayscue and the 70-year-old Sir Joseph Jordan, as vice- and rear-admiral respectively. Sandwich became admiral of the blue, with Sir Edward Spragge and Sir John Harman beneath him. This careful plan was upset by the death of Ayscue just before the start of the campaign. To preserve the principle of seniority, ten changes of ship or flag were necessary; in the most important moves, Spragge and Harman moved to the red, Jordan became vice-admiral of the blue, and Sir John Kempthorne became rear-admiral of the same squadron.[9]

Charles and James attempted to show similar impartiality in the appointments to individual commands. These were divided almost equally between interregnum and tarpaulin officers on the one hand, and Cavaliers and gentlemen on the other. Of seventy-six captains in the main fleet in April 1672, ten were interregnum officers, twenty-five were tarpaulins, seven were Cavaliers, and twenty-six gentlemen. In the first- to third-rates, interregnum officers and tarpaulins held fourteen commands, Cavaliers and gentlemen seventeen.[10] These bare figures conceal a number of significant features. James's personal preference for gentlemen officers had been reinforced by the inclinations of his secretary Matthew Wren, and the appointments in James's red squadron were therefore more obviously weighted in favour of gentlemen and Cavaliers, while Sandwich's blue squadron contained a higher proportion of interregnum officers and tarpaulins.[11] Another development was the appointment to important commands of aristocrats with very limited seagoing experience, a reversion to Tudor and early Stuart practice which had been considered, but rejected, at the start of the previous war. The earl of Ossory moved to a second-rate at the beginning of the campaign, while the young earl of Mulgrave was appointed to command a second-rate later in the summer.[12] The new dependence on gentlemen officers, which contrasted sharply with the domination of the fleet by interregnum officers in the previous war, attracted criticism. The Venetian ambassador believed that the employment of gentlemen stemmed from the government's inability to depend on the affections of its people; merchants criticized the employment of young, inexperienced commanders on warships

[9] Tanner, *Catalogue*, i. 313–15; SP 29/305, fo. 123.
[10] Analysis based on the fleet-lists in *CSPD*, 1671–2, 403–5, and Coventry MS 95, fo. 128, with differences resolved by Adm. 10/15. Cf. Appendix I, below.
[11] By August, all the captains in James's own division (except his flag-captain) were 'gentlemen': Anderson, *Journals and Narratives of the Third Dutch War*, 185–6.
[12] *Works of Sheffield, Earl of Mulgrave*, ii. 17–18.

assigned to protect trade;[13] while Pepys and others attributed the relatively large number of accidental groundings during the war to the inexperience of the captains.[14]

The administration's attempt to create a unified body of sea-officers was doomed to failure from the start. Personal and factional jealousies soon re-emerged: in particular, Sandwich's return to command after seven years ashore met with mixed reactions in the fleet. His return provided a fount of patronage both for his old clients and for younger men, notably Francis Digby, who held the most senior command after the flagship in the blue squadron and became particularly closely associated with the earl.[15] However, Sir John Chicheley, one of the most able of the gentlemen officers, was so disgusted at the prospect of serving under Sandwich that he resolved to quit the service.[16] Sandwich himself found his position uncomfortable, partly because of his opposition to the war and partly because he found it difficult to live down the memory of his unfortunate part in the 1665 campaign: 'I must do I know not what, to save my reputation', he told Evelyn, gloomily.[17] His friends and clients saw his death on the blazing wreck of the *Royal James* at the battle of Solebay as 'a sacrifice to faction'.[18] Other quarrels permeated the fleet. For instance, Captain Richard le Neve, once a page to the duke of York, had fallen out with another of the duke's favourites, John Narbrough, and was also highly critical of Parliament's proceedings, believing that it had voted too little money for the war.[19] The mutual antagonism of Spragge and Sir Robert Holmes contributed to the dismal failure of the opening naval action of the war, the unprovoked and unjustified attack on the Dutch Smyrna convoy in March 1672, when the two officers failed to unite their forces—a failure widely regarded as deliberate. The rivalry between the two former clients of Rupert had been intensifying since 1666, but

[13] *CSP Ven.*, 1671–2, 145, 218; SP 29/316, fo. 124; HMC, *Le Fleming MSS*, 84; W. D. Christie (ed.), *Letters Addressed from London to Sir Joseph Williamson while Plenipotentiary to the Congress of Cologne in the Years 1673 and 1674* (Camden Society, NS 8–9; 1873–4), ii. 14. Cf. Coventry MS 104, fo. 124.

[14] Pepys MS 2581, p. 260; *CSPD*, 1672–3, 58.

[15] SP 29/308, fo. 204; D. Ellison, 'Cavalier Captain' (unpublished paper). I am grateful to Mr Ellison for allowing me to consult this paper, which deals with Digby's naval career.

[16] Kaufman, *Tangier at High Tide: The Journal of James Luke 1670–3* (Paris, 1958), 115. Chicheley never carried out this resolution.

[17] *Evelyn's Diary*, iii. 617.

[18] Rawl. MS D. 147, fo. 6ᵛ.

[19] Kaufman, *Tangier*, 200.

the abortive attempt to intercept the convoy left Spragge temporarily in the ascendant and Holmes out of favour at court. While Spragge received the prestigious post of vice-admiral of the red, Holmes was passed over for the vacancy created by Ayscue's death in favour of Kempthorne, an officer who was debatably junior to him in the scheme of seniority used to allocate the flags.[20]

While the sea-officers feuded, the problem of manning arose once more. On the whole, payment was less of a problem in the third war than in the second: the government's financial position was stronger, and the seamen's complaints at the end of the 1672 campaign were to focus on a belief that they had been underpaid, not that they had not been paid at all.[21] The scenes of starving seamen reacting to their predicament with violence, so characteristic of the second war, were not repeated in the third. Even so, recruitment was markedly disappointing, and as early as 6 April the desperate response was made of revoking all protections until the fleet was fully manned.[22] The usual explanation, the inadequacy of naval pay, was put forward once more as the immediate cause of the problem,[23] and war again brought a rapid and substantial increase in wages in merchant ships.[24] After the rumours of 1671, there was little evidence of opposition to the war itself: as usual, seamen responded to material problems, rather than to more abstract issues. Far from opposing the war, the articulate and patriotic Edward Barlow was to query England's sudden withdrawal from it, believing that the country should have fought on until it was certain of an honourable peace.[25]

The king's determination to avoid the mistakes of the previous war led him to assume a greater degree of personal control over the movements of the fleet. Throughout the summer of 1672, Charles and his ministers discussed strategy and despatched advice to James on the best station for his fleet, the interception of the Dutch East Indies fleet, and hypotheses about Dutch strategy. Although in theory James was able to accept or reject this advice, sharp differences of opinion

---

[20] *CSPD*, 1671–2, 196–214; H. A. Hansen, 'The Opening Phase of the Third Dutch War Described by the Danish Envoy in London, March–June 1672', *Journal of Modern History*, 21 (1949), 99; Ollard, *Man of War*, 178–9.

[21] SP 29/317, fo. 36; Tanner, *Catalogue*, i. 122–5; C. D. Chandaman, *The English Public Revenue, 1660–88* (Oxford, 1975), 228–31.

[22] *CSPD*, 1671–2, 115, 122, 141, 288, 478; *CSPD*, 1672, 8, 14.

[23] See e.g. Pepys MS 2581, p. 254.

[24] Davis, *Rise of the English Shipping Industry*, 135–6.

[25] *Barlow's Journal*, i. 242.

occurred; the plan to attack the East Indies fleet originated with Lord Ashley, the future earl of Shaftesbury, and ran contrary to the flag-officers' wish to sail to the Dutch coast.[26] The frequent presence of the king and his ministers in the fleet put further pressure on the sea-officers. The landsmen might be more eager to engage the enemy than the captains: on one occasion when sails were sighted on the horizon, John Narbrough, James's second captain on the flagship *Royal Prince*, observed 'his Royal Highness and his Grace the Duke of Buckingham and the Lord Howard and the other lords and noblemen being very desirous to get up with these ships to fight them, judging they must be the Dutch fleet'.[27] Ministers attended councils of war with the flag-officers: on 10 September 1672, for example, Arlington, Ashley, Clifford, Buckingham, and Osborne were all present at such a meeting.[28] When the hoped-for decisive victory failed to materialize, disquiet over central interference in naval planning came to the surface. Spragge blamed the fleet's lack of preparedness at the start of the battle of Solebay on 'ill measures . . . taken at Court', while Digby attacked the 'domestic advisers' who brought the fleet into danger.[29] However, the senior officers may have brought some of their problems onto their own heads by not speaking their minds: Rupert believed that 'Some Flagg officers will say one thing to the King & another to others.'[30]

The indecisive and unsatisfactory battle of Solebay on 28 May 1672 brought to the fore the arguments among the sea-officers. James him-self received fulsome praise, but his subordinates squabbled furiously over each other's conduct. Sir Joseph Jordan, perhaps considered an easy target because of his great age, was singled out for particular censure. When Sandwich's *Royal James* was fighting her losing battle against the Dutch rear squadron, the flag-captain (Richard Haddock) noted that 'Sir Joseph Jordaine . . . passed by us very unkindly to windward . . . and took no notice at all of us'.[31] This criticism was echoed by others, but in official accounts Jordan's courage was praised and, in one of the changes necessitated by Sandwich's death, James

[26] BL, Landsdowne MS 1236, fos. 139–42, 191–210; SP 29/307, fo. 20; SP 104/77, fos. 25, 29–30, 79 *et passim*; Anderson, *Journals and Narratives*, 22–4; Hansen, 'Opening Phase', 104.
[27] Anderson, *Journals and Narratives*, 89.
[28] Ibid. 152; Lincolnshire Archives Office, Jarvis MS IX/1/A/3, 10 Sept. 1672.
[29] Anderson, *Journals and Narratives*, 159–60; SP 29/308, fo. 204.
[30] SP 104/177, fo. 79.
[31] Thompson, 'Haddock Correspondence', 18.

made him vice-admiral of his own squadron.[32] More general criticisms were directed at the majority of the captains, but as in the
previous war it proved remarkably difficult to pin blame successfully on
individuals.[33] More significant in the long term were the criticisms
levelled at the French squadron. Although official accounts praised the
French, they were censured by Spragge, by Dutch agents, and by
coffee-house opinion in London.[34] The same opinion was held by at
least one sea-officer with no ulterior motive for attacking the French: a
few days after the battle, the captain of a fourth-rate in James's
squadron wrote that 'we have the creditt of keeping the sea, but
Monseiur got noe honour in this dispute. I hope hee will doe better
next time.'[35] Though the king could state that he intended to 'stick
firme' to his French alliance,[36] naval and public opinion was already
moving in a different direction.

Well before the end of the 1672 campaign it was being said that
James would leave the command of the fleet and that Rupert would be
appointed in his place. As in 1665, fears were expressed for the health
of the heir to the throne; James himself wished to take command of the
expeditionary force which was to be landed in the Netherlands following a successful naval campaign in 1673.[37] The death of Sandwich had
reduced the very small number of potential successors to James, and
Charles appointed Rupert. Purely in terms of seniority, the prince,
who had become vice-admiral of England on Sandwich's death, was
the obvious choice, and he was the only experienced English admiral
of sufficiently high social rank to command a combined fleet. However, his attitude to the French was known to be cold, and their
admiral, d'Estrées, was reportedly alarmed at the prospect of serving
under him.[38] Despite the risks involved in appointing Rupert, Charles

[32] SP 29/310, fo. 35; Coventry MS 95, fos. 399–400; Anderson, *Journals and Narratives*, 21.

[33] 'A Letter Written by an Unknown Hand, Whereof Many Copies were Dispersed among the Commanders of the English Fleet' (1672), *Lord Somers' Tracts*, 8 (1812), 19–20; BL, Lansdowne MS 1236, fos. 209–10.

[34] Anderson, *Journals and Narratives*, 156–7; SP 29/310, fo. 178; SP 29/311, fos. 18, 52; H. T. Colenbrander, ed., *Bescheiden uit vreemde archieven omtrent de groote Nederlandsche zeeorlogen 1652–76* (The Hague, 1919), ii. 126. Cf. *Memoirs of Sir John Reresby*, ed. A. Browning (Glasgow, 1936), 85; BL, Addit. MS 37951, fos. 4–5.

[35] BL, Addit. MS 21948, fo. 205.

[36] BL, Lansdowne MS 1236, fo. 209.

[37] BL, Addit. MS 21948, fo. 258; SP 29/310, fo. 153; SP 29/311, fo. 17; SP 104/177, fo. 62; Colenbrander, *Bescheiden*, ii. 127.

[38] PRO, PRO 31/3/128, fo. 15; Colenbrander, *Bescheiden*, ii. 127.

may have seen political advantage in choosing him; the parliamentary session which began in February 1673 was critical of the war and suspicious of the duke of York's Catholicism, and this disquiet culminated in the passing of the Test Act. Rupert, though, was of known 'zeal for the Reformed Protestant Profession of Religion', and had been popular with the Commons since his exposure of naval miscarriages in 1667, so Charles may have hoped that the prince's appointment would restore parliamentary enthusiasm for the war.[39]

The king took steps to reduce the risks involved in appointing Rupert. Charles restricted the prince's ability to appoint sea-officers directly, a move which, far from preventing faction, made Rupert resentful of what he saw as a tying of his hands, and angered some of his clients, who argued that Rupert would not be able to rely on the loyalty of his officers.[40] The prince's main difficulties stemmed from the allocation of the flags. Spragge became admiral of the blue: he had moved away from his former patron to such a degree that Rupert's clients saw him as one of the leaders of a faction, closely tied to the duke of York, which sought to denigrate the prince.[41] Spragge's appointment also thwarted Rupert's wish to have Sir Robert Holmes in the fleet. Spragge refused to serve with Holmes, who was still out of favour at court—notably with James, who blocked Holmes's ambition to become governor of Tangier.[42] At various times during the 1673 campaign, Rupert appealed for Holmes to be sent to the fleet, but Charles simply could not contemplate the risks of allowing the two temperamental Irishmen to serve together.[43] For the subordinate flag-posts, the aged Jordan was overlooked and Harman and Kempthorne were appointed vice-admirals of the red and blue respectively, with Sir John Chicheley becoming rear-admiral of the red.[44] The remaining flag post caused some problems: it was originally allocated to John Narbrough, but he was in command of a force near Tangier and was not likely to be back for the start of the campaign, so to avoid contention the inexperienced Ossory was appointed to the vacancy.[45]

[39] Anderson, *Journals and Narratives*, 372.

[40] BL, Harleian MS 6845, fo. 185ᵛ; Anderson, *Journals and Narratives*, 374.

[41] *CSP Ven.*, 1673–5, 59, 67.

[42] *Tangier Papers*, 245; Sir H. Cholmeley, *An Account of Tangier* (1787), 236–7. However, Holmes had been proposed by the king in Sept. 1672 as commander of a projected expedition to the East Indies: SP 104/177, fos. 88–9.

[43] SP 29/335, fo. 152; SP 29/336, fos. 242, 288.

[44] Tanner, *Catalogue*, i. 313–15.

[45] Anderson, *Journals and Narratives*, 22, 25, 375; SP 29/335, fo. 109.

These appointments were not to the liking of some of Rupert's clients. Their views were expressed most forcibly in the pamphlet *An Exact Relation of the Several Engagements and Actions of His Majesty's Fleet under the Command of His Highness Prince Rupert*,[46] supposedly written by a captain in the fleet, which implied that Harman was too sick with gout to command properly, that Chicheley was a 'a person of honour and quality, yet but of late a seaman', and that Narbrough's appointment would have caused offence, 'for, though he were a good seaman, yet there were many others in the fleet that were of better merit, and longer service'.[47] The pamphlet also attacked the king's restriction of Rupert's powers of appointment, Spragge's conduct in the summer's engagements, and the behaviour of the French squadron. It seems to have been disseminated widely from the autumn of 1673 onwards, and may have helped to shape Burnet's very similar, partial treatment of the summer's campaign.[48] The best modern work on the naval war accepts *An Exact Relation* uncritically as an accurate account of the events of 1673.[49] However, the pamphlet was not unchallenged in its own day: at least two manuscript counterblasts were drafted, though there is no evidence that either was published. Both argue that the author of *An Exact Relation* could not have been present in the fleet during the campaign. The first, 'A Full Answer to a Trayterous Seditious Lybell Intituled, An Exact Relation . . .', is a distorted, even hysterical account penned by a self-confessed landsman: it charges Rupert with cowardice, homosexuality, atheism, ambitions on the throne, and (because of his German origins and strong Dutch connections) treachery. The second account, a heavily corrected and unfinished letter to an anonymous correspondent, is a far less partial and more detailed critique of *An Exact Relation*: its author was evidently present in the fleet and was almost certainly George Legge, later Lord Dartmouth, and one of Rupert's seconds in his division.[50]

[46] Printed in Anderson, *Journals and Narratives*, 371–86.

[47] Ibid. 375. However, Narbrough's appointment was consistent with the scheme of seniority, as he had been flag-captain to the admiral of the fleet in 1672, a post which traditionally conferred a right to the first vacant flag.

[48] Staffordshire RO, MS D(W)1778/Ii/355, 'Legge Rejoinder', fo. 1 (for this source, see below, n. 50); Burnet, *History*, ii. 14–15.

[49] Anderson, *Journals and Narratives*, 371–86.

[50] Both accounts survive in Staffordshire RO, MS D(W)1778/Ii/355, a bundle of anonymous and often fragmentary accounts of naval events in the third Dutch war. They are distinguished hereafter as 'A Full Answer' and 'Legge Rejoinder'. The identification of Legge as the author of the latter is based on internal evidence, notably a comparison of handwriting.

Legge replied to *An Exact Relation*'s criticism of Rupert's sub-ordinate officers by observing that many of these were actually of the prince's own recommendation, and that the captains of his own division were entirely men of his own choosing.[51] Legge emphasized the ability of both Harman and Chicheley, stressed Narbrough's right to the vacant flag, and praised Spragge's loyalty and conduct; he also praised the administrators' diligence in setting out the fleet.[52] Legge provided a thorough account and justification of the fleet's tactics and concluded with a stinging attack on d'Estrées, accusing him of openly disobeying Rupert's orders to attack.[53] The significance of Legge's version of the events of 1673 lies in the light it sheds on the balance of factions in the fleet. Some of Rupert's clients took the uncompromis-ing position outlined in *An Exact Relation*, while others in and out of the navy (such as the author of 'A Full Answer') took the opposite line, favouring the duke of York and Spragge. Legge, whose career owed much to both Rupert and Spragge, may have represented a middle ground of sea-officers, not totally dependent on either of the extreme parties and alarmed at the dissension in the officer corps.[54] Unfor-tunately for this group of naval *politiques*, Rupert was not being misled by the insinuations of others:[55] the prince genuinely believed that he was being badly served by his superiors and subordinates alike.[56]

Rupert's lack of love for the naval administration, previously dem-onstrated in 1666, had not been mollified by his service as *de facto* head of that administration in 1672. As early as April 1673 he was critical of the many wants and disorders in the fleet, while by early May he was imposing supposedly unrealistic deadlines on the dockyard officers, and by June he was making regular complaints about the poor standard of supplies and victuals (despite receiving assurances that the admin-istration was making every effort 'as farr as the great engine money will give leave'), as well as complaining about the treatment of sick and wounded men.[57] The full force of Rupert's wrath was reserved for

---

[51] 'Legge Rejoinder', fos. 3, 4, 7. This contention is supported by the fleet-list of Apr. 1673 (BL, Sloane MS 2032, fos. 6–8).
[52] 'Legge Rejoinder', fos. 4–5, 6.
[53] Ibid., fo. 16 *et passim*.
[54] For a similar manifestation of 'neutralist' sentiment in 1690 among sea-officers who realized that faction fighting would damage the fleet's chances of victory, see HMC, *Finch MSS*, ii. 365.
[55] 'Legge Rejoinder', fo. 9.
[56] BL, Harleian MS 6845, fos. 163, 184–5.
[57] SP 29/335, fos. 72, 261; BL, Addit. MS 34727, fo. 115; Adm. 106/25, fos. 312,

James's new secretary, Sir John Werden, and the Navy Board. The prince accused Werden of sending letters which were 'mysticall and out of alle roads', and of undermining his authority with the captains by sending them orders without reference to him. Rupert earnestly requested 'that I may be comanded by His R[oyal] Highness only and not be stinted by his Secretaryes'.[58] He also attacked what he saw as the inadequate preparation of the fleet by the Navy Board, and it was popularly believed that on his first visit to London from the fleet he had caned some of the principal officers and commissioners for their failings.[59] The main difficulty faced by the board and the sea-officers was again the manning of the fleet. By July 1673 the wages due to the seamen totalled over £600,000, and men responded in the usual way, with many deserting to the merchant service, or claiming that they were landsmen in an attempt to avoid being turned over (as able seamen were) into other ships without receiving payment.[60] The Navy Board could only attempt a holding operation: 'Wee pay noe wages but only to prevent Clamer' was its line by the end of August.[61] Individual ships were severely undermanned, and often the men they had were not seamen; captains had to beg for men from each other, or took men out of warships bound for foreign stations; eventually, the administration resorted to a threat to press the masters of merchant ships lying in the Thames unless they provided seamen in lieu.[62] The reluctance of the seamen to serve was matched by a decline in enthusiasm for the service among their social betters. Rupert's attitude towards gentlemen volunteers was distinctly cooler than James's, though the volunteers themselves were less enthusiastic about serving at sea if the duke was absent.[63]

The prince's difficulties were compounded by the continuing determination of Charles and James (even after his resignation as lord high admiral) to play a dominant role in the direction of naval strategy.

316, 318; Adm. 106/26, fos. 22, 30, 40 (quotation from fo. 30); Adm. 106/281, fo. 168; Adm. 3/275, p. 3; Christie, *Letters to Williamson*, i. 19.

[58] SP 29/335, fos. 87, 94, 141. Werden's relations with the sea-officers in general were bad: Kaufman, *Tangier*, 200.

[59] SP 29/335, fo. 261; Christie, *Letters to Williamson*, i. 48.

[60] Adm. 1/3545, p. 98; Adm. 8/1, fos. 6–11; Pepys MS 2265/18; Pepys MS 2581, pp. 261, 263.

[61] NMM, SER/1, unfol. board minutes, 27 Aug. 1673.

[62] BL, Addit. MS. 34727, fos. 115, 117–18; NMM, AGC/24/1; BL, Sloane MS 2439, fo. 5ᵛ; Adm. 106/26, fos. 58, 76, 78; Adm. 106/282, *passim*; Adm. 3/275, p. 2. Cf. *CSPD*, 1672–3, 1673, *passim*.

[63] *CSP Ven.*, 1673–5, 42; Cooper, *Savile Correspondence*, 38.

Throughout the summer they sent advice to Rupert on appropriate stations for his fleet and possible tactics,[64] but the prince suspected that dangerous tactics which other admirals would not have contemplated, notably the strategy of fighting the Dutch in the shallow waters of the Schooneveld and the Flanders coast, were being foisted on him. For once the naturally aggressive Rupert was cast in the unlikely role of the advocate of caution, drawing off his fleet when he considered that the danger of the coastal sands had become too great.[65] One result of this attempt to control Rupert's movements was his uncharacteristic deference to Whitehall throughout the summer: he made frequent requests to know the king's intentions, and sought reassurance that Charles approved of his tactics.[66] Rupert's resentment of the restrictions placed on him, and his frustration at the fleet's lack of success in the two battles of Schooneveld in May and June, culminated in his attempt to get a commission with wider powers. Above all, he sought personal control over the yards, victuallers, and stores, effectively bypassing the much-maligned Navy Board; he also sought the strongest available fleet, not weakened by the removal of vessels for convoy or other duties, full powers of martial law over the fleet, and *carte blanche* for offensive operations against the Dutch.[67] Some of his demands were met on 16 June, the day after James laid down the office of lord admiral, when the prince received a new commission as commander-in-chief of the fleet. Among other things, this gave him the authority to remove and appoint sea-officers as he saw fit.[68]

Despite Charles's hope that Rupert would now be able to keep the fleet in better order,[69] the prince again proved unable to control the jealousies and faction fights among the sea-officers; indeed, he was deeply implicated in those struggles himself. He was under pressure from some of the duke of York's clients, who were prepared to criticize his every move, while his tactics at the battles of Schooneveld were censured by some in the fleet.[70] Disputes over tactics were now at the heart of his quarrels with Spragge, and the disagreement between the two admirals was the talk of the London coffee-houses by the middle

[64] BL., Lansdowne MS 1236, fos. 147, 149, 156, 172–3, 178–9, 201.
[65] BL., Harleian MS 6845, fo. 184; SP 29/335, fo. 230; HMC, *Abergavenny MSS, etc.*, 182.
[66] SP 29/336, fos. 96, 106; Coventry MS 2, fo. 34.
[67] BL., Harleian MS 6845, fo. 163, Cf. Christie, *Letters to Williamson*, i. 52.
[68] SP 29/336, fo. 7. Cf. NMM, AGC/C/2.
[69] BL., Harleian MS 6845, fo. 185ᵛ.
[70] HMC, *Le Fleming MSS*, 103; PRO, PRO 30/53/7, fo. 182.

of June.[71] Rupert got into another argument with his flag-captain, Richard Haddock, whom he accused of various shortcomings, including cowardice and inconsistent, dangerous tactics. He demanded and obtained the removal of the captain, who was moved ashore to a commissioner's place at the Navy Board—supposedly 'with the approbation & advice of our most Deare Cosen Prince Rupert'.[72] Schomberg, the commander of the army which Rupert was to land in the Netherlands, accused him of being unwilling to accept advice and of being dominated by his 'former page', the recently knighted Captain Sir William Reeves.[73] Rupert's own tactlessness further contributed to his problems. After the first battle of Schooneveld at the end of May he sent an account to the secretary of state, Arlington, which praised by name the conduct of some of his own clients, including Reeves, John Holmes, and John Wetwang. The letter and the names were published as an official account of the engagement, and immediately caused a 'babble' of jealousy in the fleet: Rupert hastily wrote another letter to Arlington, regretting that the praise of individuals had been published and that others who had done equally well had been slighted. Even so, the prince went on to appoint Reeves and Wetwang as first and second captains of his new flagship, the *Sovereign*.[74]

Each campaign during the war of 1664–7, and the campaign of 1672, had seen only one or two major fleet engagements; that of 1673 saw three, all indecisive and frustrating, and the failure to secure a decisive victory over the Dutch led to bitter recriminations. Spragge attacked Rupert's disposition of the fleet and his tactics in battle; in turn, Rupert's clients and others censured Spragge, particularly for his remarkable and fatal 'duel' with the Dutch admiral, Tromp, at the battle of the Texel.[75] Sir John Kempthorne was criticized for his conduct in the same battle, and responded by attacking his former rear-admiral, the earl of Ossory, who had been promoted after the Texel to the prestigious post of vice-admiral of the red over the heads of the likes of Kempthorne.[76] Ossory found criticism of his division's

[71] BL, Harleian MS 6845, fos. 184–5; Anderson, *Journals and Narratives*, 322–8; Christie, *Letters to Williamson*, i. 52.
[72] BL, Harleian MS 6845, fo. 184; Adm. 3/275, p. 4; Adm. 2/1736, p. 11; Anderson, *Journals and Narratives*, 324. Cf. 'Legge Rejoinder', fo. 9.
[73] SP 29/336, fo. 157.
[74] SP 29/335, fos. 230, 231, 232, 286; SP 29/336, fo. 75.
[75] Anderson, *Journals and Narratives*, 322–8, 381–4; J. C. M. Warsinck, *Admiraal de Ruyter: de zeeslag op Schooneveld, juni 1673* (The Hague, 1930), 121–3.
[76] Anderson, *Journals and Narratives*, 53–5; Bod. Lib., Carte MS 38, fos. 30–1, 34–5.

conduct 'nonsensical or malicious' and petitioned the king in the strongest possible terms, rejecting Kempthorne's insinuation 'that by their [i.e. Spragge's and Ossory's divisions] ill behaviour ... the opportunity was lost of destroying Admiral Trumps whole squadron which attacqued them', and asserting that Kempthorne himself had displayed cowardice by exposing Spragge's flagship and Ossory's division to danger.[77] The matter was quickly resolved in Ossory's favour; Kempthorne was examined and retracted all the charges he had made, but Ossory continued to bear a grudge against him for the rest of his life.[78] The recriminations in the fleet went beyond the jealousies of the flag-officers, however. Sir Thomas Allin, controller of the navy, said of the English captains at the Texel: 'Some did little and Some nothing, had all done well it might have proved the greatest defeat they ever had.'[79] At least one pair of captains fought a duel over mutual accusations of cowardice, while a lieutenant from Spragge's flagship unsuccessfully took two captains of sloops to courts-martial on similar charges.[80] Rupert was instructed to prepare an account of the conduct of his captains at the Texel, but as usual it proved remarkably difficult to single out individual officers for blame. Even so, the jealousies of the captains attracted widespread public comment, and were even likened to the accusations and threats of impeachment being traded between the 'cabal' ministers in the autumn of 1673.[81]

The rival sea-officers and factions could agree on one target, however: the conduct of the French squadron under the Count d'Estrées at the battle of the Texel. In the early stages of the 1673 campaign, Rupert was careful, despite his own inclinations, to comply with the king's wishes for a close working relationship with the French; even so, his personal relations with d'Estrées were poor, and deteriorated further as the summer progressed.[82] After the first battle of Schooneveld, Rupert observed cryptically that 'the French behaved them selfs as well as could be expected', and this line was maintained in official accounts of the second battle a week later, though privately Rupert was convinced that the French had failed to support him or

[77] Ibid. fo. 52; SP 29/336, fo. 297.
[78] BL, Egerton MS 928, fo. 155; Bod. Lib., Carte MS 38, fo. 53; Staffordshire RO, MS D(W)1778/Ii/474.
[79] Adm. 106/284, fo. 158.
[80] SP 29/337, fo. 135; Rawl. MS A. 314, fos. 4, 6ᵛ.
[81] Adm. 3/275, pp. 52, 68, 71–3; SP 29/335, fos. 135, 184.
[82] Thompson, *Hatton Correspondence*, i. 106; Christie, *Letters to Williamson*, i. 84, 93.

obey his orders.[83] The latent tension between the allies came to a head
after the indecisive battle of the Texel on 11 August. The most
dispassionate accounts, those of junior sea-officers in the English
fleet with no ulterior motive for attacking French conduct, criticized
d'Estrées's squadron for tacking too late, and, when it had tacked, of
making no use of its advantage of being to the windward of the enemy;
for most of the day the French lay idle, and, with Spragge also on the
periphery of the action, Rupert and the red squadron bore the brunt of
the Dutch pressure.[84] The first reports of poor French conduct
reached London by the 15th, were in full cry by the 17th, and were
soon supplemented by letters from officers and seamen and verbal
reports from wounded sailors coming ashore from the fleet.[85] Nevertheless, Rupert himself stayed aloof from the argument for almost a
fortnight, merely reporting the discontent of some of the French
officers against their admirals and the Dutch opinion that the French
had behaved badly.[86] He was under pressure from Charles, who wrote
on 20 August to the effect that 'I am sorry to heare of the jealousys
fallen into the fleete concerning the French . . . whatever the matter
hath been . . . suppresse the effects of them all you can, least the enimy
gaine a greater advantage upon us that way, then they can possibly have
by fighting'.[87] When Rupert finally took a public stance, he carefully
avoided a general criticism of the French and concentrated his attack
exclusively on their admiral, d'Estrées. He praised the subordinate
French officers, whom he believed to be equally ashamed of their
admiral's conduct; on 23 August he informed Arlington that

I find that Msr d'Estree intends to make great excuses for his not beareing into
the enemy, not understanding the signes & many other fine things, I only say
this that when ever it comes in question, I will justify his Majesty and the whole
world that his squadron was to windward of the enemy drawne up in very good
order & never bore within cannon shott of the ennemy . . . my wittnesses shall
be his owne officers & mariners and the rest of both fleets freinds & foes. This
I hope will not be interpreted as an intention to breed an animosity between
the nations for accusing the commander . . . att the same time I doe assure you

[83] SP 29/335, fo. 230; Christie, *Letters to Williamson*, i. 19; BL, Harleian MS 6845, fos. 184–5.
[84] BL, Egerton MS 840B, fo. 7 (log of Thomas Culpepper, *York*); Adm. 51/3817 (log by Capt. Richard Carter, *Crown*). For a detailed and fair account of the battle, see Anderson, *Journals and Narratives*, 46–53.
[85] Christie, *Letters to Williamson*, i. 162, 168–9, 170; Adm. 106/284, fo. 339.
[86] SP 29/336, fo. 259.
[87] BL, Lansdowne MS 1236, fo. 174.

that I am satisfyed that most of the comanders are as forward as our owne in the service, & are ashamed of what was done, I could say more of this but it being a subject not very acceptable I shall end.[88]

Indeed, this interpretation of events was supported by an account of the battle by Martel, the French vice-admiral, and copies of his relation were circulated widely in England.[89]

Rupert's carefully worded distinction between the French admiral and the French *per se* was not appreciated by public opinion, and his popular standing was greatly enhanced. His frequent visits to Shaftesbury's house were seen as signs that he was involved in the earl's complex intrigues against the French alliance,[90] but this view may have been simply a misinterpretation of Rupert's close business connections, and unlikely personal friendship, with 'the false Achitophel'.[91] Regardless of Rupert's role, it was clear in the autumn of 1673 that naval opinion was an important element in the formulation of broader public opinion. Letters and verbal reports from the fleet circulated widely in coffee-houses and elsewhere, the pro-Rupert pamphlet *An Exact Relation* gained widespread acceptance, and Parliament threatened to summon Rupert to hear his version of the French fleet's conduct.[92] The outburst over the poor conduct of the French at the Texel provided a focus for the more general discontent with the French alliance: it was more tangible proof of French perfidy than higher matters of diplomacy and politics, just as the Dutch raid on the Medway in 1667 had been the most tangible proof of maladministration during the previous war.

The final months of 1673 and early months of 1674 constituted a period of confusion in the affairs of both state and navy. London abounded with rumours about the factions at court and possible new combinations of ministers, and this uncertainty was reflected in the appointments to flag posts in the fleet. After the Texel, Rupert

[88] SP 29/336, fo. 286.
[89] SP 29/337/9, fo. 1; PRO, PRO 31/3/129, fo. 62; Christie, *Letters to Williamson*, i. 189–90; ii. 1–5; Bod. Lib., Carte MS 50, fo. 105; O. Airy (ed.), *Essex Papers* (Camden Society, NS 47; 1890), i. 121.
[90] Christie, *Letters to Williamson*, ii. 21–2; PRO, PRO 31/3/129, fos. 21, 56; O'Malley, 'The Whig Prince', 340–2.
[91] Ibid. 339–40.
[92] Christie, *Letters to Williamson*, i. 170, 173–5, 194–6; ii. 1–3; Thompson, *Hatton Correspondence*, i. 113–15; Airy, *Essex Papers*, i. 121, 131; Harris, *London Crowds*, 93.

redistributed the flags, elevating Narbrough, John Holmes, and John Berry; these appointments offended others, notably George Legge, who claimed to have a better right to a flag than Holmes.[93] At the end of August, Rupert left the fleet and Harman succeeded him, but when the latter became ill in September contention among the flag-officers was prevented by the elevation of Ossory to command-in-chief, despite his own desire to be at home and his modest opinion of his ability as a seaman.[94] Ossory's social rank and popularity made him an obvious choice, though the recent return to political prominence of his father, the duke of Ormonde, may also have been significant in this respect.[95] A more long-term problem was the chief command for the projected 1674 campaign, plans for which were being made in October and November.[96] At one point, Charles seems seriously to have considered his illegitimate son, the 24-year-old duke of Monmouth, as a possible figurehead commander-in-chief, but nothing came of this scheme.[97] Rupert would have been the popular choice for this new campaign, but it was generally believed that factions in the fleet and at court, together with pressure from the French, would prevent his appointment.[98] By the turn of the year, even a return to sea by the duke of York was being predicted.[99] Such speculation was rendered academic by the lack of money to continue the war. The signing of peace in February 1674 created an entirely new set of conditions in the navy, conditions dominated by a prolonged and severe retrenchment and the problems which that retrenchment created.

[93] SP 29/336, fo. 247.
[94] Adm. 3/275, p. 43; Adm. 2/1736, pp. 109–10, 145; SP 29/336, fo. 284.
[95] Airy, *Essex Papers*, i. 132.
[96] Adm. 3/275, pp. 74–5, 95–6, 97–8, 101–2.
[97] *CSP Ven.*, 1673–5, 78, 120; Tanner, *Catalogue*, ii. 40, 52.
[98] Christie, *Letters to Williamson*, ii. 8–10, 101; SP 29/337, fo. 3.
[99] Christie, *Letters to Williamson*, ii. 87; SP 29/360, fo. 113.

10

THE YEARS OF PEACE

DESPITE their importance, the two Anglo-Dutch wars occupied less than five of the twenty-eight years during which Charles II and James II ruled England. For the country and the navy, peace at home was the normal state of affairs for most of the period, and as the largest spending department of the state, the navy in peacetime was an obvious target for those who sought to retrench government expenditure. Only the smallest viable force was sent to sea each year; consequently, too many sea-officers with war experience and grandiose ambitions chased too few vacancies. After the end of the third Dutch war, in particular, the character of the navy seemed to change. The great naval patrons and ambitious, aggressive officers who had dominated the 1660s and early 1670s, men like Albemarle, Sandwich, Penn, Spragge, and Holles, were dead, as were many of their clients; the duke of York was no longer lord high admiral; Prince Rupert was ageing and increasingly distant from naval affairs. The prospect of England becoming involved in another European war was resurrected seriously just once, in 1678, when it suited the purpose of the chief minister, Danby, and the mood of Parliament, to go to the verge of war with France. A naval mobilization took place, Anglo-Dutch negotiations paved the way for a jointly conducted naval war which foreshadowed in many ways the war strategy of the 1690s, and Sir Thomas Allin took many of Charles II's great ships for a pointless summer's cruise in the Channel. Charles certainly did not want war with France, and the war scare was over before the mobilization was complete. Pepys bemoaned 'the great disappointment which our poore Commanders & L[ieutenant]s will meet with in their being soe soon discharged from the service . . . But it must be submitted to.'[1]

However, although no war took place in northern waters, the navy *was* at war for almost the whole of the two reigns. The threat to English

[1] Pepys MS 2854, p. 236. I am preparing a more detailed study of the importance to the navy of the 'war scare' of 1678; on the navy as a political issue in this period, and on its response to the 'exclusion crisis', see my 'The Navy, Parliament, and Political Crisis in the Reign of Charles II', *Historical Journal*, forthcoming.

merchant shipping from the corsairs of North Africa ensured that fleets had to be based almost continually in the Mediterranean. With the active fleet in home waters decimated by successive retrenchment programmes, the Mediterranean fleet became the main focus for the sea-officers' professional ambitions, and the main battleground in which they fought out their professional jealousies.

An English commitment against the Barbary corsairs was nothing new at the Restoration: James I had sent an expedition against Algiers in 1620, and Blake's exploits in the 1650s were still fresh in many memories. The acquisition of Tangier in 1662, as part of Catherine of Braganza's marriage dowry, gave England a permanent foothold in the area, although optimistic plans to use the colony as a major naval base came to nothing because of its lack of shelter for shipping.[2] Squadrons which varied in size from over thirty vessels (under Narbrough in the late 1670s) to fewer than a dozen (under Herbert and his successors in the 1680s) struggled for years to prevent attacks on English shipping from the vessels of Algiers, Tunis, Tripoli, and 'Sallee' (Salé, in Morocco). The earl of Sandwich, Sir John Lawson, and Sir Thomas Allin commanded in the area before the second Dutch war; Allin went out again in 1668, leaving the command to Sir Edward Spragge in 1670. The Mediterranean was practically abandoned by the navy when the third Dutch war began, but Sir John Narbrough led a force to the area in 1674, arranged treaties with Tunis and Tripoli, and (apart from a brief return to England in 1676–7) remained in the area until 1679, when Arthur Herbert succeeded him in the command. It was Herbert who finally procured a lasting peace with Algiers in 1682, and when he returned to England in the following year he left Captain Cloudesley Shovell with a few ships to continue the war against Sallee. Shovell's successors Henry Priestman and Henry Killigrew maintained the campaign until the start of the great war with France.[3]

Attitudes within the navy to service in the Mediterranean were by no means uniform. Shore officials, condemned to permanent service in one place, had the most jaundiced view: Pepys's eccentric brother-in-law Balthazar St Michell, navy storekeeper at Tangier in the early 1680s, described the place as 'this hell, this hell of brimston and fire, and Egipts Plagues (which god eternally curse)', while his successor at Gibraltar in the late 1680s, Jonathan Gauden, called the future bastion

---

[2] See Hornstein, 'The Deployment of the English Navy', ch. 6 *et passim*.
[3] Ibid. 22–5 *et passim*.

of Britain's Mediterranean policy 'this hole . . . this land of oblivion'.[4]
The seamen's reactions were predictable. On arriving in the area, they
happily over-indulged in drink and the brothels of the Mediterranean
ports, until the notoriously poor victuals provided on the station began
to change their outlook.[5] Prolonged absence from home also affected
morale, even to the extent of making some men aboard the *Europa* in
1676 desperate enough to plot to burn their ship.[6] Absence had other
repercussions at home, where the families of men on long deployments
often had difficulty making ends meet: in 1686, for example, the wives
of the ship's company of the *James Galley* petitioned for some allowance, arguing that the ship had been in the Mediterranean for six years
and that no money had come through from their husbands in that
time.[7] For the commissioned officers, too, a lively social life was one
attraction of Mediterranean service. Lieutenant Daniel MacDonnell
was almost certainly not the only sea-officer to spend time pursuing
'the Cadiz ladies', and dining was, if anything, even more of an
obsession in the 'Straits fleet' than in the rest of the navy.[8] The centre
of the officers' social lives was Tangier. Naval men sometimes bought
houses in the town; most moved in an exclusive social circle which
included the governor and his staff, army officers from the garrison,
and prominent local merchants, and many dinners were attended by
cosmopolitan cross-sections drawn from these groups.[9] Such meetings
provided opportunities to establish friendships and alliances, to gossip
about the society of the town, and to discuss political issues of both
local and national significance. In due course, the alliance, factions,
and enmities which had been formed at Tangier were to exert a
significant influence on the revolution of 1688, as recounted in the
next chapter.

Mediterranean service was popular among the commissioned
officers for reasons other than the purely social, and, indeed, convoy
duty or service in the Straits fleet was generally regarded as the most

[4] Rawl. MS A. 190, fo. 42; NHL., MS 169, pp. 119–20. After the demolition of
Tangier in 1683, the navy maintained a base at Gibraltar by arrangement with the
Spanish authorities: Hornstein, 'Deployment', 166–73.
[5] KAO, U. 1515/O. 8, unfol., Narbrough to Pepys, 6 Nov. 1678 (second fo., *verso*);
Baltharpe, *Straights Voyage, passim; Barlow's Journal*, i. 52, 59–61, 162–4.
[6] Rawl. MS C. 972, fos. 9–14.
[7] Adm. 7/687, pt. 3, no. 164. Cf. SP 104/176, fo. 289ᵛ.
[8] NHL., MS 169, p. 132; *Teonge Diary*, 44, 63, 82–3, 126, 228, 233.
[9] HMC, *Dartmouth MSS*, iii. 38–9; Kaufman, *Tangier at High Tide*, 37, 56, 57–8,
89–90, 92–3, 140 *et passim*; E. M. G. Routh, 'The English at Tangier', *EHR* 26 (1911),
471–2.

attractive proposition in the navy. Pepys put the matter succinctly, as usual: 'there can never want enough of Comanders to whom it will be an obligation to take that voyage to the Streights', he wrote in 1678.[10] Pepys knew that two things underlay this popularity, money and the chance of preferment. Mediterranean service provided several means for a captain to enhance his personal fortune. With England at peace in northern waters, the wars against the corsairs provided the only opportunity for earning prize-money, and even commanders of convoys could expect to receive substantial presents for their exertions. Captains competed ruthlessly for the plum convoys, and failure to gain such a command occasioned grave disappointment, as well as providing cause for new personal animosities among the sea-officers: Pepys referred to 'the just dissatisfaction which gratifying of one Man this way occasions to half a score that think themselves to have as much Right to the favour as he'.[11]

However, the most important means of enriching oneself on the Mediterranean station lay in the opportunity for private trading, either officially (by carrying gold or silver) or unofficially (by carrying other merchant goods). In the Mediterranean, particularly in the mid-1670s when England was a neutral in a sea of warring navies, captains could attempt to justify their taking in merchants' goods on the grounds that the local English merchants wanted them to, either because there were no suitable merchantmen available, or because the seas were too dangerous.[12] However, this practice attained epidemic proportions in 1674–5, and led to complaints from other groups of merchants against the carriage of goods in warships, while some port authorities, notably at Leghorn, threatened to impose customs duties on English warships.[13] In November 1674, a squadron returned to England resembling a fleet of argosies: its cargo included sugar, silk, wine, raisins, carpets, bees' wax, and two thousand elephants' 'teeth'.[14] Matters had plainly got out of hand, and the administration attempted

---

[10] Pepys MS 2854, p. 398. Pepys later claimed that this preference only began under his bitter rivals, the Admiralty commissioners of 1679–84: Pepys MS 1534, p. 34. In fact, Sir William Coventry had noted a similar preference in the 1660s: Coventry MS 95, fo. 271.

[11] Pepys MS 2855, p. 49. Cf. Adm. 2/1752, p. 251.

[12] Rawl. MS A. 178, fo. 275; SP 29/362, fo. 8; Hornstein, 'Deployment', 75–81.

[13] Tanner, *Catalogue*, ii. 337; Rawl. MS A. 178, fo. 289.

[14] Adm. 1/3546, pp. 305–23. Whether the intended recipients of these goods knew beforehand that they would be shipped in warships is debatable, but if they did, considerable doubt is cast on the administration's seriousness in dealing with this problem: the recipients included the king, the duke of York, and Samuel Pepys.

to clamp down. Its attitude to the practice of carrying merchants'
goods had always appeared to be consistent, if not always effective:
the carrying of merchandise was prohibited by the fortieth general
instruction to commanders as bringing dishonour to the service and
defrauding the king of customs duties,[15] and all orders and instructions issued to commanders sailing to the Mediterranean included an
injunction against engaging in the practice.[16] Even so, in 1669 widespread complaints against captains who had traded forced the administration to restate its position and to announce that all future cases
would be referred directly to the king and the lord high admiral.[17] The
reaction to the 'boom' in trading by warships after the third Dutch
war was quick and effective, and exemplary punishments of fines
and imprisonment were given to captains who had traded.[18] Stern
warnings were issued to captains then in the Mediterranean, and apart
from isolated incidents the practice was kept largely under control; by
the early 1680s it was accepted that most captains kept within the legal
limits imposed for their carrying of merchandise.[19]

However, those legal limits still gave captains a great deal of scope
for making money. The fortieth general instruction permitted them to
carry gold, silver, and jewels, though they could do so only within the
limits of their operational instructions, which meant in theory that they
could only carry plate to ports to which they were already ordered; in
1673 the captains' personal gain from such voyages was fixed at 1
per cent interest on all plate carried.[20] Even such an uncommercial
rate could be attractive if the cargo was large enough. In 1670, John
Kempthorne was said to have had 700,000 pieces of eight aboard at
Cadiz, while John Holmes was reported to have made 12,000 pieces
for himself and his admiral.[21] At about the same time, Captain John
Waterworth made what was later regarded as the most profitable single
voyage of all, 'making £2,500 freight at once'.[22] The security afforded
by a warship was an obvious attraction for many merchants, and this

---

[15] NMM, ADL/A/4.
[16] See Adm. 2/1, *passim*.
[17] PRO, PC 6/1, pp. 380–1.
[18] Tanner, *Catalogue*, iv. 65–6, 70–1, 80–2, 83–6; Rawl. MS A. 314, fo. 12.
[19] Tanner, *Catalogue*, iii. 6, 17; iv. 236; *Tangier Papers*, 144.
[20] NMM, ADL/A/4; NHL, MS 121/9, p. 77.
[21] SP 101/91, fos. 192, 196. In 1686 a group of captains were bitterly disappointed to
get only 100,000 pieces of eight between three ships: NHL, MS 169, p. 172.
[22] *Tangier Papers*, 166. Many voyages probably netted much less. In the early 1680s,
one voyage was expected to net £160 between two captains: KAO, U. 1515/O. 11, p. 82.

became even more marked in the years of England's neutrality. Ships
which berthed in Cadiz soon after the arrival of the Spanish plate-fleet
from America were counted particularly fortunate. In March 1677, for
example, it was reported that 'All our English fregates which have gone
from Cadiz Northwards or Eastwards since the arrival of the flota
last November, have carried much treasure for English, French,
Dutch and Italian accompts, to the very great advantage of the
Commanders'.[23]

The competition between captains for these 'good voyages' was
intense, and was caused by the inadequacy of their wages and the considerable expenses which were often incurred in the Mediterranean,
facts which were recognized by captains and administrators alike.[24]
Captains solicited for voyages with indecent desperation: obvious
targets for requests were the flag-officers commanding the fleets, but
anyone who might possess some influence could be a potential target
(Pepys, the admiral's secretary, found himself in this position on Lord
Dartmouth's expedition to Tangier in 1683).[25] The allocation of
profitable voyages gave rise to jealousies among the commanders and
helped to shape the factions which existed in the Mediterranean
fleet;[26] moreover, Pepys and his associates believed that the clamour
for these voyages affected the operational efficiency of the navy. They
accused captains of making any excuse to get an order to put in to
Cadiz, or any other port where a plate cargo might be obtained,[27] and
of inventing reasons to stay there until a sufficiently profitable cargo
appeared. Scrutiny of ships' journals suggested to Pepys that some
captains were staying in port for up to, or in some cases more than, half
of their time in the Mediterranean.[28] It is difficult to establish the exact
amount of truth, or otherwise, in these charges. Some English consuls
and merchants in the area upheld Pepys, and complained that warships
should have been concerned more with pursuing Algerine corsairs
than private profit.[29] On the other hand, Sari Hornstein's recent study
of the navy in the Mediterranean suggests that it was perfectly natural

[23] SP 101/92, fo. 34. Cf. SP 94/56, fo. 92; SP 94/63, fo. 326; KAO, U. 1713/C. 1,
fo. 45.
[24] Pepys MS 2581, p. 228; Pepys MS 2853, p. 337; *Tangier Papers*, 240–1; Rawl. MS
A. 189, fo. 267.
[25] *Tangier Papers*, 141–3.
[26] Ibid. 213.
[27] Ibid. 139, 141.
[28] Rawl. MS A. 185, fos. 110, 299; Pepys MS 2351, p. 201.
[29] See e.g. SP 101/91, fo. 197; Adm. 2/1752, pp. 96–7.

for warships to spend long periods in port for legitimate reasons, such as repairs or weather conditions—considerations which were largely ignored by Pepys. Even if captains bent their orders to benefit themselves at times, they did carry out those orders.[30] Ultimately, as Dr Hornstein has pointed out,[31] the problem in assessing the sea-officers' motives for putting in to or remaining in port centres on the obvious fact that they would not mention selfish motives in their official correspondence or ships' journals, which, with few exceptions, are all that survives. Moreover, there are hints of collusion between captains and some local consuls or officials: the navy agent at Gibraltar in the mid-1680s and his contacts among the Cadiz merchants may not have been the only Englishmen actively to co-operate with captains' aspirations for 'good voyages'.[32] In conclusion, there were certainly abuses, but they were not, on the whole, to the detriment of English naval policy in the Mediterranean.

The naval administration's responses to the problems with the plate-carriage system lacked credibility. The solution was obvious, and was always recognized by Pepys and his colleagues: plate-carriage had to be abolished completely, and wages raised to a level which would remove temptation from the captains' paths.[33] In the 1670s and first half of the 1680s, however, the financial conditions which would permit such a reform did not exist. The administration could only fall back on cosmetic measures to curb the worst excesses, and even in this it was handicapped by the inconsistency of the administrators themselves. Pepys occasionally attempted to warn captains against going into port too often, but this depended on the co-operation of the local commander-in-chief;[34] attempts to get English merchants or consuls to report on the length of time spent in port by English warships were equally half-hearted.[35] Pepys was by no means entirely critical of the captains, and sympathized with the financial plight which drove them

---

[30] Hornstein, 'Deployment', 49, 68–75, 81; Cf. KAO, U. 1515/O. 8, unfol., Narbrough to Pepys, 6 Nov. 1678, third fo. *recto*. For the deep concern of two captains to reconcile their personal gain with their orders, see HMC, *Downshire MSS*, i. 235; SP 94/63, fo. 126ᵛ.

[31] Hornstein, 'Deployment', 81.

[32] NHL, MS 169, pp. 145, 152, 155, 157, 159, 162, 172.

[33] Rawl. MS A. 464, fo. 174; BL, Egerton MS 3383, fo. 129; *Tangier Papers*, 148, 227; HMC, *Dartmouth MSS*, iii. 131.

[34] See e.g. Pepys MS 2854, p. 361; Pepys MS 2856, p. 60; KAO, U. 1515/O. 8, unfol., Narbrough to Herbert, 9 Mar. 1679.

[35] See e.g. Tanner, *Catalogue*, iii. 371.

to seek plate cargoes.[36] The main complaint made by Pepys was not so much against the principle of the voyages, but against their iniquitous distribution, so that a few gentlemen officers with influence gained voyages and others did not;[37] indeed, he even suggested that abolishing the 'good voyage' would end the distinction between gentlemen and tarpaulins, because it would take away the main bone of contention between the two types of sea-officer.[38] However, attempts by Pepys and his rivals in the Admiralty commission of 1679–84 to deal with the problem foundered on the tolerance shown by Charles and James towards their captains. Both believed that captains had to be given 'good voyages' to encourage them, at least until Parliament voted more money for the navy, and officers therefore relied on their easy access to the king and duke to apply for such voyages. Captain Thomas Hamilton, lying in Alicante harbour in 1678, wrote to his kinsman and patron, the earl of Ossory, asking him to represent to the king and duke that he had not yet been sent on a profitable voyage.[39] Even when, in 1682, the Admiralty court-martialled two captains for spending too much time at Cadiz, Charles intervened on the officers' behalf.[40] Pepys bemoaned the fact that commanders would conclude from this incident that they would never be punished for their misdemeanours in the Mediterranean.[41]

The commanders-in-chief of the Mediterranean squadrons had come to the same conclusion many years earlier. Sir John Berry, who served in the area in each decade of Charles II's reign, recalled that the practice of admirals taking a share of their subordinates' profits from 'good voyages' began under Allin, and continued under Spragge, Narbrough, and Herbert.[42] The accusations against Allin certainly seem to have had some foundation; when he returned to England in 1669, it was common knowledge that he had indulged in large-scale trading, and his subordinates accused him of taking a 50-per-cent 'cut'

---

[36] Pepys MS 2853, p. 337; Pepys MS 2855, p. 15. It is also possible that Pepys might have benefited financially from some voyages: certainly, Sir John Narbrough kept his profits from such voyages with Pepys's servant Will Hewer at the Admiralty secretary's house (KAO, U. 1515/O. 8, unfol., Narbrough to Capt. Langston, 12 Mar. 1679).

[37] *Tangier Papers*, 120, 150, 206–7, 213.

[38] Ibid. 214.

[39] Bod. Lib., Carte MS 38, fos. 621–2. Cf. Davies, 'Pepys and the Admiralty Commission', 40–1.

[40] Ibid. 40.

[41] *Tangier Papers*, 227.

[42] Ibid. 183.

from plate-carriage.[43] Indeed, the outcry against Allin prompted the administration to reiterate its prohibition of merchant voyages, but at the end of 1669 Allin returned once again to the Mediterranean as admiral.[44] Opinions on Herbert's time as admiral must be treated with caution, as explained later in this chapter, but he was accused among other things of corruptly arranging promotions in favour of men who would give him a larger share of their profits, and of deliberately prolonging the war with Algiers to enhance his personal profit.[45] Even Lord Dartmouth, Pepys's epitome of an enlightened admiral, found himself unable to resist the pressure from his subordinates for orders or excuses to visit Cadiz, and it was subsequently reported that Dartmouth's fleet had returned to England with plate worth £600,000 for merchants' accounts.[46] The problems caused by plate-carriage were finally dealt with at their root by James and Pepys in July 1686, when the practice was prohibited (except in certain specifically authorized cases) in favour of a substantial increase in captains' wages and allowances.[47] The end of the long peace two years later obscured one important flaw in this apparently far-sighted Pepysian reform: the new allowances were never paid.[48]

The officers of the Straits fleet were concerned to make money, but not to the exclusion of everything else. The wars against the corsairs provided opportunities for glory, and included both daring attacks on fortified harbours and some of the most famous single ship actions before the time of Nelson, such as Sir John Kempthorne's defence of the *Mary Rose* against seven Algerine ships in 1669, or his son Morgan's heroic action in the *Kingfisher* in 1681.[49] Hand in hand with the chance of earning a reputation for bravery went the chance of gaining promotion. At a time when promotion in home waters was severely restricted, the Mediterranean provided opportunities for

---

[43] Pepys MS 2581, pp. 190, 228; BL, Addit. MS 36916, fo. 136. Cf. SP 94/56, fo. 92.

[44] Narbrough, too, was punctilious in insisting on his 'Customary' share from voyages: KAO, U. 1515/O. 8, unfol., Narbrough to Capt. Langston, 12 Mar. 1679. Cf. *Tangier Papers*, 183.

[45] Ibid. 159–60, 182, 195–6, 199–203 *et passim*; BL, Egerton MS 3383, fos. 126–30.

[46] *Tangier Papers*, 144–5, 205–6; Bod. Lib., MS Film 295, Newdigate newsletter 1518 (original at the Folger Shakespeare Library, Washington, DC).

[47] Establishment printed in *Pepys' Memoires of the Royal Navy 1679–88*, ed. J. R. Tanner (Oxford, 1906), 55–68.

[48] NHL, MS 121/11, p. 5; BL, Addit. MS 11602, fos. 76, 77.

[49] Kempthorne, 'Sir John Kempthorne', 302, 311–14.

advancement which did not depend on influence at court, or months of soliciting in the galleries of Whitehall. Through their patrons, young volunteers sought places on ships going to the Straits, and the quotas of volunteers on such ships were invariably full.[50] Mortality provided a natural means of succession. Although the Straits fleet was never as notorious as the West Indies squadron became in the eighteenth century, the combination of deaths from natural causes and enemy action did provide a large number of vacancies: for example, the death of Captain Thomas Gardiner of the *Assistance* in April 1679 led to the elevation of his lieutenant, John Jenifer, while the death of Captain Edward Pinn of the *Hampshire* in July 1680 allowed three officers to move into larger commands.[51] However, Jenifer's promotion was automatic, whereas the elevation of Pinn's successors depended on the personal preference of the commander-in-chief, who held full powers of appointment on the station. The favour of the admiral was vital if an officer aspired to a vacancy which occurred in the Mediterranean.

Like flag-officers in home waters, admirals in the Mediterranean naturally attempted to gather as many of their friends and clients around them as possible. Arthur Herbert, going out as vice-admiral to Narbrough in the spring of 1678, sought places for several young men who were later to gain commissions through his patronage, including Francis Wheeler, Anthony Hastings, and Charles Kirke.[52] Many of the problems and personality clashes which blighted the Mediterranean fleet in the early 1680s may be attributable to Herbert's almost total domination of the means of patronage; with only one flag-officer, unlike the situation in earlier fleets, promotion was restricted chiefly to his own 'pool' of clients. However, several officers made a successful transition from Narbrough's patronage to Herbert's when the command changed hands in 1679, among them the future national heroes George Rooke and Cloudesley Shovell.[53] Similarly, George Aylmer (brother of another Herbert protégé, Matthew Aylmer) adjusted smoothly from being a client of his 'good patrons' George Legge and the earl of Ossory in home waters to becoming 'a swearing idle fellow' in the circle of Herbert's crony Colonel Kirke at Tangier, before reverting to Legge's patronage when, as Lord Dartmouth, he

---

[50] See Pepys MS 2856, p. 201; Adm. 2/1749–51, *passim*.

[51] Adm. 106/343, fo. 315; Herbert Lbk, 129.

[52] Ibid. 2, 4, 7; P. Le Fevre, 'Charles Kirke', *MM* 68 (1982), 327–8.

[53] Herbert Lbk, 97–8, 120, 129, 222; Rawl. MS A. 228, fo. 38; *Tangier Papers*, 141, 186–7. However, Herbert certainly knew of both Rooke and Shovell from earlier years.

brought a fleet to evacuate the town.[54] Even so, Aylmer was quite prepared to abandon Dartmouth again if he did not get the command he wanted.[55] It made sense to cultivate any potential patron, particularly as there were few such men in the Mediterranean. When the king's bastard son, the duke of Grafton, came to the area as a volunteer in 1679, Shovell quickly became 'one of his great favourits'; eight years later Grafton returned to the Straits as vice-admiral of England, with Shovell as his flag-captain.[56]

For those who were unwilling to cultivate the favour of the commander-in-chief or the very few other men of influence, or for those who fell out with them, life in the Straits fleet could be extremely uncomfortable. When Captain Henry Barnardiston fell out with his admiral, Spragge, in 1671, he soon found himself with orders to sail home.[57] Such incidents were comparatively isolated until Herbert took command, but his unprecedented domination of the fleet led to a faction fight of an intensity unseen since the Dutch wars; by 1681 it was said that the Straits fleet was 'divided into 2 implacable factions, & the differences between them irreconcilable'.[58] The sea-officers who tended to oppose Herbert were men of his own or of an older generation, captains who had gained their first commands in the Dutch wars and may have resented the elevation of their equal. In 1678, even before he assumed the chief command, Herbert got into a dispute with Anthony Langston, 'a man that . . . knows not how to govern himself'; in 1666 Langston had been in command of a second-rate when Herbert was still a lieutenant.[59] More significant in the long term were Herbert's clashes with his second-in-command, Edward Russell, and with two long-serving tarpaulins, John Wyborne and William Booth. By the summer of 1681, Russell was said to have fallen out with his 'Quondam Amigo' and wrote that 'I lye under the same unhappy circumstances with Admirall Herbert that all other mankinde dos'; their uneasy relationship would have important repercussions in later years, when they were the two admirals entrusted with the defence of William III's crown and the 'revolution settlement'.[60]

[54] Rawl. MS A. 181, fos. 381, 387; *Tangier Papers*, 194–5; Adm. 2/1754, p. 95; HMC, *Dartmouth MSS*, i. 86; Pepys MS 2858, pp. 303, 366.
[55] *Tangier Papers*, 151.
[56] BL, Addit. MS 19872, fo. 40.
[57] Rawl. MS A. 174, fo. 380.
[58] Rawl. MS A. 183, fo. 190.
[59] Herbert Lbk, 35; Adm. 10/15, pp. 64, 79.
[60] Rawl. MS A. 183, fo. 190; HMC, *Finch MSS*, ii. 117; Rawl. MS A. 228, fo. 123. Cf. Ehrman, *The Navy in the War of William III*, chs. 9 and 10.

Wyborne, a friend of Pepys (whom Herbert detested),[61] was bitterly critical of Herbert's conduct, though Wyborne had always shown a liking for 'good voyages' and might have felt aggrieved at the admiral's allocation of those excursions.[62] Booth's break with Herbert came in 1681, when he and the admiral's client Francis Wheeler disputed the capture of an Algerine prize. Herbert took Wheeler's side and accused Booth of 'setting up for makeinge faction in the fleet, but I know very well he hath only malice, but neither merit nor sense enough to bring it about';[63] although Herbert later attempted a reconciliation, Booth remained embittered, at least in part because he, too, felt that he was not getting his fair share of profitable voyages.[64] At the end of Herbert's time in the Mediterranean, another of his opponents observed that 'no man can expect to get anything but those who are his favourites';[65] the exclusivity of Herbert's circle, with young men like Shovell, Wheeler, Matthew Aylmer, and Anthony Hastings monopolizing the admiral's favour in appointments and the allocation of voyages, was a source of considerable resentment to those outside it.[66] This preference was regarded as one manifestation of Herbert's supposed opposition to tarpaulins,[67] but it should really be seen as a preference for younger men who were personally loyal to him: Herbert furthered the careers of several young tarpaulins, notably Shovell and John Benbow, both of whom went on to flag-rank and international fame, and he also tried to assist older men who had served under him.[68]

In his relations with authority, Herbert was hampered by his rough, plain-speaking manner and violent temper, failings of which he was well aware.[69] He quarrelled with successive governors of Tangier, regarding the earl of Inchiquin's behaviour as 'preposterous' and accusing Colonel Sackville of 'sloath and want of integrity'.[70] He fell out with Henry Shere, the engineer of the Tangier breakwater or

---

[61] Rawl. MS A. 178, fo. 39; Herbert Lbk, 222; *Tangier Papers*, 139.

[62] Rawl. MS A. 190, fo. 41; Rawl. MS A. 194, fo. 123ᵛ; *Naval Minutes*, 36; Tanner, *Catalogue*, iv. 83–4; *Tangier Papers*, 141, 213.

[63] Herbert Lbk, 199; P. Le Fevre, 'The Dispute over the *Golden Horse* of Algiers', *MM* 73 (1987), 313–17.

[64] Herbert Lbk, 186–7, 193–4, 197–200, 208; HMC, *Finch MSS*, ii. 190.

[65] Ibid. ii. 185.

[66] *Tangier Papers*, 141, 186–7 *et passim*.

[67] See e.g. ibid. 123.

[68] W. A. Benbow, *Brave Benbow: The Life of Vice-Admiral John Benbow, 1653–1702* (Victoria, BC, 1986), 15–17; Herbert Lbk, 139.

[69] See e.g. Rawl. MS A. 228, fos. 122, 150; Herbert Lbk, 115.

[70] Ibid. 23–4, 173–4 *et passim*. Cf. HMC, *Finch MSS*, ii. 103–4, 107, 110–11.

'mole', because he regarded it as inadequate to protect shipping and therefore ordered his ships to Gibraltar for cleaning.[71] His relations with the authorities at home were even worse. Herbert attacked Pepys for failing to maintain a regular correspondence;[72] his concern to receive royal approval of his actions and to counter the 'unhandsome & unjust proceedings of my enemies' was almost obsessive.[73] He criticized the poor provision of stores for his fleet, on one occasion instructing John Brisbane (Admiralty secretary from February 1680, and Herbert's personal friend) in the most dramatic terms, *'for God of heavens sake speak that wee may have stores'*.[74]

Herbert also found fault with his instructions. When he assumed command of the fleet in 1679 he was restricted to the waters immediately adjacent to Tangier, which was then under threat from the Moors. Although the Admiralty clearly intended these orders as a means of helping to defend the garrison, Herbert found them nonsensical in terms of his main objective, the war against Algiers. He sought unrestricted freedom of movement, without which he believed that the continued stationing of a squadron in the Straits was pointless.[75] Closely related to this question was Herbert's attempt to gain an admiral's flag for himself. When he became commander-in-chief after Narbrough's departure, he retained the title of vice-admiral and had no powers to hold courts-martial, and he maintained a correspondence with successive Admiralty secretaries in an attempt to gain more power for himself.[76] He received the powers to hold courts-martial in October 1679,[77] but the admiral's flag proved more difficult to obtain. Herbert claimed that he needed it to define the extent of his power over his subordinates and to treat with the Algerines, who only had respect for an admiral's commission.[78] The Admiralty proved reluctant to comply with his request: they thought it absurd that a full admiral should command so few ships, and there may have been a suspicion among at least some of the commissioners that Herbert's chief aim was his own aggrandizement.[79] Nevertheless, the interven-

---

[71] Herbert Lbk, 143, 159, 170–1, 222–3; BL, Lansdowne MS 193, fos. 16, 19, 67, 68^v, 69^v, 71^v, 72, 74^v; Hornstein, 'Deployment', 162.

[72] Herbert Lbk, 19, 73.

[73] Ibid. 173–4.

[74] Ibid. 125–6. Cf. Hornstein, 'Deployment', 65–8 and ch. 6 *passim*.

[75] Herbert Lbk, 61–2, 65–7, 114–16; Hornstein, 'Deployment', 116–20.

[76] Herbert Lbk, 68, 73, 82–3, 88–91.

[77] Ibid. 93.

[78] Ibid. 114–16, 128.

[79] Adm. 3/277, pt. 1, 175; Adm. 2/1749, p. 198.

tion of his patron, the duke of York, brought Herbert the desired result, and in July 1680 he was commissioned admiral.[80] Despite this success (or perhaps because of it), his relations with the Admiralty remained strained, and, if anything, deteriorated.

The parliamentary Admiralty commission set up by Charles II in the spring of 1679 as a sop to a vociferously anti-Catholic House of Commons has received a uniformly bad press, due largely to Pepys's devastating indictments of its record.[81] Much of this criticism was justified, but in his eagerness to score points over political rivals Pepys seriously distorted the truth about the commission. Its members were certainly inexperienced and torn by factional jealousies, but they made a genuine effort to stamp out abuses; the real culprits for the deterioration of the material condition of the navy between 1679 and 1684 were the Treasury commissioners, who were unable or unwilling to respond to the Admiralty's often desperate appeals for money. Pepys's famous figures which charted the decline of the navy from seventy-six ships in service in 1679 to just twenty-four in 1684 were lifted impudently out of context: had it not been for the inability of the Admiralty commission which he had served to pay off the massive fleet mobilized in 1678, Pepys himself would have regarded twenty-four ships as an acceptable size for the summer fleet of 1679, or any other year. Pepys's enduring and colourful libel of the commission's record should not be seen as the unvarnished truth, but as one element in the struggles which dominated naval affairs in the 1680s. Central to those struggles was the re-emergence, after almost a decade, of men who moved constantly and comfortably between the two worlds of the navy and court politics.

The first of these men was Arthur Herbert. The Admiralty commissioners never had much faith in him: they took Inchiquin's side in his dispute with Herbert, and demanded the admiral's recall in July and October 1679, and again in February 1680. On each occasion, only the king's support prevented Herbert's return in disgrace.[82] From February 1680 onwards, the Admiralty was more divided in its attitude to its admiral in the Straits: Daniel Finch, the new leading figure in the commission,[83] opposed Herbert, but the new secretary, John Brisbane,

---

[80] Rawl. MS A. 228, fo. 69ᵛ.

[81] This paragraph is based on Davies, 'Admiralty Commission', 34–53.

[82] Adm. 3/277, pt. 1, pp. 80, 170; pt. 2, pp. 15, 17.

[83] Viscount Brouncker was nominally first commissioner until 1682, by virtue of social rank alone: Davies, 'Admiralty Commission', 35–6.

proved very friendly to him, and relations between the two administrators were sour from the beginning.[84] The high favour which
Daniel and the rest of the Finch family enjoyed throughout 1681 was
detrimental to Herbert's and Brisbane's interests, and the secretary
regularly informed the admiral of the strong criticisms which were
being made of his strategy and immoral life-style, and of the favour
which the 'mighty multitude' of their opponents enjoyed at court.[85] In
June 1681, Herbert suggested that a possible alternative to the expense
of an offensive war or the disgrace of a hasty peace would be a change
to a defensive strategy based on a comprehensive convoy system. Finch
vigorously opposed this project, on the grounds that Herbert would be
able to line his pockets by extorting fees from merchantmen, but the
Admiralty's professional advisers—'those great men for the Sea soe
often mentioned at the council board', as Herbert called them—also
put forward convincing strategic reasons for rejecting this scheme.
Herbert hastily protested his innocence, saying that he had only
suggested the plan as one option, and defended himself against
Finch's charges of seeking his own gain (a charge which was unfounded, as Herbert had never proposed to have the convoys under his
own control).[86] However, 1682 saw important changes in the relative
positions of the protagonists. Finch lost ground at court, and Henry
Savile and Sir John Chicheley, both clients of the duke of York and
well disposed towards Herbert and Brisbane, joined the Admiralty
commission at the earl of Halifax's instigation.[87] Even more significant
was the return to favour and high office of the earl of Sunderland, 'who
hath beene a very excellent friend to you & I doe answeare will prove
so', Brisbane told Herbert.[88] The successful conclusion of a peace
with Algiers further raised the admiral's stock, as Brisbane observed in
October 1682: 'your enemies will all flatter you, when you come, for
your success & the Kings continued bounty hath overcome their hopes
of ruining you.'[89] The secretary was being over-optimistic. The end of

[84] Leicestershire RO, Finch political papers 148, fo. 6; Horwitz, *Revolution Politicks*,
ch. 2 *passim*.
[85] Rawl. MS A. 228, fos. 89, 94, 108, 122; Horwitz, *Revolution Politicks*, 28–31.
Another of Herbert's correspondents warned him of the charge that he did 'not whore
decently': BL, Addit. MS 39757, fo. 108.
[86] Leicestershire RO, Finch political papers 148, fo. 6; Herbert Lbk, 188–90,
213–15; Rawl. MS A. 228, fos. 125–6, 127–8; P. Le Fevre, 'Arthur Herbert and his
Scheme for Establishing Convoys in the Mediterranean', *MM* 64 (1978), 134.
[87] Longleat House, Thynne MS 41, fo. 286.
[88] Rawl. MS A. 228, fo. 169ᵛ; Horwitz, *Revolution Politicks*, 32–5.
[89] Rawl. MS A. 228, fo. 153.

the war made Herbert's recall inevitable,[90] while his high position in the navy itself was beginning to come under threat from two different directions.

While Herbert commanded in the Mediterranean, two rivals were gaining increasing favour at court. George Legge had not served at sea since the third Dutch war, but his command of a second-rate at that time gave him a place on the half-pay list, and he kept in close touch with naval affairs; Sir Roger Strickland, rear-admiral of Narbrough's fleet, was a close friend, his governorship of Portsmouth gave him a natural point of contact with the navy, and as late as 1679 Legge was associated with a group of gentlemen captains who opposed Pepys.[91] By the end of 1682, Legge had become master of the ordnance, had been raised to the peerage as Baron Dartmouth, and had already become 'convinc'd abundantly of the ignorance of those Gentlemen', the Admiralty commissioners (even though Daniel Finch was an old school-friend).[92] His rise had been due to the high favour he enjoyed with the duke of York, though he regarded himself as competing for that favour with John Churchill, a close friend of Herbert.[93] Dartmouth became regarded as a leader of a group of Anglican tories at court; in the spring of 1683 he was heavily involved in intrigues with the earl of Rochester against the rising influence of Sunderland, the new secretary of state.[94] The other sea-officer to rise to prominence at this time, the duke of Grafton, did so by very different means. The natural son of Charles II and the duchess of Cleveland, he served as a volunteer in the Mediterranean between 1679 and 1681 before succeeding Prince Rupert as vice-admiral of England in January 1683.[95] Grafton naturally had fewer connections among the sea-officers than either Herbert or Dartmouth, but he became closely associated with the new first commissioner of the Admiralty, Finch, who succeeded to the earldom of Nottingham in December 1682.[96]

Herbert sought to capitalize on his success in the Algerine war by

---

[90] Ibid. Cf. Adm. 3/278, pt. 3, p. 61.

[91] HMC, *Dartmouth MSS*, i. 132–3; NMM, LBK/8, p. 891.

[92] Legh, *Lyme Letters*, 80, 129–30; G. E. C., *Complete Peerage*, s.n. 'Dartmouth'; Rawl. MS A. 194, fo. 277ᵛ; Horwitz, *Revolution Politicks*, 2–3, 30.

[93] Staffordshire RO, MS D(W)1778/Ii/615. For the friendship of Herbert and Churchill see Rawl. MS A. 228, fo. 148.

[94] *Reresby Memoirs*, 294; J. P. Kenyon, *Robert Spencer, Earl of Sunderland 1641–1702* (1958), 91, 93.

[95] A. Fitzroy, *Henry, Duke of Grafton 1663–90* (1921), 9–11.

[96] Leicestershire RO, Finch political papers 148, fo. 7.

joining the Admiralty board, an appointment favoured by the duke of York, but resisted strongly by Nottingham, Dartmouth, and Grafton; the king supported Herbert's case, and in August 1683, shortly after his return from the Mediterranean, Herbert became a supernumerary member of the board.[97] By that time, naval preparations centred on an expedition to demolish Tangier, a drastic step which its proponents, Charles, James, Sunderland, and Rochester, saw as an essential cost-cutting exercise.[98] Despite the lively social life which they had enjoyed there, few sea-officers mourned the loss of Tangier. It had never been a success as an operational base, and commanders-in-chief from Allin to Herbert had doubted its value.[99] Nevertheless, the expedition to destroy the town was undertaken in extraordinary secrecy,[100] and this even extended to the chief command of the expedition. In April 1683, Grafton was commissioned admiral and commander-in-chief in the narrow seas, and on 5 July he joined the third-rate named in his honour, the *Grafton*, to take command of a force which included two other third-rates—the most powerful naval force England had sent to sea for five years.[101] It is unlikely that Grafton was ever seriously intended to command the Tangier expedition, and at some point in July it was decided to remove him from the command. On 27 July Grafton was suddenly recalled to Whitehall, and six days later Dartmouth boarded the *Grafton* as admiral, his commission having been signed in haste on the very day he took command;[102] the Admiralty was ignored completely, and still believed that Grafton was in command the day after he was recalled.[103] Grafton and his mother, the duchess of Cleveland, were bitterly disappointed and remarked 'that Wm Legs son should not have been disparaged to go Vice-admirall under the Kings son'.[104] In most respects, however, Dartmouth was a better choice for the task in hand. The response of the Moors, the French, and the Spanish to the English expedition was

[97] Rawl. MS A. 228, fo. 178; Horwitz, *Revolution Politicks*, 35; Appendix II, below.

[98] Horwitz, *Revolution Politicks*, 35 n; PRO, PRO 31/3/155, fo. 104.

[99] Rawl. MS A. 190, fos. 66–69; Cholmeley, *Account of Tangier*, 147; Hornstein, 'Deployment', ch. 6 *passim*.

[100] Bod. Lib., Carte MS 217, fo. 37; Bod. Lib., MS Film 295, Newdigate newsletters 1413, 1416, 1418, 1445; A. Bryant, *Samuel Pepys: The Years of Peril* (1935), 393–401.

[101] Tanner, *Catalogue*, i. 313; Adm. 51/407, pt. 1, *Grafton* log.

[102] Ibid., 27 July, 2 Aug. 1683; Adm. 51/3863, *Henrietta* log, 27 and 30 July 1683; Tanner, *Catalogue*, i. 313.

[103] Adm. 3/278, pt. 3, pp. 97, 102. For the secrecy with which Dartmouth's commission was drafted, see Davies, 'Admiralty Commission', 42.

[104] Bod. Lib., Carte MS 40, fo. 108. Cf. PRO, PRO 31/3/155, fo. 113.

uncertain, and Dartmouth had the advantages of having commanded ships in battle, of having several years' military service behind him, and of having experience in ordnance matters. He had also been involved in the secret planning of the expedition from the beginning, and had resolutely opposed the sale of the town to France—a move which had been strongly supported by the king's mistress (the duchess of Portsmouth) and the French envoy Barrillon, but which was defeated largely by Dartmouth's obstinacy.[105]

Nevertheless, in the broader political context Dartmouth's position was extremely delicate. His departure weakened the court tories opposed to Sunderland,[106] while the demolition of Tangier was an act of outstanding importance which was bound to attract considerable opposition at home.[107] Dartmouth and the Admiralty board were well aware of their dislike of each other; ideally, Dartmouth wanted to bring down the board, end the influence of Grafton and Herbert in naval matters, and secure the duke of York's return to the Admiralty.[108] Ironically, in the short term Dartmouth's departure from England weakened his chances of bringing about these changes. Like Herbert before him, he had to look constantly over his shoulder and keep in mind the influence his enemies would exert at court while he was away: 'I do not doubt my task is easy at Whitehall, though I am sure few of them could go through with it,' he wrote to his friend William Trumbull, while in December 1683 he informed Rochester that 'I am very sensible what advantage my enemies will endeavour to take of my long stay here,' and identified 'all the ill practices and arts of [John] Churchill' as one of the main obstacles to his interest.[109] Dartmouth therefore had to move cautiously, taking care not to offend those who might bring influence to bear against him at court: this entailed a great deal of swallowing of pride, with Dartmouth being unable to impose discipline on well-connected captains in his fleet or to criticize those involved in the government of Tangier, notably Percy Kirke, Herbert's close friend and Dartmouth's predecessor as governor of the colony.[110]

---

[105] All Souls College, Oxford, MS 317, fos. 7–9.
[106] Kenyon, *Sunderland*, 94.
[107] See e.g. Grey, *Debates of the House of Commons*, vii. 97–101; viii. 4–20, 99–106.
[108] HMC, *Dartmouth MSS*, i. 93; iii. 121, 124; *Tangier Papers*, 218–19.
[109] HMC, *Downshire MSS*, i. 20; *The Correspondence of Henry Hyde, Earl of Clarendon, and of his Brother Laurence Hyde, Earl of Rochester*, ed. S. W. Singer (1828), i. 92. Cf. All Souls College, Oxford, MS 317, fo. 12; Staffordshire RO, MS D(W)1778/Ii/959.
[110] *Tangier Papers*, 164, 174, 186, 221, 244.

Bound up closely with Dartmouth's grandiose objective of reforming the Admiralty was a more immediate task, the overthrow of his rival Herbert in the duke of York's favour. Dartmouth even compared their rivalry to that of Sir Edward Spragge and Sir Robert Holmes, quoting Spragge's remark 'that he was willing to leave it to the King which he would choose . . . and that it would spoil his whole service to make use of them both'.[111] Dartmouth's fleet abounded with enemies of Herbert. His flag-captain was Sir William Booth, recently knighted but still nursing a grudge against Herbert, and another new naval knight who detested Herbert, Sir John Wyborne, was also in the squadron.[112] Henry Shere was on the expedition, still bitter at Herbert's contempt for the mole which he had built, and was now employed to demolish.[113] Pepys's former clerk Samuel Atkins was also aboard the *Grafton*; he had failed to get a lieutenancy from Herbert in 1682, and resented the admiral's treatment of him. Atkins attributed Herbert's failure to promote him to his connection with Pepys, and during Herbert's command of the Straits fleet Atkins had informed Pepys of the admiral's implacable opposition to the former Admiralty secretary and all connected with him.[114] Indeed, Herbert and Brisbane had long believed that Pepys was intriguing against them, and that he was responsible, among other things, for inciting Booth to oppose Herbert.[115] The most significant passenger aboard the *Grafton*, therefore, was Pepys himself, serving as Dartmouth's secretary and assiduously collecting every story or rumour which might serve to discredit Herbert.[116]

Pepys made few concessions to fair-mindedness. His sources of information were all Herbert's enemies, Dartmouth, Shere, Booth, Wyborne, Atkins, and Sir John Berry (captain of the *Henrietta* in Dartmouth's squadron, and an old friend of both Pepys and Shere).[117]

---

[111] Ibid. 245.

[112] In addition to other sources cited, much of this and the next paragraph is based on P. Le Fevre, 'Arthur Herbert and the Tangier Papers of Samuel Pepys' (unpublished paper).

[113] All Souls College, Oxford, MS 317, fo. 9.

[114] Rawl. MS A. 178, fos. 184, 186; Rawl. MS A. 183, fo. 190; Rawl. MS A. 194, fos. 257–8.

[115] Rawl. MS A. 228, fos. 108–9.

[116] For Pepys's and the fleet's activities at Tangier, the best account (albeit heavily biased in favour of Pepys's view) is A. Bryant, *Samuel Pepys: The Saviour of the Navy* (1938), chs. 1–5. Unfortunately, Pepys is silent on the process which had brought him and Dartmouth together since 1679.

[117] *Tangier Papers, passim*; Le Fevre, 'Arthur Herbert and the Tangier Papers', *passim*.

Between them, they assembled a mass of anecdotes about Herbert's supposed immorality and corruption, though there is a strong element of wish-fulfilment in many of the stories which Pepys recorded in his 'Tangier papers'. There was undoubtedly a considerable amount of truth in many of the stories—sexual morality, for example, was never the strong point of either Arthur Herbert or Tangier itself, and tales of 'good voyages' were easy to come by in the Straits fleet—but others were distorted by personal animosity, and some were entirely concocted. Pepys made much of Herbert's mocking attitude to ships' journals, noting that the admiral had never kept and never would keep one; Pepys evidently did not know or did not care that Herbert had kept a competent journal in his own hand for his flagship, the *Bristol*.[118] Pepys faithfully noted Dartmouth's statement that 'Herbert did make two captains at sea that had never been lieutenants, Wheeler and Hastings, the latter being his valet de chambre and both his vicious confidants and such as were privy to things, he durst not but oblige them.'[119] The second part of the story may have contained an element of truth; the first part was pure fiction, as Pepys must have known. Anthony Hastings became a lieutenant in 1673, commanded a ketch in 1676, and served as first lieutenant of a first-rate in 1678, all long before Herbert gave him a captain's commission in 1681.[120] Wheeler served as a lieutenant for some time before gaining a command;[121] Pepys had actually secured approval of his first appointment as a lieutenant, even though it transgressed the strict terms of the lieutenants' establishment of 1677.[122] The Tangier papers were designed and fashioned for self-interested ends, and are full of comments which Pepys's colleagues evidently knew he wanted to hear. Their purpose was to provide raw material to discredit Herbert and his clients; if that end was achieved, it might lead to Dartmouth attaining an unchallenged position in the duke of York's favour and, perhaps, to the return of the duke and Pepys to the Admiralty. They were emphatically not an accurate account of Arthur Herbert's command of the Straits fleet.[123]

Over the winter of 1683–4, Dartmouth's fleet lay before Tangier

---

[118] *Tangier Papers*, 225; Adm. 51/4131, pt. 3.

[119] *Tangier Papers*, 117–18.

[120] Tanner, *Catalogue*, i. 362; Adm. 10/15, p. 62.

[121] Tanner, *Catalogue*, i. 422.

[122] Herbert Lbk, pp. 7, 11; Rawl. MS A. 228, fo. 34ᵛ.

[123] Le Fevre, 'Arthur Herbert and the Tangier Papers', which also contains several other important examples of Pepys and his friends manufacturing or distorting evidence.

while the process of evacuation and demolition went on. His friends in England worried that the duration and expense of the operation would tell against him, and that he would have a hard time when he returned.[124] Dartmouth's enemies remained in high favour, and in January 1684 Arthur Herbert was elevated to the new, honorific, but prestigious post of rear-admiral of England.[125] The circumstances were inauspicious, therefore, when Dartmouth's fleet returned to England at the end of March, and he fully expected to find himself in disgrace.[126] His problems increased when he immediately accused the Admiralty of sending orders to ships in his fleet without reference to him, and an acrimonious correspondence ensued.[127] Dartmouth's treatment strengthened his resolve to come to a reckoning with the Admiralty, as he informed Pepys on 8 April:

> The Admiralty have already beene playing of tricks with me, endeavering to lessen my command, though I hope it is likely to continue but very short under them . . . let the Duke know of theire so unpresidented proceedings, which I apprehend was procured by Brisbane on purpose to put a slight upon me, but I hope the Duke will not thinke it his service to let me be quite thrown off from the Fleete, which now he hath an oppertunety to serve himself & protect my future pretentions in great measure at least; for upon my Lord Brunckards death he hath an oppertunity to bring you to the Admiralty, & if my Lord Nottinghame can help out Brisbane Mr Sheeres with your assistance, may againe put some life into the sea service . . . [128]

Dartmouth's plans for a limited reform of the Admiralty show his natural caution and concern for his enemies' proceedings, that he hoped to be able to work with his old friend Nottingham, and that he was out of touch (naturally enough) with the new groupings which had formed at court, where the duke of York, the duchess of Portsmouth, and the earl of Sunderland had formed an unlikely alliance which sought to restore James to the Admiralty and isolate Sunderland's rival Halifax,[129] whose influence over the Admiralty board had increased after he had arranged the appointments of Savile and Chicheley as

---

[124] HMC, *Downshire MSS*, i. 26–7. Cf. Bod. Lib., Carte MS 220, fo. 36.

[125] Adm. 3/278, pt. 3, p. 164; *Tangier Papers*, 327.

[126] Staffordshire RO, MS D(W)1778/Ii/1029.

[127] HMC, *Dartmouth MSS*, iii. 48–9; Adm. 2/1751, p. 54; Adm. 3/278, pt. 3, p. 199. Cf. Rawl. MS A. 190, fo. 115.

[128] Rawl. MS A. 190, fo. 113. The Admiralty commissioner Lord Brouncker had died on 5 April.

[129] Kenyon, *Sunderland*, 96–8; Horwitz, *Revolution Politicks*, 37.

commissioners in 1682.[130] Halifax's enemies had already scored an important success by securing the appointment of Lord Godolphin as secretary of state at the beginning of April, and they then turned their attentions to the Admiralty.

After seeing James at Whitehall, Dartmouth proceeded to Windsor on 11 April with Samuel Atkins, who noted that the king's reception of his admiral was 'very Gratious and kind'.[131] Praise of Dartmouth was unexpectedly generous and widespread, and his position seemed far stronger than had been anticipated.[132] For instance, Captain Randall MacDonnell was 'dismissed by the duke of his querries place, as well as of his ship for haveing wrote a letter to Admirall Herbert reflecting on Lord Dartmouth who had been his patron & brought him into his H[ighness']s service'.[133] Dartmouth spent April at court, conferring occasionally with his agents, Atkins and Captain David Lloyd;[134] the latter had connections in the duchess of Portsmouth's household, and may have acted as a 'go-between' for Dartmouth and his former adversaries Portsmouth and Sunderland, now all temporarily united by their wish to see change at the Admiralty.[135] However, their objectives were not attained immediately. Charles filled the vacancy on the board by appointing Herbert a full member, and he issued a new patent to the board on 17 April which added Halifax's new son-in-law, Lord Vaughan, as a supernumerary member.[136] The pressure on the king from the Dartmouth–Pepys group on the one hand, and the more powerful York–Portsmouth–Sunderland group on the other, finally had the desired effect in the following fortnight. Charles, with the court at Windsor, had decided by the beginning of May to part with an Admiralty which was largely the domain of the increasingly isolated Halifax, but he may have delayed the announcement while James went to London to attend his wife, who had suffered a miscarriage on the

---

[130] Longleat House, Thynne MS 41, fo. 286; *The Life and Letters of Sir George Savile, Bart, First Marquis of Halifax*, ed. H. C. Foxcroft (1898), i. 311, 313, 335–6.

[131] NMM, JOD/173, p. 217.

[132] *Reresby Memoirs*, 335; HMC, *Downshire MSS*, i. 29.

[133] Bod. Lib., Carte MS 216, fo. 482.

[134] NMM, JOD/173, pp. 217–18. The evidence for Lloyd's links with Dartmouth and Pepys is circumstantial but strong: see Pepys MS 2855, p. 313; Rawl. MS A. 183, fo. 190; *Tangier Papers*, 134, 225.

[135] Ibid. 330.

[136] J. C. Sainty, *Admiralty Officials 1660–1870* (1975), 21; F. Jones, 'The Vaughans of Golden Grove', *Transactions of the Honourable Society of Cymmrodorion* (1963), 132, 135–6.

6th.[137] On 10 May the Admiralty board met as usual, making plans for the following week's business and clearly unaware of what was about to happen; on the 11th, the king declared in council that the patent of the Admiralty commission was revoked. Charles took the nominal authority of the Admiralty into his own hands, leaving its executive powers to James.[138]

Herbert may not have been too disappointed at losing the commissioner's salary he had gained so recently; he remained in high favour with the duke of York, as the honours he received at James's accession a few months later showed.[139] The chief blow to his interest was the replacement of the pliant Brisbane as secretary of the Admiralty by the antipathetic Pepys. Ironically, in the short term it was Dartmouth who suffered. The caution he had shown at Tangier evaporated as a result of the favourable welcome he received, to be replaced by over-confidence. He tried to set up a new faction at court, opposed both to dissent and to Catholic, Francophile influences, but Sunderland, who had so recently sought his friendship, quickly scotched these ambitions. After several weeks of lobbying in late May and June, Dartmouth's interest collapsed, and with it his physical and mental health.[140] Nevertheless, he remained in favour with the king and duke, although his struggle with Herbert remained unresolved. The Admiralty commission of 1679–84 disappeared, and Pepys turned his attention from Herbert to the commission's posthumous memory. He succeeded so well that one of the greatest historians of the seventeenth-century navy, J. R. Tanner, could describe Pepys's 'Memoires' of the years 1679–84 as 'extraordinarily methodical, temperate, and fair'.[141] When Samuel Pepys set out to destroy the reputation of an opponent, the qualities of method, temperance, and fairness were noticeable only by their absence.

---

[137] PRO, PRO 31/3/158, fos. 26, 33; HMC, *Seventh Report*, 376. The timing of the announcement might also have been affected by the departure of one of the Admiralty board's likely defenders, Grafton, for France at the end of April: Bod. Lib., MS Film 295, Newdigate newsletter 1527.

[138] Adm. 3/278, pt. 3, pp. 212–13; NMM, JOD/173, pp. 219–20; PRO, PRO 31/3/158, fos. 33, 35–6, 38.

[139] See *DNB*, s.n. 'Herbert, Arthur'. If Pepys did pass on some or all of the material he had gathered on Herbert to Charles or James, it evidently had little effect.

[140] *Reresby Memoirs*, 335; HMC, *Downshire MSS*, i. 31–3.

[141] *Pepys' Memoires*, p. xv.

11

THE REVOLUTION OF 1688

THE navy was one part of James II's kingdom which might have been expected to greet his accession with unbridled enthusiasm. James himself perceived a special relationship, and told his sea-officers of his pride in having been their admiral before he was their king.[1] The navy soon benefited in a material sense from the new reign: the large sums voted by the Parliament of 1685 for the upkeep of the navy, and the increase in the yield from ordinary sources of revenue, freed the service from the financial constraints under which it had laboured since 1679, and the Navy Board was reorganized on Pepys's initiative to undertake a major programme of refurbishment.[2] Nevertheless, the essential problem of the peacetime navy, the lack of employment, persisted: throughout 1685 and 1686, the combined total of frigates on the two main stations, the Channel and the Mediterranean, came to less than a dozen.[3] More ships were hurriedly made ready for service during Monmouth's rebellion, but the short duration of that emergency served only to dash expectations, notably those of Arthur Herbert, the commander of the new fleet.[4] Herbert (the new master of the robes) was still competing for the royal favour with Dartmouth, master of both the horse and the ordnance,[5] and Grafton, who was developing his interest in the army as colonel of the first regiment of foot guards.[6] In particular, contemporaries perceived a struggle for favour between Dartmouth and Herbert's ally John Churchill: if one was believed to be on the way up, the other was clearly on the way down.[7]

---

[1] Dr William's Library, MS 31P, p. 585; *Memoirs of Thomas, Earl of Ailesbury, Written by Himself* (1890), i. 102–3, 131.

[2] Davies, 'Pepys and the Admiralty Commission of 1679–84', 43–52.

[3] Adm. 8/1, fos. 186–210.

[4] Pepys MS 2858, pp. 105–6. Cf. ibid. 1–138 *passim*, for the fleet's involvement in the Monmouth rebellion.

[5] 'Two such places as have rarely been in one Subjects hand': Dr William's Library, MS 31Q, p. 145.

[6] C. Dalton, *English Army Lists*, ii. 19.

[7] Davies, 'James II . . . and the Admirals', 87–8.

The relative positions of the leading flag-officers began to change when James introduced a new rival for the highest levels of naval preferment, Sir Roger Strickland. The former rear-admiral of the Straits fleet had been living in retirement on his Yorkshire estates for five years, making regular but unsuccessful attempts to solicit a command from the Admiralty; within four days of ascending the throne, James invited him to return to the service.[8] Strickland immediately attempted to assert himself, claiming the right to fly a flag at all times and to receive only the best commands—claims which Pepys disputed hotly.[9] However, Strickland's position at court was strong: his brother was James's vice-chamberlain, and his interests were also being promoted by his close friend Dartmouth.[10] Although he had been accused of Catholicism in 1679, as noted in Ch. 6, it is unlikely that Strickland was an overt adherent to that faith as early as 1685; indeed, James made no immediate move to introduce a Catholic element into his navy. The first appointment of an avowed Catholic was made only in July 1686, when the veteran Captain John Tyrwhitt, one of the two naval casualties of the 1673 Test Act, was commissioned to a port guardship.[11] Although elements in the army soon began to express concern about the influx of Catholic officers,[12] the navy was almost entirely free of such tensions for at least the first eighteen months of James's reign.

Other actions by James were more important in creating disquiet in the navy during this period. In the autumn of 1685, the king permitted French officers to search for escaping Huguenots aboard his royal yachts *en route* from France to England. One of the most senior and respected captains in the navy, William Davies of the *Catherine Yacht*, found the order 'astonishing' and collaborated in the smuggling of refugees on several occasions; he was eventually dismissed for this in May 1687. However, Davies's case could be one instance of James's ambiguous attitude to the whole Huguenot question. The dismissal might have been engineered to placate the French, for Davies was recommissioned to his post within a month, and when he was appointed flag-captain to the commander-in-chief in 1688

---

[8] Adm. 3/278, pt. 3, pp. 66, 205; Pepys MS 2857, pp. 164, 319.

[9] Pepys MS 2858, pp. 208–9, 227, 368, 379, 406–7, 543–4, 555–6.

[10] Pepys MS 2860, p. 277; HMC, *Dartmouth MSS*, i. 132–3.

[11] Tanner, *Catalogue*, i. 417.

[12] J. Childs, *The Army, James II, and the Glorious Revolution* (Manchester, 1980), 42, 46–7.

he was said to be 'a person of . . . much weight in the King's owne Estimation'.[13] Conflict also developed between the men of the fleet and the rapidly expanding standing army. By the autumn of 1686, clashes between seamen and soldiers were occurring at both Chatham and Portsmouth, usually taking the form of alehouse brawls, and the warrant-officers of the ships in ordinary at Portsmouth objected strongly to the quartering of troops from the garrison in their houses ashore.[14] James's controversial policies also affected the navy in other ways. In the summer of 1686, for example, the appointment of naval chaplains was taken away from the bishop of London, Henry Compton (whom James had suspended for opposing his religious policy), and given to the notoriously pliant bishop of Durham, Nathaniel Crewe.[15]

These tensions were developing as a more prominent Catholic element was being introduced into the fleet, for at some point during the winter of 1686–7 Sir Roger Strickland's conversion became public.[16] The change of faith was hardly a difficult step to take, given the nature of Strickland's family ties and dependence on James's patronage, but there were also sound professional reasons for it. Strickland's attempts to consolidate himself in the service had not been entirely successful: his desire for a flag or pennant of distinction had been blocked by Pepys, and in April 1686 the Admiralty secretary had warned Strickland that he was not guaranteed a place at sea that summer.[17] Regardless of its motivation, Strickland's conversion had far-reaching implications. Most of his close circle of clients also went over to Rome, notably Thomas Ashton, his lieutenant in 1678–9 and 1685, and Thomas Conaway, his lieutenant in 1672–4 who served under him again in 1686–7.[18] Strickland may have attempted to convert another client, John Laton, who served as his lieutenant in 1685–7 and for whose 'principles' Strickland assumed responsibility when recommending him for a command in 1687; similarly, an attempt may have been made to convert Captain Matthew Aylmer, who was granted dispensation from the oaths of allegiance and supremacy

---

[13] All Souls College, Oxford, MS 317, fos. 22, 41; Pepys MS 2860, pp. 88–9; Pepys MS 2861, pp. 210–11; Tanner, *Catalogue*, i. 343.
[14] Pepys MS 2859, pp. 261, 268, 376, 386; Adm. 106/380, pt. 1, fos. 170, 174, 179–84.
[15] Bod. Lib., Tanner MS 30, fo. 87; Pepys MS 2860, p. 25.
[16] *Reresby Memoirs*, 582.
[17] Pepys MS 2858, pp. 406–7, 420, 429–30; Pepys MS 2859, pp. 49, 173–4, 178.
[18] Charnock, *Biographia Navalis*, ii. 134; Pepys MS 2857, p. 392; Adm. 10/15, pp. 5, 31; BL, Harleian MS 7504, fos. 14–15; Rawl. MS A. 186, fo. 40.

in July 1687.[19] Though these attempts were unsuccessful, a small group of sea-officers not directly connected with Strickland was also converted. Randall MacDonnell, who had been cleared of a charge of papism in 1679, returned to his father's faith in a move which may have been designed in part to recover some of a County Antrim estate, lost to the family since the civil war,[20] and a small number of more junior officers were also converted.[21]

The existence of a new 'pool' of Catholic sea-officers was reflected in the appointments for the summer of 1687, when the converts were rewarded with promotion and for the first time James made a serious attempt to introduce a significant Catholic element into the officer corps. When Strickland attempted to get Ashton a command in August 1686, Pepys told him that with so many captains unemployed 'and some of them wanting bread', it would be unfair to bring in 'new ones over their heads, who had never yet Comands', but in April 1687 James appointed Ashton to a command.[22] In the same batch of appointments, John Tyrwhitt was given a seagoing command and Randall MacDonnell was promoted to a larger ship.[23] Strickland himself benefited most dramatically. Despite Pepys's bitter opposition, he was commissioned vice-admiral in Grafton's small Mediterranean fleet in the summer of 1687, and shortly afterwards he succeeded the recently disgraced Herbert as rear-admiral of England, a post which James had originally intended to keep vacant after Herbert's fall.[24] His influence on naval patronage increased throughout 1687 and 1688,[25] though his patronage of his Catholic clients was discreet: in May 1688 he wrote to a priest at James's court, asking him to recommend Thomas Conaway, 'an Honorable Sea officer having served as Leif [tenant] under many Comand [sic] ... the which I have not been wanting I laying favourable [sic] before the secretary of the Navy omitting only his being a Catholick'.[26]

Though the number of Catholics commissioned into the fleet was

[19] Pepys MS 2877, p. 341; *CSPD*, 1687–9, 23.
[20] Ibid. 53.
[21] See Gooch, 'Catholic Officers', 278–9, though Gooch's criterion for identifying Catholic sea-officers (i.e. selecting all those who did not serve after 1689) is erroneous: his list contains several known Protestants.
[22] Pepys MS 2859, p. 203; Pepys MS 2860, pp. 66–7.
[23] Ibid. 63–4; Tanner, *Catalogue*, i. 381.
[24] Pepys MS 2860, pp. 274–9; Pepys MS 2877, pp. 336–54; Pepys MS 2862, p. 34; Tanner, *Catalogue*, i. 315.
[25] Pepys MS 2861, pp. 210–11, 393; Rawl. MS A. 186, fos. 31–40.
[26] BL, Addit. MS 21483, fo. 31.

small in absolute terms, they still formed 10 to 12 per cent of the commissioned officer corps, and their presence was deeply resented by many sea-officers, notably the flag-officers Grafton and Sir John Berry.[27] Nevertheless, the position of the Catholic sea-officers was precarious. Once Strickland's clients and the other converts had been commissioned, there was virtually no 'reserve' of Catholics in training, in warrant-posts, or in the merchant service, to maintain the proportion should the fleet be expanded. By 1 December 1688 the commissioned-officer corps of the fleet had doubled in size, compared with the summer, to 157 men, but the number of Catholics remained at its previous level of nine, only 6 per cent of the new total.[28] The only 'new' Catholic captain brought into the service during the mobilization was William Constable, the future Viscount Dunbar, an army officer with barely a year's experience at sea.[29] As with so many of James's other projects, there was simply no time for a systematic programme of training young Catholic sea-officers to be carried through. Furthermore, there was no realistic prospect of introducing a substantial Catholic element onto the lower deck of the fleet until recruitment from Ireland became more feasible.[30] Without a strong body of co-religionists among the seamen and warrant-officers, the Catholic officers' influence was necessarily limited; even so, their presence influenced the factional divisions within the service, and had an important bearing on the reactions of the rest of the fleet to the events of 1688.

The 'Catholic factor' probably contributed, at least in part, to the most dramatic change in the relative positions of the leading sea-officers, the fall of Arthur Herbert from the royal favour. Early in March 1687, the king closeted Herbert as part of his campaign to secure the agreement of major office-holders to the repeal of the tests. James fully expected Herbert to comply, and was startled when the admiral refused on grounds of conscience—though as Herbert himself admitted, that conscience had been generally overlooked because of his notorious immorality. James responded by dismissing him from his places, an action which caused a great stir in the political nation; Herbert's dependence on the income from his offices was well known,

---

[27] Davies, 'James II . . . and the Admirals', 89–91.
[28] Adm. 8/1, fos. 239–40.
[29] G. E. C., *Complete Peerage*, s.n. 'Dunbar'; *CSPD*, 1687–9, 104; Gooch, 'Catholic Officers', 278–9.
[30] For earlier rejections of such recruitment, see above, p. 75.

and one observer remarked that 'some thought if any subject had made his station necessary it had been this man'.[31] After his dismissal, Herbert sought royal permission to go into the Venetian service against the Turks; James told him brusquely that 'he might go where he pleased for he had no service for him', but the king later changed his mind and Herbert was forbidden to leave the country.[32]

Herbert's stand on the issue of repeal was wholly out of character. Burnet, who learnt the measure of the admiral's mind while they discussed invasion plans together in 1688, probably got closest to the heart of the matter: 'his private quarrel with the lord Dartmouth, who he thought had more of the king's confidence than he himself had, was believed the root of all the sullenness he fell under towards the king, and of all the firmness that grew out of it.'[33] Even so, the issue of the repeal of the tests was a strange one to take up, given that the bitter jealousy of Herbert and Dartmouth was of such long standing. However, Herbert's politics had been somewhat ambiguous for several years. Despite his ties to James, he was closely related to, and on friendly terms with, whig politicians like Lord Mordaunt and Lord Herbert of Cherbury, and had once tried to gain a parliamentary seat through the latter's influence.[34] These associations do not make Herbert one of the 'first whigs', but they do suggest that he was open to more influences than those of his tory, courtier friends and of his patron, James. Herbert may also have been concerned at the prospect of repeal of the tests leading to a greater influx of Catholic officers into the navy: James was planning the appointments for the summer of 1687 by the beginning of March, and the intention to promote Catholics may therefore have been known before Herbert resigned.[35] Certainly, Strickland's conversion was already common knowledge, and his rise in the service (with the prospect of even more significant advancement if the tests were repealed), together with his friendship with Dartmouth, might in Herbert's eyes have posed such a threat to his influence on naval patronage that it could only be answered with a dramatic and desperate gesture of defiance.

By July 1688 James had an augmented summer guard at sea under

---

[31] *Bishop Burnet's History*, iii. 95–6; PRO, PRO 31/3/168, fos. 51–3; Dr Williams's Library, MS 31Q, pp. 81–2. Cf. PRO, PRO 30/53/8, fos. 42, 47.

[32] Longleat House, Thynne MS 42, fos. 137, 144; BL, Sloane MS 3328, fos. 58, 65; Luttrell, *Brief Historical Relation*, i. 396–7.

[33] *Bishop Burnet's History*, iii. 261.

[34] Davies, 'Navy, Parliament, and Political Crisis'.

[35] Pepys MS 2859, p. 490.

Strickland to monitor certain unexplained Dutch naval preparations.[36] Throughout his time in command, Strickland displayed a remarkable combination of arrogance and indiscretion: Pepys, for one, was bemused by Strickland's willingness to quibble for months on end over technicalities of status.[37] More significant was his introduction into the fleet of Catholic priests who attempted to say mass aboard ship, and officers and men alike reacted violently.[38] The king visited the fleet on 18 and 19 July, and went to each ship in an attempt to placate the seamen with kind words and money, putting the priests ashore and guaranteeing liberty of conscience to the men, but Strickland was retained in command.[39] James also spoke to each captain about Herbert's recent defection to Holland, an event which the king was clearly unable to comprehend; he railed against Herbert's 'ingratitude', but ominously found the captains unwilling to condemn the admiral's conduct.[40] The mood of the lower deck was unenthusiastic, and recruitment throughout the summer and autumn of 1688 was erratic: many seamen believed that they would not be paid if war came, and it was suggested (albeit chiefly by Dutch diplomats and English exiles, who may have been indulging in wishful thinking) that the seamen were not keen to fight their fellow Protestants, the Dutch. As in the earlier wars against the Dutch, desertion was commonplace.[41] Even before the full-scale mobilization to counter the Dutch threat began in September, therefore, the fleet's mood was tense, and its attitude uncertain.

That uncertainty was heightened by the defections of several leading sea-officers to the Netherlands. Edward Russell had been travelling to and from Holland since at least the beginning of 1687, ostensibly paying visits to a sister who lived there; by April 1688 he was privy to William's intention to invade England later that year. Herbert crossed over in July, landing at Rotterdam on the 14th.[42] The roles played by

[36] Ehrman, *The Navy in the War of William III*, 211.

[37] Pepys MS 2861, pp. 71–2, 241–2, 245–6, 310–11, 340–1, 351.

[38] Davies, 'James II . . . and the Admirals', 90.

[39] Longleat, Thynne MS 42, fo. 154ᵛ; BL, Addit. MS 34487, fo. 17; *Bishop Burnet's History*, iii. 248–9.

[40] PRO, PRO 30/53/8, fo. 67.

[41] BL, Addit. MS 34510, fo. 145; Addit. MS 34512, fos. 95, 108, 114; *Bishop Burnet's History*, iii. 248–9. For the manning of the fleet, see Ehrman, *Navy . . . of William III*, 229–33.

[42] Pepys MS 2859, pp. 446, 449; *Bishop Burnet's History*, iii. 229; N. Japikse (ed.), *Correspondentie van Willem III en van Hans Willem Bentinck* (The Hague, 1927–37), I. i. 36; BL, Addit. MS 41816, fo. 104. For his earlier political connections, see Davies, 'Navy . . . and Political Crisis'.

both men in the clandestine negotiations preceding William's invasion are well known; Russell as a signatory of the letter of invitation to the prince, and Herbert as its courier, ensured places for themselves in the pantheon of heroes of the revolution, and also ensured (if the revolution succeeded) that they would dominate the highest commands in the navy, the machinery of naval administration, and the means of patronage.[43] In the short term, the defections were expected to lead to a more general exodus of sea-officers. By the end of July, a strong rumour was circulating to the effect that Sir Richard Haddock (the controller of the navy) and other leading officers had defected, but Haddock vigorously denied the report.[44] The most prominent of the lesser defectors was Captain David Mitchell, who had risen in the Mediterranean fleet under the patronage of both Herbert and Russell.[45] Captain John Votier was dismissed for transporting wool contrary to customs regulations, and fled to Holland; James's envoy there, d'Albeville, reported that Votier was 'compell'd by meer necessity to abscond himselfe; he would return, if he might be assur'd of a subsistence'.[46] A few warrant-officers and a significant but indeterminate number of ordinary English and Scots seamen also entered the Dutch service, though as usual these were motivated more by the prospect of Dutch money than by any idealistic desire to liberate their nation.[47] Though the number of defections was small, the psychological effect was considerable: Mitchell was reported as stating that 'divers others will come over before the fleet will set sayle', and James himself at least half-believed the rumour that some of his captains might go over.[48]

After a long period of vacillation, James finally ordered a large-scale mobilization at the end of August and authorized pressing in the third week of September.[49] As the fleet grew in size, James took the belated step of replacing Strickland as admiral. The candidates for the post were few; virtually all the flag-officers of the Dutch wars were

[43] See J. R. Jones, *The Revolution of 1688 in England* (1972), ch. 8.
[44] Longleat, Thynne MS 42, fos. 156–8; Thompson, 'Haddock Family, Correspondence', 35–6.
[45] Herbert Lbk, 5; Rawl. MS A. 228, fo. 178; Adm. 6/428, 1679–84 lieuts' list, no. 32; Rawl. MS A. 186, fo. 33ᵛ; Davies, 'James II ... and the Admirals', 87.
[46] BL, Harleian MS 7504, fos. 11–12; BL, Addit. MS 41816, fo. 177ᵛ.
[47] Ibid., fos. 124ᵛ, 172, 177ᵛ, 181, 189.
[48] Ibid., fo. 209ᵛ; PRO, PRO 30/53/8, fo. 67.
[49] See Ehrman, *Navy ... of William III*, 211–15, 229; Jones, *Revolution of 1688*, 254–62.

dead, Sir John Narbrough having died only a few months earlier on
an extraordinary treasure-hunt in the Caribbean.[50] James's choice
of Dartmouth was therefore quite predictable, partly because of
his strong position at court, and partly because his friendship with
Strickland ensured that the Catholic admiral could be retained as
second-in-command. Moreover, Dartmouth's appointment coincided
with James's abrupt abandonment of his 'alliance' with the dissenters,
and his attempt to rebuild his relations with the church of England.
Given that he was one of the leading Anglican courtiers, Dartmouth's
commission to command the fleet could have been seen as an important gesture by the king to the established church. Dartmouth's hatred
of Herbert, too, may have contributed to the appointment. Although
he was appointed admiral before it was known that Herbert would
command the invasion fleet,[51] it was natural to assume that Herbert
would have a prominent place in that fleet, and Dartmouth's known
antipathy to Herbert might have suggested to James that he would
engage if he got the chance.[52] Dartmouth's appointment also meant
passing over the duke of Grafton, who could claim a right to command
the fleet through his office of vice-admiral of England. James's blunt
response to this problem was to abolish the office outright. Faced with
such a clear affront, and the disgrace of being overlooked in favour of
Dartmouth for the second time in five years, Grafton (who was already
increasingly disillusioned with James's policies, and in close touch with
John Churchill) paid an immediate and surreptitious visit to William in
the Netherlands.[53] He went on to play a central role in the conspiracies
against James in both the navy and army.

With Grafton out of contention, James allocated the flags on a basis
which was logical in terms of seniority, but unsound in other respects.
Dartmouth and Strickland could be expected to work well together,
but the rear-admiral, Sir John Berry, was a firm opponent of Catholic
influence in the fleet. The next most senior officer after the flagmen,
Dartmouth's flag-captain on the *Resolution*, was the same William
Davies whom James had dismissed for smuggling Huguenots out of
France. Also present at councils of the flagmen was Captain Lord

[50] P. Earle, *The Wreck of the Almiranta: Sir William Phips and the Hispaniola Treasure*
(1979), 215–16 *et passim*.
[51] Dartmouth's commission was dated 24 Sept., and news of Herbert's appointment
reached England in mid-Oct.: BL, Addit. MS 41816, fo. 228.
[52] For Dartmouth's remarkable attempt to challenge Herbert to duel in Sept. 1688,
see Davies, 'James II . . . and the Admirals', 88.
[53] Rawl. MS D. 148, fos. 1–2; Davies, 'James II . . . and the Admirals', 88.

Berkeley of Stratton, whose conduct from the beginning of the 1688 campaign revealed that he was one of James II's most active opponents in the fleet. Dartmouth was no more decisive and dominating in 1688 than he had been in 1683–4, and lacked both the experience and the self-confidence to impose his will on this disparate group. Moreover, he lacked the essential prop of clear, unambiguous advice from above. Throughout the campaign, James put Dartmouth in a difficult position for an independent commander, giving his admiral theoretical freedom of action but immediately adding riders which set out his preferred course.[54] Inexperienced, confronted with contrary advice from above, and facing the almost unprecedented prospect of commanding a major naval campaign in winter, Dartmouth inevitably had to rely on the advice of his senior subordinates and the consensus opinion of councils of war.

In mid-October, Dartmouth's fleet took up its station behind the Gunfleet shoal, off the Essex coast. The anchorage was far from ideal for intercepting a Dutch fleet sailing south-west into the Channel, but English strategy was based on the assumptions (gleaned from inaccurate intelligence from the Netherlands) that the Dutch would attempt to engage before convoying their transports, and that their objective was the east coast of England; moreover, the chief alternatives, the buoy of the Nore and the Downs, had at least as many disadvantages as the Gunfleet.[55] Indeed, James himself held a poor opinion of that anchorage, and had originally advised Dartmouth against using it.[56] Even so, by the end of October the king was fully convinced by the intelligence reports of a northern or eastern landing. His original instructions to Strickland, in August, had included provisos 'for preventing the States Ships passing by undiscovered to the westward',[57] but the possibility that the Dutch might adopt such a

---

[54] Ibid. 94–5, 101–2.

[55] E. B. Powley, *The English Navy in the Revolution of 1668* (Cambridge, 1928), 20–1, 46–7, 60, 62. For analyses of the English and Dutch strategies, see C. Jones, 'The Protestant Wind of 1688: Myth and Reality', *European Studies Review*, 3 (1973), 201–21; J. L. Anderson, 'Combined Operations and the Protestant Wind, 1688', *The Great Circle*, 9 (1987), 96–107; id., 'Prince William's Descent upon Devon, 1688: The Environmental Constraints', in S. Fisher (ed.), *Lisbon as a Port Town, the British Seaman, and Other Maritime Themes* (Exeter, 1988), 37–55; A. W. H. Pearsall, 'The Invasion Voyage: Some Nautical Thoughts', in C. Wilson and D. Proctor (eds.), *1688: The Seaborne Alliance and Diplomatic Revolution* (1989), 166–74; Davies, 'James II . . . and the Admirals', 83–5.

[56] J. Burchett, *Memoirs of Transactions at Sea during the War with France, Beginning in 1688, and Ending in 1697* (1703), 9; Anderson, 'Prince William's Descent', 39.

[57] Burchett, *Memoirs*, 4–5.

strategy was quietly discarded during the following two months. For their parts, William and Herbert possessed excellent intelligence which told them that the English were expecting a landing in the north-east, while Herbert already favoured sailing to the south-west if the wind was favourable. As he knew from his experiences in the Dutch wars, such a wind would trap Dartmouth in the Gunfleet.[58] Despite such a reasonably optimistic strategic situation, William had to attempt to minimize the risk of encountering the English fleet at sea. The Dutch wars were far too recent for him to rely on Dartmouth and his men immediately and enthusiastically complying with his intended design to save the Protestant faith in England. Therefore, elaborate precautions were made to undermine the fleet's loyalty to James, hoping that disaffection would make it incapable of interfering with William's invasion—or better still, would lead it to join in actively on his side.[59] Two declarations, one by Herbert and one by William, were aimed specifically at the English fleet, both stressing the religious issue.[60] Although the second declaration (William's) was not circulated until after the landing, controversial literature was certainly circulating around the fleet while it lay at the Gunfleet. In mid-October, Dartmouth complained of 'caballing' among his captains, and noted how easily pamphlets and newsletters were reaching the ships.[61]

More direct methods were also being used to subvert the loyalty of the fleet. From the beginning of October, or possibly earlier, Captain Matthew Aylmer and Lieutenant George Byng had been making soundings of naval officers on behalf of a group of army conspirators headed by the duke of Ormonde and Colonel Percy Kirke, and believed that they had secured undertakings not to oppose William from several prominent captains.[62] In October, too, Grafton paid a secretive visit to the fleet, in another initiative designed to win over as many captains as possible.[63] Dartmouth had some idea, albeit a very incomplete one, of what was going on. He reported his suspicions of

[58] BL, Addit. MS 34510, fos. 152ᵛ, 169; Anderson, 'Prince William's Descent', 38–43; Davies, 'James II . . . and the Admirals', 84.

[59] Japikse, *Correspondentie*, I. i. 46–7.

[60] Davies, 'James II . . . and the Admirals', 85.

[61] Japikse, *Correspondentie*, I. ii. 618–19; HMC, *Dartmouth MSS*, i. 259.

[62] Laughton, *Torrington Memoirs*, 27–8.

[63] Rawl. MS D. 148, fo. 10ᵛ; Clarke, *Life of James the Second*, ii. 208. For the problematical evidence of Grafton's visit(s) to the fleet, see Davies, 'James II . . . and the Admirals', 88, 99.

Grafton's activities, and of those of Lord Berkeley, who had also been covertly spreading 'strange notions' around the fleet.[64] Nevertheless, Dartmouth remained convinced that most of the captains would prove loyal to their king.[65] He had little real alternative: a court-martial *pour encourager les autres* would almost certainly have backfired for lack of evidence, and would in any case have damaged morale at a critical time. Moreover, several of those who were most involved in the 'caballing', notably Matthew Aylmer, were regarded by Dartmouth as personal friends.[66] The admiral concentrated instead on the side-issue of the tardiness of some captains in leaving the court to join their ships, but in itself this was not suspicious: the worst culprit, loitering in the king's bedchamber long after he should have sailed, was Dartmouth's own client, the Catholic William Constable.[67]

On 26 and 28 October, the English fleet's council of war debated the strategy, strongly advocated by king and court, of sailing to the Dutch coast to intercept William when he put to sea. Almost unanimously, the council decided that such a course of action was impractical and dangerous in the stiff autumnal gales. The Dutch were expected to be aiming for Harwich and the Thames Estuary, in which case Dartmouth's ships would certainly intercept them.[68] The English attempted to sail on 30 October, having received intelligence that the Dutch were about to leave Hellevoetsluis, but the easterly winds which favoured William ensured that Dartmouth could only get as far as a position due east of the Naze, still unable to clear the Long Sand bank to the south.[69] Therefore, when William sailed on 1 November, James II's fleet was unable to move to intercept it. The winds did not allow the English to move until 3 November, after some stragglers from the invasion fleet had been sighted and one of them had been captured by Dartmouth's scouts. When William landed at Brixham on 5 November, Dartmouth was no nearer than Beachy Head. Even so, if the wind had remained easterly, the English could have expected

[64] HMC, *Dartmouth MSS*, i. 260–1; *Memoirs of . . . Ailesbury*, i. 186.
[65] HMC, *Dartmouth MSS*, i. 260–1, 264; iii. 61.
[66] Pepys MS 2858, pp. 366–7.
[67] HMC, *Dartmouth MSS*, i. 145–6, 148, 166, 172, 177, 179, 181, 188. However, the subsequent failure of three of the leading naval conspirators, Captains Aylmer, Churchill, and Hastings, to get their ships to sea quickly enough *was* widely regarded as suspicious, though their excuses (lack of men and supplies, and contrary winds) were plausible enough: BL, Addit. MS 34510, fo. 163ᵛ.
[68] Davies, 'James II . . . and the Admirals', 93. On 1 Nov., the frigate *Saudadoes* was sent north 'to discover the Dutch fleet': Adm. 51/3965, pt. 1, *Saudadoes* log.
[69] Powley, *English Navy*, 92–4; Anderson, 'Prince William's Descent', 43, 46.

to reach Torbay in less than forty-eight hours. Had they done so, and attacked the Dutch fleet as it lay at anchor, disembarking and unloading, much of William's equipment would have been destroyed, his supply and escape route would have been cut off, and his whole enterprise would most probably have been defeated. However, at a council of war on the 5th, Dartmouth's captains accepted the intelligence gleaned from the officers of the captured Dutch transport, namely that William's fleet had almost double the number of major warships as the English. 'It was not thought fit to hazard the fleet at such Odds & to noe purpose', one captain observed, and the council therefore decided not to attack.[70] The decision had already been made before, later in the day, the wind blew up from the west. By 7 November, Dartmouth's fleet was back in the Downs, and William's disembarkation proceeded unhindered.

Courtiers at the time, James II and Jacobite apologists during their long exile, naval officers who took part in the 'Orangist conspiracy', historians of the 'Glorious Revolution', and even the present prince of Wales,[71] have all taken the view that the decisions of the councils of war were the result of a highly successful campaign of canvassing by the conspirators. According to these accounts, the officers of the fleet had decided beforehand that they would not fight against William, and their views prevailed. Indeed, some convincing evidence can be marshalled in support of this interpretation. Not long after William's landing, Russell reported to Herbert that at least eight of Dartmouth's captains had resolved to abandon him and defect to William: his list included two members of the council of flagmen, Berry and Berkeley, together with such prominent captains as George Churchill (brother of John), Matthew Aylmer, Cloudesley Shovell, and Anthony Hastings.[72] The councils' decisions were in fact effectively taken beforehand, by the elite council of flagmen, and this body was largely dominated by men with grudges against James, or who were actively working for the prince of Orange.[73] Moreover, many captains and junior officers had ample cause for conspiring against James. Anti-Catholicism could work both on an idealistic level and on a more

---

[70] Adm. 51/4322, pt. 2, *Ruby* log; Davies, 'James II . . . and the Admirals', 93–4.
[71] See the foreword to Wilson and Proctor (eds.), *1688: The Seaborne Alliance and Diplomatic Revolution* (1989).
[72] BL, Egerton MS 2621, fo. 47.
[73] Davies, 'James II . . . and the Admirals', 94–5.

immediate, professional one: Strickland's arrogance and indiscretion in religious matters were widely disliked,[74] as were the apparently preferential promotions of more junior Catholic officers. Fear of popery, for mariners as much as for any landsman in 1688, went hand in hand with fear of France. Suggestions that the English fleet might be reinforced with French ships, or that James II had an actual military alliance with Louis XIV, led to an outcry from the fleet. Berry and Grafton had been known as vigorous opponents of pro-French policies long before the 1688 campaign began, and James II himself believed that the officers of his fleet had a 'natural aversion' to the French. The memory of the battle of the Texel, fifteen years before, lived on in the navy, ensuring that any prospect of yet another joint Anglo-French naval operation was anathema to most of James II's captains.[75]

More personal influences could also have created disaffection in James's fleet. Of the 'naval conspirators' named by Russell, all, with the exception of Berry and Berkeley, had close connections with Herbert from his time in command of the Straits fleet in 1679–83, and many other former protégés of Herbert were in Dartmouth's fleet.[76] The loyalty of Herbert's clients to their patron was to be manifested most clearly after the battle of Beachy Head two years later, when many of the potential witnesses and members of the court were known to be favourable to the then earl of Torrington through ties of friendship or patronage; in many cases, these sea-officers were the same men who had commanded in 1688.[77] However, many captains were friends or clients of both Herbert and Russell: in 1688, their interests in the fleet were not mutually exclusive. Some men were influenced more by the defection of one than the other; George Byng, for example, seems to have been influenced more by Russell's lead, and was certainly closer to Russell after 1689.[78] Contrary to the mistaken opinion of James's courtiers (such as Ailesbury, and even Dartmouth himself),[79] many more officers owed direct obligations to Herbert than to Russell, but taken together the names of the two prominent naval defectors had considerable influence in the fleet.

[74] Ibid. 89–91.
[75] Clarke, *James the Second*, ii. 187; Davies, 'James II . . . and the Admirals', 91–2.
[76] Ibid. 86–7.
[77] See HMC, *Rutland MSS*, ii. 129; *Conduct of the Earl of Nottingham*, 82; Stephens, *Plain Relation*, 13–14; P. Le Fevre, 'Tangier, the Navy and its Connection with the Glorious Revolution of 1688', *MM* 73 (1987), 187–90.
[78] Laughton, *Torrington Memoirs*, 27, 65–6.
[79] *Memoirs of . . . Ailesbury*, i. 291; HMC, *Dartmouth MSS*, i. 260–1.

William's decision to appoint Herbert to command the invasion fleet was therefore less surprising than has been suggested; moreover, Herbert had the advantage of having commanded a fleet in wartime (albeit a very small fleet in a very small war), and had an undoubted right of seniority over Russell. Indeed, historians who give Russell the title of 'admiral' in 1688 exaggerate his importance in the navy before that date: although he had been second-in-command in the Mediterranean, he had never risen above the rank of private captain.[80] Ironically, Russell's immediate promotion to full admiral in 1689 was far more spectacular, rapid, and against all the conventions of the navy than had been James II's much-resented promotion of Sir Roger Strickland.

Herbert and Russell were not the only influences on the allegiance of sea-officers in the autumn of 1688. Another of the officers on Russell's list, Cloudesley Shovell, had been one of Herbert's closest colleagues, but also enjoyed the favour of the duke of Grafton,[81] and Anthony Hastings also had close links with the duke; indeed, when Grafton went to the fleet as a volunteer he joined Hastings's ship.[82] Grenville Collins, master of Dartmouth's *Resolution*, had become hydrographer royal through Grafton's patronage.[83] In addition to the duke's purely naval clientage, however, his influence in the fleet also reveals a wider element of the Orangist conspiracy, the close connection between intrigues in the fleet and those in the army. Hastings was a captain in Grafton's first regiment of foot guards; so, too, were Sir Francis Wheeler and Captain Ralph Delaval.[84] George Churchill and Wolfran Cornwall were officers in Lord Cornbury's and the earl of Oxford's regiments respectively, both of which defected to William. Lord Berkeley was a major in John Churchill's horse guards regiment; William Davies, George Byng, and Richard Carter were all officers of the queen's regiment of foot, whose commanders went over to the prince early in the land campaign;[85] Matthew Aylmer was a captain in the regiment commanded by Lord Lumley, one of the signatories of the letter of invitation to William, and also enjoyed the favour of John

[80] See S. Baxter, *William III* (1966), 230–1; Jones, *Revolution of 1688*, 233; W. A. Speck, *Reluctant Revolutionaries: Englishmen and the Revolution of 1688* (Oxford, 1988), 75.

[81] Pepys MS 2861, p. 201.

[82] HMC, *Dartmouth MSS*, i. 176–7, 261.

[83] *Naval Minutes*, 189, 388.

[84] Dalton, *English Army Lists*, ii. 129.

[85] Ibid. ii. 59, 120, 126, 135.

Churchill.[86] Several of these men had been with their regiments until mid- or late October before joining their seagoing commands, and therefore would have been exposed to all the intrigue, discussion, and covert decision-making going on at the Hounslow Heath army camp.[87] Most of the leading figures in the army conspiracy, notably Churchill, Ormonde,[88] Kirke, and Grafton, therefore possessed several contacts or agents in the fleet; the overlap in personnel between the two forces ensured that the conspiracies were inextricably linked.[89]

Despite such a close relationship, the outcomes of the army and navy conspiracies appear to be very different. It is possible to take the view that the naval conspiracy succeeded, in that the conspirators managed to prevent an engagement between the two fleets, whereas the outcome of the army conspiracy at least disappointed William, who had wanted a far larger part of James's field army to defect to him.[90] On the other hand, it is also possible to take the view that the naval conspiracy failed, in that the fleet might still have fought if it had got close enough to the Dutch, but that the defection of just a few senior army officers was enough to break James II's nerve.[91] Each of these interpretations has something to commend it: when dealing with something as shadowy as a conspiracy, the evidence of 'success' and 'failure', and even the definitions of the terms, are inevitably extremely tentative. As far as the naval conspiracy is concerned, anyone remotely connected with it would have had good cause, after the revolution, to play up the importance and success of the conspiracy, and of their own parts in it. Herbert and Russell were careful to mention the services rendered to William during the revolution by individual sea-officers when recommending them for advancement in later years.[92] George Byng's memoirs, the single most detailed source for the naval conspiracy, gives Byng such a central role that, in Hollywood fashion, he

---

[86] Ibid. ii. 78; Pepys MS 2859, p. 37.

[87] HMC, *Dartmouth MSS*, i. 171; Childs, *Army . . . and the Glorious Revolution*, 142–4, 148–59.

[88] See HMC, *Ormonde MSS*, NS, viii. 4, 6, 8, 13–14, for some of Ormonde's contacts in the fleet.

[89] See Childs, *Army . . . and the Glorious Revolution*, 138–59; Davies, 'James II . . . and the Admirals', 85–93.

[90] For the ingredients of these arguments, see e.g. Powley, *English Navy*, 94–7 *et passim*; Baxter, *William III*, 240.

[91] For this view, see above all Childs, *Army . . . and the Glorious Revolution*, ch. 6 *passim*. For the view that *both* conspiracies failed, see Speck, *Reluctant Revolutionaries*, 82–3, 86–7.

[92] Davies, 'James II . . . and the Admirals', 92.

seems almost to bring about the Glorious Revolution single-handed. The conspiracy theory also fitted neatly into James II's and the Jacobites' masochistic interpretation of how he had lost his throne through the plots of a gaggle of self-interested and dishonourable men.[93] In the years after 1688, it suited both the whig and tory interpretations of history to believe that the naval conspiracy had succeeded.

Whether this was actually the case is debatable. The conspirators were undoubtedly fortunate that whatever covert promises they had made to William were never put to the test: the strategic and climatic conditions of October and November 1688 ensured that the 'official' reasons put forward for inaction were only too plausible. When the councils of war on 26 and 28 October decided not to sail to the Dutch coast on a westerly gale, thereby risking the prospect of being wrecked on a lee shore, they were taking the only logical decision captains of large sailing ships could make. When the fleet tried to sail between 30 October and 3 November, the wind kept it behind the sandbanks. This is one of the two stages of the naval campaign on which the conspiracy might realistically have had a bearing. Pepys later wrote that Dartmouth's ignorance of the sands had prevented the fleet getting to sea at this time,[94] and it might have been relatively easy for his more competent subordinates to have deluded the admiral with false advice. However, the log-books of the English ships, and subsequent statements by the highly experienced Sir Roger Strickland, indicate that this was not the case: the fleet genuinely could not clear the sands.[95] At the council of war on 5 November, the decision not to fight was based on the assumption that the Dutch fleet was considerably larger. The assumption was wrong, the intelligence on which it was based was inaccurate, but the decision was a perfectly correct one for any council of war to take, given the information available to it. Moreover, the fact that the captains' opinions were canvassed individually, and that Catholics and future Jacobites were in complete accord with 'conspirators', indicates that the decision was not the product of some premeditated agreement.[96] The original decision to move to the Gunfleet, the other stage of the naval campaign which could conceiv-

[93] See e.g. *Memoirs of...Ailesbury*, i. 186; Clarke, *James the Second*, ii. 206–8, 235.
[94] *Naval Minutes*, 273–4.
[95] Anderson, 'Prince William's Descent', 46; Davies, 'James II ... and the Admirals', 96.
[96] NMM, DAR-16, pp. 85–6.

ably have been influenced by the conspiracy, can be regarded as
suspicious in the light of James's opposition to the decision and of what
actually happened subsequently. Certainly, the Gunfleet was known to
be a bad anchorage in an easterly wind, and would be hopeless if the
Dutch sailed south-west; but the Dutch did not decide finally on their
own destination until 1 November at the earliest, and, of course, there
was no guarantee that they would come out on an east wind alone, or
that such a wind would last long enough to bottle up the English
indefinitely.[97] Seventeenth-century naval warfare was always an unpredictable and confused business: if a captain claimed that a sudden
change of wind, or a sandbank, or the attitude of his crew, or the
sudden appearance of another ship had prevented him defecting to
William or fighting for James, there was very little that William or
James could do to prove or disprove his statement.[98]

If the majority of captains had in fact decided not to fight for James
after 5 November, they went to quite extraordinary lengths to maintain
the illusion of serving him. On 16 November, the fleet left the Downs
following the receipt of intelligence which gave the true (and much
more modest) size of the Dutch fleet, accompanied by an order from
the king to attack it at the first opportunity. Despite a severe battering
from storms, Dartmouth actually reached Torbay by the 19th and had
the Dutch in sight, but with his numbers badly depleted and the
weather worsening, any attack would have been foolhardy, at the very
least.[99] The fleet withdrew to Spithead. While it lay there, clearly
unable any longer decisively to influence events, William's supporters
among the sea-officers became more open and more prepared to take
risks; even Dartmouth noticed how men's attitudes had changed, with
some captains exaggerating the defects of their ships in attempts to
avoid active service.[100] A major stir was caused by the defection at
Plymouth of George Churchill and the *Newcastle*.[101] Sir John Berry
became increasingly assertive, taking much of the effective command
of the fleet away from Dartmouth, whose self-confidence had evaporated even before he knew that the Dutch fleet had got past his

[97] Anderson, 'Prince William's Descent', 38–42, 48.

[98] See e.g. *Memoirs of…Ailesbury*, i. 313–15; Laughton, *Torrington Memoirs*, 30.

[99] Anderson, 'Combined Operations', 104; Davies, 'James II … and the Admirals',
99–100.

[100] HMC, *Dartmouth MSS*, i. 267, 271–2, 274, 275.

[101] For the debatable motivation underlying this 'defection', see Davies, 'James II …
and the Admirals', 96–7.

own.[102] The conspirators in the fleet decided to make direct contact
with William, and despatched George Byng, who reached William's
headquarters at Sherborne on 28 November and presented an address from the prince's supporters in the fleet.[103] William sent a reply
to the officers and also sent a letter to Dartmouth, asking him to join
his fleet to Herbert's and implicitly assuring him that Herbert would
not be set above him. On his return, Byng gave the letter to Aylmer,
who smuggled it into Dartmouth's toilet; the admiral found it there on
12 December.[104]

Dartmouth's response was shaped by increasing discontent with
James's handling of affairs. The king's advice on tactical matters
had become increasingly unclear and confused, a symptom of James's
serious mental collapse in late November.[105] Dartmouth was momen-
tarily uplifted by the king's decision of 28 November to summon
Parliament, a move Dartmouth had strongly supported, and he organized an address from the officers of the fleet to thank James for his
gesture.[106] Within days, however, Dartmouth became alarmed at
James's request for assistance in smuggling the infant prince of Wales
from Portsmouth to France. Dartmouth argued vigorously against
such a move and took action to prevent it, believing that it would only
strengthen James's enemies and lead to endless war with France.[107]
When the king informed Dartmouth on 10 December both that he had
sent the prince away and that he, too, was withdrawing, Dartmouth felt
completely betrayed. Writing to James between the king's abortive and
successful escape attempts, Dartmouth expressed his deep regret that
the prince had been sent away despite all his exhortations, and that he
could not understand James's intention to leave as well, an action
which, he claimed, had 'almost broke my heart'.[108] When Dartmouth
replied to William's letter, therefore, his answer was full of grief at
James's failure to listen to his advice or the advice of a free Parliament;
Dartmouth's other letters at this time show his complete disbelief of

---

[102] Clarke, *James the Second*, ii. 233–4; C. Petrie, *The Marshal Duke of Berwick* (1953),
44.
[103] Most likely, as Dr Childs has remarked, as 'a frantic appeal for the recognition of
services not quite rendered and an apology for inaction ...': *Army ... and the Glorious
Revolution*, 145.
[104] Clarke, *James the Second*, ii. 208; Laughton, *Torrington Memoirs*, 32.
[105] Ibid. 30–2; HMC, *Dartmouth MSS*, i. 219.
[106] Ibid. iii. 268.
[107] Ibid. i. 272, 274, 278; iii. 69.
[108] HMC, *Dartmouth MSS*, i. 226, 282; Davies, 'James II ... and the Admirals', 86.

James's actions.[109] The only course left was to place the fleet under William's control.[110] Already, on 11 December, the 'provisional government' of peers at Whitehall had ordered Dartmouth to dismiss all Catholic officers, and this order was implemented at a council of war two days later. The only Catholic captains in commission on that date, Strickland, Tyrwhitt, MacDonnell, Constable, and John Grimsditch, resigned at once, as did the more junior officers.[111] In what was an obvious triumph for the 'Orangists' in the fleet, Berry was promoted to vice-admiral and Berkeley to rear-admiral, despite his lack of seniority and the prior claim of the flag-captain, William Davies.[112] However, the change of allegiance met with mixed reactions in the fleet. Within days, what seems to have been a loyalist naval conspiracy was in being. Compared with the conspiracy on William's behalf, this new intrigue appears even more shadowy, has left even less evidence of its existence, and was obviously improvised very rapidly, not planned or discussed over months. On the other hand, the loyalist conspiracy achieved what had almost certainly been its one objective in spectacular fashion: it successfully spirited the king out of England.

By the end of November, James II was convinced that the only alternatives open to him were to climb down completely and accept whatever terms William and a free Parliament might impose on him, or to flee the country and await a second Stuart restoration.[113] James's rigid personality and memory of his family's previous triumphant return from exile ensured that he always favoured the second of these options. His first priority was to secure the successful flight of the queen and prince of Wales via Portsmouth, but Dartmouth's obstinate refusal to assist in this venture delayed James's plans.[114] His alternative strategy for their and (perhaps) his own escape was hatched on or about 1 December, when he sent orders to the Catholic Captain Randall MacDonnell of the *Assurance*, then lying at Sheerness, 'to take care that a Moments time be not lost in hastening her, to bee in a

[109] F. Devon, *Vindication of the Right Honourable the First Lord Dartmouth from the Charge of Conspiracy or High Treason, Brought Against him in the Year 1691, and Revived by Macaulay in his 'History of England'*, 1855 (1856), 50–1; HMC, *Dartmouth MSS*, i. 279–80. Cf. Speck, *Reluctant Revolutionaries*, 236–7.

[110] HMC, *Dartmouth MSS*, iii. 69.

[111] R. Beddard, *A Kingdom Without a King* (1988), 38, 68–9, 176–7; HMC, *Dartmouth MSS*, i. 229, 279; iii. 69; Dr Williams's Library, MS 31Q, p. 349; Adm. I/3557, p. 803; NMM, DAR-16, pp. 166–7, 171, 175, 184.

[112] Anderson, 'English Flag Officers', 334.

[113] Beddard, *Kingdom Without a King*, 24–5.

[114] Clarke, *James the Second*, ii. 233.

Condition to Execute any Comands the King shall presently have for her . . .'.[115] Soon afterwards, a small squadron led by the third-rate *Henrietta* was ordered to leave the main fleet and make its way to Sheerness, where it was on station by 8 December, and two of the royal yachts were ordered to Erith, perhaps to await the royal party.[116] Once James had got his wife and son safely away on 9 December, partly as a result of MacDonnell's success in procuring a packet-boat,[117] he could put his own escape plan into effect. He sent word to Dartmouth to sail to Ireland with any ships which remained loyal, thereby suggesting that he had already decided on the strategy of invading Ireland which he was to adopt in 1689.[118] Then, in the morning of 11 December, the king left London, and hired a boat at Sheerness. His flight ended abruptly when he was taken prisoner at Faversham, where the vessel was taking on ballast. Quite what James had intended remains unclear, but it seems probable that he had expected either to sail out to the *Assurance*, or to have her and some or all of the other ships in the Sheerness squadron escort his boat to France—an optimistic scheme, in view of the Dutch domination of the Channel. Certainly, James was visibly taken aback when told in the evening of the 11th that the Sheerness squadron was believed to be about to surrender to William, while early on the 13th the *Assurance* 'weighed bound to Marget Road, but at 9 (hearing the news of the Kings being taken) came back into the Swale'.[119] On the following day, after a 'consult' aboard the *Henrietta*, that vessel, the *Assurance*, the *Crown*, and the other three ships at Sheerness surrendered to William, and MacDonnell laid down his command.[120] James began his journey back to London on the 15th, arriving there the next day.

Ths shape of the escape plot in the following week is particularly shadowy, but it seems that James continued to pin his hopes for a successful get-away on the officers of the Sheerness squadron. The

---

[115] Pepys MS 2862, p. 449.

[116] Adm. 52/49, pt. 6, *Henrietta* log, 8 Dec. 1688; A. Strickland, *Lives of the Queens of England, from the Norman Conquest*, v (1873), 86.

[117] Ibid. v. 84–6; McDonnell, 'Irishmen in the Later Stuart Navy', 101.

[118] HMC, *Dartmouth MSS*, i. 226; Beddard, *Kingdom Without a King*, 32–3.

[119] Adm. 52/3, *Assurance* log. Aboard another component of the squadron, the *Crown*, on the 13th, 'being about to send our lower teare of gunns ashore, upon a sudden privat information we took them in again . . .': Adm. 51/3797, pt. 2, *Crown* log. For a description of James's reaction, see H. and B. van der Zee, *1688: Revolution in the Family* (1988), 198.

[120] See the relevant logs: Adm. 51/3797, pt. 2, *Crown*; Adm. 52/3, *Assurance*; Adm. 52/49, pt. 6, *Henrietta*.

commander-in-chief of that force, the veteran Cornishman Richard
Trevanion of the *Henrietta*, had gone to London on the 14th to discuss
his squadron's disposition with William. He was still there when James
re-entered his capital, and could conceivably have seen the king some
time on the 16th or 17th.[121] James evidently still had the Medway
escape route firmly in mind when, having been told that William
wanted him to withdraw to Ham House at Richmond, he said he
would prefer to go to Rochester. The king went down river by barge
and arrived there on the 19th. Once again, the immediate preliminary
to his escape plan was an attempt to contact Dartmouth, who had been
ordered by William (as James presumably knew) to take his fleet round
to the buoy of the Nore.[122] On the 21st, James wrote to ask him
whether he planned to obey this order or to remain where he was. The
king's purpose was so secret that it could not be committed to paper,
but was to be conveyed verbally by another captain from the Sheerness
squadron, Edmund Elliott.[123] The first serious historian of the navy in
1688, E. B. Powley, speculated that the verbal message might have
involved either James fleeing to the fleet, or ensuring that Dartmouth's
ships did not interfere with the king's escape. Given James's dis-
enchantment with the fleet's performance in the preceding campaign,
the second of these interpretations is more plausible, but the exact
content of the message must remain open to debate. Dartmouth
claimed that he sailed immediately in response to James's message:
this was probably just a canard invented to cover him in all eventualities, for there is no record of Dartmouth, his ship, or any other vessel,
leaving the main fleet at this time.[124]

Equally puzzling is the fact that Elliott never delivered the message
to Dartmouth. It was actually conveyed to the admiral by his old friend
and agent from the early 1680s, Captain David Lloyd, whose precise
role in the events of December 1688 is perhaps one of the most
intriguing aspects of all. Lloyd's ship, the *Sedgemoor*, only arrived at
Plymouth from the Mediterranean on 17 December. Nevertheless, he
had somehow made his way to Dartmouth's fleet within five days,
bearing the king's cryptic message. Despite its captain's absence, the

[121] Ibid.
[122] E. B. Powley, *The Naval Side of King William's War* (1972), 26; Beddard, *Kingdom Without a King*, 58–60.
[123] HMC, *Dartmouth MSS*, i. 238. Elliott was captain of the *Sallee Rose*, lying in Queenborough Swale. He was absent from his ship between 20 and 26 Dec. 1688 (Adm. 51/3970, pt. 7).
[124] Powley, *English Navy*, 155.

Sedgemoor, too, was probably intended to play some part in the royal escape. It was reported on Christmas Day that James had intended to go aboard her at Deal, in order to sail to France; in fact, the *Sedgemoor* seems to have put in to Boulogne bay on the previous day in order to land the king's illegitimate son, Henry FitzJames, who had been serving aboard her as a volunteer.[125] Lloyd was still absent from the ship when she was wrecked on the Kent coast on 2 January 1689.[126] Meanwhile, on 22 December, James had finally decided on his own course of action, believing that if he remained in England any longer his life would be in certain danger. William was only too happy to facilitate the king's escape, as it would resolve several pressing political problems—especially the question of the precise division of power between the vanquished uncle and the victorious nephew. Consequently, no guards were posted on the Medway side of James's temporary residence. During the night of the 22nd, the king made his way to a rowing-boat in the river and set off downstream, accompanied by several attendants and by FitzJames's brother, the duke of Berwick. Their objective was Trevanion's ship, the *Henrietta*: the captain had returned from London on the 21st, and now took charge of the escape plan. At first, the royal party were unable to find the *Henrietta*, and in any case Trevanion was doubtful of the affections of his crew, though he believed his officers would stand by him. The fugitives therefore took refuge aboard another unit of the Sheerness squadron, the guardship *Eagle* (Captain Robert Wilford).[127] Wilford's loyalty was assured: he had been the court candidate for Queenborough in 1688, and had been proposed as one of the new Kent JPs who would agree to repealing the Test Act.[128] When daylight broke on the 23rd, Trevanion was able to get the king and his party aboard the *Henrietta*'s smack, where they were joined by another of the loyalist conspirators, Randall MacDonnell. After a rough crossing, the royal party landed at Ambleteuse on Christmas Day.[129]

Trevanion and MacDonnell were soon joined in France by Sir Roger Strickland, David Lloyd, and another long-serving Protestant

---

[125] Bod. Lib., MS Film 296, Newdigate newsletter 1952; Adm. 33/132, *Sedgemoor* pay-book, ticket no. 170.

[126] Adm. 1/5253, fos. 69–74.

[127] Clarke, *James the Second*, ii. 275–8.

[128] Ibid. 276; G. Duckett, *Penal Laws and Test Act* (1882), 350, 361, 364–5; Speck, *Reluctant Revolutionaries*, 132.

[129] Adm. 51/3863, pt. 2, and Adm. 52/49, pt. 6, *Henrietta* logs; Clarke, *James the Second*, ii. 275–7.

captain, Sir William Jennens, who had disgraced himself in a quarrel with an aristocratic French volunteer.[130] A small number of other dismissals or sudden departures for France took place in the early months of 1689, particularly after the accession of William and Mary. By March, rumours of an imminent purge of disaffected officers were circulating in the fleet. In fact, only Captains James Montgomery and Thomas Smith left their commands, followed in April by Edmund Elliott.[131] The most extraordinary case was that of Sir William Booth, commissioner of the navy, former parliamentary candidate, and captain of the third-rate *Pendennis*. In the middle of March, he discussed with his lieutenants and Captain Wilford a scheme to take the *Pendennis* and *Warspite* to France, arguing that they would be the first of many to go over and that nobody would dispute the orders of a commissioner. The other sea-officers decried the scheme as foolhardy, impractical, and disloyal, and the exasperated Booth ended the discussion by announcing, 'Damme if you won't, I'll goe up & trimme.'[132] However, Booth was too heavily committed, and was forced to flee across the Channel. The most prominent exiled sea-officers, Strickland, Booth, Jennens, Lloyd, and Trevanion, served in the French fleet between 1689 and 1693, acting as advisers, interrogators of captured English seamen, and propagandists;[133] Jennens was particularly active in despatching letters which denigrated the Dutch and exalted James's good intentions, while carefully praising the conduct in battle of English sailors, and in 1692 he was involved in planning a French attack on the Medway as part of the projected invasion.[134] After the failure of the military efforts to restore James, several of the former sea-officers, both Protestant and Catholic, took up household posts at Saint-Germain, while David Lloyd became one of the leading Jacobite agents of the 1690s.[135] Commanding the Jacobite privateers which operated from French ports was probably regarded as beneath the dignity of former captains of great ships,

[130] Bod. Lib., MS Film 296, Newdigate newsletter 1952; HMC, *Dartmouth MSS*, i. 233–4, 238–9, 242, 245–6.
[131] Adm. 106/389, fos. 344, 346; Adm. 3/279, pp. 7, 9; Powley, *Naval Side*, 151.
[132] Adm. 1/5253, fos. 75, 129–32.
[133] *CSPD*, 1689–90, 375–6; Luttrell, *Historical Relation*, ii. 63–4; HMC, *Finch MSS*, iv. 190.
[134] BL., Addit. MS 42586, fos. 93–4; C. de La Roncière, *Histoire de la marine française*, vi (Paris, 1932), 65–6.
[135] 'A View of the Court of Saint Germain, Between the Year 1690 and 1697', *The Harleian Miscellany*, 6 (1810), 390–7; *DNB*, s.n. 'Lloyd, David'.

though Thomas Smith did captain a ship in the regular French service until 1707; most of James's privateer captains were renegade
Irishmen.[136]

Measuring the relative importance of disinterested loyalty to James
against the more mundane motives which might have determined
the allegiance of these officers would be an abstract and unrealistic
exercise. Although Jennens, for example, stressed his concern to
restore the lawful king and punish rebellion, less altruistic factors also
pushed him and most of the others towards Jacobitism. Although
helping the *de jure* king to escape was, of course, not treason, and had
indeed served William's purpose, it would not have been easy for the
likes of Lloyd, Elliott, and Trevanion to have convinced the new
regime of their loyalty to it. Moreover, the success of the invasion
inevitably entailed the triumph of Herbert and Russell, who were
certain to dominate naval patronage. Both Booth and Lloyd could
expect little from Herbert because of their past opposition to his
interest and their associations with Dartmouth, whose departure from
the fleet in January 1689 effectively ended his influence in naval
matters.[137] Even so, Booth's behaviour in particular appears surprising, given his comparatively strong position as a commissioner of
the navy. He admitted that it was very much a spur-of-the-moment
decision, 'that he had thought of it 24 houres . . . let us push at our
fortunes . . .'.[138]

Others might have thought out the implications of the change of
government more fully. Jennens and Trevanion had depended heavily
on the personal favour of James; moreover, both were captains of over
twenty years' standing, and could expect younger men of proven loyalty
to the new regime to be preferred ahead of them.[139] In Jennens's case,
his chances under the new government were limited still further by his
past role in the 'tory reaction', when he had acted as a prosecution
witness in the trial of the whig martyr Stephen College.[140] Supporting
a successful restoration of James was the only realistic chance for

[136] Charnock, *Biographia Navalis*, ii. 192–3; J. S. Bromley, 'The Jacobite Privateers
in the Nine Years War', in E. A. O. Whiteman, J. S. Bromley, and P. G. M. Dickson
(eds.), *Statesmen, Scholars, and Merchants: Essays in Eighteenth-Century History Presented to
Dame Lucy Sutherland* (Oxford, 1973), 19–21, 22–4, 36, 40–1.
[137] *DNB*, s.n. 'Legge, George'; Powley, *Naval Side*, 29–30.
[138] Adm. 1/5253, fo. 132.
[139] Trevanion: A. L. Rowse, *The Byrons and Trevanions* (1978), 98–100; Jennens:
DNB, s.n.
[140] *CSPD*, 1682, 106, 615.

either Jennens or Trevanion to gain any further advancement in the navy. Similarly, Edmund Elliott's patrons in 1688—King James, Lord Godolphin, and Sir Roger Strickland—were hardly ideal men to ensure his survival in the service after 1688.[141] Many of James's, Dartmouth's, and Strickland's clients survived because they already possessed, or were quick to establish, connections with the new patrons, but some were too closely associated with the fallen authorities to continue in the service after 1689.

Both socially and professionally, there was little difference between the conspirators and the Jacobites. In October 1688, Dartmouth had suspected that most of those involved in intrigues were 'young men',[142] but a comparison of the careers of nine captains named as being privy to aspects of the Orangist conspiracy, and of the twelve captains (both Catholic and Protestant) who were displaced, suggests that members of both groups had been commanding ships for about eleven years, on average: veterans like Berry and John Ashby supported William, their contemporaries Jennens, Trevanion, and Strickland supported James; younger men like Hastings and Cornwall were implicated in the conspiracy, while their contemporaries Elliott and MacDonnell left the country. Berry and Shovell came from tarpaulin backgrounds, as did Booth and Wilford of the Jacobites. Scots, Welshmen, Irishmen, and west country men featured in both groups. The insufficiency of these wider generalizations to explain the choice of allegiance in the fleet suggests that patronage, the employment problem, and personal animosities, together with individual reactions to royal policies, were the most important factors motivating the commissioned officers, regardless of age, social origin, or other considerations. However, the active conspirators and the Jacobites were the extremes: taking Catholics and Protestants together, between 10 and 15 per cent of the 157 commissioned officers in service on 1 December 1688 resigned or were dismissed between then and April 1689, while at least 15 to 20 per cent were either involved in the conspiracy or had strong past associations with Herbert, Russell, or Grafton.[143] Probably well over half the officers of the fleet were uncommitted, and ready to

---

[141] Rawl. MS A. 186, fo. 425ᵛ; HMC, *Dartmouth MSS*, i. 209; Pepys MS 2861, pp. 402–3.

[142] HMC, *Dartmouth MSS*, i. 260.

[143] Analysis based on Adm. 8/1, fos. 239–40. Inevitably, these figures are tentative: several others never served after 1689, but only positive evidence of dismissal or resignation has been taken as a criterion. Even so, my assessment of the scale of the

comply with orders from any undisputed authority. The one great common denominator in the conduct of the commissioned officers in 1688 was concern for their careers. It was this concern which prevented many officers from becoming too closely involved in the Orangist conspiracy; it was this concern which made Sir William Booth's lieutenants reject his proposal to defect to France.[144] It was this concern which made the captain's clerk of the distant Sallee squadron transform the tone of his journal from an extravagant panegyric on James II's character into an assault on him and 'his pernicious popish councellors' as each succeeding despatch arrived from England.[145] Paradoxically, it was this concern, too, which turned several sea-officers into Jacobites. Herbert and Russell had gained power, glory, and riches for organizing a successful invasion by William; there was every reason to believe that a Jennens or a Trevanion would benefit in the same way if they organized a successful invasion by James.

On the lower deck, the seamen's response to the revolution echoes their response to the restoration in 1660.[146] In an interregnum, with no certain direction in naval administration, the men's chief concerns were for material considerations and the preservation of their arrears of pay. Mutinies began in January 1689. Aboard the *Ruby*, the men 'grumble[d] mightily' over the lack of cold-weather clothing and the uncertainty over what was to happen to their ship.[147] The *Bristol*'s men attacked the house of the resident commissioner at Portsmouth, Sir Richard Beach, to complain about the lack of victuals, and when they were ordered to change ships 'they swore and damned themselves they would not stirr out of theire shipp till they had theire money . . . '.[148] Beach suggested that there might have been faint Jacobite undertones to the disturbances at Portsmouth: the discontent had begun aboard the *Mary*, Strickland's old flagship, whose crew 'have been the Ring-

---

'purge' is far more conservative than that of Johnston, 'Parliament and the Navy', 426–7. His estimate that two-thirds of Dartmouth's captains did not serve William III is not supported by the evidence, while his comparison of the officer corps in 1688 and 1699 seems to ignore the fact that, in a war, warriors do get killed.

[144] Davies, 'James II . . . and the Admirals', 92–3 *et passim*.

[145] BL., Addit. MS 19302, fos. 11ᵛ, 17ᵛ, 246ᵛ, 247, 252–6, 278.

[146] There is very little evidence of the response of the navy's 'middle class', the warrant-officers. It was reported in Feb. 1690 that the only case of overt opposition to the new government in the fleet had come from the gunner of a third-rate: Adm. 1/5253, fo. 133.

[147] Adm. 106/389, fos. 49, 330; Pepys MS 2862, pp. 532–3, 540.

[148] Adm. 106/387, fos. 100, 106.

leaders of all the rest... being a choice companie of Sir Roger Stricklands picking out of the whole fleet, are such Stubborne Rogues that they neither feare God nor the Devill...'.[149] The protests of the seamen were only quelled by ordering £20,000 out of the treasury.[150] Apart from the possible implications of the mutiny on the *Mary*, the only overtly political action by the lower orders took place in New England, where in April 1689 the warrant-officers and some of the men of the *Rose* arrested the captain and lieutenant to protest at their refusal (and that of Governor Andros) to accept William's authority, though the lieutenant also believed that the men were intent primarily on overthrowing a ship's hierarchy consisting of 'Church of England people'. The crew's action was atypical of the fleet's reaction to the revolution, partly because of the isolation of the *Rose* from the rest of the navy, partly because of the peculiar local political circumstances, and partly because many of the ship's company were probably recruited locally.[151]

The English declaration of war on France on 7 May 1689 completely changed the circumstances of the navy.[152] At first sight, some things would have seemed to have changed little since the Dutch wars: the ordinary was fitted out, the great ships were made ready, and a hugely expanded fleet was put to sea. This created many more opportunities for employment. Herbert and Russell, emulating the roles of Lawson and Mountagu as the naval architects of a change of regime, took the highest commands available, but there were finally vice- and rear-admirals' flags available for the likes of John Ashby, Ralph Delaval, and Henry Killigrew, men who had been deprived of advancement in the long period of peace. There were many lesser posts to be filled: men who had gained their first lieutenancies only in 1688 were captains in 1689, warrant-officers like John Benbow gained their first commissions, and men who had been away from naval service for many years returned to gain commands once again.[153] The fleet had to be

[149] Ibid. fos. 57, 70, 75 (quotation from fo. 75).
[150] Pepys MS 2862, pp. 540, 542, 543, 545, 549, 559; Ehrman, *Navy... of William III*, 255, 263.
[151] *CSP Col.*, 1689–92, 33, 66–8, 92–4; Adm. 51/3955, pt. 7, *Rose* log, fos. 134–5; Adm. 33/123, *Rose* pay-book; J. M. Sosin, *English America and the Revolution of 1688* (Lincoln, Nebr., 1982), 92–3.
[152] For the navy after 1689, the standard work remains Ehrman, *Navy... of William III*, though aspects of it are likely to be modified by the ongoing research of John Hattendorf. Cf. also Johnston, 'Parliament and the Navy'.
[153] Capp, *Cromwell's Navy*, 392.

manned, and the first half of 1689 saw all the old voluntary and compulsory procedures of the Dutch wars revived, together with all their attendant problems.

However, if certain things remained the same, others were markedly different from the beginning, and even more profound differences became apparent as the war went on. The prospect of the first prolonged naval war against France for a century and a half entailed a complete break with the strategic assumptions of the Dutch wars. The Channel and the Atlantic, not the North Sea, would be the main theatres of war. Wholly different wind, weather, and tide conditions prevailed, and the threat of a full-scale invasion of the British Isles—never a serious prospect in the Dutch wars—was a constant preoccupation of William III's admirals. Portsmouth therefore became increasingly important, and a new base had to be built at Plymouth.[154] Though a large fleet in the Mediterranean was something familiar to all naval men in 1689 (Sir John Berry, veteran of Charles II's Straits fleet, was its first wartime commander), the concepts of a large permanent squadron in the West Indies and of prolonged operations by many ships off Ireland and Scotland were quite new. Above all, the sheer length of the French wars had a cumulative effect. The state might have needed to develop new governmental and financial methods to cope with the vast armed forces required for a constant state of war, but the armed forces themselves also had to adapt. The navy was faced with questions of how to acquire, retain, and pay seamen, who would be required in greater numbers and for considerably longer periods than in the past. It was faced with the problem of getting a sufficient number of competent officers, and ensuring that they could be promoted and encouraged fairly. It was faced with administrative and strategic problems on a scale unknown since the last era of prolonged world-wide warfare, the 1650s. Indeed, in many respects the problems and commitments of the navy between 1689 and 1713 ensured that perhaps it had more in common with the navy of Cromwell than with that of Charles II. Historians may continue to debate the significance of the Glorious Revolution in political, religious, and social terms, but for the navy, which had played such a decisive role in determining the outcome of that revolution, 1688–9 marked one of the most important watersheds in its history.

---

[154] On the changed strategic situation, see J. R. Jones, 'Limitations of British Sea Power in the French Wars, 1689–1815', in J. Black and P. Woodfine (eds.), *The British Navy and the Use of Naval Power in the Eighteenth Century* (Leicester, 1988), 33–49.

CONCLUSION

THE navy's actions during, and its responses to, the events of 1688 conformed to a broad pattern which had been evident at the time of the Restoration, and which continued to characterize the attitudes of the seagoing personnel to events ashore for the whole of the period. The commissioned officers, at least, were constantly aware of, and influenced by, the attitudes, decisions, and prejudices of the court, parliament, and the 'political nation' in general: their own backgrounds and connections, notably the maintenance of ties with family and friends ashore, ensured that it could not be otherwise. The very nature of naval employment during this period, with the majority of commissioned officers spending long periods ashore awaiting new posts, provided another important 'bridge' between the fleet and the nation it served. The very poorest tarpaulin commissioned officers, the warrant-officers, and seamen, who could enjoy more continuous employment and who came from lower orders of society, with fewer concerns ashore, were more truly a different race, concerned primarily with material issues and possessing the distinctive dress, speech, songs, and mannerisms which Restoration playwrights loved to caricature; but even they were influenced by ties ashore, and possessed a rough-and-ready patriotism and Protestantism which made them true, if slightly unusual, Englishmen.

One of the most impressive characteristics of the navy during this period is the way in which all these disparate elements among the officers and men combined together into an effective fighting force. Certainly, there were lasting petty jealousies, religious differences, serious defects in the recruitment system, conflicts between officers, antagonism between officers and men, and (among many of those who served on the lower deck) a strong dislike of many aspects of the navy in which they served. Yet these were less significant, and arguably less damaging to the fleet's ability to fight a war, than the serious regional conflicts which blighted the Dutch navy, or the far greater divide between officers and men which characterized the French fleet.[1] By

---

[1] Extensive research is now being carried out on both services. See e.g. J. R. Jones, 'The Dutch Navy and National Survival in the Seventeenth Century', *International*

concentrating on the conflicts, contemporaries and historians alike have produced a distorted image of the Restoration navy, an image which ignores the factors which might bind officers and men, or men and men, to one another. These factors—neighbourhood or family ties, the workings of patronage, the pursuit of fortunes or reputations, shared notions of patriotism or xenophobia, the very nature of shipboard life—were more potent, in the final analysis, than those which divided them.

Even the divisive elements have generally been seen in isolation from their wider context. For one thing, the constant interplay of the influences of sea and shore affected the nature of naval faction. Internal, purely naval, patronage, and purely naval objectives, shaped these factions to a considerable extent, but during the second and third Dutch wars, for example, naval factions often reflected divisions at court, and in turn the divisions in the fleet accentuated differences of opinion ashore. Attacks on the conduct of high-ranking officers were often concerned less with the actual failings of those officers than with efforts to undermine the standing of such men and their patrons. Similarly, in the 1680s the mutual jealousies of the leading flag-officers, and the considerable influence which they possessed at court, ensured that naval faction did not exist in isolation. Although as yet few naval MPs sat in Parliament, and there is little evidence of an extension of the 'whig–tory' divide into the fleet during the exclusion crisis,[2] the seeds were already sown for the identification of naval faction with political affiliation, an identification which was to exert considerable influence on the nature of the officer corps in the next century.[3]

Although naval factions were never entirely separate from court and political intrigue, the contending cliques would probably have regarded themselves as competing, above all, for strictly professional ends, and the greatest of those ends was the quest for employment. Many of the Restoration navy's problems stemmed from the fact that it was popular. To gentlemen and tarpaulins alike, it provided a means of coming to the attention of the king, the heir to the throne, and the administration, and it held out the prospects of enriching oneself, or—for a fortunate few low-born officers—of achieving the kind of

---

History Review, 10 (1988), 18–32; J. R. Bruijn, 'The Dutch Navy in its Political and Social Setting of the Seventeenth Century', in Wilson and Proctor (eds.), *1688: The Seaborne Alliance*, 45–58 (and sources cited therein); Symcox, *The Crisis of French Sea Power 1688–97*, 23–9.

[2] Davies, 'The Navy, Parliament and Political Crisis'.

[3] See e.g. Rodger, *Wooden World*, ch. 8.

significant social advancement which would have been difficult or impossible to attain in almost any other sphere or profession. The result of this popularity was, during peacetime, ferocious competition between many sea-officers for the few posts available; during war, the freer availability of posts only whetted the thirst for advancement, and competition centred on appointments to flag-posts and promotion to higher rates. Concern to remain in employment, or to secure advancement in future, helped to shape many sea-officers' responses to the restoration of the monarchy and the revolution of 1688. This concern does not preclude the possibility of sea-officers holding strong political or religious views, as indeed many did throughout the period, but it does suggest that for many, such views were being subordinated to the paramountcy of professionalism.

Paradoxically, then, the officers competed to get into the navy with the same zeal with which many seamen sought to get out of it. The officers' desires to remain within the service suggest that many already regarded themselves as professional naval men: the merchant navy or the army existed as alternatives, but many saw these as responses to an absence of employment in the navy, not as ends in themselves. Self-perception, as Geoffrey Holmes has pointed out, was arguably the most important criterion for defining a profession during the late seventeenth century.[4] In many respects, the sea-officers had acquired such a degree of self-perception: the formation of what may have been the naval officers' first formal club in 1674 is a particularly clear sign of this growth of *esprit de corps*.[5] The development of professional attitudes stemmed, consciously or unconsciously, from their families and social equals ashore. A sense of family honour translated easily into a sense of the honour of the profession and the nation: sea-officers and their ships were the most visible defenders of the state, and their insistence on the 'salute to the flag' and on their personal rights as officers of the king's ships were signs that they appreciated the responsibility of their position. If these notions of honour were largely brought into the service by gentlemen officers after 1660, they blended easily into an officer corps which had already become more career-orientated as a result of the almost continuous employment available in the 1650s[6]—or at least, blended easily until the crisis of 1688 presented them with the impossible choice between honour and career.

[4] G. Holmes, *Augustan England: Professions, State and Society, 1680–1730* (1982), 6.
[5] NMM, SOC-21.
[6] See Capp, *Cromwell's Navy*, 179–80.

A sense of professional solidarity also developed, paradoxically, as a reaction against the efforts by the administration to improve the quality of the profession. The general instructions to commanders, the regulating of the format of ships' journals, the attempts to restrict leave, and so on, were all worthy attempts to reform the service. However, the shortcomings of each, most notably the mixture of rigidity and inconsistency with which the administrators applied them, created resentment among the sea-officers and led not only to a widespread flouting of the rules, but also to a closing of ranks to resist the administrators. Pepys and his colleagues deserve credit for attempting to regulate the sea-officers: above all, Pepys deserves credit for introducing the lieutenants' examination in 1677, an innovation which gave the officer corps another vital criterion of professionalism, that of formal training culminating in a professional qualification. The sea-officers, on the other hand, certainly indulged in financial and other abuses which needed to be checked. The difficulty with much of the historiography of the Restoration navy has been a tendency to leave the story at that point. In fact, the administration's reforms were by no means uniformly successful, and the sea-officers were by no means as black as they have sometimes been painted. The abuses in which they indulged did not magically appear in 1660, and did not vanish overnight in 1689; many could be justified, financially if not morally, on the grounds that the regular pay was inadequate to support an officer, his family, and, less tangibly, the image of guardian of the nation's honour which he was meant to sustain. Furthermore, the highest and most important branch of the naval administration, the monarch and lord high admiral, took the sea-officers' side on this point, and tolerated or even encouraged the quest for a fortune. 'Counter-revisionist' historians, no doubt, would regard this as proof of Charles's and James's dilettante approach to the navy, and of their lack of regard for its best interests.[7] In fact, it is really just one aspect of the most important and abiding (and least visible) way in which the Stuart brothers controlled their navy, namely their ultimate, very real, and constant control of the

---

[7] e.g. Jones, *Charles II: Royal Politician*, 99; R. Hutton, *Charles II: King of England, Scotland, and Ireland* (Oxford, 1989), 221, 302. Dr Hutton's work appeared too late to be used in the main body of this book. His assertions about the navy appear to be based on a reading of Turnbull, 'The Administration of the Royal Navy 1660–73', esp. pp. 21, 30–5, which seems not to be supported either by Turnbull's evidence or his conclusions, and (for the period post-1673) on printed sources—notably Tanner, *Catalogue*, which provides an incomplete picture. Cf. Pepys MS 2879, p. 223, for a very different picture of the mechanics of higher naval administration in the period 1673–9.

appointment of officers of all ranks, and their direct involvement in deciding on the deployment of warships.[8] Even if Pepys's implicit claim (made explicit by his subsequent enthusiasts) to have been the architect of the naval profession during this period has to be rejected, his high praise of the royal brothers' understanding of, and involvement with, the navy, must remain inviolate.

However, other aspects of his interpretation of the history of the navy during this period require revision. As Richard Ollard has observed, Pepys was just as factious as the squabbling sea-officers whom he condemned:[9] in the diary years, his positions as a member of the naval administration and as a client of the earl of Sandwich coloured his view of men and events, making him naturally sympathetic to certain sea-officers and viewpoints, and antipathetic to others. Similarly, his association with certain factions and policies in the 1680s produced accounts of the Admiralty commission of 1679–84, and of Arthur Herbert's command of the Mediterranean fleet, which were overladen with factional bias and filled with ingeniously subtle distortions and exaggerations. Misled by a myth of Pepysian infallibility, historians have consequently perpetuated a false picture of the later Stuart navy, and this is particularly apparent in Pepys's treatment of the 'gentleman–tarpaulin' conflict. This conflict was very complex: it involved differences in social status, conflicts between old and young officers, and, above all, competition for employment and lucrative voyages, with gentlemen, who possessed influential connections at court and elsewhere, able to obtain these ahead of the disadvantaged tarpaulins. Pepys understood some of these elements, but his own prejudice against the gentlemen officers, assimilated early in the 1660s from his mentors Sandwich and Coventry, prevented him from viewing the whole issue dispassionately. Moreover, his insistence on characterizing the struggle as being between incompetent, highborn gentlemen on the one hand, and able, low-born tarpaulins on the other, has perpetuated the view that essentially the issue was in the same state as it had been in the 1620s and 1630s. In fact, the distinctions between (and struggles of) gentlemen and tarpaulins were often subordinate to other divisions, those which existed between the many factions and cliques in the fleet, and the relative balance between

---

[8] See Davies, 'Pepys and the Admiralty Commission', 42–3, for a 'counter-counter-revisionist' view of Charles's role in the later period. Turnbull, 'Administration', strangely ignores the issue of appointing officers.

[9] Ollard, *Pepys*, 160.

the different kinds of officer changed dramatically between 1665 and 1685, altering the basis of the issue in a way which Pepys seems unable or unwilling to comprehend: he adhered to the prejudices of his youth, rather than the truisms of his middle age. Moreover, the dividing-line between gentlemen and tarpaulins was already blurred in the early 1660s, and became increasingly difficult to draw in later years. Even some of the first generation of gentlemen officers possessed considerable technical skill, and their successors, particularly those commissioned under the auspices of the lieutenants' establishment, were generally competent ship-handlers, even if they did not necessarily know the name of every knot or rope on the ship. This blurring of the distinctions was partly the result of the deliberate royal policy of continuing to encourage officers from all backgrounds, but it was also assisted by the fierce competition for employment. A sea-officer could rise to command because of the influence of his patrons alone, but there were many officers in competition for places, and many influential patrons. To prove oneself more competent than one's competitors, therefore, was an important advantage, and the navy of Charles and James already contained many examples of that supposedly eighteenth-century hybrid, the well-born officer who possessed considerable technical skill. There *were* gentlemen who were seamen, and seamen who were gentlemen, in the navy of Charles the Second.

APPENDIX I

THE 'GENTLEMAN–TARPAULIN' CONTROVERSY: A STATISTICAL ANALYSIS

By adopting the criteria given in the Introduction and Ch. 2, it has been possible to ascertain the career patterns of 784 sea-officers commissioned between May 1660 and December 1688 (62% of the total number). In terms of numbers of men, interregnum officers constituted 15% of the 784; Cavalier officers 4.1%; gentlemen officers 21.4%; and tarpaulin officers 53.7%. 'Borderline' cases, of men whose careers reveal some elements of both 'gentleman' and 'tarpaulin' career patterns, constitute 4.8%, and 'others' (foreigners, or former buccaneers and privateer captains) 1%. These figures are deceptive as they stand, for they reveal nothing of changing appointment patterns within the period under consideration. Consequently, a sample of 260 sea-officers (20% of the total number commissioned in 1660–88) was drawn from the initial group of 784. This sample was divided into categories of career structure according to the proportions given above: further selection within the sample was at random. All subsequent analysis has been based on the individual commissions granted to each officer. In all, the 260 sea-officers accumulated a total of 962 commissions, an average of 3.7 each. Lieutenants' and captains' commissions have been considered separately.

Two other criteria were used in compiling the tabular analysis. First, the period 1660–88 divided naturally into seven periods: from the Restoration to the mobilization for the second Dutch war; the course of the war, from September 1664 to September 1667; from October 1667 to the mobilization for the third Dutch war; from October 1671 to the end of that war; from April 1674 to the establishment of a new Admiralty commission in the wake of the 'popish plot'; from June 1679 to Pepys's return to the Admiralty; from May 1684 to the flight of James II. Secondly, several rates of ship have been considered together. First-, second-, and third-rates, the largest and most prestigious units which were usually set out only in wartime, have been considered as one category. The fourth- and fifth-rates have also been considered together: as the backbone of the peacetime navy they also provided most of the opportunities for employment. The term 'sixth-rate' has been extended to include royal yachts, fire-ships, and all lesser craft. These vessels generally carried no lieutenants, and the very few cases of lieutenants' commissions within this category have been included with the captains' commissions.

TABLE 1. *Analysis of Commissions Granted to Sea-officers, May 1660–December 1688 (%)*

	Interregnum		Cavalier		Gentlemen		Tarpaulins		Borderline		Others	
	Lts.	Capts.	Lts.	Capts.	Lts.	Capts.	Lts.	Capts.	Lts.	Capts.	Lts.	Capts.
May 1660–Aug. 1664												
Rates 1–3	8.3	38.5	0	61.5	75	0	16.7	0	0	0	0	0
Rates 4–5	0	61.2	0	20.4	38.5	8.2	61.5	10.2	0	0	0	0
Rate 6	—	68	—	12	—	0	—	20	—	0	—	0
Sept. 1664–Sept. 1667												
Rates 1–3	2.9	50	0	12.5	26.5	7.5	58.8	17.5	8.8	12.5	2.9	0
Rates 4–5	0	37.5	2.9	1.1	17.1	15.9	74.3	45.4	5.7	0	0	0
Rate 6	—	4.1	—	5.5	—	1.4	—	87.7	—	1.4	—	0
Sept. 1667–Sept. 1671												
Rates 1–3	0	27.3	0	18.2	27.3	27.3	36.4	9.1	27.3	18.2	9.1	0
Rates 4–5	0	20.6	0	11.8	42.9	20.6	35.7	41.2	14.3	5.9	7.1	0
Rate 6	—	10	—	5	—	15	—	60	—	10	—	0

Oct. 1671–Mar. 1674

Rates 1–3	2.2	21	0	10.5	30.4	36.8	54.4	23.7	8.7	5.3	4.3	2.7
Rates 4–5	16.7	4	0	0	50	48	22.2	16	11.1	20	0	12
Rate 6	—	4.1	—	2	—	2	—	89.8	—	2	—	0

Apr. 1674–May 1679

Rates 1–3	5.9	5.6	0	5.6	47	55.5	35.3	27.7	11.8	5.6	0	0
Rates 4–5	0	2.9	0	0	63.2	50	26.3	32.3	10.5	14.8	0	0
Rate 6	—	0	—	0	—	14.7	—	85.3	—	0	0	0

June 1679–Apr. 1684[a]

Rates 1–3	—	—	—	—	—	—	—	—	—	—	—	—
Rates 4–5	0	0	0	0	63.2	75	15.8	21.4	21	3.6	0	0
Rate 6	—	0	—	0	—	15.8	—	84.2	—	0	—	0

May 1684–Dec. 1688

Rates 1–3	0	0	0	7.1	27.3	57.1	54.5	28.7	18.2	7.1	0	0
Rates 4–5	0	0	0	6.5	80	64.5	0	25.8	20	3.2	0	0
Rate 6	—	0	—	0	—	16	—	76	—	8	—	0

[a]Too few commissions were granted in first- to third-rate ships to enable a reliable analysis to be made.

The figures given in the table are percentages of the numbers of commissions granted to sea-officers within the sample of 260 in each category of ship. Therefore, during the period 1660–4 61.2% of captains' commissions in fourth- and fifth-rates were granted to interregnum officers, while in 1674–9 35.3% of lieutenants' commissions in first- to third-rates went to tarpaulin officers.

APPENDIX II

THE CONCERNS OF A 'GENTLEMAN CAPTAIN'

Letter of Francis Wheeler, captain of the *Nonsuch*, to his father, Sir Charles Wheeler (British Library, Addit. MS 28054, fo. 208).

Giblatore Bay [*sic*], 24 February,
1680/1.

Sir

Since my leaving England I have had two letters from you of the 1st & 8th of September, in which you chide mee for not writeing, of which fault you are I hope satisfied to the contrary long since. Wee left Tangier with our men and shipps above two months, there being nothing but peace & quiettness soe that the place is voyd of news, onely that the Ambassadour Sir James Lashly is preparing for his journey with all Expedition to [name unclear] where the King of Fes keeps his court, Wee all expect a firme peace will be concluded, both partys being very willing. I am now a Carreening my shipp in this port,[1] which I hope will be performed in ten dayes, when I have good reason to judge shee will sayle very well, & then to try my fortune with the Argerins [*sic*]. The Admirall[2] has privately told mee he intends my shipp home with the shipps that went upp the straits with Herrings,[3] shee haveing been soe long abroad that tis not convenient for the Kings service to keepe her out longer, the men haveing soe much pay due, that makes 'um very much dissatisfied. The Admirall is a contriving to gett an Exchange [for me] with Capt. Coleman, Commander of the *James Gally*, he being very uneasie to be Comanded by Capt. Russell, a junior captain, but I am affraid 'twont doe; however, he has promised to give mee oppertunity to gett some money from Cadiz in our homeward bound voyage, soe that now the favour I desire of you is to try your interest with the Commissioners of the Admiralty, that if the defects of the shipp does not absolutely require it, when wee come home shee may not be payd off quite but to twelve or six monthes, which if they are not my Enemys 'tis not hard to be done, especially at this time, money being not very plenty

---

[1] The process of careening involved hauling the ship ashore or into shallow water, then using ropes to pull it onto its sides to facilitate the cleaning of the ship's bottom. For the popularity of Gibraltar as a careening facility in this period, see Hornstein, 'The Deployment of the English Navy', 159–66.

[2] Arthur Herbert, admiral of the Mediterranean or 'Straits' fleet, 1679–83.

[3] On naval protection for the English herring trade with the Mediterranean, see Hornstein, 'Deployment of the English Navy', 51–2.

& the ship sayling with 150 men a small Charge, & a good sayler, soe consequently very Usefull for the Service. I know I shall not want our Admirall's letter of request in this point. Lord Bruncker & Mr Hales has offered to be very Civill to mee when I was in England, & Mr Finch, who is a leading man.[4] I hope you have interest to prevaile with in this point.

I hear since I came abroad Severall Lts of the Kings Regment is dead & severall Ensigns preferred soe that I am sure I am within one of being the Senior by Comission in the whole Regment, soe that if Coll. Russell is not invetiratly my enemy I may have hopes of some advancement there. Since it soe happens that I shall come home soe soone as three monthes, I meane from the time of my departure out of these seas, I should be very glad that the things I desired you to send mee may not come; if they are allready on their way, 'tis too late to repent. Pray doe mee the favour to give my service to Mr Prescott, & tell him his Sonn is well & resolves to be a good seaman but that I have not had one letter from him since I left England. When my shipp is Cleane depends a great deale of my future sattisfaction in haveing the good fortune to meet with & outsayle a Turks man of warr. I hope I shall not want your good wishes & prayers. Twas extreame joye to mee to heare by your letter that my mother had recover'd her health, please to give her my humble duty & to tell her I dayly pray for its continuance and that I am as well her Ladyshipp's as

                Sir
                Your Most Obedient Sonn & humble Servant

                Francis Wheler

My humble service to my Sister, I'll not fayle to write her by the next conveyance. I suppose my Brother is still at Plymouth, where I believe he intends to continue. I expect to heare in your next, about the Admirall's money owing from my Ld Plimouth.

[4] Brouncker, Hales, and Finch were all members of the Admiralty commission, the first named being the first commissioner at this time.

BIBLIOGRAPHY

I. MANUSCRIPT SOURCES

All Souls College, Oxford

All Souls MSS
  240   Owen Wynne papers
  317   Papers of Sir William Trumbull

Bodleian Library, Oxford

Carte MSS
  34–40, 46–50   Correspondence of the dukes of Ormonde
  73–5   Correspondence and papers of Edward Mountagu, earl of Sandwich
  215, 217   Letters to Ormonde, 1664–8
  219   Letters of Ormonde, 1660–83
  220   Letters of Ormonde, 1684–7
  222   Newsletters, 1660–85
  223   Correspondence of Sandwich, 1643–70

Clarendon MSS 66–72   Correspondence of Edward Hyde, earl of Clarendon, 1659–60

English History manuscripts (MSS Eng. Hist.) c. 236   Journal of Thomas Baker, consul at Tripoli, 1677–83

Microfilms (MSS Film) 295–6   Newdigate newsletters, 1683–9 (originals at Folger Shakespeare Library, Washington DC)

Rawlinson MSS, A
  170–95   Official and unofficial correspondence and papers of Samuel Pepys, 1660–89
  228   In-letter book of Admiral Arthur Herbert, 1672–83
  230   Chatham Chest papers
  234   Warrants and orders, 1673–9
  299   Chatham Chest papers
  314   Court-martial papers, 1673–9
  316   Journal of Captain James Jenifer, 1672
  342   Letters to Sir Henry Shere, 1676–9
  464   Papers on the state of the navy, 1684–6
  468   The earl of Sandwich's account of the 1665 campaign

Rawlinson MSS, C

  199   Chatham Chest papers
  255   Ships' journals, 1682–5
  972   Mediterranean fleet, court-martial papers 1675–6

Rawlinson MSS, D

  147   Drafts of naval essays by Sir Henry Shere
  148   Colonel Norton's account of conspiracy in the army, 1688
  861   Alington family papers
  919   Army and navy miscellanies
  924   Miscellaneous papers (including accounts of the second Dutch war)

Tanner MSS 30, 39, 44   Miscellaneous letters and papers

British Library

Additional MSS

  9302–5, 9307   Navy papers, 1618–1707
  9311   Navy orders, reports, etc., 1660–97
  9316   Papers relating to the navy, 1661–98
  10117   The diurnal of Thomas Rugge
  11531   Account-book of the purser Edward Gregory
  11602   Richard Gibson's naval papers
  11606   Journals of John Kempthorne, jun.
  12097   Autographs of statesmen and noblemen (letters of Prince Rupert)
  12424   Journals of Sir William Beeston
  14286   Diary of Sir William Clarke, 1666
  15857   Original letters, 1626–1712
  17484   Journal of Captain Francis Digby, 1666–8
  18447   Correspondence of James II and George Legge, Lord Dartmouth, 1679–89
  18986   Papers relating to the navy, 1644–89
  19302   Journal of the Sallee squadron, 1686–9
  19367   Autograph letters on naval affairs
  19399   Royal and noble autographs
  19872   Letters of Sir Henry Shere
  20085   Papers relating to the navy, 1655–1724
  21417–18, 21427   Papers of Captain Adam Baynes (letters etc., of John Lawson)
  21483   Letters to James II and others
  21947–8   Correspondence of the duke of Richmond
  22546   Papers relating to naval affairs, 1643–77
  28053–4   Leeds correspondence (letters from Captain Francis Wheeler)
  29554–6   Hatton-Finch correspondence (letters from Captain Henry Carverth)
  32094   Correspondence and papers of Sir William Coventry

34487   Mackintosh collection, vol. i: newsletters, 1685
34510   Mackintosh collection, vol. xxiv: van Citters letters
34512   Mackintosh collection, vol. xixv: van Citters despatches, 1685–8
34727   West papers (correspondence and papers of Prince Rupert)
36916   Newsletters to Sir Willoughby Aston, 1667–72
37820   Nicholas papers
37951   Miscellaneous autograph letters
39757   Autographs from the Morison collection
41816   Middleton papers
42586   Brockman papers (letters from Sir William Jennens)
51511   Notes by the marquis of Halifax
60386   Correspondence and papers of Sir Henry Capel, 1679–80
70100   Portland naval papers, 1640–96

Egerton MSS

840B   Ships' journals, 1673–8
928   Papers of Sir John Kempthorne
2521   Correspondence of the Haddock family
2539, 2543   Nicholas papers
2621   Correspondence of Arthur Herbert, 1680–90
3383   Leeds papers

Harleian MSS

6277   Papers of naval affairs
6287   Naval tracts
6843   Papers relating to naval affairs
6845   Historical papers, sixteenth and seventeenth centuries (correspondence of Prince Rupert)
7504   List of officers of the navy, 1672–84

Lansdowne MSS

193   Correspondence of Sir Henry Shere, 1679–80
1236   Letters of royal and noble persons (correspondence of the duke of York and Prince Rupert)

Sloane MSS

505   Journal of a Lisbon voyage, 1661
1745   Journals and correspondence of Lieutenant Thomas Browne
2032   Naval affairs, 1660–78
2439   Journal of Captain Charles Wylde, 1673
3328   'Papers and notes on natural curiosities' (including newsletters of 1684–8)
3671   Journals of John Kempthorne, jun.

Cumbria Record Office, Carlisle

Lonsdale MSS D/Lons/L/boxes 1–7   Lowther naval papers

Devon Record Office, Exeter

DQS 1/10–11   Quarter sessions order-books
QS 128   Petitions for relief from maimed soldiers and seamen

Doctor Williams's Library, London

31P–31R   Roger Morrice's entering-books, 1677–91

Kent Archives Office

U. 269/C. 298, C. 320   Fitzharding papers (correspondence of Sir William
    Berkeley and Charles Berkeley, earl of Falmouth)
U. 269/O. 29   Sackville papers (fifth earl of Dorset's magistracy papers:
    returns of reputed seamen in Sussex, 1673)
U. 1515/O. 3, O. 6, O. 8, O. 11, O. 12   Journals, accounts, and corre-
    spondence of Sir John Narbrough and Sir Cloudesley Shovell
U. 1713/C. 1–4   Dering–Southwell correspondence

Leicestershire Record Office

Finch MSS, political papers, 148   Fragment of an autobiography of Daniel
    Finch, earl of Nottingham

Lincolnshire Archives Office

Jarvis MSS IX/1/A   Journals of Captain Christopher Gunman

Longleat House

Manuscripts in the possession of the Marquis of Bath:
Coventry MSS
    1   Royal autographs, 1665–80
    2   Select letters and papers, 1656–80
    95–9, 101–2, 104–5   Correspondence and papers of Sir William
        Coventry, 1660–86
Thynne MSS 41–2   Newsletters to Thomas Thynne

Magdalene College, Cambridge

Pepys MSS
    1490   Papers relating to the special commission of 1686–8
    1534   The state of the navy, 1684
    2265–6   Abstract of naval papers collected for Parliament
    2350–1   Naval journals and abstracts annotated by Richard Gibson
    2554   Pepys's defence of the conduct of the navy in the second Dutch war
    2581   The 'navy white book'
    2611   Sir William Penn's naval collection
    2849–62   Admiralty secretary's out-letters, 1673–9, 1684–9
    2867   Admiralty and naval precedents
    2869–79   Naval miscellanies
    2902   Pepys's day collection

National Library of Wales, Aberystwyth

Deposit MS 38B   Journal of Captain Grenvill Collins aboard the *Leopard*, 1680–1

Herbert papers 9346B   Letter of Lord Herbert to Admiral Herbert, 22 December 1679

Powis papers Parcel 14, 7a   Journal of Captain Henry Herbert, 1671–2

National Maritime Museum, Greenwich

ADL/A/4   Printed copy of the general instructions to commanders
ADL/L   Petitions of officers and seamen
AGC/6   Papers of Sir Frescheville Holles
AGC/19   Miscellaneous papers of Samuel Pepys
AGC/24/1   Letter of the earl of Ossory, 1673
AGC/C/2   Instructions to Prince Rupert, 1673
AGC/L/1   Letter of Sir John Lawson, 1664
AND/9   Original letters of navy commissioners at Chatham
CHA/E/1/A   Letters to the clerk of the cheque, Chatham, 1671–5
CLU/7   Copies of naval letters and papers
DAR/16   Lord Dartmouth's order-book, 1688–9
DAR/27   Dartmouth's order-book, 1683–4
JOD/173   Journal of Samuel Atkins, 1680–4
LBK/8   Correspondence of Samuel Pepys, 1662–79
LBK/47   Letter-book of the duke of Albemarle, 1665
MAT/17a   Marsham-Townshend collection (notes on Sir Cloudesley Shovell)
NVT/8   Navigational work-book, 1686
POR/B/2   Portsmouth yard correspondence, 1675–9
RUSI/NM/135   Copy of the general instructions
SER/1–18   Navy board minutes, 1673–89
SOC/21   Constitution of the officers' club, 1674
TRN/39   Admiral Russell's annotated list of officers, 1691
WYN/   Correspondence and papers of Sir William Penn

Naval Historical Library, Ministry of Defence
121   Thomas Corbett's collection of naval precedents
169   Letter-book of Jonathan Gauden, navy agent at Gibraltar, 1686–8

Norfolk Record Office
C/52/3   Quarter sessions orders, 1669–81
Townshend MSS, Holkham Hall   Muster-roll of seamen in the county of Norfolk, 1664 (consulted at, and by arrangement of, Norfolk Record Office)

Public Record Office

Admiralty papers (Adm.)
1/3545–58   Admiralty, in-letters from Navy Board, 1673–89

1/5138–9   Orders in council, 1673–89
1/5253   Reports of courts-martial, 1680–93
2/1   Orders and instructions, 1665–79
2/169   Admiralty, lords' letters, 1689
2/377   Admiralty, secretary's out-letters, 1689
2/1725–7   Orders and warrants, 1660–88
2/1731–9   Orders, instructions, and warrants, 1659–79
2/1740–3   Orders, letters, and warrants, 1660–89
2/1745–6   Duke of York's out-letters, 1660–84
2/1747–51   Letters and warrants, 1674–84
2/1752–4   Admiralty, secretary's out-letters, 1679–84
3/274   Admiralty, board minutes, orders, and warrants, 1658–60
3/275–8   Admiralty, board minutes, 1673–84
3/279–80   Admiralty, board minutes, 1689–90
6/425   Services of officers, 1673–84
6/428   Applications and recommendations for employment, 1673–89
7/549   Lists of ships and captains, 1651–1737
7/630   Register of passes, 1662–8
7/687   Memorials, reports, and petitions, 1674–88
8/1   Disposition lists, 1673–89
8/2   Disposition lists, 1689–92 (includes list of captains and their recom-
      menders, 1692)
10/10   Lists of commissioned officers, 1660–1746
10/15   Lists of commissioned officers' services, 1660–85
33   Treasurer's pay-books
51–2   Captains' and masters' journals
82/3, 12, 128   Chatham Chest papers
106/1–69   Navy board, in-letters from Admiralty, 1660–89
106/281–394   Navy board, in-letters from captains, dockyards, etc.,
      1673–89
106/2908   Masters' certificates
106/3023   Bounty papers, 1675–84
106/3520   Memoranda and notes, 1660–88
106/3537–40, 3544   Miscellaneous papers, 1650–90

High Court of Admiralty

1/9   Oyer and terminer records
13/73–9   Depositions and examinations

Privy Council 6/1   Committee for Admiralty and naval affairs, 1660–74

Public Record Office, gifts and deposits

30/24   Shaftesbury papers
30/32   Leeds papers
30/53   Powys papers

31/3 Baschet's transcripts from French archives (reports of French ambassadors)

E/M/21/58 Typescript continuation of the *Calendar of State Papers, Venetian*, for 1676–8

Probate

4, 5 Prerogative court of Canterbury, inventories
11 PCC wills

State papers

18 Domestic: interregnum
29 Domestic: Charles II
31 Domestic: James II
46, pt. 4 Domestic: supplementary: Admiralty papers, 1646–73
71 Foreign: Barbary states
79 Foreign: Genoa
84 Foreign: Holland
89 Foreign: Portugal
93 Foreign: Sicily and Naples
94 Foreign: Spain
101/80, 91–2 Foreign: newsletters
104/176–80 Committee for foreign affairs

Staffordshire County Record Office

Dartmouth MSS D(W)1778/Ii Papers of George Legge, Lord Dartmouth

Yale University Library

James Marshall and Marie Louise Osborn Collection, shelf no. Fb 96: Letter-book of Admiral Arthur Herbert, 1678–83

2. PRINTED PRIMARY SOURCES

Unless otherwise stated, all sources were published in London.

AILESBURY, THOMAS BRUCE, earl of, *Memoirs of Thomas, Earl of Ailesbury, written by Himself*, 2 vols. (1890).

AIRY, O. (ed.), *Essex Papers* (Camden Society, NS 47; 1890).

ALLIN, SIR T., *The Journals of Sir Thomas Allin*, ed. R. C. Anderson (2 vols; Navy Records Society, 79–80; 1939–40).

ANDERSON, R. C. (ed.), *Journals and Narratives of the Third Dutch War* (Navy Records Society, 86; 1946).

BALTHARPE, J., *The Straights Voyage*, ed. J. S. Bromley (Luttrell Society, 20; Oxford, 1959).

BARD, N. P. (ed.), 'The Earl of Warwick's Voyage of 1627', *The Naval Miscellany*, 5 (Navy Records Society, 125; 1985).

BARLOW, E., *Barlow's Journal of his Life at Sea in King's Ships, East and West Indiamen, and other Merchantmen from 1659 to 1703*, ed. B. Lubbock, 2 vols. (1934).

BAUGH, D. A. (ed.), *Naval Administration 1715–50* (Navy Records Society, 120; 1977).

BOND, M. F. (ed.), *The Diaries and Papers of Sir Edward Dering, Second Baronet, 1644–84* (1976).

BURCHETT, J., *Memoirs of Transactions at Sea during the War with France, Beginning in 1688, and Ending in 1697* (1703).

BURNET, G., *Bishop Burnet's History of his Own Time*, ed. M. J. Routh, 7 vols. (Oxford, 1823).

Calendar of State Papers, Colonial Series, America and West Indies (1880–1901).

Calendar of State Papers, Domestic Series (1886–1939, 1960–72).

Calendar of the State Papers relating to Ireland (1905–10).

Calendar of State Papers and Manuscripts, Relating to English Affairs, Existing in the Archives and Collections of Venice, and in other Libraries of Northern Italy (1931–47).

CHOLMELEY, Sir H., *An Account of Tangier* (1787).

CHRISTIE, W. D. (ed.), *Letters Addressed from London to Sir Joseph Williamson while Plenipotentiary to the Congress of Cologne in the Years 1673 and 1674*, 2 vols. (Camden Society, NS 48–9; 1873–4).

CLARENDON, EDWARD HYDE, earl of, *The Life of Edward Earl of Clarendon ... in which is Included a Continuation of his History of the Grand Rebellion*, 2 vols. (Oxford, 1827).

CLARENDON, HENRY HYDE, earl of, *The Correspondence of Henry Hyde, Earl of Clarendon, and of his Brother Laurence Hyde, Earl of Rochester, &c.*, ed. S. W. Singer, 2 vols. (1828).

CLARKE, J. S., *The Life of James the Second*, 2 vols. (1816).

COLENBRANDER, H. T. (ed.), *Bescheiden uit vreemde archieven omtrent de groote Nederlandsche zeeorlogen 1652–76*, 2 vols. (The Hague, 1919).

COOPER, W. D. (ed.), *Savile Correspondence* (Camden Society, 71; 1858).

CORBETT, J. S. (ed.), *Fighting Instructions 1530–1816* (Navy Records Society, 29; 1905).

COXERE, E., *Adventures by Sea*, ed. E. H. W. Meyerstein (Oxford, 1945).

DALTON, C., *English Army Lists and Commission Registers, 1661–1714* (6 vols. 1892).

DAVENANT, SIR W., *News from Plymouth* (Dramatists of the Restoration, 9; 1878).

DENNIS, J., *An Essay on the Navy* (1702).

DEVON, F., *Vindication of the Right Honourable the First Lord Dartmouth from the Charge of Conspiracy or High Treason, Brought against him in the year 1691, and Revived by Macaulay in his 'History of England', 1855* (1856).

'Enquiry into the Causes of our Naval Miscarriages, An' (1707), *The Harleian Miscellany*, 1 (1808).

EVELYN, J., *The Diary of John Evelyn*, ed. E. S. de Beer, 6 vols. (Oxford, 1955).

FIRTH, C. H. (ed.), *The Clarke Papers*, iv (Camden Society, NS 62; 1901).

—— (ed.), *Naval Songs and Ballads* (Navy Records Society, 33; 1908).

Flagellum Parliamentarium: Being Sarcastic Notices of Nearly Two Hundred Members of the First Parliament after the Restoration (Aungervyle Society reprints, 1st ser., Edinburgh, 1881).

FOSTER, J. (ed.), *Alumni Oxonienses . . . 1500–1714*, 2 vols. (Oxford, 1891–2).

Gloria Britannica: or, the Boast of the British Seas (1690).

GRANT, J. (ed.), *The Old Scots Navy from 1689–1710* (Navy Records Society, 44; 1914).

GREY, A., *Debates of the House of Commons from the Year 1667 to the Year 1694*, 10 vols. (1763).

GUMBLE, T., *The Life of General Monck, Duke of Albemarle* (1671).

HALIFAX, GEORGE SAVILE, marquis of, *The Life and Letters of Sir George Savile, Bart, First Marquis of Halifax*, ed. H. C. Foxcroft, 2 vols. (1898).

—— *The Works of George Savile, Marquis of Halifax*, ed. M. N. Brown, 3 vols. (Oxford, 1989).

Historical Manuscripts Commission, reports and appendices:

—— *Sixth Report, with Appendix* (1877).

—— *Seventh Report, with Appendix* (1879).

—— Tenth report, appendix, vi: *The Manuscripts of the Marquis of Abergavenny, Lord Braye, G. F. Luttrell, Esq., &c.* (1887).

—— Eleventh report, appendix, ii; twelfth report, appendix, vi; thirteenth report, appendix, v; fourteenth report, appendix, vi; new series: *The Manuscripts of the House of Lords* (1887 onwards)

—— Eleventh report, appendix, v; fifteenth report, appendix, i: *The Manuscripts of the Earl of Dartmouth*, i, iii (1887, 1896).

—— Twelfth report, appendix, vii: *The Manuscripts of S. H. Le Fleming, Esq., of Rydal Hall* (1890).

—— Thirteenth report, appendix, ii: *The Manuscripts of His Grace the Duke of Portland, Preserved at Welbeck Abbey*, ii (1893).

—— *Calendar of the Manuscripts of the Marquess of Ormonde, K.P., Preserved at Kilkenny Castle*, NS 1–8, 8 vols. (1902–20).

—— *Calendar of the Stuart Manuscripts, belonging to His Majesty the King, Preserved at Windsor Castle*, 1–4, 4 vols. (1902–23).

—— *Report on the Manuscripts of Allan George Finch of Burley-on-the-Hill, Rutland*, 4 vols. (1913–65).

—— *Report on the Manuscripts of the Marquess of Downshire, Preserved at Easthampstead Park, Berkshire*, 1 (1924).

—— *Supplementary Report on the Manuscripts of the Late Montague Bertie, Twelfth Earl of Lindsay, Formerly Preserved at Uffington House, Stamford, Lincs.* (1942).

HOLLOND, J., *Two Discourses of the Navy (1638 and 1659) by John Hollond, Also a Discourse of the Navy, 1660, by Sir Robert Slyngsbie*, ed. J. R. Tanner (Navy Records Society, 7; 1896).

Hue and Cry after P. and H., and Plain Truth, A (n.d.; actually 1680).

INGRAM, B. S. (ed.), *Three Sea Journals of Stuart Times* (1936).

JAMES, duke of York, *Memoirs of the English Affairs, Chiefly Naval, from the Year 1660 to 1673* (1729).

JAPIKSE, N. (ed.), *Correspondentie van Willem III en van Hans Willem Bentinck*, 4 vols. (The Hague, 1927–37).

JEAFFRESON, J. C. (ed.), *Middlesex County Records* (4 vols., 1888).

Journals of the House of Commons, 8–9.

Journals of the House of Lords, 11–12.

JUSSERAND, J., *A French Ambassador at the Court of Charles the Second* (1892).

KAUFMAN, H. A. (ed.), *Tangier at High Tide: The Journal of James Luke, 1670–73* (Paris, 1958).

KERR, R. J., and DUNCAN, I. C. (eds.), *The Portledge Papers* (1928).

LAUGHTON, J. K. (ed.), *Memoirs Relating to the Lord Torrington* (Camden Society, NS 46; 1889).

'Letter written by an Unknown Hand, Whereof Many Copies were Dispersed Among the Commanders of the English Fleet, A' (1672), *Lord Somers' Tracts*, 8 (1812).

List of Officers Claiming to the £60,000, &c., Granted by his Sacred Majesty for the Relief of his Truly-loyal and Indigent Party, A (1663).

LUDLOW, E., *Ludlow's Memoirs*, ed. C. H. Firth, 2 vols. (Oxford, 1894).

LURTING, T., *The Fighting Sailor Turn'd Peaceable Christian* (1710).

LUTTRELL, N., *A Brief Historical Relation of State Affairs, from September 1678 to April 1714*, 6 vols. (Oxford, 1857).

MACKY, J., *Memoirs of the Secret Services of John Macky, Esq.* (1733).

MAGALOTTI, L., *Travels of Cosmo III, Grand Duke of Tuscany, through England, during the Reign of King Charles II* (1821).

MANWARING, Sir H., *The Life and Works of Sir Henry Manwaring*, ii, ed. G. E. Manwaring and W. G. Perrin (Navy Records Society, 56; 1922).

MARGOLIOUTH, H. M. (ed.), *The Poems and Letters of Andrew Marvell* (2nd ed.; Oxford, 1952).

MARTIN, S., *The Life of Captain Stephen Martin, 1666–1740*, ed. C. R. Markham (Navy Records Society, 5; 1895).

MARTIN-LEAKE, S., *The Life of Admiral Sir John Leake*, ed. G. A. R. Callender, 2 vols. (Navy Records Society, 51–2; 1920).

MAYDMAN, H., *Naval Speculations, and Maritime Politicks* (1691).

MERRIMAN, R. D. (ed.), *Queen Anne's Navy* (Navy Records Society, 103; 1961).

—— *The Sergison Papers* (Navy Records Society, 89; 1950).

MILWARD, J., *The Diary of John Milward*, ed. C. Robbins (Cambridge, 1938).

MONSON, Sir W., *The Naval Tracts of Sir William Monson*, ed. M. Oppenheim, 5 vols. (Navy Records Society, 22–3, 43, 45, 47; 1902, 1912–14).

MORDAUNT, JOHN, Viscount, *The Letter Book of John, Viscount Mordaunt, 1658–60*, ed. M. Coate (Camden Society, 3rd ser., 69; 1945).

MULGRAVE, JOHN SHEFFIELD, earl of, *The Works of John Sheffield, Earl of Mulgrave, Marquis of Normanby, and Duke of Buckingham* (1740 edn.).

NOTTINGHAM, DANIEL FINCH, earl of, *The Conduct of the Earl of Nottingham*, ed. W. A. Aiken (New Haven, 1941).

'P. C.', *The Three Establishments Concerning the Pay of the Sea-Officers* (2nd edn., 1714).

PENN, G., *Memorials of the Professional Life and Times of Sir William Penn, Knt*, 2 vols. (1833).

PEPYS, S., *The Diary of Samuel Pepys*, ed. R. C. Latham and W. Matthews, 11 vols. (1970–83).

—— *Further Correspondence of Samuel Pepys, 1662–79*, ed. J. R. Tanner (1929).

—— *Letters and the Second Diary of Samuel Pepys*, ed. R. G. Howarth (1932).

—— *The Letters of Samuel Pepys and his Family Circle*, ed. H. T. Heath (Oxford, 1955).

—— *Pepys' Memoires of the Royal Navy 1679–88*, ed. J. R. Tanner (Oxford, 1906).

—— *Samuel Pepys's Naval Minutes*, ed. J. R. Tanner (Navy Records Society, 60; 1926).

—— *Shorthand Letters from Samuel Pepys's Official Correspondence, 1662–79*, ed. E. Chappell (Cambridge, 1933).

—— *The Tangier Papers of Samuel Pepys*, ed. E. Chappell (Navy Records Society, 73; 1935).

PERRIN, W. G. (ed.), *Boteler's Dialogues* (Navy Records Society, 65; 1929).

POWELL, J. R., and TIMINGS, E. K. (eds.), *The Rupert and Monck Letter Book, 1666* (Navy Records Society, 112; 1969).

RERESBY, Sir J., *Memoirs of Sir John Reresby*, ed. A. Browning (Glasgow, 1936).

RODGER, N. A. M. (ed.), *Articles of War* (Havant, 1982).

ROUTLEDGE, F. J. (ed.), *Calendar of the Clarendon State Papers Preserved in the Bodleian Library*, iv–v (Oxford, 1932–70).

ST LOE, G., 'England's Safety, or, a Bridle to the French King' (1693), *Lord Somers' Tracts*, 11 (1814).

SANDWICH, EDWARD MOUNTAGU, earl of, *The Journal of Edward Mountagu, First Earl of Sandwich*, ed. R. C. Anderson (Navy Records Society, 64; 1929).

SAVILLE, R. V. (ed.), 'The Management of the Royal Dockyards, 1672–8', *The Naval Miscellany*, 5 (Navy Records Society, 125; 1985).

SHADWELL, C., *The Fair Quaker of Deal: Or, The Humours of the Navy* (1715 edn.).

SLUSH, B., *The Navy Royal: Or, a Sea-Cook turn'd Projector* (1709).

SMITH, J., *The Seaman's Grammar* (1652 edn.).

The Statutes of the Realm, 11 vols. (1810–28).

STEPHENS, E., *A Plain Relation of the Late Action at Sea, between the English and Dutch, and the French Fleets, from June 22nd to July 5th last, with Reflections thereupon, and upon the Present State of the Nation* (1690).

TANNER, J. R. (ed.), *A Descriptive Catalogue of the Naval Manuscripts in the Pepysian Library at Magdalene College, Cambridge*, 4 vols. (Navy Records Society, 26–7, 36, 57; 1903–4, 1909, 1922).

TEONGE, H., *The Diary of Henry Teonge 1675–9*, ed. G. E. Manwaring (1927).

THOMPSON, E. M. (ed.), 'Correspondence of the Family of Haddock', *The Camden Miscellany*, 8 (Camden Society, NS 31; 1883).

—— *Correspondence of the Family of Hatton* (Camden Society, NS 22; 1878).

THURLOE, J., *A Collection of Papers, Containing Authentic Memorials of the English Affairs from 1638 to the Restoration*, ed. T. Birch, 7 vols. (1742).

VENN, J. and J. A. (eds.), *Alumni Cantabrigienses . . . Part 1, From the Earliest Times to 1751*, 4 vols. (Cambridge, 1922).

'View of the Court of Saint Germain, Between the Year 1690 and 1697, A ', *The Harleian Miscellany*, 6 (1810).

WARD, E., *The Wooden World Dissected*, ed. G. A. R. Callender (1929).

WYCHERLEY, W., *The Plain Dealer*, ed. L. Hughes (1968).

YONGE, J., *The Journal of James Yonge (1647–1721), Plymouth Surgeon*, ed. F. N. L. Poynter (1963).

3. SECONDARY SOURCES

AIKEN, W. A., 'The Admiralty in Conflict and Commission, 1679–84', in W. A. Aiken and B. D. Henning (eds.), *Conflict in Stuart England, Essays in Honour of Wallace Notestein* (1960), 203–25.

ALDRIDGE, D. D., 'Admiral Sir John Norris, 1670–1749', *The Mariner's Mirror*, 51 (1965), 173–83.

ANDERSON, J. L., 'Combined Operations and the Protestant Wind, 1688', *The Great Circle*, 9 (1987), 96–107.

—— 'Prince William's Descent upon Devon, 1688: The Environmental Constraints', in S. Fisher (ed.), *Lisbon as a Port Town, the British Seaman, and Other Maritime Themes* (Exeter, 1988), 37–55.

ANDERSON, R. C., 'English Flag Officers, 1688–1713', *The Mariner's Mirror*, 35 (1949), 333–41.

—— *List of English Naval Captains, 1642–60* (1964).

ANDREWS, J. H., 'The Thanet Seaports, 1650–1750', *Archaeologia Cantiana*, 66 (1954), 37–44.

ANDREWS, K. R., 'The Elizabethan Seaman', *The Mariner's Mirror*, 68 (1982), 245–62.

AVELING, J. C. H., *The Handle and the Axe: The Catholic Recusants in England from Reformation to Emancipation* (1976).

BALLEINE, G. R., *All for the King: The Life Story of Sir George Carteret (1609–80)* (Jersey, 1976).

BARBER, V. C., 'The *Sapphire*, a British Frigate, Sunk in Action in Bay Bulls, Newfoundland, in 1696', *International Journal of Nautical Archaeology and Underwater Exploration*, 6 (1977), 305–14.

BAUGH, D. A., *British Naval Administration in the Age of Walpole* (Princeton, 1965).

BAUMBER, M., *General at Sea: Robert Blake and the Seventeenth-Century Revolution in Naval Warfare* (1989).

BAXTER, S., *William III* (1966).

BEDDARD, R., *A Kingdom Without a King* (1988).

BENBOW, W. A., *Brave Benbow: The Life of Vice-Admiral John Benbow, 1653–1702* (Victoria, BC, 1986).

BOXER, C. R., 'Some Second Thoughts on the Third Anglo-Dutch War, 1672–4', *Transactions of the Royal Historical Society*, 5th ser., 19 (1969), 67–94.

BROMLEY, J. S., 'The Jacobite Privateers in the Nine Years War', in E. A. O. Whiteman, J. S. Bromley, & P. G. M. Dickson (eds.), *Statesmen, Scholars, and Merchants: Essays in Eighteenth-Century History Presented to Dame Lucy Sutherland* (Oxford, 1973), 17–43.

BROWNING, A., *Thomas Osborne, Earl of Danby*, 3 vols. (Glasgow, 1951).

BRUIJN, J. R., 'Dutch Men-of-War—Those on Board, c. 1700–50', *Acta Historiae Neerlandicae*, 7 (1974), 88–121.

—— 'The Dutch Navy in its Political and Social Setting of the Seventeenth Century', in C. Wilson and D. Proctor (eds.), *1688: The Seaborne Alliance and Diplomatic Revolution* (1989), 45–58.

BRYANT, A., *Samuel Pepys: The Man in the Making* (1933).

—— *Samuel Pepys: The Years of Peril* (1935).

—— *Samuel Pepys: The Saviour of the Navy* (1938).

CALLENDER, G. A. R., 'Sir John Mennes', *The Mariner's Mirror*, 26 (1940), 276–85.

CAPP, B., *Cromwell's Navy: The Fleet and the English Revolution 1648–60* (Oxford, 1989).

CHALKLIN, C. W., *Seventeenth-Century Kent: A Social and Economic History* (1965).

CHANDAMAN, C. D., *The English Public Revenue, 1660–88* (Oxford, 1975).

CHAPPELL, E., *Samuel Pepys as a Naval Administrator* (Cambridge, 1933).

CHARNOCK, J., *Biographia Navalis: Or, Impartial Memoirs of the Lives and Characters of Officers of the Navy of Great Britain*, i–iii (1794).
—— *An History of Marine Architecture* (1800).
CHEALE, H., *The History of Shoreham* (1921).
CHILDS, J., *The Army of Charles II* (1976).
—— *The Army, James II, and the Glorious Revolution* (Manchester, 1980).
CLEAVELAND, E., *A Genealogical History of the Noble and Illustrious Family of Courtenay* (1735).
CLOWES, W. L., *The Royal Navy: A History*, 7 vols. (1897–1903).
C[OKAYNE], G. E., *The Complete Baronetage* (1900–9).
—— *et al.*, *The Complete Peerage* (1910–53).
COLEMAN, D. C., 'Naval Dockyards under the Later Stuarts', *Economic History Review*, 2nd ser., 6 (1953–4), 134–55.
COLLINGE, J. M., *Navy Board Officials 1660–1832* (1978).
COPINGER, W. A., *The Manors of Suffolk*, 7 vols. (1905–11).
CRESWELL, J., *British Admirals of the Eighteenth Century: Tactics in Battle* (1972).
DAVIES, J. D., 'More Light on Irishmen in the Stuart Navy, 1660–90', *The Irish Sword*, 16 (1985–6), 325–7.
—— 'Wales and Mr Pepys's Navy', *Maritime Wales*, 11 (1987), 101–13.
—— 'Pepys and the Admiralty Commission of 1679–84', *Historical Research*, 62 (1989), 34–53.
—— 'James II, William of Orange, and the Admirals', in E. Cruickshanks (ed.), *By Force or by Default? The Revolution of 1688–9* (1989), 82–108.
—— 'Devon and the Navy in the Civil War and the Dutch Wars, 1642–88', in S. Fisher, B. Greenhill., and J. Youings (eds.), *A New Maritime History of Devon* (forthcoming).
—— 'The Navy, Parliament, and Political Crisis in the Reign of Charles II', *Historical Journal* (forthcoming).
DAVIS, R., *The Rise of the English Shipping Industry* (1962).
DE BEER, E. S., 'Reports of Pepys' Speech in the House of Commons, March 5th 1668' *The Mariner's Mirror*, 14 (1928), 55–8.
DUCKETT, G., *Penal Laws and Test Act*, 2 vols. (1882).
DYER, F. E., *The Life of Admiral Sir John Narbrough* (1931).
EARLE, P., *The Wreck of the Almiranta: Sir William Phips and the Hispaniola Treasure* (1979).
EHRMAN, J., *The Navy in the War of William III* (Cambridge, 1953).
ELIAS, N., 'Studies in the Genesis of the Naval Profession', *British Journal of Sociology*, 1 (1950), 291–309.
ELLISON, D., 'Lend me a Frigate', *The Mariner's Mirror*, 68 (1982), 81–2.
FARRANT, J. H., 'The Rise and Decline of a South Coast Seafaring Town:

Brighton, 1550–1750', *The Mariner's Mirror*, 71 (1985), 59–76.
FITZROY, A., *Henry, Duke of Grafton, 1663–90* (1921).
FOREEST, H. A. VAN, and WEBER, R. E. J., *De vierdaagse zeeslag, 11–14 Juni 1666* (The Hague, 1984).
FOX, F., *Great Ships: The Battlefleet of King Charles II* (1980).
'G. E. C.' *see* C[okayne].
GEITER, M. K., and SPECK, W. A., 'The Reliability of Sir John Reresby's "Memoirs" and his Account of the Oxford Parliament of 1681', *Historical Research*, 62 (1989), 104–12.
GILLINGWATER, E., *An Historical Account of the Ancient Town of Lowestoft, in the County of Suffolk* (1791).
GOOCH, L. C., 'Catholic Officers in the Navy of James II', *Recusant History*, 14 (1977–8), 276–80.
HANNAY, D., *Naval Courts-Martial* (1914).
HANSEN, H. A., 'The Opening Phase of the Third Dutch War Described by the Danish Envoy in London, March–June 1672', *Journal of Modern History*, 21 (1949), 97–108.
HARLAND, J., *Seamanship in the Age of Sail* (1984).
HARRIS, F. R., *The Life of Edward Mountagu, K. G., First Earl of Sandwich*, 2 vols. (1912).
HARRIS, T., *London Crowds in the Age of Charles II* (Cambridge, 1987).
HARTMANN, C. H., *Clifford of the Cabal* (Kingswood, 1937).
—— *The King's Friend* (Kingswood, 1951).
HENNING, B. D. (ed.), *The Commons 1660–90*, 3 vols. (History of Parliament Trust, 1983).
HOLMAN, R. G., 'The *Dartmouth*, a British Frigate Wrecked off Mull, 1690: 2. Culinary and Related Items', *International Journal of Nautical Archaeology and Underwater Exploration*, 4 (1975), 253–65.
HOLMES, G., *Augustan England: Professions, State and Society, 1680–1730* (1982).
HORNYOLD, H., *Genealogical Memoirs of the Family of Strickland of Sizergh* (Kendal, 1928).
HORWITZ, H., *Revolution Politicks: The Career of Daniel Finch, Second Earl of Nottingham, 1647–1730* (Cambridge, 1968).
HUTTON, R., *The Restoration: A Political and Religious History of England and Wales, 1660–7* (Oxford, 1985).
—— *Charles II: King of England, Scotland, and Ireland* (Oxford, 1989).
JONES, C., 'The Protestant Wind of 1688: Myth and Reality', *European Studies Review*, 3 (1973), 201–21.
JONES, F., 'The Vaughans of Golden Grove', *Transactions of the Honourable Society of Cymmrodorion* (1963), 96–136.
JONES, J. R., *The Revolution of 1688 in England* (1972).

—— *Charles II, Royal Politician* (1987).

—— 'Limitations of British Sea Power in the French Wars, 1689–1815', in J. Black and P. Woodfine (eds.), *The British Navy and the Use of Naval Power in the Eighteenth Century* (Leicester, 1988), 33–49.

—— 'The Dutch Navy and National Survival in the Seventeenth Century', *International History Review*, 10 (1988), 18–32.

JUNGE, H.-C., *Flottenpolitik und Revolution: Die Entstehung der englischen Seemacht während der Herrschaft Cromwells* (Stuttgart, 1980).

KEEVIL, J. J., *Medicine and the Navy, 1200–1900*, ii (1958).

KEMPTHORNE, G. A., 'Sir John Kempthorne and his Sons', *The Mariner's Mirror*, 12 (1926), 289–317.

KENNEDY, D. E., 'Naval Captains at the Outbreak of the English Civil War', *The Mariner's Mirror*, 46 (1960), 181–98.

—— 'The Crown and the Common Seamen in Early Stuart England', *Historical Studies, Australia and New Zealand*, 11 (1964), 170–7.

KENYON, J. P., *Robert Spencer, Earl of Sunderland, 1641–1702* (1958).

—— *The Popish Plot* (1972).

KNIGHT, C., 'Carpenter Master Shipwrights', *The Mariner's Mirror*, 18 (1932), 411–22.

LA RONCIÈRE, C. B. DE, *Histoire de la marine française* (Paris, 1899–1934).

LAVERY, B., *The Ship of the Line*, i. *The Development of the Battlefleet 1650–1850* (1983).

—— *The Ship of the Line*, ii. *Design, Construction and Fittings* (1984).

—— *The Arming and Fitting of English Ships of War 1600–1815* (1987).

LE FEVRE, P., 'Arthur Herbert and his Scheme for Establishing Convoys in the Mediterranean', *The Mariner's Mirror*, 64 (1978), 134.

—— 'Sir George Ayscue, Commonwealth and Restoration Admiral', *The Mariner's Mirror*, 68 (1982), 189–202.

—— 'Charles Kirke', *The Mariner's Mirror*, 68 (1982), 327–8.

—— 'Another False Misrepresentation', *The Mariner's Mirror*, 69 (1983), 299–300.

—— 'Arthur Herbert's Early Career in the Navy', *The Mariner's Mirror*, 69 (1983), 91.

—— 'John Tyrrell (1646–92): A Restoration Naval Captain', *The Mariner's Mirror*, 70 (1984), 149–60.

—— 'Sir Cloudesley Shovell's Early Career', *The Mariner's Mirror*, 70 (1984), 92.

—— 'Tangier, the Navy, and its Connection with the Glorious Revolution of 1688', *The Mariner's Mirror*, 73 (1987), 183–90.

—— 'Matthew Aylmer', *The Mariner's Mirror*, 73 (1987), 206–8.

—— 'The Dispute over the *Golden Horse* of Algiers', *The Mariner's Mirror*, 73 (1987), 313–17.

LEGH, E., *Lyme Letters 1660–1760* (1925).

LEWIS, M., *The Navy of Britain: A Historical Portrait* (1948).

LLOYD, C., 'Bartholomew Sharpe, Buccaneer', *The Mariner's Mirror*, 52 (1966), 291–301.
—— *The British Seaman* (1968).
LOUNSBURY, R. G., *The British Fishery at Newfoundland 1634–1763* (New Haven, 1934).
MACAULAY, T. B., *The History of England from the Accession of James the Second*, ed. C. H. Firth, 6 vols. (Oxford, 1913).
MCDONNELL, H., 'Irishmen in the Later Stuart Navy, 1660–90', *The Irish Sword*, 16 (1985–6), 87–104.
MCGOWAN, A., 'The Dutch Influence on British Shipbuilding', in C. Wilson and D. Proctor (eds.), *1688: The Seaborne Alliance and Diplomatic Revolution* (1989), 89–98.
MARKHAM, C. R., *The Life of Robert Fairfax of Steeton* (1885).
MARSDEN, P., and LYON, D., 'A Wreck Believed to be the Warship *Anne*, Lost in 1690', *International Journal of Nautical Archaeology and Underwater Exploration*, 6 (1977), 9–20.
MARTIN, C. J. M., 'The *Dartmouth*, a British Frigate Wrecked off Mull, 1690: 5. The Ship', *International Journal of Nautical Archaeology and Underwater Exploration*, 7 (1978), 29–58.
MARTIN, P. F. DE C., 'The *Dartmouth* . . . 4. The Clay Pipes', *International Journal of Nautical Archaeology and Underwater Exploration*, 6 (1977), 219–23.
MAY, W. E., 'Midshipmen Ordinary and Extraordinary', *The Mariner's Mirror*, 59 (1973), 187–92.
MERRIMAN, R. D., 'Captain George St Lo, R.N., 1658–1718', *The Mariner's Mirror*, 31 (1945), 32 (1946).
—— 'Sir John Ernle: A Confusion of Identities', *The Mariner's Mirror*, 33 (1947), 97–105.
MILLER, J., *James II: A Study in Kingship* (Hove, 1978).
NUTTALL, G. F., 'Dissenting Churches in Kent Before 1700', *Journal of Ecclesiastical History*, 14 (1963), 175–89.
OLLARD, R., *Man of War: Sir Robert Holmes and the Restoration Navy* (1969).
—— *Pepys: A Biography* (1974).
O'MALLEY, L. C., 'The Whig Prince: Prince Rupert and the Court vs Country Factions during the Reign of Charles II', *Albion*, 8 (1976).
OPPENHEIM, M., *A History of the Administration of the Royal Navy and of Merchant Shipping in Relation to the Navy from 1509 to 1660* (1896).
PEARSALL, A. W. H., 'The Invasion Voyage: Some Nautical Thoughts', in C. Wilson and D. Proctor (eds.), *1688: The Seaborne Alliance and Diplomatic Revolution* (1989), 165–74.
PETRIE, C., *The Marshal Duke of Berwick* (1954).
PITCAIRN JONES, C. G., 'Midshipmen', *The Mariner's Mirror*, 40 (1954).
POWELL, J. R., *The Navy in the English Civil War* (1962).
—— 'Talbot and the Division of the Fleet in 1666', *The Mariner's Mirror*, 53 (1967).

POWER, M., 'Shadwell: The Development of a London Suburban Community in the Seventeenth Century', *The London Journal*, 4 (1978), 29–48.

POWLEY, E. B., *The English Navy in the Revolution of 1688* (Cambridge, 1928).

—— *The Naval Side of King William's War* (1972).

REDIKER, M., *Between the Devil and the Deep Blue Sea: Merchant Seamen, Pirates, and the Anglo-American Maritime World, 1700–50* (Cambridge, 1987).

ROBERTS, C., 'The Impeachment of the Earl of Clarendon', *Cambridge Historical Journal*, 13 (1957), 1–18.

—— 'Sir Richard Temple: "The Pickthank Undertaker" ', *Huntington Library Quarterly*, 41 (1977–8), 137–55.

RODGER, N. A. M., *The Wooden World: An Anatomy of the Georgian Navy* (1986).

ROGERS, P. G., *The Dutch in the Medway* (1970).

ROUTH, E. M. G., 'The English at Tangier', *English Historical Review*, 26 (1911), 469–81.

—— *Tangier: England's Lost Atlantic Outpost* (1912).

ROWSE, A. L., *The Byrons and Trevanions* (1978).

ST MAUR, H., *Annals of the Seymours* (1902).

SAINTY, J. C., *Admiralty Officials 1660–1870* (1975).

SCHOENFELD, M. P., 'The Restoration Seaman and his Wages', *The American Neptune*, 25 (1965), 278–87.

SCOTT, D., *The Stricklands of Sizergh Castle* (Kendal, 1908).

SEAWARD, P., 'The House of Commons Committee of Trade and the Origins of the Second Anglo-Dutch War, 1664', *Historical Journal*, 30 (1987), 437–52.

—— *The Cavalier Parliament and the Reconstruction of the Old Regime, 1661–7* (Cambridge, 1989).

SHELLEY, R. J. A., 'The Division of the English Fleet in 1666', *The Mariner's Mirror*, 25 (1939), 178–96.

SOSIN, J. M., *English America and the Revolution of 1688* (Lincoln, Nebr., 1982).

SPECK, W. A., 'The Orangist Conspiracy against James II', *Historical Journal*, 30 (1987), 453–62.

—— *Reluctant Revolutionaries: Englishmen and the Revolution of 1688* (Oxford, 1988).

STREETE, L., *An Uncommon Sailor: A Portrait of Admiral Sir William Penn* (Bourne End, 1986).

STRICKLAND, A., *Lives of the Queens of England, from the Norman Conquest*, v (1873).

SYMCOX, G., *The Crisis of French Sea Power, 1688–97: From the Guerre d'Escadre to the Guerre de Course* (The Hague, 1974).

TANNER, J. R., *Samuel Pepys and the Royal Navy* (Cambridge, 1920).

TAYLOR, G., *The Sea Chaplains* (Oxford, 1978).

TEDDER, A. W., *The Navy of the Restoration* (Cambridge, 1916).

THORNTON, A. P., *West India Policy under the Restoration* (Oxford, 1956).

[TYRWHITT FAMILY], *Notices and Remains of the Family of Tyrwhitt* (1858).

VALE, V., 'Clarendon, Coventry, and the Sale of Naval Offices, 1660–8', *Cambridge Historical Journal*, 12 (1956), 107–25.

WARSINCK, J. C. M., *Admiraal de Ruyter: de zeeslag op Schooneveld, juni 1673* (The Hague, 1930).

WHITLEY, W. T., *The Baptists of London 1612–1928* (1928).

WILSON, C., *Profit and Power* (1957).

—— and PROCTOR, D. (eds.), *1688: The Seaborne Alliance and Diplomatic Revolution* (1989).

WITCOMBE, D. T., *Charles II and the Cavalier House of Commons, 1663–74* (Manchester, 1966).

ZEE, H. and B. VAN DER, *1688: Revolution in the Family* (1988).

4. UNPUBLISHED THESES, PAPERS, AND TYPESCRIPTS

COGAR, W. B., 'The Politics of Naval Administration, 1649–1660', D.Phil. thesis (Oxford, 1983).

ELLISON, D., 'Cavalier Captain' (unpublished paper).

HAMMOND, W. N., 'The Administration of the English Navy, 1649–60', Ph.D. thesis (British Columbia, 1974).

HORNSTEIN, S., 'The Deployment of the English Navy in Peacetime 1674–88', D.Litt. thesis (Leiden, 1985).

JOHNSTON, J. A., 'Parliament and the Navy, 1688–1714', Ph.D. thesis (Sheffield, 1968).

LE FEVRE, P., 'Arthur Herbert and the Tangier Papers of Samuel Pepys' (unpublished paper).

PITCAIRN JONES, C. G., *et al.*, 'The Commissioned Sea Officers of the Royal Navy, 1660–1815' (National Maritime Museum; typescript, 1954–).

SCOTT, W. F., 'The Naval Chaplain in Stuart Times', D.Phil. thesis (Oxford, 1935).

TURNBULL, A., 'The Administration of the Royal Navy from 1660 to 1673', Ph.D. thesis (Hull, 1975).

INDEX

Lawson, Sir John 36, 63, 70, 95 n.,
108–9, 119, 129, 133, 134, 135,
137, 139, 142, 143, 148, 157, 177,
226
attitude to political change (1659–60)
120–6
leave of absence 48–9, 100
Legge, George, later Lord
Dartmouth 32, 37, 39, 51, 61–2,
65, 115, 167–8, 175, 184, 185–6,
199–200, 204, 212, 213, 219, 223
and Admiralty commission of 1679–
84: 191–8
command of fleet in 1688: 207–11,
215, 216–18, 220
Leghorn (Livorno) 102, 179
Le Neve, Richard 31, 162
Leopard 77
Ley, James, earl of Marlborough 111
lieutenants 11, 18, 52–3, 89
qualifying examination for (1677)
40–1, 53, 195, 231
Lilburne, Henry 107
Lincolnshire 74
'line-of-battle' 10, 14, 139–40
Lisbon 92, 94, 112
Littleton, Sir Thomas 157
Llewellyn, Francis 105
Lloyd, David 197, 220–1, 222, 223
Loades, Edmund 25
London 28 n., 56, 68–9, 72, 120–1, 122,
138, 173
London 9, 70
London, bishop of 20, 106, 108
Long Sand Bank 210
lord high admiral 11, 13, 17, 43, 60,
95–6, 157
Lowestoft 29
battle of (1665) 138–40, 150, 153,
155, 156
Lumley, Lord 213
Lurting, Thomas 107–8
Lynch, Sir Robert 32
Lynch, Sir Thomas 19

Macaulay, Lord 34, 87, 90, 92, 94
MacDonnell, Daniel 178
MacDonnell, Randall 115, 197, 202,
218–19, 221, 224
Magdalene College, Cambridge 2
Maine, John 24
Malta 94

Marlborough, earl of, *see* Ley
Martel, French vice-admiral 174
Mary 225–6
Mary Rose 184
masters 11, 19–20, 28 n., 41–2, 59, 89
see also Warrant Officers
'master and commander' 11, 61
masters-attendant 21, 44
Maydman, Henry 101
Mediterranean fleet 12, 52, 56, 94, 102,
115, 177–89, 227
appointment of officers in 13, 23, 184–
7
'good voyages' in 50, 179–84, 187
Medway 13, 71, 220–1, 222
Mennes, Sir John 123, 130
merchant ship commanders 17, 27, 28,
58–9
messes 88
Middleton, Thomas 146
midshipmen 11, 40
midshipmen extraordinary 52, 88
miscarriages, parliamentary committee of
(1667–8) 149–50, 152–3, 155
Mitchell, David 206
Monck 131
Monck, George, duke of Albemarle 5,
24 n., 35, 36, 101, 108, 116, 126,
129, 138
and parliamentary enquiries of 1667–
8: 150–2, 155, 157
attitude to, and role in, second Dutch
war 133, 134, 141–7
role in Restoration (1659–60) 120–1,
122, 124–5, 127
Monmouth, duke of *see* Scott
Montgomery, James 30, 222
Mordaunt, Lord 204
Mordaunt 94
Morris, John 105
Mountagu, Edward, earl of Sandwich 5,
28, 35, 36, 56, 70, 95, 108, 111, 116,
123, 126, 129, 137, 164–5, 177,
226, 232
attitude to 'gentlemen officers' 132
attitude to, and role in, second Dutch
war 134, 139, 140–3, 155–6
attitude to, and role in, third Dutch
war 159, 161–2
role in Restoration (1659–60)
119–21, 126–7
Mountague 92, 94
Mulgrave, earl of, *see* Sheffield